FACTA DUCIS VIVENT, OPEROSAQUE
GLORIA RERUM——OVID, IN LIVIAM, 255.
THE HERO S DEEDS AND HARD-WON
FAME SHALL LIVE.

DEMOSTHENES

WITHDRAWN

Heroes of the Nations

A Series of Biographical Studies presenting the lives and work of certain representative historical characters, about whom have gathered the traditions of the nations to which they belong, and who have, in the majority of instances, been accepted as types of the several national ideals.

FOR FULL LIST SEE END OF THIS VOLUME

THE ACROPOLIS OF ATHENS

DEMOSTHENES

AND THE LAST DAYS OF GREEK FREEDOM

384-322 B.C.

BY

A. W. PICKARD-CAMBRIDGE

FELLOW OF BALLIOL COLLEGE, OXFORD

Arthur Wallace

32236

G. P. PUTNAM'S SONS

NEW YORK AND LONDON

The Knickerbocker Press

1914

The Knickerbocker Press, New York

PREFATORY NOTE

IN the main body of this book, references have
been given throughout to the chief original
authorities on which the statements in the text
are based. It seemed less necessary, and indeed
scarcely possible, to do this in those portions of the
work (especially Chapters II, III, and beginning
of Chapter IV) which are of the nature of an
introductory summary: and readers who wish for
fuller information must consult the larger Greek
histories and works on the Athenian constitution.

The work has been based on a study of the
original authorities throughout, but I have considered carefully the treatment of the period in the
leading Greek histories, and have made particular
use of the histories of Grote, Holm and Beloch, and
of Schäfer's *Demosthenes und seine Zeit*, which, in
spite of the corrections which later work on the
subject has rendered necessary, can never be
superseded. I wish also to express my obligation
to Hogarth's *Philip and Alexander of Macedon*,
Blass' *Attische Beredsamkeit*, and Butcher's *Demosthenes* (in Macmillan's Classical Writers series).
Among other works which I have consulted with
profit have been Francotte, *Les Finances des Cités*

Grecques; W. S. Ferguson, *Hellenistic Athens;* Edward Meyer, *Isokrates' zweiter Brief an Philipp;* J. Sundwall, *Epigraphische Beiträge zur sozial-politischen Geschichte Athens im Zeitalter des Demosthenes;* M. P. Foucart, *Les Athéniens dans la Chersonese de Thrace au IVᵉ siècle;* W. Reichen-bächer, *Die Geschichte der athenischen und makedonischen Politik;* A. Cartault, *De causa Harpalica;* A. Motzki, *Eubulos von Probalinthos;* U. Kahr-stedt, *Forschungen zur Geschichte des ausgehenden fünften und des vierten Jahrhunderts;* E. Schwartz, *Demosthenes' erste Philippika* (in the Festschrift für Th. Mommsen); J. Rohrmoser, *Ueber den philokrateischen Frieden;* P. Wendland, *Beiträge zur athenischen Politik u. Publicistik des vierten Jahrhunderts;* E. Radüge, *Zur Zeitbestimmung des Euboischen u. Olynthischen Krieges;* J. Kromayer, *Antike Schlachtfelder;* and other writings to which reference is made in the notes.

It must be admitted that, time after time, the evidence which has come down to us is not sufficient to give certainty to the conclusions based upon it. For the greater part of the period with which this book deals, a historian has to be content with Diodorus, who is notoriously untrustworthy in certain respects, particularly in chronology; with the meagre summary of Justin; with Plutarch, to whom the moral was perhaps as important as the truth of his story; and with the statements of orators about themselves and about one another, made, as a rule, in moments of strong feeling, and by members of a nation by which strict truthfulness was never felt to be one of the most obligatory virtues. Here and there we receive valuable help from inscriptions, but other contemporary sources, apart from the orators, are almost wanting, and we are obliged to rely upon allusions in writers who lived centuries after the events with which we are concerned. There are many points at which the explanation of Demosthenes' conduct and policy can only be conjectured, and different writers have found it possible on the same evidence to construct diametrically opposite theories of his character and motives. I have attempted to estimate these as impartially as possible, and it is hoped that the account given in this book will be found to be in accordance with the evidence, and that, where gaps have to be filled by conjecture, the conjectures may be thought reasonable and consistent with the more certain conclusions.

As regards the illustrations, I am indebted to Lord Sackville for the permission given by him to photograph the statue of Demosthenes at Knole; to Dr. G. B. Grundy for a photograph of Thermopylæ and a sketch of the hills about Cytinium; to Mr. M. S. Thompson for a photograph of the Lion of Chæroneia; to Mr. A. B. Cook for a photograph of Calaureia; to my wife for a drawing of the view from Thermopylæ; to Messrs. Fradelle and Young for permission to reproduce their photograph of Lamia; to the Committee of the Egyptian Exploration Fund for leave to photograph the papyrus which appears at p. 317; to Dr. G. F. Hill for casts of the coins which are reproduced in this book; to Herr J. Kromayer and Messrs. Weidmann for leave to reproduce maps of Chæroneia and the neighbourhood; and for other help to Prof. Percy Gardner and Mr. A. J. Toynbee. To all of these my best thanks are offered.

I have also to thank the Delegates of the Oxford University Press for permission to reprint passages from my translation of the Public Speeches of Demosthenes. I could have wished to quote much more freely from the Speeches, which give a far more truthful impression of Demosthenes than can be given by any description; but the limitations of space imposed by the plan of this series did not allow this; and I hope that the translation and the present volume may be treated as companion works, and that each may be allowed in some small degree to atone for the many deficiencies of the other.

Postscript.—Since the above was written, it has been found possible to insert some more illustrations. For these I have to thank my wife, Messrs. Alinari, and the English Photographic Company in Athens.

CONTENTS

vii

ILLUSTRATIONS

PAGE

CHRONOLOGICAL TABLE

[The chronology of this period is often uncertain and there are many differences of opinion among historians in regard to it. The order of events in the years 355–348 is especially disputed. The dates here given must therefore be regarded only as those which the author himself regards as probable, and which he has followed in the text. The table only includes events which fall within the scope of the book, and makes no claim to completeness].

B.C.

404 Athens capitulates to Sparta; the Long Walls are destroyed, and the Peiræus dismantled. The "Thirty Tyrants" established.

403–2 The "Thirty Tyrants" overthrown and democracy restored.

400 The Spartans begin hostilities against Persia in Asia Minor.

395 Artaxerxes II. sends Timocrates to rouse the Greek States against Sparta. Sparta sends help to the Phocians against the Thebans and Locrians, but Lysander is slain at Haliartus.

394 Beginning of Corinthian War, in which the Athenians and allies oppose the Spartans. Spartan forces recalled from Asia Minor. Conon defeats the Spartan fleet off Cnidos, and Athens refortifies the Peiræus.

393 The Long Walls of Athens rebuilt. Iphicrates in the Peloponnese.

392 War continues in the Peloponnese, between Sparta and Argos, Corinth etc. (aided by Athens). Iphicrates destroys a Spartan division. Abortive mission from Sparta to Artaxerxes.

391 War in Peloponnese continues. Sparta also sends troops to Asia Minor against the Persian general.

B.C.

373   Spartans devastate Corcyra, and are opposed first by Timotheus, then by Iphicrates and Chabrias. Thebes destroys Platææ. Isocrates' *Platæicus.*

372   Iphicrates continues to operate against Sparta in the West.

371   Athens makes peace with Sparta, and Sparta and Amyntas acknowledge her claim to Amphipolis. Thebes will not join in the Peace. Battle of Leuctra. Theban supremacy established.

370   A congress at Athens confirms the Peace of Antalcidas. Mantineia rebuilds its walls, and the Arcadians found Megalopolis. Democratic movements in Argos, Tegea, etc.

         The Thebans massacre the people of Orchomenus. Jason of Pheræ murdered; Alexander acquires his power.

369   The Thebans invade the Peloponnese to help the Arcadians against Sparta. Athens makes alliance with Sparta. The Thebans make the Messenians independent of Sparta, and build Messene.

         Death of Amyntas III.

368   The Thebans (under Pelopidas) unite Thessaly against Alexander of Pheræ, and bring Macedonia into alliance, taking Philip as a hostage to Thebes. Perdiccas III. becomes King of Macedonia.

         Hostilities in the Peloponnese continue. Philiscus summons a congress at Delphi, but without result.

367   The Thebans again in the Peloponnese. Embassies from the Greek States to Persia.

366   The Congress of Greek States at Thebes rejects the Peace proposed by Artaxerxes; Timagoras executed at Athens.

         The Thebans are unsuccessful in Thessaly. Themison of Eretria gives Oropus to Thebes.

         The Arcadians make peace with Athens, and begin hostilities with Elis. Corinth and Phleius make peace with Thebes.

         Timotheus helps Ariobarzanes in revolt against Persia, and conquers Samos. Isocrates' *Archidamus.*

365–4   Hostilities continue between Thebes and Alexander of Pheræ, and between Arcadia and Elis.

B.C.

359   Death of Perdiccas III. Accession of Philip. He acknowledges the title of Athens to Amphipolis, but Athens neglects to garrison it.

358   Chares enforces the cession of the Chersonese to Athens. Timotheus liberates Eubœa from Theban control. Demosthenes co-trierarch with Philinus.

Social War. Chios, Cos, Rhodes, and Byzantium revolt against Athens; defeat and death of Chabrias at Chios.

Philip, after a campaign against the Pæonians and Illyrians, attacks Amphipolis, which appeals to Athens. Secret arrangement between Athens and Philip with regard to Amphipolis and Pydna.

357   Social War continued. Prosecution of Iphicrates and Timotheus.

Philip takes Amphipolis. Olynthus, rejected by Athens, makes alliance with Philip. Philip takes Pydna.

Law of Periander.

357-6   Philip takes Poteidæa.

356   Birth of Alexander the Great. Philip takes Mt. Pangæus, and founds Philippi. Athenian alliance with Lyppeius, Grabus, and Cetriporis.

Chares helps Artabazus against Persia; the Persian King helps the allies in their revolt, and Chares is recalled to Athens.

Androtion's commission to recover arrears of war-tax. Isocrates *On the Peace.*

355   Philip conducts campaigns against the Illyrians and Pæonians, and builds a fleet.

End of Social War. Athens recognises the independence of the allies. Mausolus of Caria establishes oligarchies in Rhodes, Chios, and Cos. Athens makes agreement with the Messenians. Athens sends cleruchs to Samos.

Sacred War. The Phocians under Philomelus seize Delphi, and the Locrians fail to defeat them. War is declared against the Phocians.

Demosthenes' Speech against Androtion.

(*End of year*) Philip attacks Methone. Neapolis applies to Athens for help. Isocrates' *Areopagiticus.*

B.C.

352   Philip returns to Macedonia. Olynthus makes over-
       tures to Athens.

       Hostilities continue between Sparta and the Arcadians.

351–348 Sacred War continues indecisively between the Pho-
       cians and the Thebans, Thessalians and Locrians.

351   Philip conquers the Bislatæ and threatens Olynthus;
       he afterwards goes to Illyria and Epirus. He
       intrigues with parties in Eubœa and Olynthus; his
       ships commit aggressions against Athens.

       Chares is sent to the Hellespont, inadequately supplied.

       Artemisia succeeds Mausolus. The exiled Rhodians
       apply to Athens for aid, but are refused. Demos-
       thenes' Speech for the Rhodians and First Philippic.

350   Athens quarrels with Corinth and Megara.

       Communications between Athens and Orontas (in revolt
       against Persia); Phocion assists Euagoras of Cyprus
       against Persia.

       Peace between Sparta and the Arcadians.

       Philip's party gain ground in Olynthus. Olynthus
       again appeals to Athens.

       Demosthenes' Speech for Phormio.

349   Philip requests Olynthus to surrender Arrhidæus.
       Demosthenes' First and Second Olynthiacs. Athens
       makes alliance with Olynthus, and sends Chares,
       but recalls him. Philip invades Olynthian territory,
       but withdraws in order to reduce Thessaly to order.
       Athens transfers Charidemus from the Hellespont
       to Olynthus, but he achieves only slight results.
       Demosthenes' Third Olynthiac (in autumn). Apol-
       lodorus' decree respecting the Theoric money pro-
       posed.

       Trial of Stephanus.

348   (*February*) Phocion is sent to help Plutarchus of Eretria
       against Philip's friends. Battle of Tamynæ. Plu-
       tarchus is thought to have played Athens false.
       (*March*) Demosthenes, when choregus at the
       Dionysia, is assaulted by Meidias. Phocion drives
       Plutarchus from Eretria and Callias from Chalcis,
       but his successor is a failure. The Eubœans obtain
       their independence of Athens (*about June*). Demo-
       sthenes' Speech against Bœotus.

B.C.

348 Philip takes Mecyberna and Torone, and besieges Olynthus. (*July*) Philip expresses desire for peace with Athens. Philocrates proposes to negotiate with him. (*August*) Philip captures Olynthus, and destroys Chalcidic towns. Lycinus prosecutes Philocrates, who is defended by Demosthenes. (*Autumn*) Athens sends embassies to rouse the Greek States against Philip. Æschines in Arcadia.

347 Informal communications between Philip and Athens. Dissensions arise among the Phocians.

(*July*) Demosthenes becomes a Councillor for the year 347–346.

(*Late Summer*) Thebes invokes Philip's aid against the Phocians. The Phocians appeal to Athens, but when Athens sends Proxenus to Thermopylæ, he is insultingly treated by Phalæcus Demosthenes abandons prosecution of Meidias.

346 Philip sends Parmenio to help Pharsalus against Halus. (*Early Spring*) First Embassy from Athens to Philip. (*April*) Debates upon proposed Peace. Philip takes Thracian strongholds, and takes Cersobleptes prisoner. (*May, June*) Second Embassy; Peace of Philocrates ratified. (*July*) Return of Second Embassy. Third Embassy sets out. Philip occupies Thermopylæ; the Athenians refuse to join him in settling the Sacred War. Phalæcus surrenders Philip, who becomes master of Phocis. Isocrates' *Philippus*. (*Late Summer*) The Phocian towns dismantle 1. Demosthenes and Timarchus announce their intention of prosecuting Æschines. (*September*) Philip presides at Pythian games. Demosthenes' Speech on the Peace. (*Winter*—probably) Mission of Eucleides to Philip.

Demosthenes' Speeches against Pantænetus and against Nausimachus and Xenopeithes.

345 Timarchus prosecuted by Æschines and condemned. Philip organises the internal government of Macedonia. Communications between Athens and Philip with regard to Thracian towns. Repair of fortifications of Athens and the Periaeus.

B.C.

341   (*Spring*) Philip protests to Athens against the conduct of Diopeithes. Demosthenes' Speech on the
Chersonese. Philip continues his conquests in
Thrace. (*Summer*) The Third Philippic. Demosthenes makes alliance (for Athens) with Byzantium and Abydos, and with Thracian and Illyrian
princes: Hypereides renews alliance with Rhodes
and Chios. The Persian King sends money to
Diopeithes. Athens makes alliance with Callias of
Chalcis, and expels Philistides from Oreus and
Cleitarchus from Eretria. Demosthenes and Callias
organise a league against Philip. Chares stationed
at Thasos. (*Late*—or early in 340) Callias and
Athenian ships commit acts of hostility against
Philip's ships, etc.

340   (*Early*) Demosthenes crowned at the Dionysia. Execution of Anaxinus as a spy. Formation of league
continues. The Byzantines refuse to help Philip
against the Athenians in the Chersonese. (*Summer*)
Philip besieges Perinthus and Byzantium. After
his seizure of Athenian merchant ships, Athens formally declares war. Chares in command at Byzantium;
then Phocion. Demosthenes reforms the trierarchy.
(*Autumn*) At the meeting of the Amphictyonic
Council, Æschines accuses the Amphisseans of
sacrilege.

339   (*Early*) The Amphictyonic Council declares war on
the Amphisseans, but the war is ineffectively conducted. Philip raises the siege of Byzantium, makes
an expedition into Scythia, and is defeated by
the Triballi on his way back to Macedonia. (*Early
Summer*) Philip appointed commander against the
Amphisseans. (*September*) Philip occupies Elateia.
Demosthenes makes alliance between Athens and
Thebes. (*Autumn and Winter*) Demosthenes carries financial reforms; the Theoric money applied
to military purposes. Athens and Thebes win some
successes against Philip.

338   (*First half*) Demosthenes again crowned at the
Dionysia. Philip takes Amphissa and (perhaps)
Naupactus; Athens and Thebes reject his proposals

B.C.

323   (*Early*) Alexander receives embassies from the Greek States at Babylon. (*June*) Death of Alexander. Athens forms a confederacy for the liberation of Greece, and recalls Demosthenes. Leosthenes with the allied army defeats Antipater and shuts him up in Lamia; but after Leosthenes' death, Antipater escapes and joins Craterus. (*Winter*) Funeral Oration of Hypereides.

322   The Athenian fleet is thrice defeated, and finally (in August) the army of the confederacy is defeated at Crannon. Athens submits to Antipater, and receives a Macedonian garrison, and a less Democratic constitution. (*October*) Death of Hypereides and of Demosthenes.

DEMOSTHENES

CHAPTER I

THE YOUTH AND TRAINING OF DEMOSTHENES

THE subject of this book is the last struggle of
the Hellenes for liberty, and the part played
in that struggle by Demosthenes. We shall see
him confronting, on the one hand, the external
enemies of his country's freedom—Philip, Alexander, and Antipater; on the other, the orators who,
for whatever reason, viewed the resistance to the
Macedonian power with disfavour, and above all
Æschines, his lifelong opponent. It will not be
maintained that the conduct of Demosthenes was
at all points admirable or blameless; but since he
represented worthily, throughout a most critical
period, the highest traditions and instincts of his
fellow-countrymen, and expressed them in a series
of orations the eloquence of which was not only
worthy of their theme, but at its best has never
been surpassed, he is entitled to a distinguished
place among those heroes of the nations, the

memory of whom is among the noblest possessions
of mankind.

Demosthenes the orator was the son of Demosthenes of Pæania,[1] a town lying at the foot of the
eastern slope of Mount Hymettus, about ten miles
from Athens. His mother, Cleobule, was the
daughter of Gylon of Kerameis. Gylon, according to the story told by Æschines,[2] had been banished from Attica, not having dared to face a trial
on the charge of having betrayed Nymphæum
—a town dependent upon Athens, and situated on
the Tauric Chersonese, a few miles south of Pan-
ticapæum,[3] on the western shore of the Cimmerian
Bosporus. (All around lay the fertile corn-lands
whence Athens derived a considerable part of
her supply of grain.) After his banishment from
Athens, Gylon continued to live in the neighbourhood of the Cimmerian Bosporus, and received
from the Spartocidæ (the princes who ruled the
league into which the towns on both sides of the
strait were united) the place on the eastern side
called Kepoi, "the Gardens." There he married
a rich wife who was said to have been of Scythian
descent. She bore him two daughters, whom he
sent to Athens, where one of them married an
Athenian named Demochares; the other married
the elder Demosthenes, and became the mother
of the orator.

The facts with regard to the alleged treachery

---

[1] Now Liopesi.   [2] *In Ctes.*, §§ 171, 172.
[3] The modern Kertch.

of Gylon cannot be certainly ascertained; but it is
at least probable that Gylon's crime amounted to
no more than the transference of Nymphæum,
towards the end of the Peloponnesian War, when
the Athenians were no longer powerful enough to
retain their outlying possessions, into the strong
and friendly hands of the Spartocidæ, whose cor-
dial relations with Athens proved to be of great
advantage to her during the following century.
This wise step may easily have been misrepresented
at Athens, and may have led to Gylon's condemnation. The penalty inflicted was probably a fine,
with banishment until the fine was paid. But
Demosthenes himself tells us[1] that although his
grandfather at one time owed money to the State,
the debt was wiped off before his death; and Gylon
may even have lived his last years in Attica.

Æschines also taunts Demosthenes with his
descent from a Scythian mother.[2] It is possible
that he is exaggerating, and that Gylon's wife was
the daughter of a Greek settler in this "Scythian"
district. But if she was in reality of Scythian
origin, it would have involved no serious stigma
in the eyes of the Athenians. In fact, if Gylon's
daughters were born before the archonship of
Eucleides (B.C. 403–2) they would have been
legally in the same position as the daughters of
two Athenian parents[3]; and it is doubtful whether

---

[1] *In Aphob.* II, §§ 1, 2.   [2] *Cf.* Deinarchus *in Dem.*, § 15.

[3] Dem. *in Eubulidem*, § 30.   Plutarch, *Dem.*, iv., was unable to
test the statement as to Demosthenes' Scythian descent.

the status of the children of an Athenian father by a foreign mother was ever actually disputed, even if they were born after the year of Eucleides. As the date of the loss of Nymphæum to Athens cannot be exactly determined, Cleobule's position must remain uncertain; but it is probable that she was not more than about twenty-two years old when her son was born.

Demosthenes the elder was the owner of a large number of slaves, of whom (at the time of his death) thirty-three were engaged in the manufacture of cutlery—whence he was named "the cutler"—and twenty in making couches, and he had considerable sums of money invested in loans at interest. With a property which, as reckoned up by his son, amounted to nearly fourteen talents, he was considered a wealthy man. He had performed his obligatory services to the State not merely punctiliously but generously, and was regarded by his contemporaries with respect.[1]

The year of the orator's birth was probably 384 B.C.[2] In 376, before he had reached his eighth birthday, his father died, leaving him with his mother and his five-year-old sister. The dying man entrusted his affairs to his two nephews— Aphobus, his brother's son, and Demophon, son of his sister and Demon; and with them he joined

---

[1] Dem. *in Aphob.* I, *passim;* Æsch. *in Ctes.*, § 171; Plut., *Dem.*, iv. See also Note 1 at the end of the Chapter.

[2] Note 2.

a lifelong friend, Therippides of Pæania.[1]   Aphobus was to marry his widow, who was still young,
and to receive with her a dowry of eighty minæ;
he was also granted the use of the house and fur-
niture, until Demosthenes should come of age.
The little girl was to be betrothed to Demophon,
and he was to receive a legacy of two talents.
Therippides was to enjoy the interest on seventy
minæ during Demosthenes' minority, and in all
other respects the property was to be administered
for Demosthenes' benefit.   But the trustees mismanaged the property for their own advantage,
and neglected the provisions of the will.   Had
these instructions been followed, Demosthenes
might reasonably have expected, after ten years,
to receive at least twenty talents, if not more:
instead of which, the estate, when handed over to
him, was not worth more than seventy minæ, or
about one twelfth of its value at the time of his
father's death.[2]

While Demosthenes' estate was being treated in
this disastrous fashion, how was he himself faring?
A boy of poor physique, thin and sickly,[3] he is said
to have been forbidden by his mother to take part
in the vigorous exercises which were an element in
the education of a young Athenian; his delicate
appearance exposed him to the ridicule of other
boys; and Æschines,[4] when they were both almost

---

[1] The account of Demosthenes' guardians and their conduct
is based on the three Speeches against Aphobus.
[2] Note 3.   [3] Plutarch, *Dem.*, iv.   [4] *In Ctes.*, § 255.

old men, upbraided him with his early indifference to his physical condition, and his neglect of the chase. So, we may perhaps infer, he grew up solitary and unsociable; and in the defects of his early upbringing may possibly be found the origin of a certain want of geniality in him, of which his enemies in later days did not fail to make the most, [1] and which perhaps caused him to take an unduly severe and unsympathetic view of the social pleasures in which his contemporaries and colleagues participated. As for his intellectual education, he went, he tells us, [2] to the schools which befitted the son of a man of position, though in another place [3] he accuses Aphobus of depriving his tutors of their fees. Æschines, indeed, several times, [4] taunts him with being uneducated, but the context proves that he is thinking of a want of tact and of taste, rather than of mental equipment. So far as he was really deficient in these qualities, the fault was probably the consequence of his early unsociability; and the deficiency in good taste was shared in no small degree by Æschines himself.

The determination of Demosthenes to become a great political orator was formed, so Plutarch tells us, [5] in his boyhood, and was prompted by

---

[1] *Cf.* Dem., *de F. L.*, § 46, *Phil.* II, § 30; and his attitude towards the enjoyments of his colleagues in the Embassy.

[2] *De Cor.*, § 257.   [3] *In Aphob.* I, § 46.

[4] *In Timarch.*, § 166; *de F. L.*, § 113, 153; *in Ctes.*, § 130.

[5] Plut., *Dem.*, v.

admiration of Callistratus, whom he heard speak either in the Assembly,[1] or when making his defence upon a charge of treason in connection with the loss of Oropus.[2] "When he saw Callistratus escorted and congratulated by numbers of persons," Plutarch tells us, "he admired his fame and marvelled even more at his eloquence, as he observed in him the strength of a born master and tamer of men's passions. And so he abandoned all other studies and the pastimes of his boyhood, and trained himself in speaking by hard practice, determined to be some day an orator himself." Whatever be the truth of this story, Demosthenes must often have had the opportunity of hearing Callistratus, before the latter was driven into exile in 361, and may well have felt inspired to emulate his example.

As the boy grew up, he naturally became aware of the mismanagement of his affairs by his guardians; he determined to demand restitution or compensation; and no sooner had he come of age, in the summer of 366, than he instituted proceedings against them for breach of trust, suing each separately and claiming ten talents from each. In preparing his case, he sought the aid of Isæus, the most skilled practitioner of the time in cases

[1] *Vit. X Orat.* 844b.

[2] This is Plutarch's version; but as the trial with regard to Oropus cannot have taken place until 366, the speech which roused Demosthenes' emulation was probably delivered on some earlier occasion.

of disputed inheritance, and unrivalled in the
thoroughness and ingenuity with which he applied
every argument of which his case admitted.[1]

The suit against Aphobus, of which alone we
have any record, came on first, and the case was
submitted, in the first instance, to arbitration.
Aphobus persuaded Demosthenes to entrust the
decision to three acquaintances, nominated, according to custom, one by each party, and one by
consent of both.   But the law of Athens allowed
either party to withdraw the case from arbitration
at any time before the verdict was given, and
Aphobus, on ascertaining that the verdict would
be unfavourable to himself, took advantage of this
possibility, and withdrew.   The matter then came
before one of the public arbitrators, who were
annually chosen by lot from among the jurors
appointed for the year.   Aphobus tried various
shifts in vain, and the arbitrator pronounced
against him, but instead of giving a final decision
himself, referred the case (as he was entitled to do
at his discretion) to a law-court.

But four or five days before the trial, which
took place late in 364 or early in 363, Aphobus,
with the help of his friends, made a clever attempt
to evade justice.   Under the Athenian naval

---

[1] Various stories are told of the financial relations of Demosthenes to Isæus, and of a futile application for instruction which
he made to Isocrates; but the stories are inconsistent with each
other, and rest on bad authority.   (*Vit. X Orat.*, 837d, 839e,
844b; Suidas, s. v. 'Ισαῖος.)

system, the duty of equipping and commanding each trireme for service, when need arose, was laid upon one or more citizens of sufficient means: but any citizen who felt that another was more capable than himself of bearing the burden (which was a heavy one) might challenge him either to undertake it or to exchange property with himself. Now a certain Thrasylochus, a friend of Aphobus, had been called upon to share the duties of trier-arch with a colleague, and his share of the cost had been estimated at twenty minæ, on payment of which his colleague (or a third party, a con-tractor) had agreed to discharge the actual duties. Thrasylochus was persuaded without difficulty to challenge Demosthenes to exchange property or to undertake the co-trierarchy. The result of the exchange would have been that all claims connected with Demosthenes' estate, and with them the right to prosecute the trustees, would pass from Demosthenes to Thrasylochus (who of course had an understanding with Aphobus), and that Demosthenes would be left without any chance of obtaining redress from his guardians. At first, as the property which had actually been handed over to him was quite insufficient to bear the burden, Demosthenes was inclined to give a provisional consent to the exchange, intending to appeal afterwards to a tribunal which should decide finally whether the burden of the trierarchy should fall on himself or on Thrasylochus, and expecting to win his appeal by demonstrating the fraudulency of his opponents' proceedings. Upon his consenting to the exchange, Thrasylochus had the right to inspect and value Demosthenes' property; and in the course of the inspection, he and his brother Meidias, of whom more will be heard hereafter, did wilful damage to Demosthenes' house, used indecent language in the presence of his young sister, and uttered all kinds of abuse against himself and his mother. Worst of all, they gave the former trustees of the estate a discharge from all claims. Their proceedings appear to have caused some sensation in Athens, and as time was pressing, and the suit against Aphobus was due for hearing in a few days, Demosthenes broke off the negotiations for the exchange, and paid Thrasylochus the twenty minæ, though he was obliged to mortgage his house and his other property in order to do so. He subsequently prosecuted Meidias for his foul language. Meidias made no appearance, and was condemned; but Demosthenes never succeeded in recovering the damages awarded him.[1]

In the action against Aphobus, Demosthenes conducted his own case. His opening speech was a clear and businesslike exposition of the value of the original estate, of the manner in which the guardians had dealt with it, and of the flagrancy of their neglect of the testator's instructions. In a second speech, he replied briefly, but convincingly, to a plea put in by Aphobus at the last moment,

[1] *In Meid.*, §§ 76–81; *in Aphob.* II, § 17.

when there was no time left for the production of evidence to rebut it, and concluded with a pathetic appeal to the jury in the name of himself and of his sister, who would depend upon him for her marriage-portion.

There can be little doubt of the guilt of Aphobus. Had he been innocent, his case must have been susceptible of proof in a simple and straightforward manner; and his subsequent proceedings afford a strong presumption against his honesty. The jury found him guilty. Onetor, his brother-in-law and a pupil of Isocrates, entreated them to assess the damages at one talent only, and promised himself to guarantee payment of that sum; but the jury awarded Demosthenes ten talents—the whole amount claimed.

Instead, however, of paying the sum, Aphobus departed to Megara, and took up his residence there as a domiciled alien. Demosthenes was of course entitled to seize Aphobus' property, though the State gave no assistance in the first instance in the recovery of damages awarded by a court: but before his departure, Aphobus had taken steps to render it as difficult as possible for Demosthenes to obtain effectual satisfaction. He dismantled his house, tore down the doors, broke up the wine-vat, and removed the slaves. He made a present to his friend Æsius of a block of buildings which he owned, and to Onetor of his land, in order that Demosthenes might be forced to institute proceedings against them if he wished to seize the property. Besides this, he made an attempt which, if successful, would have secured the virtual reversal of the verdict against him. He prosecuted Phanus, one of Demosthenes' witnesses at the trial, for perjury, and was assisted in the preparation of the case (and also, as Demosthenes asserts, in the procuring of false witnesses) by Onetor. Demosthenes defended Phanus, and had no difficulty in proving his case. But his troubles were not yet at an end; for when he attempted to take possession (as he was entitled to do) of a piece of land belonging to Aphobus, he was driven out of it by Onetor, who professed to have a prior claim to the land; and he was forced to prosecute Onetor for this action. The trial took place in 362: its result is nowhere recorded, but Demosthenes' proofs of collusion between Aphobus and Onetor appear to be unanswerable, and he was doubtless successful.

The five extant speeches delivered by Demosthenes in the course of his attempt to recover his property are strongly reminiscent of Isæus. Some phrases, and even (in the First Speech against Onetor) a whole passage on the value of evidence given under torture, are taken *verbatim* from his teacher. Yet these speeches already show promise of greater work than Isæus ever produced. In his complete mastery of his subject, in the clear exposition of facts, in the skill with which the narrative and the argument are dovetailed one into the other, and in the ability which is shown not

only in formal proofs, but in argument from prob-
abilities and indications (particularly in the
Speeches against Onetor), Demosthenes is the
follower of his teacher. But in the eloquence of
the more pathetic passages he surpasses all his
predecessors; and though now and then the expressions of strong indignation which he uses have the
appearance of being studied, rather than quite
spontaneous, and stand out rather too conspicuously in the somewhat dull and uniform texture of
the main part of the speeches, there is even in
these some evidence of power, not yet entirely
conscious of itself, nor entirely under control, but
obviously capable of development. It is said[1]
that the fierceness which Demosthenes displayed
in his attack upon his guardians earned for him
the nickname of Argas—the name of a venomous
serpent; and it is not improbable that these early
experiences engendered in him a certain bitterness
—a quality which was always liable to show itself
in him in later days, when he was strongly moved.

We do not know what terms Demosthenes made
with Therippides and Demophon, or whether he
came to terms with them at all. But it is scarcely
likely that, after the verdict which had been given
against Aphobus, they did not attempt to make
some arrangement with him. We hear, however,
of lawsuits against Demophon's father and brother,
Demon and Demomeles. The elder Demosthenes
had lent money at interest to Demomeles,[2] and

---

[1] Æsch., *de F. L.*, § 99; Plut., *Dem.*, iv.   [2] *In Aphob.* I, § 11.

Demosthenes may have tried to recover from the father what was due from one or both of his sons. Against Demomeles he brought an action before the Council of Areopagus[1] on account of a wound in the head which Demomeles had inflicted upon him—possibly in the course of disputes with regard to the property but afterwards abandoned the case, and accepted a sum of money in compensation for the injury.[2] Æschines states that Demosthenes inflicted the injury upon himself, and accused Demomeles of causing it, in order to extract money from him. Such a statement from such a source carries no weight; but it is plain that the long series of quarrels with his relations cannot have contributed to the young orator's peace of mind or good temper, and also that he was himself already a dangerous person to quarrel with.

In spite of the verdicts of the courts, it is uncertain how much Demosthenes recovered of his estate. Plutarch says that he failed to get back even the smallest fraction, but this must be an exaggeration: there can be little doubt, for instance, that he took possession of Aphobus' house,[3] and it is unlikely, as we have seen, that he recovered nothing at all from the two other guardians. For some years indeed he followed the profession of a writer of speeches, but we cannot be sure that it

---

[1] This Council dealt with cases of actual or attempted murder.
[2] *De F. L.*, § 93.
[3] This is implied in the Second Speech against Onetor, § 1.

was poverty that obliged him to do so. Æschines asserts[1] that Demosthenes made money out of rich young men, and particularly out of the half-witted Aristarchus, whom he deluded with the pretence that he could make him a great orator. The story of Demosthenes' relations with Aristarchus is more than doubtful, and no other pupil of Demosthenes is known to us by name. But it is probable that down to the year 345 or thereabouts he was ready to teach young men the art of speaking[2] and to compose speeches for others, though he did not appear in court as an advocate for others in person after he entered political life.[3]

The profession of speech-writer was not one which was in good repute in Athens. This was partly due to the feeling that a good case needed no professional ingenuity to support it; and so not only did Lysias and other[4] orators deprecate the deceitfulness of the "clever speaker" and treat his skill as a proof of his dishonesty, but Isocrates, who in his earlier days wrote speeches for clients, afterwards actually denied having done so, and spoke of the practice with contempt. Besides this, the fact that the professional advocate or speech-writer was paid for his work[5] suggested a certain unscrupulousness to the Athenian mind, which disapproved of the making of money either

[1] *In Timarch.*, §§ 170–2; *de F. L.*, § 148; *in Ctes.*, § 173. See Note 4.
[2] This is implied by Æsch. *in Timarch.*, §§ 117, 173, 175.
[3] Pseudo-Dem. *in Zenothemim*, § 31.
[4] See below, p. 19.   [5] Note 5.

by rhetorical practice or by philosophical teaching. Demosthenes' opponents, Æschines and Deinarchus, make the most of the supposed iniquity of the profession, though Demosthenes returns the charge upon Æschines' own head with some force.[1]

But Demosthenes' real motive for undertaking the composition of speeches for others may have been the desire, not to make money, but to acquire practice in the art for himself, with a view to his intended career. Plutarch[2] tells us that he also profited by the speeches and litigation of others, going over each case again, when he returned from the court,—reflecting upon the arguments used, considering how the matter might have been better treated, and remodelling the expressions which he remembered, until he was perfectly satisfied with them; applying, in fact, the same process of castigation and revision to which in later days he appears to have subjected his own work.

Nor was this all. It was doubtless during the ten or twelve years after he came of age that Demosthenes acquired the knowledge of Greek history which he so often displays. The story of his having copied out Thucydides eight times[3] is

---

[1] Æsch. *in Timarch.*, i., §§ 94 (with schol.), 125, 175; *de F. L.*, §§ 99, 165; Isocr., *de Antidosi*, §§ 37–44; *de Sophistis*, §§ 19 ff.; Deinarch. *in Dem.*, § 111; Dem., *de F. L.*, § 246.

[2] Plut., *Dem.*, viii.

[3] Lucian, πρὸς τὸν ἀπαίδευτον, § 4. Equally apocryphal is the tale in Zosimus' Life of Demosthenes that when the library at Athens was burnt, and the MS. of Thucydides destroyed, Demosthenes wrote out the historian's work from memory.

indeed apocryphal. But that he was thoroughly familiar with the historian, the evidence of his earlier style leaves no doubt; and he also displays the same habit of referring events and past and present conditions to their causes, the same serious view of the moral aspect of political affairs, and the same manner of stating and applying general principles of action and policy, as does Thucydides, both in the speeches included in his history, and in his own reflections upon events. In the history of Thucydides he must have studied the portraits of statesmen of widely different types, and familiarised himself with the better and the worse methods which statesmen could employ. For him, as for modern readers, Thucydides was doubtless a school of political instruction without a rival, as well as a collection of masterpieces in the older style of Athenian eloquence.[1]

The style, however, of Thucydides could not be made suitable, without great modification, to the practical affairs of the middle of the fourth century. His stiffness and compression were ill-fitted for carrying away the jury or the Assembly, and the perpetual use (which was characteristic of him) of the antithetical figures of speech, valuable as these always remained for certain purposes, would have seemed artificial and monotonous

---

[1] The speeches in Thucydides' history were probably less widely removed than is commonly supposed from the style actually adopted by Pericles; but this is not the place to argue the point.

to the audiences which Demosthenes addressed. In parts of the first extant speech of Demosthenes to the Assembly—the Speech on the Naval Boards, delivered in 354—these Thucydidean characteristics are somewhat conspicuous; but he became more discriminating in his use of them before long.

Since the history of Thucydides had been written, two new styles had sprung up. The one, of which Lysias had been the greatest master, was particularly serviceable for private lawsuits. It consisted in a studied simplicity, an apparent innocence of all artifice, which must have been (as it still is) extremely attractive, especially when so modified in the case of each litigant as just to suit his particular character. Almost every speech of Lysias appears as if it were the absolutely natural and unstudied utterance of the client for whom it was composed. Only in prologue and epilogue, and sometimes in moralising upon the actions or the characters described, the tone is somewhat heightened, and some of those artifices which distinctly separated oratory from conversation reappear, though even so they are not thrust forward. A more artificial style is also to be seen in the four speeches of a public character which Lysias composed. But in general the effect of Lysias' writing is that of conversation in which, without any sign of effort on the speaker's part, every word is just the right one, and is uttered in just the right place. The arrangement of the speech is almost invariably simple—introduction, narrative, argument, and conclusion following one another artlessly and straightforwardly. From many indications[1] it is clear that the mistrust of the "clever speaker," to which allusion has already been made,[2] was strong in the days of Lysias, and there was always a risk that suspicion would be aroused if a private person spoke in an ingenious, elaborate, or artificial manner. In the same spirit, Æschines and others made it a reproach against Demosthenes himself that he elaborated his phrases and arguments like a sophist; and the reason which Plato gives[3] for the fact that the great speakers of the fifth century had not published their speeches was that they were afraid of being thought sophists. In the speeches composed for clients by Demosthenes himself, it is noteworthy in what apologetic tones the speaker is made to introduce arguments which show an acquaintance with law or with precedents beyond the range of the ordinary man's knowledge; and how more than one speaker emphasises his own want of familiarity with the courts and compares it with his litigious opponents' long practice in conducting lawsuits. Even in speeches dealing with matters of public interest, Demosthenes makes his client warn the jury against the "clever speaker."[4]

---

[1] *e. g.*, Lysias, xii., § 86, xviii., § 16, xxvii., § 5, xxx., § 24. Lysias was already writing speeches before 399, when Socrates was condemned partly for making the worse cause appear the better.

[2] See above p. 15.　　　　　　　　　[3] *Phædrus*, 257d.

[4] *e. g. in Androt.*, §§ 4, 37; *in Aristocr.*, § 5.

Demosthenes' speeches have not, it is true, the
absolute and artless simplicity of Lysias. For
although in certain cases of a trivial kind the time
allowed was so short that only a concise statement
of the facts and recital of the laws was possible,
in most of his speeches the arrangement is carefully planned so as to emphasise the important
points; and the narrative, the proofs, and the reply
to the actual or anticipated arguments of the
opponent are interlaced (after the example of
Isæus) in a manner which is artistic without ceas-
ing to be lucid, and which offers more variety to
the hearer than a merely consecutive treatment of
the several elements in the speech. The arguments, especially those which are drawn from
considerations of general morality or of public
interest, are often more like those of a statesman
than of a plain man, and the contentions of the
speakers on points of law are sometimes subtle and
ingenious. Dionysius of Halicarnassus (an admirable critic of the last century B.C., and a very
discerning student of the great orators in particular)
says that, as compared with Lysias, Demosthenes,
like Isæus, aroused suspicion even when he had a
good case.[1] But modern readers, more familiar
with the ingenuity of lawyers, and more conscious
that legal questions can only be settled by the
careful sifting of legal arguments, are less likely
to feel this; and in fact the private speeches, at
least, of Demosthenes display, to a degree only

[1] Dion. Hal., *de Isæo*, iv.

surpassed in the work of Lysias himself, the art of adapting the language and tone of the oration to the characters of the several speakers, and of giving an impression of innocence and honesty. They show also on occasion, as do the speeches of Lysias, a sense of humour which rarely appears in the political orations.

The other style which influenced Demosthenes (coming into prominence soon after that of Lysias) was the style of Isocrates, itself a development of that of Thrasymachus, of whom as an orator we know little except that it was he who first introduced the deliberate use of rhythms into oratory. While Isocrates employs the antithetical figures, at times to excess, he does not merely arrange antithetical clauses in pairs, but builds up periods of a more elaborate kind out of clauses symmetrically arranged and characterised by dominant and often corresponding rhythms. Such work is pleasing for a while, but its rhythmical character and its studied symmetry are too obtrusive; its obvious artificiality soon cloys; its regularity becomes monotonous. It is not surprising that Isocrates' speeches could not be declaimed in the Assembly or the Law-Courts, and that his influence was achieved through the circulation of his writings in many copies.

But the value of rhythmical effects and of a periodic structure in oratory, and particularly in oratory addressed to an æsthetically sensitive people, such as the Athenians were, did not escape

Demosthenes; and his mastery of all the varieties of oratorical rhythm must have been largely acquired in his early years.　He is never the slave of rhythm, and is never bound to a single type of sentence-structure, but uses every type as he requires it, and never allows any to pall.　For such complete mastery long practice must have been needed.　Some of Isocrates' greatest writings were issued before Demosthenes' first extant public oration was delivered,—the *Panegyricus* in 380, the *Platæicus* in 373, the *Archidamus* in 366, the *Speech on the Peace* probably in 356, and the *Areopagiticus* in 355.[1]　There is no need to take literally the story[2] that Demosthenes obtained surreptitiously the technical treatises of Isocrates and other rhetorical teachers of the time and learned them by heart.　The principles of Isocrates' art must have been well known, in the days of Demosthenes' youth, to all who were interested in rhetoric, through his pupils, and through his and their works; and it was doubtless by the close study of these works that he was enabled to adapt the principles to the purposes of practical oratory.

With the matter of Isocrates' writings Demosthenes can have been little in sympathy, and it is only in his earliest work that we seem to have any unmistakable echo of Isocrates' sentiments.　It is true that Isocrates, like Demosthenes, traced much of the evil of his times, first, to the prevail-

[1] For the dates see Drerup, *Isocratis opera omnia*, I, pp. cliii. ff.
[2] Plut., *Dem.*, v.

ing love of pleasure and the unwillingness of the citizens of Athens to undertake personal service for the good of the community; and secondly, to the refusal of the Athenian people even to listen to those wise advisers who would not prophesy smooth things. He was also, like Demosthenes, deeply impressed by the perpetual discord of the Greek States with one another, and by the cruelties and the mischief perpetrated by the mercenary armies which the cities employed to do their work; he expressed, as Demosthenes did (particularly in middle and later life), the strongest Panhellenic feeling, and aspired to bring about a union of all the Hellenes, with Athens as their centre. The two writers had, moreover, many ideas in common in regard to the history and traditions of Athens, and appealed to the same outstanding examples of her action in the past. But nothing could be more alien from Demosthenes than the academic suggestions by which Isocrates sought to remedy the mischiefs of the age—the vague sentiment (not altogether unjustified as a sentiment, but quite unpractical as a policy) in favour of some kind of monarchy, whether it was to be exercised by Jason of Pheræ, or by Dionysius of Syracuse, or by Philip; the fancy that Philip could be converted into a regenerator of Hellas, or a purely unselfish leader of a voluntary Panhellenic coalition; the dream of a return of the city to the form of government which existed in the days when the Council of Areopagus was supreme; the idea of healing the

disunion of the States by causing them to undertake a united campaign against Persia under the
leadership of Athens and Sparta, or of Archidamus,
or of Philip himself. When Demosthenes himself
made a proposal on any subject, every point was
worked out in detail, in a practical and businesslike manner: the half-thought-out generalities of
Isocrates must have been almost repulsive to him;
and as for Isocrates' favourite nostrum—a united
war against Persia—it must have been perfectly
obvious that, so far from it being possible to achieve
union by organising a campaign against Persia,
no such campaign was possible until some kind of
unity was enforced: and when in fact, after Isocrates' death, Philip and Alexander imposed a
formal unity, and Alexander led an army drawn
from many of the Greek States into Asia, no real
or effective union—certainly no union of spirit—
between the States at home was after all achieved.
Isocrates' attitude both towards Philip and towards
Persia was the exact opposite of that which Demosthenes adopted when his policy was fully matured.
Isocrates wished to set Philip at the head of the
Greeks in order to crush Persia: Demosthenes (at
least in 341, as will appear later[1]) desired the alliance of Persia in order to prevent Philip from
becoming the head of the Greeks. Moreover,
Isocrates' generally anti-imperialistic attitude is
just the reverse of the attitude of Demosthenes
towards empire, even though many passages in

[1] See below, pp. 316, 340–343, 409, 417.

Isocrates' writings may express in more fulsome
and artificial language the sentiments which
Demosthenes himself held with regard to the
degeneracy of the People and their behaviour
towards the politicians who advised them.

Yet, poles apart as Isocrates and Demosthenes
were, the younger man learned much from the
elder. Above all, he probably learned from him
the possible influence of speeches published as
political pamphlets. There can be little doubt
that at two very critical times—those of the Social
War, and of the peace-negotiations in 346—public
opinion was prepared for the measures to which
the policy of Eubulus led, by the writings of
Isocrates; and there can be even less doubt that
the influence of Demosthenes' own speeches was
immensely extended by their publication. The
view, which some recent scholars have maintained, [1]
that the speeches which we have were not delivered
at all, but are simply political pamphlets, and that
Demosthenes' real speeches in the Assembly were
far rougher in form and more violent in language,
is based upon very inadequate evidence; and it is
probable that, although the speeches were subjected to some revision before publication, the
divergence between the spoken and the published
form was not great. But it is beyond question
that they owed much of their influence on the
course of events to their appearance as pamphlets;
and although some few political pamphlets [2] seem

---

[1] *E. g.*, Hahn and Wendland. See Note 6.   [2] Note 7.

to have been issued towards the end of the fifth
century, Demosthenes was the first great practical
statesman to make use of methods, the effectiveness of which in some degree anticipated the power
of the press in modern times; and it was from
Isocrates that he must have learned to use them.

Whether or not Demosthenes came at any time
under the influence of Plato, who died in 347–6, is
doubtful. Cicero, Quintilian, and Tacitus all
allege that he was a reader and even a pupil of
Plato; but the tradition on which they relied
seems to rest on very weak authority,[1] and although it is most improbable that he did not know
the philosopher's writings, he can have felt little
sympathy with his opinions. Much as Demosthenes lamented the weaknesses of the Athenian
people, he was a whole-hearted believer in democracy—the constitution which Plato placed lowest
but one in his enumeration of the several types of
State; and the fact that the philosophic ideal was,
from the point of view of the practical statesman,
unpatriotic and selfish, would also render Demosthenes unfriendly to such speculations.

During the years between 365 and 355—the
years of preparation for his public career—
Demosthenes must not only have familiarised
himself with the work of his predecessors and older
contemporaries, with Greek history and Athenian
law, but must also have written many of those

---

[1] See Sandys' note on Cicero's *Orator*, iv., §16, and the references
there given.   See also Note 8 below.

typical passages which formed part of an orator's stock-in-trade. For nearly every speaker, and certainly every rhetorical teacher, formed a collection of prologues and epilogues, and of passages dealing with each of the more frequently recurring topics; these he adapted, as might be convenient, to the purposes of the particular speech upon which he was engaged. Rhetorical teachers appear not only to have imparted such collections to their pupils, but also to have published them, and hence we find not only verbal or almost verbal repetitions in different orations of the same speaker, but also passages which are identical in the speeches of different composers.[1] Moreover, the rhetorician or sophist wrote passages both for and against particular views, and was ready to be of service to either side; and the writer of speeches for clients doubtless found such passages useful.[2] Nor could the politician, who had already formed his view and chosen his side, despise the advantage of having his opinions upon certain topics, which were sure to present themselves, reduced to the best form which he was capable of giving to them: and many of the general reflections which abound in Demosthenes' speeches (and particularly those reflections which occur in more than one context[3])

---

[1] Compare the procœmium of Andocides, *de Mysteriis*, with those of Lysias, *Or.* xix., and Isocr., *Or.* xv.; and Andocides *de Pace*, §§ 3–12, with Æschines, *de F. L.*, §§ 172–6. See also Spengel, *Artium Scriptores*, pp. 106, 107.   [2] Note 9.

[3] Compare (*e. g.*) *Phil.* I, § 2, and III, § 5; *de Chers.*, § 34, and

may owe their origin to his early studies. In his earlier speeches, when one or another of these passages is inserted, we can sometimes detect the joints; but after a few years, though many of the generalisations found in the speeches had probably been worked up beforehand, they are so perfectly fitted into their place, and seem to arise so naturally out of their context, that the artificiality is almost imperceptible.

An orator must learn not only to compose his speeches, but to deliver them. It was here that Demosthenes' greatest difficulties lay. He began his practice weak-voiced, lisping, and short of breath; the letter R was especially troublesome to him; and it has been noticed that, in the statues of him which are known, the lower lip comes much less forward than the upper—a defect which is inimical to clear enunciation. We are told that he overcame these physical disadvantages by practising with pebbles in his mouth, repeating many times the line,

ῥοχθεῖ γαρ μέγα κῦμα ποτὶ ξερὸν ἠπείροιο,[1]

trying to shout down the breakers on the shore at Phalerum (where, in Cicero's day, the local guides were able to show the exact spot where the young orator's efforts were made[2]), reciting while running

---

Phil. III, § 4; *in Aristocr.*, §§ 207, 208, and *Olynth.* iii., §§ 25, 26. See also Note 10.

    [1] *Odyssey*, v., 402.   [2] Cic., *de Fin.*, V, ii., § 5.

up hill, learning to deliver many lines in one breath, and speaking before a mirror to correct his gestures. More than once he failed, when he rose to address the People. At his first attempt his periods fell into confusion, and he was met with shouts of laughter. As he wandered in depression up and down the Peiræus, an old friend, Eunomus of Thria, met him, and rebuked him because, when he had a speech to deliver that was worthy of Pericles, he sacrificed his opportunity from want of pluck and manliness—from timidity before the crowd and lack of proper physical exercise. On another occasion, when he had failed, the actor Satyrus came to his aid. Demosthenes complained to Satyrus that, although he had sacrificed his health out of devotion to his studies, the People would not listen to him, but preferred the speeches of drunken sailors and fools to his own. Satyrus bade him recite from memory a speech of Euripides or Sophocles. Demosthenes did so, and Satyrus then taught him to speak it in a manner, and with a spirit, that befitted the character. So effective were these lessons that Demosthenes came to regard action, or delivery, as incomparably the most important of all the elements in the art of oratory. He built, we are told, an underground chamber (which was shown for centuries afterwards), where he daily practised his voice and delivery, sometimes for two or three months at a time, shaving one side of his head in order that he might resist the temptation to go out into the

streets. The amount of truth that there is in
these tales cannot be estimated; but we need not
hesitate to believe that Demosthenes showed a
heroic perseverance in his determination to overcome the physical defects with which he began his
career, and that he made himself perfect in that
"actor's art," which, he told an enquirer, was
first, second, and third among the requirements of
an orator.[1]

Plutarch tells a story which illustrates the importance attached by Demosthenes to the tone
of the voice. A man came to him and asked him
to plead for him, explaining that he had been
assaulted. "Indeed," said Demosthenes, "you
have not really suffered any injury at all." The
man thereupon raised his voice and cried out,
"What? Do you mean to say that I have suffered
no injury?" "Ah!" said Demosthenes, "now I
hear the voice of an injured man!" Plutarch adds
that Demosthenes' own delivery captivated the
majority of his hearers, though the more refined
of them thought that he carried his action to a
point at which it became ignoble and effeminate.
The same reproach was brought (so we infer from
Aristotle[2]) against the dominant school of contemporary tragic actors.

[1] Cic., *Brutus*, § 142. Most of these stories are found in
Plutarch. He derived some of them from Demetrius of Phalerum
who professed to have heard them from Demosthenes himself.
Some say that the actor by whom he was assisted was Neoptolemus or Andronicus, and that Demosthenes gave him 10,000
drachmæ for his help. See Note 11.   [2] *Poetics*, xxvi.

THE STATUE OF DEMOSTHENES IN THE VATICAN

PHOTO BY ALINARI

Nervousness was less easy to overcome than defective utterance: and on one or two important occasions of Demosthenes' life this weakness seems to have recurred.[1] Indeed it was always so far present that he seldom ventured to speak without preparation. Whether he really increased his natural lack of robustness by wearing soft raiment and neglecting bodily exercises, as his enemies affirmed, we do not know; and the question is of no importance. He had at least the courage to pursue his way, undeterred by every obstacle, to the goal which he had set before himself—that of becoming a statesman and an orator worthy of Athens.

APPENDIX TO CHAPTER I

(*On the Private Speeches*)

In a study which is particularly devoted to the public career of Demosthenes there is no need for any detailed account of his Private Speeches; and the subject is rendered difficult by the doubts which exist as to the genuineness of many of those which have descended to us under his name, and the uncertainty of the criteria by which their genuineness is tested. But they are sufficiently illustrative of his versatility as an orator to demand a brief notice.

The Private Speeches which there is good reason to consider genuine mainly fall between the years 357 and 345. (The dates of the Speeches against Spudias and against Callicles—both of which may be quite early,—and of the Speech against Conon, are unknown.) The short Speech on the Trierarchic Crown was composed on behalf of Apollodorus, son of Pasion the banker,[2] who seeks to make good his claim to the crown offered by the

---

[1] Especially on the First Embassy to Philip (see below, p. 243). Compare Dem., *de F. L.*, § 206, *de Chers.*, § 68.   [2] Note 12.

State to the captain whose ship was first manned and ready for sea, and to disprove the claim of his opponents. The expedition for which the fleet was ordered out was probably that of the year 360, in which Demosthenes himself served, and the trial took place two years later. The interest of the Speech lies in the light which it throws on the Athenian naval system—a subject with which we shall be concerned in a later chapter. The concluding portion is chiefly devoted to a denunciation of paid advocates, which falls oddly from Demosthenes, and is of course one of the tricks of the trade. The trenchant directness of the Speech, and its outspoken criticism of the attitude of the Athenians towards defaulting captains, are entirely in his own style; and we can see already the interest in naval affairs which led him a few years later to propose, and many years later to carry out, a reform of the Trierarchic system.

The Speech against Spudias, dealing with a quarrel arising out of a family arrangement, which had been broken by Spudias, need not detain us. In its tone and style it resembles the Speeches against Aphobus and Onetor. The case was a comparatively trivial one, and is briefly, but convincingly, treated.

The Speech against Callicles is more interesting. It is admirably written in the vein of a good-natured man who only wants a quiet life, but is wantonly attacked by his neighbour, and so has to appear in court. The speaker and Callicles occupied adjacent farms, between which ran a road. The speaker's father, finding that the water which was carried down from the hills was making a channel for itself in his land, had built a wall, which diverted the flow. Many years later, a torrent due to a violent storm broke down an old wall on Callicles' property and did some mischief. Callicles then brought an action for damages, and the reply, composed by Demosthenes, not only gives an interesting picture of Attic country-life, but is also the most graceful and humorous of his speeches, and shows that, given a good case, not of too serious a nature, he could adopt a less solemn tone than was usual with him.

The Speech against Conon is also admirably conceived. A respectable and even priggish young man claims damages for a somewhat brutal assault—the culmination of a good deal of "ragging" on the part of a number of men who had formed themselves into a club of a lively and dissolute character; and he expresses himself in a manner, the unconscious humour of which must have given a good deal of pleasure to the composer of the Speech and to the jury.[1]

The Speeches for Phormio (350 B.C.) and against Stephanus (350 or 349), delivered in the course of litigation mainly concerned with banking, raise a problem which so nearly touches the character of Demosthenes as an advocate and a man, that they must be more fully treated at a later point in the narrative.

The Speech against Bœotus "On his name" was written in 348 for a certain Mantitheus, who brought an action against his half-brother Bœotus for illegally taking the same name as himself. It is composed in the manner of a blunt and direct speaker, fond of putting pointed questions one after another, and displaying some humour in the pictures which he draws of the inconveniences which must arise from the failure of other people to distinguish between himself and the much less respectable person who has taken his name. We do not know, however, what was to be said on the other side; and, for whatever reason, the speaker lost his suit.

The two Private Speeches which were probably composed in or about the year 346 are (like the Speech for Phormio) instances of a *paragraphé* or plea in bar of action, based principally on the fact that the plaintiff had already given the defendant a release from all claims. In the Speech against Pantænetus, the claim made by Nicobulus against Pantænetus was the result of a series of complicated transactions in regard to the ownership of a mine; and the case was tried under the special law regulating mines. This law required a speedy decision and imposed certain stringent conditions on the litigants; and it is part of Nicobulus' plea that the case was not one which properly fell under that law, and that a number of causes of action which should have been brought before different courts had been illegally merged in one suit. The Speech is written for a man possessed of a good deal of the "humility that humbly commends itself to notice," and conscious of the prejudice which must have been aroused by Pantænetus' representation of him as a money-lender and a person whose very manner was suspicious; and it combines some

---

[1] The date of the Speech is uncertain; but it may have been delivered about 355 B.C.

3

very able character-drawing with great ingenuity in legal argument.

The other *paragraphé* was pleaded to bar an action brought by Nausimachus and Xenopeithes, who claimed a large sum of money from the sons of their former guardian Aristæchmus. The speaker pleads that a discharge given to Aristæchmus had covered all matters connected with the trust, and that the plaintiffs' action was barred by the Statute of Limitations. The Speech is short, lucid, and businesslike, except for a piece of rhetorical ingenuity at the close, where the speaker replies to the plaintiffs' claim to consideration on account of their large expenditure in the service of the State, by arguing that such a plea brings discredit upon the city, since it implies that the city makes excessive demands upon her citizens.

The last of the Private Speeches which can with any probability be ascribed to Demosthenes himself was directed against Eubulides, in the year 345. The speaker, Euxitheus, charges Eubulides with having brought about his exclusion from the list of citizens (in a revision which took place in 345) by the use of unfair means, and appeals to the jury, as he was entitled to do, to restore his name to the list. He speaks as an honest and straightforward man, not ashamed of his poverty—his mother sold ribbons and had served as a nurse—and is confident in the strength of his case, which is clearly and vigorously presented.

These speeches sufficiently illustrate the variety of the aspects of human nature with which an Athenian advocate had to deal, and the skill of Demosthenes in dealing with them. While adapting himself to the character of the speaker, he yet remains, in most cases, recognisably himself. Even if his more forceful characteristics are repressed in the main part of the speech—his irony, his moral indignation, his merciless incisiveness—they are apt to break out in sudden flashes; and he constantly succeeds in giving the impression that he stands on a higher moral level than his adversary, and can afford either to treat him with scorn or to fall upon him without mercy. But when once he had attained a position of responsibility in public life, we can understand that he would naturally abandon this lower branch of oratory, just as, from the time when he first began to take part in political debates, he ceased to appear personally in court in the interest of his clients,—doubtless from a desire not to prejudice his political prospects by exposing himself to the ill-favour with which the professional advocate was regarded. It was not until after 345 that he was in a position really to control the policy of Athens, and up to that time, while he was in opposition, his political occupations were probably not so absorbing as to leave him no time to write speeches for clients. But after this date we find no more such speeches from his pen; for the suggestion[1] that after the accession of Alexander the Great he may have found himself cut off from political activities and resumed for a time the profession of advocate (composing among others the Speeches against Phænippus and against Phormio) rests on no solid foundation.

NOTES

1. It is not easy to give the value of the estate according to modern standards. At the present price of silver, the weight of silver in a talent (about 57 lbs. avoirdupois) would be worth little more than £100 (see Goodwin, *Demosthenes' Meidias*, § 80, note). But its purchasing power would be much greater. The wages of an unskilled labourer were about 1½ drachmæ a day in the 4th century B.C. (see Beloch, *Griech. Gesch.*, ii., pp. 358, 359); they are now perhaps 3s. a day (all told) in England, and at this rate a talent would buy £600 worth of unskilled labour. Again, if the price of wheat be taken as a standard, wheat in Athens in Demosthenes' time (*in Phorm.* § 39) cost 5 drachmæ a medimnus—about 27 dr. a quarter. It now costs (March, 1913) 36s. a quarter in London; and at this rate a talent would be the equivalent of about £400.

2. The date of Demosthenes' birth cannot be exactly determined, as he himself gives two inconsistent accounts of his age. In the first Speech against Onetor, § 15, he says that Aphobus was married in the last month of the archonship of Polyzelus, *i. e.*, about June, 366 B.C.; and that immediately afterwards he himself came of age, *i. e.*, reached his eighteenth birthday. If so, he was born soon after the middle of 384. Again, in the first Speech against Aphobus, §§ 4, 17, 19, he says that he was seven years old at his father's death, and was ten years under guardianship before coming of age in 366. This also fixes his birth in the archon-year 384-3. Hypereides (*in Dem.*, Col. 22) refers to him in

---

[1] Butcher, *Demosthenes*, p. 140.

324-3 as over sixty; and this also points to 384. But in the Speech against Meidias, § 154, he speaks of himself as thirty-two years old. The date of this speech is disputed, but it was probably composed (see below, p. 226) late in the summer of 347; and, if so the orator's birth was assigned to 379. Even if the words δύο καὶ τριάκοντα are a corruption of τέτταρα (δ') καὶ τριάκοντα (as in Thucyd., ii., 2, τέσσαρας μῆνας is a generally accepted emendation of δύο μῆνας), this only brings us back to 381 B.C.—the date given also by Dion. Hal., *ad Ammæum*, I, iv. If the speech was delivered in 349, as many scholars suppose, the discrepancy is less, but there are strong reasons against this dating. The date of Demosthenes' birth given in *Vit. X Orat.*, p. 845d, is the archonship of Dexitheus, B.C. 385-4.

3. The real value of Demosthenes' estate has been minutely discussed by Beloch, Kahrstedt, and others, but the discussion (which turns upon the interpretation of some difficult passages in the Speeches against Aphobus and against Polycles) is too often vitiated by an obvious desire to prove Demosthenes to have been lying. Demosthenes perhaps exaggerates slightly the original value of the estate, and slightly underrates the amount which he actually received, but there is no reason to suppose that he seriously misstates the facts. The scope of this book does not permit a more detailed examination of the evidence.

4. Æschines states further that when at a later time Aristarchus was forced to go into exile on account of a peculiarly shocking murder of which he was accused, Demosthenes, himself an instigator of the crime, managed to retain three talents which he ought to have given to Aristarchus; and Deinarchus (*in Dem.*, §§ 30, 47) repeats the story with little variation. Demosthenes himself (*in Meid.*, §§ 104-7, 117-20) stated that the whole story was a malicious slander, invented and spread by Meidias; and this is as likely as any other to be the true version of the matter. No ancient orator is to be trusted when he speaks of the private life of his opponents, and if there was among the clients or pupils of Demosthenes a rich young man who afterwards became notorious, it would be quite in accordance with the character of Meidias and the practice of Athenian orators to add the details necessary to involve Demosthenes in the same infamy. The details themselves are very suspicious. According to Æschines (*de F. L.*, § 148) the murdered man, Nicodemus, had accused

Demosthenes of desertion. The occasion referred to was probably the spring of 348, when Demosthenes returned from service in Eubœa to perform his duty as choregus at the Dionysia. But from the Speech against Meidias, § 103, it appears that the charge was made, not by Nicodemus, but by Euctemon, at the instigation of Meidias; and if so, the reason for Demosthenes' alleged animosity against Nicodemus vanishes. In § 116 Demosthenes accuses Meidias of charging Aristarchus falsely with the murder.

5. We do not know whether the profession of speech-writer was really lucrative. The only indication of the fees charged is found in a fragment of the defence of Antiphon (edited from a papyrus by M. Jules Nicole in 1907) in 411 B.C., in which Antiphon says, "My accusers assert that I wrote court-speeches for others, and got my twenty per cent. for it." But as Antiphon was suspected of avarice, we cannot be sure that all speech-writers demanded twenty per cent. of the sum at issue,—still less that the rate was the same in the time of Demosthenes, half a century later.

6. There can really be little doubt that the extant speeches of Demosthenes were delivered substantially in their present form: and the arguments to the contrary are singularly weak. It is of course clear that they underwent a certain amount of revision and alteration, especially through the insertion of passages here and there to meet the objections of opposing speakers, and possibly through the modification of some phrases in the light of the debate. Perhaps also the formal proposals of resolutions may have been omitted when the speeches were published; such purely formal sentences would have little interest for readers. But they may never have stood in the text of the speech at all. In all probability motions were handed in to the clerk or the president, and read aloud by him. The objection, which has been raised against holding the extant speeches to have been spoken orations, viz., that they contain no definite motions, is to be answered, partly by these considerations, partly by pointing out, first, that some of the speeches obviously did accompany definite motions, and that they do make quite definite proposals, though not in formal shape; secondly, that some of the speeches may well be replies to motions; thirdly, that there is no reason why either Demosthenes or any other speaker should necessarily

have moved a motion in every speech.   Other objections that
have been raised are:

(1) That the speeches range over too wide a ground to have
been made upon definite motions in debate.   But we do not
know what limits were imposed upon irrelevancy in Athens,
and the alleged irrelevancy has been greatly exaggerated; for
the objectors (particularly Hahn) have actually treated as
irrelevant the arguments which Demosthenes bases on broad
grounds of policy and public morality.   It is true that the
extant debating speeches of Andocides and Hegesippus do not
make much use of such arguments; but this is part of the difference between them and Demosthenes, and not a necessary
feature of debating speeches.

(2) That the speeches are not such as Plutarch's description
of Demosthenes' manner would lead us to expect.   This
however is a great exaggeration of the truth.   It is true that
Plutarch and Æschines quote some phrases from Demosthenes
more violent than any but a few which are found in the extant
orations; but there are close approximations to them, and the
fact that they must have occurred in speeches which Demosthenes either spoke *ex tempore,* or else did not think worth
publication, does not prove that the speeches which he did
think worth publication were never spoken.

The utmost that can be said is that in one or two cases—and
particularly in that of the Third Philippic—there were two
versions of the speech current, possibly owing to a reissue, with
alterations, by Demosthenes himself.   But it has now been
shown to be highly probable that versions of some of Demosthenes'
speeches were made up by Anaximenes for his history, partly by
copying passages in genuine published speeches of the orator,
partly by invention or by alteration of genuine passages.   To
this or similar causes we almost certainly owe the Speech on the
Constitution (at the time of the Olynthian crisis) and the Reply
to Philip's Letter,—possibly also Philip's Letter itself and the
Fourth Philippic; and it is possible (though not likely) that one
of the versions of the Third Philippic may have arisen in the same
way, or may have been influenced by such spurious rhetorical
work.   For the rest, it is hard to understand how an unprejudiced
reader can regard the speeches as they stand as unfit for a debate.
Even a feeble imagination should be able to form some concep-

tion of their tremendous power, when spoken with the unique delivery of Demosthenes. But imagination is not always one of the gifts of the scholar.

7. Such pamphlets were the pseudo-Xenophontic *Constitution of Athens* (425–4 B.C.); Andocides' Speech πρὸς τοὺς ἑταίρους (shortly after 415); Antiphon's περὶ τῆς μεταστασέως (in 411); and the περὶ πολιτείας ascribed to Herodes, but probably the work of a member of Theramenes' circle in 404. (See Drerup's edition, p. 110 ff.)

8. A story is told by a Scholiast on Galen, de Nat. Fac. II, § 172, that Demosthenes was expelled by Plato from his class, because he would only attend to the form and not to the argument of the remarks made; but that he found his way in by the garden-gate, and listened for a long time without being detected. Hence arose the Greek proverb, "to get in by the garden-gate." (See Probst, in *Neue Jahrbücher* xxxi, p. 307.)

9. We find in Antiphon's Speech against the Stepmother strong assertions of the supreme value of evidence given by slaves under torture; and in the same orator's Speech on the Murder of Herodes an equally strong condemnation of this kind of evidence, as likely to be simply the evidence which will enable the slave to escape from the torture most quickly.

10. Whether the repetitions in Demosthenes are as numerous as was supposed by Lord Brougham (in his *Dissertation on the Eloquence of the Ancients*) may be doubted. The question really turns on the view taken of the origin of the Fourth Philippic (see below, pp. 342, 356). He accounts for them by supposing that the orator "desires to gratify, to please, as well as to persuade; and that they are come to enjoy a critical repast, as well as to expatiate and discourse their State-affairs. In this case, the repetition would heighten the zest at each time; as they who love music or take pleasure in dramatic representations are never so much gratified with the first enjoyment of any fine melody or splendid piece of acting as with its subsequent exhibition." That Athenian audiences appreciated an oration as a work of art is undoubted; but it is too much to suppose that they were so strongly affected by the particular passages which in fact we find repeated (at considerable intervals of time) as to welcome them in the manner imagined by Lord Brougham.

11. Dr. Johnson was never tired of denouncing the use of

"action" in oratory. "Action can have no effect upon reasonable minds. It may augment noise, but it never can enforce argument. If you speak to a dog, you use action; you hold up your hand thus, because he is a brute; and in proportion as men are removed from brutes, action will have the less influence upon them." *Mrs. Thrale:* "What then, Sir, becomes of Demosthenes' saying, 'Action, action, action'?" *Johnson:* "Demosthenes, madam, spoke to an assembly of brutes—to a barbarous people." (Boswell.)

12. The theory of Blass that Demosthenes composed the speech on his own behalf (after he had served as trierarch in 360), and that Libanius is wrong in saying that Apollodorus was the speaker, seems to rest on insufficient grounds; but there is no real reason to doubt that Demosthenes did write the speech.

CHAPTER II

GREECE FROM 404 TO 359

THE condition of the Greek world at the time when Demosthenes began to take an interest in public affairs cannot be satisfactorily explained without a brief review of the course of Greek history since the downfall of Athens at the end of the Peloponnesian War. To this the present chapter will be devoted.[1]

So far as Athens herself was concerned, the calamity, despite the apparent completeness of her overthrow at the moment, proved to be less great than might have been expected. The tyranny of the Thirty, who established themselves in power shortly after the capitulation of the city to Sparta, was soon over; and it had at least one beneficial result, that it brought oligarchy into lasting disrepute. The democratic constitution was restored; and although rival orators might accuse one another of employing oligarchical methods or of sympathising with oligarchical

---

[1] The summary of events here given only attempts to deal with matters which must be mentioned in order to explain the history of the succeeding period.

ideas, and theorists might hanker after a constitution more efficient in its practical working than the Athenian democracy, there was, nevertheless, —at least for eighty years or so—no serious desire for constitutional change, nor any risk of successful revolution. The laws of Athens, which had fallen into some confusion, were revised and brought into harmony with one another; the city's trade revived rapidly; her external splendour and her position as the chief centre both of Hellenic commerce and of Hellenic culture brought strangers to her, as of old, from all countries; and, apart from some temporary relapses, her history for the next thirty years was a history of the gradual recovery of strength and prosperity.

The history of Sparta during the same period presents a different picture. After the capitulation of Athens in 404 she was for the moment the strongest State in Greece. But the governors and "Committees of Ten," which she established wherever she could, ruled tyrannically, and she came to be more and more detested. She failed, moreover, to fulfil the expectations of the principal States which had assisted her to conquer Athens,— Corinth, Argos, and Thebes. Corinth wished for the possession of Corcyra, and for undisputed supremacy in the seas west of the Isthmus, in order that her trade in those seas might be secure. Argos, though not really capable of being more than a second-rate power, at least expected some improvement in her position in the Peloponnese.

PEIRAEUS, HARBOUR OF ZEA, FROM MUNYCHIA

PHOTO BY THE ENGLISH PHOTO CO.

Thebes desired to be acknowledged as the par-
amount state in Bœotia. Sparta did not gratify
any of these desires, and all three States, as well
as Athens herself, were ready to turn upon her
when the opportunity offered itself in 395.

In that year the Persian King, Artaxerxes II.,
with whom—nominally in the interest of the Greek
cities in Asia Minor—the Spartans had been at
war since about 400, sent a Rhodian named Timocrates to the principal Greek States, with large
sums of money, to induce the leading statesmen
to cause their several cities to declare war upon
Sparta. (Whether any statesman at Athens took
the bribe is uncertain: in any case Athens needed
little persuasion.) The Thebans incited their
friends the Locrians of Opus to hostilities against
the Phocians; the latter applied for aid to Sparta;
and the Spartans under Lysander invaded Bœotia.
But Lysander was killed in an attack upon Haliartus, and when an Athenian force joined the
Thebans, his successor returned to Sparta. In
the next year (394) we find a mixed army composed
of troops from Athens, Thebes, Corinth, Argos,
and Eubœa, opposed to the army of Sparta, in
which were contingents from the smaller Peloponnesian states. At first Sparta was successful on
land: but the re-fortification of the Peiræus, the port
of Athens, was begun in July; on August 10th,
the Athenian admiral Conon, at the head of a
Persian fleet, won a great naval victory over the
Spartans off Cnidos; and in 393 he rebuilt the walls

of Athens (which had been destroyed in 404), a large body of Theban workmen assisting in the task. About the same time (probably in consequence of the revival of imperialistic ambitions in Athens) the moderate leaders who had guided Athens for some years gave way to Agyrrhius and other politicians of a more extreme type. The increase of the payment for each attendance in the Assembly to three obols made it better worth while for the masses once more to throw their weight into politics, and as their interests were on the whole best served by war,[1] a markedly militant tendency began to show itself. The demagogues unhappily resorted, not infrequently, to prosecutions of their opponents and of the wealthier citizens in order to obtain money and to find supplies for the army. The war continued with varying results for some years: on the whole the trend of events was adverse to the domination of Sparta, and she lost to a great extent her hold over the islands and more distant colonies. Brilliant generalship was displayed on both sides: the Athenian Iphicrates in particular distinguished himself by his use of the newly devised force of peltastæ—composed largely (though not entirely) of mercenaries, and more lightly armed, though equipped with longer weapons, than the heavy hoplite forces which had been customarily employed—as well as by new tactical methods, which at first were extremely successful. On one

[1] See below, p. 74.

occasion he surprised and destroyed a whole division of the Spartan army near Corinth.

In 392, the Spartans, hard-pressed for money, made an abortive appeal to Persia for the dictation and enforcement of a Peace. A similar appeal conveyed to Susa by their admiral Antalcidas in 387 was more successful; and the position of Athens at the end of the year was seriously threatened both on the Hellespont and at home: her finances were exhausted; and she had really no alternative but to submit to the Peace, which was finally concluded in the winter of 387–6. Any desire on the part of Corinth and Thebes to resist was quelled by the mobilisation of the Spartan army; and when the Great King's letter was read to the assembled representatives of the Greek States, the terms of the Peace were generally accepted. They seemed, indeed, to provide a temporary solution, if not altogether an honourable one, both of the disputes between the Greek States themselves, and of the position of the Greek cities in Asia Minor in relation to the King. These cities, with the islands of Clazomenæ and Cyprus, were now to become part of the King's Empire. All other Greek cities were to be independent, except that the islands of Lemnos, Imbros, and Scyros were still to belong to Athens. The King declared his intention of making war upon any State which would not accept the peace; and although Thebes made an effort to obtain the recognition of her supremacy in Bœotia, she was obliged to give way, and to allow the towns of Orchomenus, Platææ, and Thespiæ to be established as independent centres—centres, that is, at first of Spartan, and before long of Athenian, influence within Bœotia.

The ratification of the Peace of Antalcidas is an event of the highest importance for the history of the next half-century. On the one hand, the Peace provided as it were a charter of liberty to all the smaller States; and it could always be appealed to by a larger State desirous of putting a rival in the wrong by accusing it of menacing the autonomy of weaker cities.[1] But, on the other hand, the final abandonment of the Asiatic Greeks to the Persian Empire, and the acknowledgment of the right of the King of Persia to dictate terms to the Greek States, are very significant of the difference between the spirit of the fourth century and that of the fifth, when any concession to Persia was thought of as treason to the cause of liberty. From this time onwards, the possibility of Persian interference in the internal affairs of Greece was always in the background of men's thoughts, whether they thought of such interference as a means of securing their own ends, or as a danger to be guarded against; and the influence of Persia by means of the "Persian gold," of which we hear so much, became from time to time a real and a very unfortunate element in Greek political life, creating suspicion everywhere, and

[1] Comp. Xen., *Hell.*, VI, iii, §7, etc.

affecting for the worse both the course of debate in the councils of Athens and the administration of justice in her courts.

The Peace of Antalcidas, however, did not in fact allay hostilities in Greece itself. It did indeed put an end for the time to direct hostilities between the Greek States and the Persian Empire: for although the rebellious subjects of the Empire—particularly Euagoras in Cyprus, and Tachos and Nectanebos in Egypt—were greatly assisted by Athenian generals and soldiers, these were not acting in the name of Athens, and the Athenians were more than once obliged to recall their generals at the request of the King. But in Greece itself the Peace was not perfectly satisfactory to any one. Athens, though the retention of the three islands was a concession to her dignity and an advantage of the first importance to her trade, was ashamed of the affair, got rid of the statesmen who had influenced her in the matter, and for many years followed the lead of Callistratus in their stead. The antagonism between Thebes and Sparta was not to be lightly healed, and the desire of the Spartans to recover their supremacy over the Peloponnese could not remain at rest for long. They did not indeed formally break the Peace. Their interferences with other States were, it seems, justified technically by the receipt of an invitation from the oligarchic party in the State interfered with, and by the pretence that that party represented the government of the State;

so that nominally they merely placed their troops and governors at the service of the local government. But the effect was the same as if they had openly broken the Peace. In 385 or 384 they compelled the people of Mantineia (the largest town in Arcadia, and generally a centre of resistance to Sparta) to destroy their walls and to live in four or five villages, each under a Spartan governor, instead of in a town in which they could fortify themselves, and could also listen more easily to the harangues of the advocates of liberty. In 379 they conquered Phleius after a siege of twenty months, and their influence throughout Greece appears for a time to have recovered rapidly. In the North the town of Olynthus, the head of the Chalcidic League, had taken advantage of the weakness of Macedonia to extend its power over the Chalcidic peninsula and (in spite of a nominal alliance with the Macedonian King, Amyntas III.) even over part of Macedonia itself. Amyntas joined two of the threatened Chalcidic cities, Acanthus and Apollonia, in an appeal to Sparta. The Spartans responded by sending an expedition against Olynthus, which, after a long struggle, was in 379 forced to become a member of the Spartan alliance. The position of Amyntas was, of course, greatly strengthened; but at the time no one could foresee that the power of the Macedonian monarchy would grow so great as to make it very regrettable that Olynthus and the Chalcidic League had not been suffered to remain as a bulwark against it.

In 383 or 382, a Spartan force under Phœbidas, on its way to Olynthus, contrived to seize the Cadmeia, the acropolis of Thebes. (The Thebans were at the time led by democratic statesmen, hostile to Sparta, and had refused to join in the campaign against Olynthus; while Phœbidas was aided by oligarchical conspirators within the walls.) The Spartans remained in possession until 379, when their garrison was expelled by the democrats, who had been living in exile in Athens, and who now formed a successful plot for the recovery of their native city. The attitude of Athens was peculiar. Strongly opposed as she had been to the policy of Sparta, the Spartan occupation of Thebes had been an advantage to her, since she had been enabled thereby to recover from Thebes the frontier town of Oropus, the possession of which was of great consequence; and the Spartans had re-established Platææ, between which town and herself there had always been friendship: she was also intimidated by the proximity of the Spartan army, and in consequence was not prepared to go to war; she even sentenced to death the generals who of their own accord had helped the Theban exiles; and she would probably have come to an arrangement with Sparta immediately, had not the Spartan admiral Sphodrias invaded Attica, and done some damage before he retreated.

The action of Sphodrias had not been ordered by the Spartans, but they refused to punish him on his return. Instead, therefore, of making peace with Sparta, the Athenians organised a new league, with the avowed object of mutual protection against the Spartans and their infringements of the Peace of Antalcidas; any States which were not subject to the Persian King were invited to join, and the terms of the Peace of Antalcidas gave some assurance to the smaller cities that they would not be oppressed, and made them the more ready to become members of the league.

The chief burden of the organisation of this Athenian confederacy (sometimes called the Second Delian League from its resemblance to the great alliance of the fifth century) was undertaken by Callistratus and the two brilliant admirals, Chabrias and Timotheus—the latter also a pupil of Isocrates, whose "Panegyric Oration" in 380 had probably done something to prepare the way for the formation of the confederacy. The arrangements were completed in 378 or 377. The synod of the allies was to be independent of the Athenian Assembly, and the consent of both was to be required to all active measures, and particularly to the declaration of war and peace. The contributions of the allies were not (as were those of the members of the former Delian League) to be regarded or designated as tribute paid to Athens,[1] and Athenians were not to hold property in any of the allied States. Some few of the allies appear to have contributed ships, but all probably contributed money; and the execution of the plan of

[1] See Note 1 at the end of the Chapter.

campaign was practically left to the Athenians. The principal cities which now, or soon afterwards, became members of the confederacy were Rhodes and Chios; Mytilene and Methymna in Lesbos; Byzantium, the great commercial city on the Bosporus; Chalcis, Eretria, and other towns in Eubœa; the important island of Corcyra in the west, and the communities of Cephallenia, Zacynthus, and Acarnania, with many others of less note. The adhesion of Thebes was also obtained—perhaps through the personal influence of the Athenian envoy Thrasybulus—but could not be counted upon for long.

The active policy pursued by Callistratus and his associates necessitated financial reforms in Athens itself. In the same year in which the League was formed, in the archonship of Nausinicus, 378–7 B.C., the war-tax (a tax upon property, which in theory was only levied in an emergency) was put upon a new basis. The property liable to taxation was valued, and divided into one hundred parts, and those who were liable to the tax were distributed into Boards or "Symmories." Every citizen except those whose property was very small—the limit is uncertain, but was possibly twenty-five minæ—was liable to the tax. By an arrangement which was made shortly afterwards, if not at once, the three hundred richest men in Athens had to advance the amount due,[1]

---

[1] They were probably distributed equally over the Symmories, three in each, of whom one was the leader of the Symmory. See Note 2.

and were left to recover it as they could from their poorer brethren. There can be no doubt that, though the system was liable to abuse, the money was forthcoming under such an arrangement more promptly than it would have been if there had been a less complete organisation, and if State-officials had been obliged to apply directly to a very large number of individual citizens for payment.

The power of the new confederacy and the efficiency of the new method of taxation were soon proved. In 376 Chabrias gained a great victory over the Spartans off Naxos, and in 375 he won over a number of towns on the Thracian coast to the alliance, while Timotheus operated successfully against Sparta around Corcyra and in the seas west of the Isthmus of Corinth.[1] In the same year, the Olynthian league was refounded—so little fear of Sparta remained in that region. But the cost of the war was heavy. Timotheus in particular was greatly embarrassed by want of funds, and the Thebans gave little help. In consequence of this, a Peace was made with Sparta in 374, by which the supremacy of Sparta on land was acknowledged by Athens, and that of Athens at sea by Sparta, and the terms of the Peace of Antalcidas were re-affirmed. But this Peace was immediately broken by acts of war on the part of Timotheus; and in order to get funds for the prosecution of the campaign in the West, he

[1] It was in these operations that Aphobus took part as trierarch.

attempted to raise fresh allies in Thrace and the islands. He seems also to have obtained the support, for a short time, of Jason of Pheræ, the most powerful ruler in Thessaly. But both Timotheus and Iphicrates, his successor in the command, found their supplies insufficient; the Thebans were becoming more or less plainly hostile (for the success of the Athenians could not but be regarded as a danger to Thebes) and in 373 they had destroyed Platææ. Accordingly peace was again made in 371. In a congress at Sparta, the autonomy of all the Greek cities was once more publicly asserted; but at the same time the right of Athens both to Amphipolis[1] and to the towns in the Thracian Chersonese was conceded. The Persian King and Amyntas, King of Macedonia, were both represented at the congress, and their admission of the title of Athens to the places in question was of some significance. But the Thebans felt themselves strong enough to refuse to join in the Peace, unless they were recognised as having authority over all the Bœotians; and since Sparta declined to acknowledge this, the Thebans were excluded from the treaty, and Cleombrotus, with a Spartan army which had gone to assist the Phocians in their hostilities

---

[1] Amphipolis had been founded by the Athenians in 437. The Spartans had captured it in 424, and in spite of various attempts, Athens had never recovered it. It was now an important city and virtually independent both of the great Greek cities and of Macedonia; but the Athenians claimed to have a right to it.

against Thebes, was instructed to attack them. He was utterly defeated in the battle of Leuctra, and the supremacy of Thebes among the Greek States was placed beyond doubt; though a second congress of envoys from Peloponnesian and other States, which assembled at Athens before the end of the year, once more confirmed the provisions of the Peace of Antalcidas.

The failure of the Spartans at Leuctra was followed by the loss of much of their influence in the Peloponnese. In one town after another, democratic and anti-Spartan revolutions took place. The Arcadian peoples asserted their independence without delay. The walls of Mantineia were rebuilt in 370; in Tegea the supporters of Sparta were overthrown; and the new town of Megalopolis was founded to be the centre of a number of Arcadian tribes and the meeting-place of their representative assembly, "The Ten Thousand." In 369, the Theban forces under Epameinondas— and among them troops sent by the Eubœans and Acarnanians, who must have deserted the Athenian alliance for the Theban—appeared in the Peloponnese to support the Arcadians, who, having been properly refused aid by Athens (now the ally of Sparta), had appealed to Thebes. The Theban army invaded the territory of Sparta, and established Messene as the capital of Messenia, at last independent after its long subjection to Spartan domination.

There is little to be gained by following in detail

THE ARCADIAN GATE, MESSENE

PHOTO BY THE ENGLISH PHOTO CO.

the kaleidoscopic movements of the various States
in the Peloponnese during the next few years.
But it is significant that two attempts were made
to establish a general peace by means of Persian
intervention. In 368-7 a congress was summoned
to meet at Delphi by Philiscus, who had been sent
by Ariobarzanes, one of the King's Asiatic satraps.
It proved a failure; for Thebes and Sparta could
not agree with regard to the independence of
Messenia, and the attempt of Philiscus to enforce
his terms by collecting an army came to nothing.
In the following year, however, representatives
of several of the great Greek powers waited upon
King Artaxerxes himself at his court in Susa,—
Pelopidas from Thebes, Archidamus from Elis,
Antiochus from Arcadia, Leon and Timagoras
from Athens. Pelopidas took the lead. The
terms he proposed stipulated for the independence
of Messenia and of Amphipolis, and the withdrawal of the Athenian war-ships from the sea.
To this Leon refused to listen; and on his return
home he prosecuted his more compliant colleague
Timagoras, who was executed as a traitor.[1] The
representatives of the Greek States, who assembled
at Thebes, also refused to accept the proposals
made in the name of the King; and both the prestige of Persia and the position of Thebes in the
Greek world were distinctly weakened.

In the year in which this congress met (366) the

[1] Comp. Dem., *de F. L.*, §§ 31, 137, 191. Demosthenes states
that Timagoras received a large bribe from the King.

Arcadians made peace with Athens. But in the course of the struggle with Elis, in which they were engaged from 365 onwards, dissensions arose among themselves as to the use to be made of the treasures of Olympia, captured from the Eleans; and the hostilities which resulted from these dissensions, and from the interferences of Thebes and Sparta, led in the end to the battle of Mantineia in 362; in which there fought on the one side the Theban army under Epameinondas (including Bœotian, Eubœan, and Thessalian troops), the Arcadians of Tegea and of Southern Arcadia generally, the Messenians and the Argives; and on the other, the Spartans, the Arcadians of Mantineia and Northern Arcadia, the Eleans and Achæans, and an Athenian contingent. The Theban side was victorious, but Epameinondas was killed, and his loss more than neutralised the advantage of the victory.

The policy of Athens had been, since the battle of Leuctra, antagonistic to Thebes and friendly to Sparta, and an incident of the year 366 had increased the hostile feeling of the Athenians towards Thebes. Themison, tyrant of Eretria, had seized Oropus,[1] and had put it into the hands of Thebes, nominally until a proper decision should be given in regard to the claim of Athens to the town. Besides this, the Thebans had further alienated the Athenians, by the destruction, in the course of the last few years, of Orchomenus,

[1] See above, p. 49.

Thespiæ, and Platææ.[1] But the Athenians were
tired of the unprofitable war, and not long after
the battle of Mantineia a general Peace was made,
Sparta alone standing out. Oropus remained in
the possession of Thebes.[2]

Before the battle of Mantineia, the Thebans
had been very active in North Greece, as well as
in the Peloponnese. In the year 370, Alexander,
the son of Jason of Pheræ, succeeded to the position of overlordship over the whole of Thessaly,
which his father had held for about five years.
But Alexander was exposed from the first to hostile
invasions from Thebes, led by Pelopidas and
Epameinondas. The invaders, though they were
not uniformly successful, proved themselves to be
on the whole the stronger power, and in 363
Pelopidas won a great victory at Cynoscephalæ,
though he lost his own life. In one of his earlier
expeditions northwards (in 368) Pelopidas had
forced the Macedonians into alliance with Thebes,
and among the hostages whom he brought to
Thebes was Philip, the future conqueror of Greece,
then not much more than a boy. But after the
death of Pelopidas and Epameinondas the Thebans
do not appear to have interfered in Thessaly, or
to have established any effective control over
Alexander.

During the greater part of the period of Callistratus' ascendancy in Athens, the Athenians had

[1] See above, p. 53.

[2] Diod., XV, lxxxix.; Plut., *Ages.*, xxxv.

remained on good terms with the King of Persia; but in time their attitude had become somewhat less guarded. The condemnation of Timagoras and the refusal of the King's proposals in 366 marked a definite change of policy. In the same year, or soon afterwards, Ariobarzanes, satrap of the Hellespont, rose in revolt against the King. At first Ariobarzanes appeared only to be at war with rival satraps, and the Athenians sent Timotheus to his assistance. As soon as his revolt against the King himself was declared, Timotheus was precluded by the terms of the Peace of Antalcidas from assisting him further. But Timotheus consoled himself by besieging and taking Samos, which was being held, in violation of the Peace, by another satrap, Cyprothemis.[1] Shortly afterwards there seems to have been a general revolt of the subordinate princes in Asia Minor and Egypt against Artaxerxes II., and not only Chabrias of Athens, but also Agesilaus of Sparta went to the aid of the rebellious Egyptians. Chabrias only returned to Athens in 359. By that time Artaxerxes II. had died, and had been succeeded by Artaxerxes Ochus, who proceeded to take all possible measures for the re-establishment of his authority throughout his dominions.

After the conquest (nominally the liberation) of Samos, Timotheus in 365 transferred his activities to the Thracian Chersonese, where the maintenance of Athenian influence was of the greatest

[1] Dem., *pro. Rhod. lib.* § 9.

importance, since the greater part of the corn-supply of Athens, coming as it did from the shores of the Bosporus and the Euxine, had to pass through the Hellespont. Athenian settlers were sent both to Samos and to the Chersonese; and Timotheus then engaged in hostilities with Cotys, who had succeeded to the kingdom of the Odrysian Thracians in 383. His predecessor Ebryzelmis had been on good terms with Athens,[1] and before him Medocus and Seuthes, who had divided the kingdom between them, had been brought into friendship with Athens by the diplomacy of Thrasybulus. Cotys, on the other hand, showed himself more anxious to maintain and extend his own power, than to assist Athens to control the Chersonese; and he gave Timotheus and other Athenian generals much trouble. Timotheus also attempted (in succession to Iphicrates, whose efforts had failed) to take possession of Amphipolis, the right of Athens to which had been conceded in the Peace of 371, both by Amyntas and by the Persian King. But though Poteidæa and Torone (two important towns on the Chalcidic peninsula) and, shortly afterwards, Pydna and Methone were brought within the Athenian alliance, Timotheus failed to recover Amphipolis. He also made no headway against Cotys; nor did better success attend any of the generals who were sent to the Hellespont

[1] See Foucart, *Les Athéniens dans la Chersonèse de Thrace*, p. 6, where a decree of the Athenians in his honour, of the year 386–5, is quoted.

in 362 and 361, only to be cashiered and prosecuted on their return.[1]   It was even worse that Alexander of Pheræ (now acting in the interests of Thebes) had built a fleet, occupied the island of Peparethus, defeated the Athenian admiral Leosthenes, and made a profitable raid upon the Peiræus itself. Moreover Epameinondas had (in 364-3) made a cruise in the northern waters with a Theban fleet, and as the result we find the Byzantines, with the peoples of Cyzicus and Chalcedon, interfering in the following year with the Athenian corn-ships.

The policy of Callistratus, who had up till now continued to direct the Athenian Assembly, seemed to have failed; he was accused in 361 of not having given the People the best advice, and went into exile; his ill-advised attempt to return to Athens shortly afterwards led to his execution. For the next few years the most influential statesman in Athens was Aristophon, a man of advanced years, who had been powerful early in the century, but whose known friendly inclinations towards Thebes had kept him out of popularity for a long period.   The Peace of 362, which has already been mentioned, was probably due to his influence, and was made none too soon.

At first, though Athens was now free from direct

[1] The events of these years, and especially the proceedings of the Athenian admirals and navy, are strikingly illustrated in the (pseudo-Demosthenic) Speech against Polycles, written by an unknown orator for Apollodorus.

hostilities on the part of Thebes, there was little improvement in the conduct of military affairs in the North. Timotheus was again defeated by the Amphipolitans in 360–59. In the same year, Cephisodotus was sent to the Hellespont; but he had more than his match in Charidemus, a captain of mercenaries, who was in the service of Cotys, and, after the assassination of Cotys in the next year, was practically the guardian and first minister, as well as the general, of Cotys' young son, Cersobleptes.

The previous relations of Charidemus with Athens had been chequered. He had served for three years under Iphicrates; and the latter, when he had taken hostages from Amphipolis, had entrusted them to Charidemus, intending to send them to Athens; but when in 364 Timotheus succeeded Iphicrates in the command, Charidemus gave back the hostages to the Amphipolitans, thus removing the strongest inducement to them to surrender the town, and himself went off to Cotys. Soon afterwards he agreed to hire his services to Olynthus, which at this moment controlled Amphipolis; but some Athenian ships captured him on his way thither; he joined the Athenian forces instead, and was rewarded with the citizenship of Athens and other compliments. He then crossed to Asia Minor, and joined in the disputes of the satraps Artabazus and Autophradates. Professing to help the former, he actually took from him (or from his relatives Memnon and

Mentor) the towns of Scepsis, Cebren, and Ilium; but he was hard-pressed by Artabazus and cut off from supplies, and in the hope of obtaining help from Athens he wrote to the newly appointed Athenian admiral, Cephisodotus, before the latter had set sail from Athens, offering to put the Chersonese in his hands. But for some unknown reason, Memnon and Mentor relented towards him, and persuaded Artabazus to let him go unmolested. He joined Cotys at Sestos (in 360), and instead of fulfilling his promise to Cephisodotus, laid siege to the Athenian towns of Crithote and Elæus in the Chersonese, openly opposed Cephisodotus for several months, and forced him to make a discreditable treaty, for which Cephisodotus was cashiered on his return home and fined five talents, only escaping condemnation to death by three votes. Demosthenes served in this campaign as trierarch[1]; Cephisodotus sailed in his ship, and (according to a statement made by Æschines)[2] Demosthenes himself spoke against Cephisodotus—whether as prosecutor or as witness does not appear—on his return home.

In the next year (359) events took a turn more favourable to Athens. Miltocythes, a Thracian

[1] He was probably co-trierarch for the year with Philippides of Pæania (*C. I. A.*, ii., 795 f.).

[2] *In Ctes.*, § 52. Demosthenes (*in Aristocr.*, § 168) speaks of the severe punishment inflicted on Cephisodotus, but makes no reference to any action of his own in the matter. (The expression which he uses does not, as some suppose, imply that he thought the sentence unduly harsh.)

prince who had risen against Cotys two years before and had received promises of support from Athens, fell into the hands of Charidemus. He handed him over to the people of Cardia, who were hostile to Athens, and they put Miltocythes and his son to death. This cruel deed was followed by a general outburst of indignation in that part of Thrace against Charidemus and Cersobleptes (the successor of Cotys); and they were forced to consent to a partition of the Thracian kingdom between Cersobleptes, Berisades, and Amadocus; the two latter being claimants to the kingdom who had entered into friendship with Athens, doubtless for their own purposes, but none the less honestly, since they stipulated in the treaty of partition for the restoration of the Chersonese to Athens. Satisfied with this, the Athenians took no proper steps to fulfil their own obligations; they despatched no funds to Athenodorus, the commander of Berisades' army, but merely sent Chabrias with one ship; so that Cersobleptes was able to disown the treaty, and to make an arrangement favourable to himself with Chabrias. This arrangement the Athenians repudiated, but it was not until 358 or 357 that Chares, who had taken command of the Athenian forces, could oblige him to make a treaty more in accordance with the original settlement. Even now, Cardia, which commanded the entry to the Chersonese from the Thracian side, was explicitly excluded from the list of places handed over to Athens. With the sequel to these proceedings in Thrace we shall be concerned in a later chapter.[1]

We have now reviewed the course of events down to the year 359, and in some cases for a year or two beyond. It remains to summarise in general terms the position of the leading States in Greece at the point which we have now reached.

Sparta, though still one of the three strongest powers, was now the least important of the three. The attainment of independence by the Messenians and Arcadians, with their newly-established centres at Messene and Megalopolis, left her with reduced territory and resources, though she was ready to make an effort, if opportunity arose, to recover lost ground, especially against the Arcadians. The Arcadians themselves were still engaged in hostilities with the people of Elis, and the possession of the district occupied by the Triphylians was in particular a matter of contention between the two peoples. The Arcadians —at least those whose meeting-place was Megalopolis—relied on the support of Thebes; and after the battle of Mantineia, a Theban force under Pammenes had been sent to help them to maintain their independence; but it appears probable (in the light of subsequent events) that before long a party gained influence which was desirous of obtaining support from Athens rather than from

[1] The chief authority for the narrative of affairs in Thrace is the speech of Demosthenes against Aristocrates. See below, Chap. V *ad fin.*

A GENERAL VIEW OF SPARTA

PHOTO BY ENGLISH PHOTO CO.

Thebes, since the aid of Thebes seemed likely to be less effective now that Epameinondas was dead. Of the other Peloponnesian states, Corinth and Phleius had concluded peace with Thebes in 366; and in 361 Athens came to an understanding with Phleius, Elis, and the Achæans; but neither these, nor Argos, which was unfriendly to Sparta, are of any importance in the period which lies before us. Indeed the Spartans themselves play but a small part in the history of the next thirty years, though they could still show from time to time that their bravery and their national dignity had not entirely left them. The relations between Sparta and Athens continued to be generally friendly.

The Thebans were fine soldiers, but they needed great men to lead them; otherwise they had not the energy or the perseverance to make the most of their opportunities; and after the deaths of Epameinondas and Pelopidas they were far less dangerous than they had previously been. They are a difficult people to characterise. The Thebans proper were a race of aristocrats—self-sufficient and contemptuous of trade and commerce, ruling or intending to rule over the inferior towns of Bœotia, but not attempting to assimilate them or consult their interests; and they were generally destitute of the humaner feelings.[1] If they shared with the Bœotians generally the gift for art and literature, they did not develop it, any more than they used their political and military opportunities.

[1] ἀναίσθητοι, as the Athenians called them.

5

except when stimulated by men of genius. So long as they could maintain their hold over Bœotia, and could occupy such a position of superiority over their neighbours, the Phocians and Thessalians, as would secure themselves against interference, they were content to live a life of self-indulgence at home; though it was of importance to them, if possible, to protect themselves against Athens by maintaining a firm footing in Eubœa, keeping Oropus in their own hands, and suppressing those towns in Bœotia which were actually or traditionally friendly towards Athens. They were entirely devoid of all concern for the interests of the Greeks as a whole. In the Persian wars they had gone over to the enemy; their alliance with Philip of Macedon was dictated by equally selfish motives; and had they not been persuaded by the extraordinary efforts and eloquence of Demosthenes to take a nobler course, they might perhaps have remained lords of Bœotia under the Macedonian domination, with leisure for the enjoyment of the pleasures to which they were so much devoted.

In Thessaly the influence of Thebes appears still to have been felt; but though the Thebans had shown their power even against so powerful a prince as Alexander of Pheræ, they do not seem to have taken steps to maintain their footing in the country, and after the assassination of Alexander in 359, his wife's brothers, Lycophron and Peitholaus, succeeded to the overlordship of Thessaly. At the same time each of the principal

towns appears to have had its own subordinate
government, and the supremacy of the tyrants of
Pheræ was not viewed with favour by rivals in
other cities, such as the Aleuadæ of Larissa. The
cavalry of Thessaly were a very valuable addition
to the forces of any power which was able to obtain
their assistance.

Farther towards the north lay the Macedonian
kingdom, which was now suffering, owing to the
death of Amyntas, from disputes as to the succession, and greatly needed a firm hand. Round the
coasts of the Thermaic Gulf were the colonies now
subject to Athens—Pydna and Methone on one
side, Poteidæa on the other—of which more will be
heard in the future; and over the Chalcidic peninsula the chief authority was wielded by Olynthus,
once more the head of a considerable league. Beyond this peninsula stretched the coasts of Macedonia and Thrace, as far as the Chersonese, and
beyond the Chersonese, the Thracian kingdom was
bounded by the Propontis and the Euxine Sea.
Amphipolis, virtually independent, occupied a position of great commercial and military importance
near the mouth of the Strymon, and not far to the
north-east rose Mount Pangæus, with its gold-
mines, worked at present by the islanders of Thasos, who were colonists from Athens. On the
Thracian coast the more important Greek towns
were Abdera, Nicæa, and Maroneia, and, between
the Chersonese and the Bosporus, Perinthus and
Byzantium, the latter exercising supremacy over

Selymbria and Chalcedon, and in virtue of its situation commanding all the traffic in corn and other commodities which passed backwards and forwards between Greece and the Euxine coasts.

We may now turn to Athens. No longer able to stand alone against a combination of other powers, and no longer generally acknowledged as the leader of the Greek States (as she had been in the great days after the Persian wars in the fifth century), Athens was nevertheless the most powerful single State in the Greek world. No city headed so extensive and important an alliance. Corcyra indeed fell away in 361, and Byzantium, with the neighbouring towns, had for some time been unfriendly; but in 359 the greater number of the members of the Second Athenian Confederacy were still loyal; and in the course of the next two years most of the Eubœan States, which had passed from the Athenian to the Theban alliance about twelve years before, were set free from the Theban domination, at their own request, by an Athenian fleet commanded by Timotheus, and became adherents of Athens. (This event made a great impression on Demosthenes, who served as trierarch in the expedition. Timotheus had roused the Athenians so effectively by his address to the Assembly, that the expedition had started within three days after it had been resolved upon.[1]) The influence of

[1] *De Chers.*, ad fin. The expedition is placed by Diodorus, XVI, vii., in the year 358–7. Kahrstedt (*Forschungen*, pp. 70, 71) decides for the late summer of 357, *i.e.* the year 357–6.

Athens thus extended over most of Eubœa, over the important islands of Lemnos, Imbros, Scyros, and Samos (as well as others), over most of the coast-towns on the Thermaic Gulf, and over the Thracian Chersonese and a number of towns on the south coast of Thrace. No other power had so numerous a fleet; her commercial activity and prosperity were unrivalled; and she was on very friendly terms with the princes who ruled the corn-lands about the Cimmerian Bosporus,[1] with which her trade was especially large. She was free from serious internal division, and her democratic constitution stood in no danger of disturbance.

Yet there were elements of weakness in her condition, which were soon to become actively dangerous. The *raison d'être* of the Second Confederacy—mutual protection against Sparta—had long ceased to exist; and her policy was becoming less and less one in which the allies had any interest. Nevertheless their contributions were still exacted, and even collected by Athenian admirals at the head of their fleet, and were used for any campaign in which they were at the moment engaged: while the resumption by the Athenians of the practice of sending out "cleruchs," or colonists who settled and held land in allied States, was contrary to the spirit, if not (in the case of the particular States concerned) to the letter, of the agreement with the allies.

Moreover there were features in the constitution

[1] See above, pp. 2, 59.

and in the financial and military arrangements of Athens which were to be a source of great weakness in the next years; and before we can pass to the events of the first years of Demosthenes' political life, we must consider at some length the political system within which, like other Athenian statesmen, he had to work.

NOTES TO CHAPTER II

1. Francotte (*Les Finances des Cités Grecques*) points out that the difference between φόρος ("tribute") and σύνταξις ("contribution") was not merely nominal. The φόρος had been practically determined by Athens; the συντάξεις were arranged by the συνέδριον of the allies, and confirmed by the Athenian Assembly. The φόρος was used by the Athenians at their own discretion; the συντάξεις were to be employed only for the objects of the Confederacy. Comp. F. W. Marshall, *The Second Athenian Confederacy* (Cambridge, 1905) and Phillipson, *International Law and Custom of Ancient Greece and Rome*, vol. ii., pp. 19–24.

2. The details of the system introduced in 378–7 are keenly disputed, and to discuss them here would take too much space. The method of προεισφορά (payment by rich men in advance) was certainly in vogue at the time of the Speech against Polycles (§§ 8, 9), *i.e.* in 360. Whether it can be proved to be earlier depends on the interpretation of Dem. *in Aphob.* I, §§ 7, 8, 9; ii., §4; *pro Phano*, § 59, etc. I believe that the payments which Demosthenes' guardians are there stated to have made were made by way of προεισφορά, and if so, this method of collection was in use in 376, and must have been the original one under the law.

CHAPTER III

THE ATHENIAN STATE IN THE FOURTH CENTURY B.C.

THE supreme power in Athens rested with the Assembly, of which every adult citizen was a member. It is obvious that in this Assembly the poor must have outnumbered the rich. We have not indeed any direct information as to the distribution of wealth at this period; but we know that in the year 358-7 the number of citizens who possessed an income which made it fair to lay the burden of trierarchy upon them was estimated at 1200 only[1]; and that in 322, out of 21,000 adult male citizens, only 9000 possessed an estate even of the low value of twenty minæ.[2] It follows that if the poor chose to make use of their numbers, they could always outvote the richer members of the Assembly; and the political interests of rich and poor respectively were so far distinct as to constitute them parties, though the word must not

[1] Dem., *de Symm.*, § 16, etc.
[2] Demosthenes' father, who was counted a rich man, possessed an estate of about 14 talents (= 840 minæ) at his death; and the wealthy banker Pasion, 30 talents. Trierarchy cost (roughly speaking) from 40 minæ to a talent.

be taken to imply the rigid organisation or the clearly-cut lines of demarcation which are characteristic of the party-system as it exists to-day.

The richer class included the landowners and the traders. Of these the traders were by far the more important. Indeed there is reason to think that, concurrently with the decline of agriculture in Attica, the most profitable land was bought up by capitalists resident in the town, and worked by means of slaves, and that apart from such estates the holdings were small, and the holders not only personally insignificant, but also unlikely to be regular attendants in the Assembly, since they would not be able to leave their work and come to town for that purpose. But the trading class clearly exercised great influence in the Assembly. In the first place, a very large part of the wealth of the country was in their hands, and wealth inevitably carries weight even in the most democratic nations. In the second place, with the increase of luxury, the rise in the standard of living, the growing variety of demand, and the consequent specialisation of trades in the city and the larger towns, the traders and the financiers, and those whose interests were connected with theirs, became more numerous and their influence ramified more widely. Above all, it was upon the traders that Athens depended for her supply of food; for the amount of home-grown corn was small; and this alone would have sufficed to give them a weight in the Assembly (under normal conditions) out of proportion to their mere numbers. The interests of the richer classes were generally better served by peace than by war.[1] The passage of merchant-vessels was naturally most secure in time of peace; and the fear of hostile invasion, and of the ravaging of the landed estates of Attica (as they had been ravaged in the Peloponnesian War) was certainly not extinct. Further, it was upon the rich that there inevitably fell the chief burden of the extraordinary taxation necessitated by war; for both the expenses of the trierarchy and the greater part of the war-tax had to be provided by the wealthy minority; and these calls upon them, which were an addition to the very large share which they contributed of the normal expenses of government, were liable to be extremely heavy. No doubt the interests of trade themselves required at times to be protected by war; and all alike were interested in maintaining at any cost the security of the great trade-route to the Bosporus and the Euxine, by way of the Ægean Sea and the Hellespont, and in taking precautionary measures against threatened invasion. (We shall see in a later chapter how these considerations affected the policy of Eubulus.) But as a rule the well-to-do classes tended to favour a pacific policy, and preferred to render trade secure by diplomacy and the formation of alliances,

---

[1] See Aristoph., *Eccles.*, 197 (392 B.C.):
> ναῦς δεῖ καθέλκειν·τοῖς πένησι μὲν δοκεῖ,
> τοῖς πλουσίοις δὲ καὶ γεωργοῖς οὐ δοκεῖ.

and even by making considerable concessions, rather than by war. Whether they had the faults which those whose interest is predominantly connected with money-making are always apt to show—whether they were indifferent to national ideals and generous sentiments, or were liable to be short-sighted, through paying too great a regard to the nearer as opposed to the more distant but greater gain—we have not much direct evidence to show. But Demosthenes at times uses language which suggests that he was conscious of such obstacles in the way of his own policy, even though he admits the patriotism of many rich men and their readiness for sacrifices.[1]

On the other hand, the masses were, generally speaking, in favour of war and of an imperialistic policy. If not the safest way of securing an abundant food-supply, victorious campaigns were often the way which seemed most obvious; and the fact that war was paid for by the rich made the poor less conscious of its disadvantages. Further, it was only through war that the poorer citizens could avail themselves of one of the chief means of earning a living that was open to them and not(apart from some very exceptional occasions) to slaves—that of service as rowers in the fleet. Besides this, the tendency of the crowd to be carried away by the kind of national conceit or swagger which is ready to go to war recklessly is illustrated by a number of references to the

[1] *De Cor.*, § 171.

orators who inflamed the Assembly by passionate appeals to the traditions of the past—to the greatest days of the Athenian Empire—and by the fact that Demosthenes himself, who certainly had no shrinking from war, even when a tamer prudence might have counselled peace, was more than once obliged to deprecate this rash folly.[1]

We have then to recognise that in Athens the tendencies of the richer and poorer classes respectively were almost exactly the reverse of those which are shown by the corresponding classes in most modern countries to-day. As a rule, imperialistic ideals, and an inclination towards militarism, are now more commonly found among the better educated and wealthier members of the community, and are supported in the name of patriotism against what are supposed to be the narrower, more domestic, and even more selfish aspirations of the less wealthy. In Athens it was the popular leaders who cried out for war; and it was those who more nearly correspond to the Conservatives of modern countries that strove to make and to maintain peace.

Unfortunately neither party, as a whole, seems to have been animated by any noble ideal. Rich and poor alike would have said that the security of the Empire, or at least the maintenance of the naval supremacy of Athens, was primarily of importance as a means to the satisfaction of the

[1] *E.g., de Symm.*, §§ 4 ff., 41; *de Pace*, § 13 ff.; comp. Isocrates, *de Pace*, §§ 5, 36, 112, etc.

hunger of the proletariat.   The masses might add
to this sentiment an enthusiasm, often somewhat
shallow and only artificially stirred up by popular
orators, for the traditions of Athens.   The richer
classes wished to steer such a middle course as
would neither involve loss of trade and the inter-
ruption of the food-supply through the insecurity
of the trade-routes, nor yet necessitate heavy
expenditure on the army and navy.   But for the
masses and the popular orators, the golden age was
in the past; and it is doubtful whether the richer
classes had any clear ideal at all, except that of
playing for safety.   Isocrates' attempt to frame
a worthy policy for Athens met with little general
acceptance.   Whether or not the policy was in fact
a good and a worthy one, it was not a time when
men's practical plans were generally conceived on
a large or generous scale; and a close student of
this period can hardly fail to be conscious of a kind
of spiritual deadness, contrasting strongly with
the feeling which the Athenians had displayed
through the first two thirds of the fifth century—
we may perhaps say, until after the Plague—and
defying any attempt which a more inspired individual might make to kindle it into warmth.[1]

[1] It would take too long to discuss here the causes of this
deadness.   But apart from the dispiriting effects of the Plague
and of the Peloponnesian War, the principal cause was the rise
and the all-pervading influence of Rhetoric, which saps the
sincerity both of those who practise it, and of those to whom it is
addressed.   Plato's criticisms of Rhetoric appear to be entirely
justified by history, and the fact that most of them are equally

THE PNYX

Demosthenes himself, who was not lacking either in ideals or in inspiration, could not restore its old life to the Athenian People, though at one great moment he fanned the flame into a final blaze of splendour.

The masses had, as has been said, a large majority in the Assembly, and could at any time outvote those who represented the agricultural, commercial, and financial interests. But we have unhappily no means of discovering with any certainty what was the *normal* composition of an ordinary meeting of the Assembly, nor (since the function of the Assembly was, as Aristotle phrases it, that of judgment, or decision upon proposals submitted to them) how far the Assembly, as normally constituted, was capable of forming judgments based upon rational grounds. There can be little doubt that there was a tendency on the part of many of the best-educated men to withdraw entirely from public life and to take no interest in State-affairs, preferring, as they did, the self-satisfied life of the cultured individual to the pursuit of the common good—regarding political power and the possession of Empire as unimportant in comparison with individual virtue, and treating the comparative sordidness of politics in a democracy as beneath the notice of the philosophic mind. Philosophy became markedly individualistic in the fourth century, and alien from the spirit of the city-state.

---

applicable to modern journalism renders them not uninteresting at the present day.

What the fellow-citizens of Socrates had felt, as to the incompatibility of his principles with those of a city-state, the more philosophic Athenians now began to feel about themselves. The withdrawal of the finer intellects from all attempt to influence the actions of the community, however few such intellects may have been, must necessarily have been a loss.

Moreover there cannot be much doubt that the payment for attendance in the Assembly, which remained at about the same figure as the wage of an unskilled labourer,[1] was likely to be more attractive to the proletariat than to the better educated or to those who had business to mind.

There is indeed something to be said on the other side. In the first place, a considerable proportion of the members of the Assembly must have acquired some training in public business, and in the art of coming to a decision upon issues submitted to them, in the sphere of local government.[2] The organisation of the demes was very thorough, and the political activity of the demes very vigorous, during this period; and a system under which every adult citizen was a member of the Assembly of his deme, and might well hold office in it, must have had a greater educational value than (for example) the English system of local government, which works by means of representative bodies, and in consequence only educates or interests a comparatively small number

[1] Note 1 at the end of the Chapter.   [2] Note 2.

of persons. In the second place, it is remarkable that of the leaders in politics, the generals, the ambassadors, and the financial and administrative officials, a very large proportion were men of wealth.[1] This not only implies the absence of strong class-feeling, but it also shows that the masses were not unready to entrust their affairs to those who felt themselves called upon to lead, and able to do so, whoever they might be.[2] It is true that they also showed some jealousy of their leaders, and even more of those officials who, when once elected, were in some degree independent of the People—generals, for instance, and ambassadors. We shall see before long how evil the effects of this jealousy were. But at least there was nothing to prevent ability from attaining the position which was its due, however perilous the position might be; and on the whole we hear extraordinarily little of the noisy and ignorant type of demagogue.

The incompetence of the Athenian Assembly may be and often has been exaggerated. At times of crisis it was certainly not incapable of

[1] This is established with a very high degree of probability by Sundwall (*Epigraphische Beiträge zur sozialpolitischen Geschichte Athens*).

[2] See esp., Dem., *de Fals. Leg.*, § 99. The statement in the text is not really inconsistent with Aristotle's characterisation of democracy as the government of the poor for the benefit of the poor, nor with Isocr., *de Antid.*, § 159 ff., who lays stress on the suspicion attaching to riches (which is abundantly illustrated in the life and speeches of Demosthenes).

responding to an appeal to the reason and good sense of its members; and under normal conditions political ability had every chance of coming to the front. Nevertheless the Athenian Assembly could not escape from the dangers which appear to beset all large bodies of men gathered together. Unless they were roused or awed by immediate and urgent danger, there was always the probability that they would respond most readily to an appeal to their sentiment or their desires. Men who are assembled in a crowd do not *think*, unless they are forced to do so by something extraordinary; it is generally the shallowest minds which are most quickly made up, and which infect the rest of the crowd by a kind of contagion; and so the art of rhetoric is different from that of reasoning. The orator has often to use arguments which no logic can defend, and to employ methods of persuasion upon a crowd which he would be ashamed to use if he were dealing with a personal friend. It must be added that in the period which we are considering the issues were often complex, and that it would not have been possible to do justice to them in the short speeches which it was customary to deliver in the Assembly; and further, that any attempt to state a complex argument was likely to expose the speaker to suspicion; for (as we have already noticed in reference to the speeches which were delivered in the law-courts) ability in argument and in exposition was not very distinct in the popular mind from the sophistry of the professional rhetorician, who was clever enough to argue for any cause—and if necessary, for either side of any case—and to make the worse appear the better. Athenian orators often warn their audience in the Assembly as in the law-courts against being deceived by the cleverness of their opponents; and even if there had not been this suspicion of cleverness, it would not have been easy to put complex proposals (for instance, on finance) before a crowd and give the true reasons for or against them.

Again, it is obvious that so large a body could only form its judgment upon the materials presented to them by the orators; it could have little or no independent knowledge of facts; and when more than one version of the facts was presented, the version most likely to be accepted was that of the speaker whose oration was best as a performance; and it was the same with rival arguments. The Athenian Assembly was probably more susceptible than most modern audiences to the theatrical effect of the oration, and more liable to be carried away by oratorical brilliance. The contests of the orators they regarded in the same light as the contests of rival actors.[1] Indeed, so great was their interest in the performance, that it was often the only interest; and the practical moral was allowed to pass without effect, when the performance was over. Demosthenes often shows himself acutely conscious of this tendency.

[1] Comp. Dem, *de Pace*, § 7.

6

"If," he cries,[1] "you sit idle, with an interest that stops short at applause and acclamation, and retires into the background when any action is required, I can imagine no oratory, which, without action on your part, will be able to save your country." And again,[2] "You have reached such a pitch of folly or distraction or—I know not what to call it, for often has the fear actually entered my mind that some more than mortal power may be driving our fortunes to ruin—that to enjoy their abuse, or their malice, or their jests, or whatever your motive may chance to be, you call upon men to speak who are hirelings, and some of whom would not deny it; and you laugh to hear their abuse of others." Both Demosthenes and Isocrates repeatedly upbraid the Athenians for their refusal even to listen to speakers who told them unpleasant truths and did not prophesy smooth things. "It has always been your way," says Isocrates, "to drive from your presence all who did not advocate your own pleasures."[3] "Under a democracy there is no freedom of speech,"[4]—so he contradicted in a sentence one of the Athenians' proudest boasts. The excessive love of pleasurable excitement, with the accompanying paralysis of the will and the inability to face unpleasant facts, were the worst moral diseases from which the Athenian People was at this time suffering. There were also defects in the constitution itself,

[1] *De Chers.*, § 77. [2] Isocr., *de Pace*, § 3.
[3] *Phil.* III, § 54. [4] *Ibid.*, § 14.

and in its practical working, which had serious consequences; and to these we must next turn.

There are two conditions apart from which government by a great assembly cannot be imagined to have any chance of success. One is the existence of a responsible ministry, changeable, of course, from time to time, but entrusted with a real leadership so long as it is in office. The other is the confinement of the functions of the Assembly to the decision of main issues, the detailed application of its resolutions being left to responsible and experienced officials or departments, with reasonable freedom of action. These two conditions were very imperfectly fulfilled in Athens. Almost all officers of State, except the generals, were elected by lot; so that there was no guarantee of their fitness for office.[1] There was no ministry charged with the duty of giving advice to the People. Everyone of the thousands of members of the Assembly stood theoretically on precisely the same level of opportunity and responsibility. No one could be called upon to make a proposal; and though in strict law no measure could be brought forward without a preliminary resolution of the Council of Five Hundred, and business no doubt began with the propounding of such a resolution for discussion, it seems clear that the Assembly had unrestricted power of amendment upon the proposition of any member—the discussions on the Peace of Philocrates illustrate this[2]

[1] See Isocr., *de Pace*, § 23. [2] See below, pp. 249 ff.

—and no obligation was apparently felt by the Assembly to give the resolutions of the Council any more respectful attention (as embodying the opinion of those who had presumably considered the matter with care) than it gave to the wildest suggestion made by a popular speaker on the spur of the moment. The administrative work of the Council, which had to see that the resolutions of the Assembly were carried out, to collect the necessary information and materials for discussion, and to perform many of the duties which in modern countries fall to the various departments of the Civil Service, does indeed appear to have been surprisingly well done, considering the nature of the body. For, annually elected by lot as it was,[1] there was no guarantee that it would be specially qualified to advise; and since it transacted most of its duties by means of committees which changed ten times a year, it could not be expected to maintain any continuous or definite policy. Further, although on the whole it did its work well, it could only take action within the terms of the resolutions of the Assembly; and had it made any attempt to frame or carry through a policy, the attempt would probably have been regarded as an oligarchical encroachment upon the absolute rights of the People, which the Assembly jealously maintained.

The want of a ministry left the Assembly the victim of its own inconsistency, and of the varying

[1] Note 3.

moods of successive meetings; and not only could no continuity of policy be relied upon from such a body, but it was quite possible that there might be no policy forthcoming at all, simply because no one was under any obligation to make a motion[1]; or that the measures resolved upon might be left imperfect, because, though a resolution to take some important step had been passed, the necessary subsidiary resolutions as to ways and means had been omitted, or inadequate provision made[2]; and in fact resolutions as to ways and means, which involved personal service as well as taxation, might easily be so unpopular that only a courageous man would move them; while the administrative officials did not dare to act without the sanction of the Assembly, even to provide means to carry out the Assembly's own decrees. In the fifth century a certain continuity had been secured by the frequent re-election of the same man to the office of general—nearly all other officials being appointed by lot; but in the fourth century the generals, though many of them were frequently re-elected, came to be more and more professional soldiers, and less and less politicians; and when not engaged in war on behalf of Athens, they were as likely as not to be fighting on behalf of some other power until Athens had need of their services again, or enjoying life in some quarter where they

---

[1] Compare the silence of all parties and persons after the news of Philip's occupation of Elateia arrived. Dem., *de Cor.*, §§ 169 ff.   [2] See below, pp. 195, 215, 427.

were not exposed to critical eyes. We hear very little, during this period, of the advice of generals to the Assembly, though Phocion when necessary played the part of a statesman as well as of a soldier. The only chance of a continuous and consistent policy lay in the possibility of some orator or statesman winning the ear of the Assembly through a sufficiently long period, either by force of character or by playing successfully upon the desires of the majority; and it is because Callistratus, Aristophon, Eubulus, and Demosthenes were able each to secure a certain degree of influence for several years, that the acts of the Athenian People during the fourth century are not merely a chaotic and incoherent succession. Even so, the moods of the Assembly made the statesman's task an unenviable one; we find no little levity and inconstancy, and much jealousy of powerful men; and the means to which statesmen were forced to resort, in order to maintain their influence long enough to give any policy a fair trial, were often of a regrettable kind.

The defects of the system of discussion by a popular Assembly were necessarily increased by the circumstances of a time when the relations between the several States of Greece were hostile, or at least needed skilful handling. The most democratic of modern States do not allow the details of international politics or projected military and naval movements to be settled by public discussion: such subjects are wholly un-

fitted for such treatment. Any delicacy of handling, and the tact which often saves a situation,
are under such circumstances out of the question;
and though the value of such tact was well known
in Athens (for instance, from the occasions when
Callistratus went as envoy to Sparta, and Thrasybulus to Thebes) the knowledge did not ordinarily
lead the Athenians to entrust their foreign affairs
to responsible ministers and give them a free hand.[1]
This would have been impossibly oligarchical, and
might even have been thought to point towards
tyranny. So the Athenians paid for the logical
carrying out of their democratic principles by the
incompetent management of their foreign and
military affairs. Philip had tact enough; but tact
is a virtue of individuals, not of crowds.

The infrequency of the meetings of the Assembly,
which took place rather less often than once a
week, was also a great disadvantage. Internal
affairs may perhaps be managed by such meetings;
but not military or international affairs, in which
not only secrecy, but rapidity and the power of
adapting measures to swiftly changing situations
are often everything. Demosthenes more than
once[2] insists on the advantage which Philip pos-

[1] The great exception is the mission of Demosthenes to Thebes
in 339 (see below, p. 373). Sundwall (*op. cit.*) shows that the ambassadors, like the generals, were usually drawn from the propertied
classes—such persons alone could afford the incidental expenses
of these offices—and this may have increased the jealousy of the
Assembly towards them.

[2] *E.g., de Fals. Leg.*, §§ 184 ff.; comp. §§ 136, 227 f., etc.

sessed in being absolute master of his own plans, under no necessity to make them public until the right time came, and able to modify them at any time without consulting any one. Extraordinary assemblies might be and sometimes were summoned, but apparently only to deal with specially important and sudden crises.

Aristotle[1] speaks of the system of election by lot and the popular control of the law-courts as the two chief marks of the sovereignty of the People. The former merely reduced the chances of obtaining the services of qualified persons; but the part which was played in political life by the law-courts was positively mischievous. A statesman might of course be quite rightly brought before the law-courts; and some specific charge had always to be made.[2] But when, whatever the specific charge, the issue at stake was in reality whether he should be punished as a criminal because his policy was unpopular or had led to failure in one respect or another, it is plain that criminal procedure was being applied to cases for which it was quite unfitted. If a statesman had committed a crime, it was right to punish him like any other man; but because the policy for which,

---

[1] Ar., *Pol.*, IV (VI), 1300a, 1301a, etc.

[2] The commonest form of proceeding was probably that of prosecution at the end of the tenure of some office, when the Board of Auditors who received the retiring official's report asked if any one had any charge to make, and if so, referred the matter to a jury.

on his proposal, the Assembly had made itself responsible had resulted otherwise than had been expected, the statesman did not on that account deserve a heavy fine or banishment or execution—least of all when the mood in which the jury was led to condemn him might be merely a transient one, due to circumstances which would be sure to change and cause them to regret their action. The list of statesmen and generals who were tried and condemned during the fourth century includes nearly all of those who displayed any ability, and the knowledge that the consequences of failure would not be (as in modern States), at the worst, dismissal from office and the obligation to cross from one side of the House to the other, but death or banishment or financial ruin, must have been paralysing to any but the bravest, and must often have prevented the statesman and the general from taking the risks which any honest man in such positions must from time to time face.

Nor were the courts representative of the best side of public opinion, or even of public opinion as a whole. The enormous size of the juries might at first lead us to suppose that this would be otherwise. But sitting on juries took time, and was only attractive to those who could not turn their time to more profitable account. For the jurors' daily pay was still only three obols—a sum which was probably less than half the wage of an unskilled labourer; and such an inducement would not appeal to any but the aged and infirm, the poor and the idle. The character of the juries is sufficiently indicated by the arguments which even leading men thought fit to address to them. (They were told, on more than one occasion, that unless they fined the accused heavily there would not be sufficient money to pay their fees.) Indeed the whole tone of the political oratory addressed to the courts is (with certain notable exceptions) lower than that of the speeches delivered in the Assembly. It is evident that the orators had to deal with those who enjoyed vulgarities and sensational pictures in black-and-white, in which truth counted for less than dramatic effect. Facts could be misrepresented with impunity, and appeals made to passion, to a degree unparalleled in the Assembly; the state of popular feeling at the moment counted more than anything else; and the jury were continually encouraged to consider not whether the accused was guilty of the charge made against him, but whether he was not as black in character as a man could be, or at least black enough to be got rid of for good, when in fact he might be merely of a respectable colour which at the moment was out of fashion. Add to this that the juries were likely to have little knowledge of law beyond what the advocates on either side chose to supply to them, that they had nevertheless to decide questions of law as well as of fact, and that the verdict was subject to no revision—and the evils of the system are sufficiently apparent.

Moreover, apart from the bad influence of such a system upon statesmen in full career, the evil effects of the actual verdicts are only too evident. The condemned man was often driven into exile either by the fear of a death sentence, or by the imposition of a fine which he could not possibly pay. Such political exile was the curse of Athenian public life. One after another, the ablest men were removed from the service of the State, which might have the utmost need of them before many months or years had elapsed. Without a proper ministry, the value of "His Majesty's Opposition" could not, of course, be appreciated; and in Athens the effect of the hot-headed oratory of the prosecutor and the inflammable passions of the jury was often to make permanent what ought to have been at most a temporary retirement from the leadership of affairs.

The defects of the Athenian jury-system were not restricted in their results to the law-courts. For it was from the jurors for each year that the Nomothetæ were chosen, with whom there rested the power to repeal or to retain laws. The Assembly merely decided whether each group of laws should remain unchanged, or whether changes should be permitted during the current year. The proposers and opponents of new laws, or of alterations in the old, then appeared before the Nomothetæ; the proceedings took the form of a trial, after which the Nomothetæ gave a final decision. It cannot therefore be said that the intelligence of the People as a whole was adequately represented in the work of legislation any more than in the administration of justice.

We pass to the financial arrangements of the Athenian State. The general principle underlying them was that the ordinary expenses of a time of peace should be provided for from the produce of such public property as the mines of Laurium, and the rent of public lands; or by indirect taxes, such as harbour- and market-dues, percentages charged on sales by auction, and the like; except that part of the cost of the great public festivals, and the duty of managing them, was imposed in the form of "liturgies," or compulsory burdens, upon wealthy citizens, who had to serve as choregi at the Dionysiac festivals, or as stewards of the games, or in sundry other capacities, and to bear the expenses which their duties entailed. But indirect taxes could not be increased without becoming too serious a burden upon trade; and therefore any extraordinary expenses, such as those of a time of war, were met by a special direct tax upon capital, while the upkeep of the fleet was a liturgy laid upon the rich in turn.

We have already seen how the collection of the war-tax was organised in the year 378–7, by the creation of the Symmories; and that the system of collection worked well on the whole is shown by the fact that on the occasion when Androtion, Timocrates, and others were appointed to get in arrears of payment, extending over a good many years, the total arrears amounted to fourteen talents only, out of three hundred that had been demanded in the time.[1] The war-tax, moreover, was not necessarily burdensome, though it might become so; in the case of Demosthenes it seems not to have exceeded one per cent. per annum on the assessed value of his property, in the ten years during which he was under guardianship. But it was in theory an extraordinary tax; there was no permanent revenue applicable to military purposes, and no regular accumulation of a surplus for use in emergencies. Eubulus (for reasons which will appear later) avoided resorting to the war-tax as far as he could; but the result was that the generals were very inadequately supplied with funds, and had to take to irregular methods of obtaining them. How far the contributions of the allies who joined in the second Athenian Confederacy were at the disposal of Athens there is no direct evidence to show. It is probable that the consent of the Synod of the allies, as well as that of the Athenian Assembly, was strictly required before any application of these funds could be made; though in the year 341 Demosthenes evidently contemplated the possibility of using them to maintain the Athenian supremacy in the Chersonese.[2] But these funds were very much diminished by the Social War. Before this war they

---

[1] Dem., *in Androt.*, § 44. The exact date of the Commission and the precise circumstances of its appointment are much disputed, but the figures are plain enough.   [2] *De Chers.*, § 21.

had amounted to 350 talents yearly; afterwards they fell at once to ninety, and in 346 the sum was no more than sixty talents. [1]

The trierarchic system, under which the fleet was equipped and manned, had also serious defects. In former times, a single citizen had been told off to equip and command each trireme. But towards the end of the Peloponnesian War, the wealth of the richer citizens had greatly diminished, and it was found necessary to authorise the sharing of the responsibility for each ship by two citizens, each of whom commanded in turn. Any one who thought himself unjustly called upon could challenge another, whom he considered to be better qualified for the task, either to undertake the trierarchy or to exchange property with him. (How this right was abused to the disadvantage of Demosthenes by Aphobus and his friends we have already seen.)

The first great defect in this system lay in the delay which it involved. [2] Not only had the Assembly to decide upon the number of ships required, and the proportions of citizens, resident aliens, and mercenaries to be called upon to serve in them—a matter upon which they were liable to change their minds more than once before doing anything,—but time had to be given in which

---

[1] Æsch., *de Fals. Leg.*, § 71; comp. Busolt, *Das zweit. Ath. Seebund*, pp. 723, 724.

[2] Comp. Dem., *de Fals. Leg.*, §§ 185–6; Phil. I., § 36.

exchanges of property could be made, and persons whose means were not immediately forthcoming could get them in readiness to discharge the liturgy. There was also great difficulty in procuring rowers and crew. Those whose names were on the lists drawn up by public officials were often inefficient, and a public-spirited trierarch often preferred to hire others. In either case the arrangement between the captain and the rowers was a personal one, and the rowers were liable to desert if they had the chance, especially if they were not punctually paid or had other causes for dissatisfaction. Again, the dilatoriness of unwilling trierarchs, though after a certain point it became punishable by law, was a further source of delays. It also happened not infrequently that trierarchs entrusted their duties to a contractor, who equipped the vessel and commanded it for a comparatively small sum, and recouped himself by committing acts of piracy at the expense of friend and foe alike.[1] The financial and other difficulties were sometimes so great that the State was obliged to ask patriotic persons to volunteer to be trierarchs, as happened in the year 358–7, when Demosthenes was one of those who volunteered, and served (as co-trierarch with Philinus) in the expedition to Eubœa.[2]

---

[1] These points are amply illustrated by the Speech on the Trierarchic Crown, and the Speeches (wrongly ascribed to Demosthenes) against Polycles, and against Euergus and Mnesibelus.   [2] Dem., *in Meidiam*, § 161.

In the same year, in view of the grave financial situation produced by the Social War, a law proposed by Periander assimilated the trierarchic system to that by which the war-tax was collected. Twenty Boards or Symmories were established to provide the sums necessary for the equipment of the triremes; there were sixty persons in each Board, and the total number of persons liable for trierarchy was therefore 1200. The management within each Board rested with the richer men (though there is no evidence that they had to advance the money, as in the case of the war-tax): but they used their power to escape their own share of payment—all members paid the same share, whatever their property—and so to overburden their poorer colleagues. The plan (which still continued to be commonly adopted) by which the work of equipment was provided for by contract, and was rather a matter of business than of personal interest or patriotism, was doubtless an unfortunate one, and in general the company-system must have diminished the efficiency and zeal of the service. But for the moment it provided what was most of all needed—a businesslike method of getting the funds required for the navy.

The worst element, perhaps, in the Athenian financial system was the distribution of "Theoric money" to the citizens to enable them to enjoy the public festivals. The exact place of the Theoric Fund in relation to the general revenues of the State has been much disputed. But it would appear that at the beginning of each year, the Assembly passed a Budget, allocating to special purposes and to particular funds as much as was required by each; and that the surplus or unallocated revenues passed in time of war into the military chest, in time of peace into the Theoric Fund, and that from the latter they were distributed to the citizens. This distribution appears to have been introduced by the strongly democratic politician Agyrrhius, early in the fourth century, and to have been a revival in principle, if not in detail, of distributions which had been made in the previous century,[1] and we shall see that about the time at which Demosthenes came forward, a special law was passed increasing the sums distributed, including (probably) a limited allocation to military purposes in the Budget, and providing that the whole of the surplus should always pass into the Theoric, not into the military fund.[2] No doubt the distribution had a certain religious colour. The festivals were all in honour of the gods, and there was at least a feeling that their hearty celebration was likely to bring good luck.[3] But however strongly piety might be

[1] Comp. Motzki (*Eubulus von Probalinthos u. seine Finanzpolitik*, pp. 49 ff.) who shows that the distribution of Theoric money was probably begun by Pericles, and was distinct from the distributions in relief of poverty instituted by Cleophon.

[2] See below, Ch. IV., p. 127.

[3] The feeling was not very deep; and the shallowness of the religious sentiment in regard to the festivals is shown by the treatment of the subject in Anaximenes' *Art of Rhetoric*, ch. ii.

pleaded in favour of the distribution, it can hardly
be doubted that pleasure rather than piety was
the basis of its popularity, and the rigidity of the
law which enjoined it was a great disadvantage
to the State. We have here one indication among
many of the reluctance of the Athenian democracy
to put the pleasure of the moment in any but the
first place. In 358 there appears for the first time
a special Board of Superintendents of the Theoric
Fund, ten in number, appointed to hold office for
four years, after which they were not re-eligible.
It may be assumed that a capable financier,
elected a member of this Board, was able to
control its policy, and that even when his own
term of office was over, he might maintain his
control through the election of one of his sympa-
thisers. Thus Eubulus was a member of the
Theoric Commission from 354 to 350, and his
supporter Aphobetus (the brother of Æschines)
from 350 to 346.[1] Æschines[2] tells us that the
members of this Board, "owing to the confidence
which the people placed in Eubulus," held all the
important financial offices[3] of State between them,

[1] Others who were members of the Commission were Diophantus of Sphettus, 358 to 354; Cephisodotus, 346 to 342; and
Demosthenes, 338 to 334.

[2] *In Ctes.*, §25.

[3] Such as the offices of the Apodectæ, who received the incom-
ing funds; and of the Financial Secretary (ἀντιγραφεύς) whose
business was to report the state of public funds to the People.
Æschines says that this state of things continued "until the law
of Hegemon was passed," *i.e.* until after 336.

and controlled practically the whole administration. It was not until a year or so before the battle of Chæroneia that Demosthenes succeeded in applying the Theoric money to military purposes; and the continuance of the Theoric Board shows that the distributions were afterwards revived. Shortly after the battle there appears a separate Treasurer of the Military Fund, appointed for four years at a time.[1]

It should be added that special needs might be met by the assignment of special commissions to individuals or to small groups of persons. Thus we hear of Commissioners of Walls, of Dockyards, and of the Fleet; of Superintendents of the Corn-Supply (an office held in 357–6 by Callisthenes, and in 338–7 by Demosthenes); and of other specially commissioned officials.

We have lastly to consider the conduct of military matters. The two points which are of most importance are the comparative independence of the generals, and the employment of mercenaries, who formed the larger proportion of almost every force. The great generals of this period, though there is no reason to doubt their loyalty, were not so closely attached to the city as those of the fifth century had been: or, rather, a distinction appears to have grown up between the relatively independent general who was responsible for the conduct of war, and his nominal colleagues who

[1] Note 4.

had to organise the preparations for war at home and to perform various duties of a civil rather than of a military character.[1] The militant general, as a rule, came less frequently to Athens. He might of course be recalled and put on his trial like any other officer of the State, and the Athenians got rid of some of their most capable commanders by this means. But for the most part he was closely attached to his men; and, if not employed in the service of Athens, he had no difficulty in finding for them under other masters the work and the pay which they expected.[2] The day of professional armies, and of an almost regimental organisation of mercenaries, each body having its general or captain, had now begun. The soldier came less and less into touch with civil life; and we hear of Iphicrates, Chabrias, Chares, and others, when unemployed, living away from Athens.[3] There is no doubt that generals who were both indispensable and independent were often regarded by the democracy with a certain mistrust, while at the same time, on account of their indispensableness, they were flattered and complimented and were awarded distinctions in a way which Demosthenes regarded as unworthy of a vigorous and self-reliant people.[4]

[1] Comp., Dem., Phil. I, § 26. Philip is said to have expressed his surprise that the Athenians could find ten generals every year, when he had found but one in all his life, viz., Parmenio (Plut., *Apophth. Phil.*, § 2).

[2] Comp. Dem., Olynth. II, § 28.

[3] See Theopompus, fr. 103 (Oxford Text).   [4] Note 5.

A number of causes had contributed to the change by which the greater part of the Athenian army came to be commonly composed of mercenaries. In the first place, the Athenian citizen had become much less ready to serve in person. That the best educated and most philosophic minds tended to think lightly of military power and imperial aims counted for something; for it could not be without effect that the great teachers did not intimately connect the good life of the individual with such ideals. But it counted for much more, that the Athenians were coming to be more and more absorbed in business, and found that their business must go to pieces if they were continuously absent for any length of time on military service; and their reluctance naturally increased, as campaigning-seasons became longer, and military operations ceased to be confined to a few months of the summer.[1]

In the second place, the art of fighting had become much more specialised, and the trained skill of the professional soldier had become almost necessary. New weapons, new and better organised kinds of troops, were employed, and every arm of the force needed practice and training.[2] The old conventional methods of warfare had given way to tactics of a more ingenious kind; and had the citizens of Athens been willing to serve in larger numbers, they could not have supplied all that was needed in an army of the fourth century.

[1] See Dem., Phil. III., §§ 48, 49.   [2] *Ibid.*, §§ 47, 49.

In the third place, there was an abundance of
men ready to be employed as mercenaries. In
former days the surplus population had been
drafted off by emigration to newly founded colonies. But the available sites for colonisation had
all been taken, and at the same time population
continued to grow, while the supply of home-grown
corn in most parts of Greece diminished rather
than increased. The pressure was particularly
felt among the agricultural peoples, with whom
the food-supply was not adequate for the numbers
and was not so easily supplemented by imported
corn, since the imported corn was mostly used up
in the towns. In a modern State there would
probably have been an inflow into the towns to
find work. To some extent this may have happened in Greece, and the numbers of the idle
proletariat were possibly swollen by such immi-
grations. But in the towns workmen were little
needed, owing to the regular employment of
slave-labour; and even if work could be found,
the existence of slavery was bound to keep the
wages of the free workmen very low both in town
and country.[1] It was more profitable, and at
the same time more exciting, to take service under
a captain of mercenaries, and to fight for the State

---

[1] This view has been contradicted by Mr. A. E. Zimmern in
the *Sociological Review*, vol. ii, Nos. 1 and 2 (1909). In spite of
his extremely interesting discussion, I do not think that the facts
which he adduces really prove his case. On the whole matter,
however, a more complete sifting of the evidence is required.

which would bid highest, or in the war in which
there was likely to be most plunder. Above all,
the result of long wars, and of political exile, and
of the revolutions which were always happening in
one State or another had been to fill the country
with homeless men, who were ready enough to
risk their lives for the wage offered, and for the
chance of adventure and booty. But though the
existence of men eager to be mercenary soldiers
and the readiness of States to employ them are
easily explained, the consequences of the mercenary system were none the less deplorable. Though
as a rule the Athenian general was loyal to his
employers, he was partly at the mercy of his men,
whose allegiance sat more loosely upon them;
and sometimes (as was the case with Charidemus)
it mattered as little to him as to them for whom
they fought. Even though we do not find at this
period any conspicuous instances of treachery or
cowardice on the part of mercenary armies, it is
clear from many statements of Demosthenes and
others that such armies could not be expected to
share the intense patriotism of a citizen-force
whose own interests were at stake. Ruskin,[1]
in a remarkable passage, insists that the soldier's
business is not killing, but being killed. The
mercenary soldier probably tended to take the
opposite view. In addition to this, the mercenary
must be always fighting, or at least plundering.
To be unemployed meant starvation. The mer-

[1] *Unto this Last*, ch. i.

cenary bands which roamed over Greece were a
terror to all; and if, when employed by Athens or
any other State, they were not punctually paid,
they helped themselves at the expense of friends
and foes alike. The allies of Athens, Demosthenes[1]
says, lived in deadly fear of the forces that Athens
sent out; and Athenian statesmen could not always
resist the temptation to avoid the imposition of
taxes, by letting the commanders and armies find
supplies for themselves, even by plundering the
towns and ships of the allies.[2]

We have now surveyed some of the principal
aspects of the public life of Athens in the middle
of the fourth century; and the conclusion must be
that the Athenian State was quite unfitted to face
the impending struggle with Philip of Macedon.
The better as well as the worse elements in aristocracy had been thrown away. It is conceivable
that a democracy in which the share taken by the
People in government was confined to the wise
choice of responsible leaders and the determination of main issues, and in which the whole of the
detailed and practical administration was placed
in skilled hands (of course with the proper safeguards), might have been successful; not only
because the part played by Athens herself could
have been better regulated, but also because
skilled statesmen and diplomatists might have
brought about such a combination of all the Powers

---

[1] Dem., *in Aristocr.*, § 139, Phil. I., § 45; cf. Isocr., *Philippus*,
120 f., *de Pace*, 44–8.　　　[2] Dem., *de Chers.*, §§ 22–26.

as no Assembly could ever have achieved. But the Athenian democracy could never have trusted its leaders enough to give them a sufficiently free hand in the conduct of military and international affairs; and its failure was largely due to its deep-seated jealousy of able men. Had it not been for this, there would have been a possibility of carrying out reforms in many departments of the State, which would have made for efficiency and success. What reforms were needed, Demosthenes, among others, shows himself well aware; but Demosthenes had not a free hand until it was too late.

It must be acknowledged that the jealousy of the Athenians was not unfounded. The possession of great or uncontrolled power seems, among the Greeks, to have been extraordinarily fatal to character. The lesson taught by tyrannies and oligarchies was that power and selfishness of the most brutal kind were never far apart; and the few instances that Greek history provided of the wise and public-spirited lawgiver were not sufficient to diminish the effect of this lesson. But in consequence of this, the Athenian democracy did not realise the one condition without which, it would seem, any democracy must go down in presence of able and determined foes—the frank acknowledgment of an aristocracy of those who have the power to think, to foresee, to plan, and to command.

Another consideration points to the same conclusion. In time of peace, government by general discussion is conceivably a possible method. But in time of war, when men throw off their civilisation and revert to primitive types of action, the more primitive types of government also seem to be necessary to success; and something like despotism—though it may be the voluntarily accepted despotism of the best or ablest men—can alone give a State the coherence, and its action the promptness and effectiveness, without which failure is almost inevitable. So far a true instinct is shown by most of the more reflective writers of the fourth century, in the strong sentiment which they display in favour of some kind of monarchy. Isocrates, for purposes of peace, favours a kind of popularly elected aristocracy of those whom he regards as the wisest men in Athens; but when he thinks of war, turns to the idea of the absolute rule of some one great man—Jason or Dionysius or Philip himself. But in the fourth century these were only the impracticable fancies of spectators. Most of those who were engaged on the Athenian side in the game of politics and war had no such sentiments; and they lost the game.

NOTES TO CHAPTER III

1. Agyrrhius (see above, p. 44) had made the pay for attendance three obols. It is generally believed that by the middle of the fourth century it had been raised to one drachma (six obols), in order that the remuneration might correspond to the rise in wages and the fall in the value of money which had taken place. But this is denied by Brandis (Pauly-Wissowa, *Real-Encyclopädie*, s. v. Ekklesia) and Sundwall (*Epigraphische Beiträge zur sozial-*

politischen Geschichte Athens, p. 68). Sundwall seems to me to underrate the preponderance of the masses in the Assembly.

2. On this subject see especially Haussouiller, *La vie municipale en Attique*. Sundwall (*op. cit.*, p. 56) thinks that it was only those who belonged to the strata of society above the poorest that took much part either in local or in State affairs. Even so, local politics would educate a large number of members of the Assembly; and the Speech against Eubulides shows that men who were quite poor might play an important part in the life of their deme.

3. Sundwall shows that the proportion of men of some property was in all probability larger in the Council than in the Assembly. No doubt the number of such persons who would be interested in politics and would feel themselves able to take part in the administration would be larger in proportion than that of the politically-minded members of the poorer class; and so the operation of the lot would not be quite so haphazard as would seem probable at first sight. But even so, there was no guarantee that the majority would be fit for their work; and though such a method of selection might seem to be the logical consequence of democracy, it is hard to imagine a sillier. (It was no doubt deliberately devised for the express purpose of preventing men of ability from obtaining continuous influence.)

4. There is not sufficient ground for dating as far back as the middle of the century the office of Superintendent of the Administration (ὁ ἐπὶ τῇ διοικήσει) which first appears in 322–1— possibly in substitution for the Theoric Board, of which we hear no more after that time. On the whole subject of the Theoric Board and other financial offices, see Sundwall, *op. cit.*, pp. 41–43, and Francotte, *Les Finances des Cités Grecques* (esp. pp. 213 ff.), in whose pages nearly all the evidence will be found. Ferguson (*Hellenistic Athens*, pp. 473–5) attempts, but inconclusively, to disprove the four years' tenure of the Theoric Commissioners. Motzki (*Eubulos von Probalinthos und seine Finanzpolitik*) also discusses the various questions raised, but on a number of points I am unable to agree with him. In view of the want of evidence and the complexity of the subject, the account given in the text must not be taken as more than probable in regard to details, though there is no doubt of the main point—the drain on the State funds caused by the Theorica, which should have been either used for war or held in reserve.

The system of providing funds for the State by raising loans at interest was very rarely resorted to in ancient Greece. See Zimmern, *Athenian Commonwealth*, p. 205.

5. A passage of the XIIIth Oration (περὶ συντάξεως) in the Demosthenic Collection—an oration which is certainly not the work of Demosthenes as it stands, but contains much Demosthenic material and doubtless represents the orator's sentiments —calls attention in a striking way to the change of tone which had taken place since old days in regard to the generals. "Your forefathers did not erect statues of Themistocles, who commanded in the sea-fight at Salamis, nor of Miltiades, the leader of the army at Marathon, nor of many others whose services were beyond all comparison with those of the generals of the present day; but they honoured them as their own equals. For the People would not then forego the credit of any of its achievements; nor would any one have spoken of the victories at Salamis and Marathon as victories of Themistocles and Miltiades, but as victories of Athens. But to-day we hear people saying that Timotheus captured Corcyra, and Iphicrates cut up a Spartan troop, and Chabrias won the sea-fight at Naxos. You give up your own claim to credit for these successes, when you pay these extravagant honours to each of your generals." The passage is found in a slightly expanded form in the Speech against Aristocrates, §§ 196 ff.

CHAPTER IV

THE BEGINNING OF DEMOSTHENES' CAREER

IT has already been narrated that Aristophon
succeeded, about the year 361, to the position
of influence from which Callistratus had been
driven in consequence of the failure of the Athenian
armies in the neighbourhood of the Chersonese,
and that in the early years of Aristophon's leadership, the Chersonese had been secured for Athens,
chiefly as the result of operations conducted by
Chares, who was himself a favourite of the People,[1]
and aided Aristophon in the execution of his policy
both then and afterwards. But the apparent
change for the better in the affairs of Athens was
very soon cut short by the outbreak of the Social
War in the year 358–7. The causes of the war were
twofold. In the first place, the Athenians had
violated the spirit, if not the letter, of their agreement with the members of the Second Confederacy,
both by sending Athenian settlers to the allied
cities, and by other high-handed proceedings. The
aggressive action of Chares towards Chios and
Rhodes and other cities was perhaps the immediate

[1] See Theopompus, fr. 205 (Oxford Text).

occasion of the outbreak, though this is uncertain.[1]
In the second place, the allegiance of some of the
allies had been weakened by the activity of Thebes,
and particularly by the naval campaign of Epameinondas in 364–3. Aristophon indeed desired to
be on friendly terms with Thebes, and his chief
opponent Eubulus shared the desire.[2] But nothing
came of it. In 358 the most powerful of the
allies declared war on Athens.

There is no need to follow the disastrous course
of the war in detail. It was marked by two
features characteristic of the time;—first the
prosecution of Timotheus and Iphicrates, who
had been the two most successful commanders
under the régime of Callistratus, and were still
probably the best admirals that Athens possessed,
by Aristophon and Chares,[3] owing to their ill-
success against the allies; and secondly, the
intervention of the King of Persia in the quarrel.
In the course of the war, Chares, while acting as
Athenian admiral, went of his own accord to the
assistance of the revolted satrap Artabazus. The
Persian King retaliated by giving his countenance
to the allies; and his vassal, Mausolus of Caria,
gave them active assistance. The Athenians
recalled Chares, on receiving a protest from the
King; and in order to avoid a war with the King,
who had to a great extent succeeded in reviving
the strength and improving the organisation of his

[1] See Dem., *pro Rhod.*, § 3.   [2] Dem., *de Cor.*, § 162.
[3] Chabrias, the third great general, was killed in the war in 358.

kingdom, they were forced also to acknowledge the independence of Chios, Cos, Rhodes, and Byzantium. Very soon afterwards Selymbria, Perinthus, Methymna, and Mytilene withdrew from the Athenian confederacy; and though the confederacy continued to exist, and the Synod of the allies still met, there remained but the shadow of the great alliance organised by Callistratus. As the disasters of the Social War gradually broke down the influence of Aristophon, his opponent Eubulus came more and more into prominence, fighting his way largely by means of judicial prosecutions,[1] and gradually gathering around him a group of able men—Æschines, for instance, who had once supported Aristophon,[2] and his brother Aphobetus—until, about the year 355, he had attained the leading position in the State. It was probably though his influence that peace was made with the allies in 355.[3]

It was during the years of the Social War that Demosthenes' first two speeches on political subjects were composed. The war had involved an intolerable strain upon the financial resources of the city: more than one thousand talents had been spent in three years upon mercenaries alone[4]:

[1] Dem., *in Meid.*, §§ 207, 218, and schol.; *de Fals. Leg.*, §§ 191, 293.   [2] Dem., *de Fals. Leg.*, § 291.

[3] Schol. ad Dem., Olynth. III, § 28.

[4] Isocr., *Areop.*, § 9. The Speech of Isocrates On the Peace illustrates the extreme exhaustion of the city. The law of Periander (see p. 96) was one of the measures designed to obtain funds promptly.

and the nervousness which evidently prevailed in regard to the finances of the city is illustrated by these speeches, both of which had their origin in proposals of a financial character.

In or about the year 356, Androtion, a pupil of Isocrates, but (if Demosthenes gives us a true portrait of him) a person of brutal temperament and immoral life, proposed the appointment of a commission to get in the arrears of the war-tax, which amounted to fourteen talents.[1] Either, Androtion declared, the sacred vessels used in religious processions must be melted down and made into coin, or there must be a fresh war-tax, or the arrears must be called in. The latter course naturally commended itself as the least objectionable; a commission was appointed, and was given the assistance of the Apodectæ (the receivers of public moneys) and of the Eleven (the chief police-officers); and among the commissioners were Androtion and his friend Timocrates. Androtion appears to have behaved with great inconsiderateness—even with some cruelty—in exacting the money due; and the feeling aroused by this encouraged two of his personal enemies, Euctemon and Diodorus, to prosecute him shortly afterwards, not on a matter arising out of the commission itself, but on a charge of proposing an illegal decree.[2]

[1] How there came to be arrears under a system by which the rich advanced the sums levied is not clear. Perhaps they had failed to advance the whole of the amounts required of them. The sums still owing were very small; hardly any one owed more than a mina. [2] Note I at the end of the Chapter.

The decree thus attacked was one awarding crowns to the Council which went out of office in the summer of 355, and of which Androtion himself had been a member. It was said to contravene two laws—first, that which required a preliminary resolution of the Council itself, before any proposal could be made to the Assembly; and secondly, that which forbade the award of crowns—the regular form of compliment to an outgoing Council —to any Council which had not built a certain number of triremes. The proposal was further stated to be unlawful, because Androtion had been guilty of immoral practices which disqualified him from taking part in public business; and Androtion's argument, that the enmity against him was really due to his public-spirited services in recovering the arrears of the war-tax, was, it was urged, quite unjustified; as was also his claim to gratitude for his treatment of certain sacred treasures, which he had melted down and recast, thereby enhancing their value: his official conduct had really been such as to deserve the utmost reprobation. Such was the case put in the mouth of Diodorus, whose speech (which followed that of Euctemon) was composed for him by Demosthenes. But Androtion could reply that a Council could not be expected to propose a vote of thanks to itself; and that the Council had actually collected the funds for building the necessary number of triremes, but that one of the officials had absconded with them. This fact certainly freed the

8

Council from blame; nor could the enormity of Androtion's personal conduct be held to justify the infliction of a stigma upon the whole Council. Androtion therefore was properly acquitted. Demosthenes, though he makes Diodorus warn the jury to beware of the unscrupulous ingenuity of his rhetorically trained adversary, himself writes to his brief, and that brief a bad one[1]; so that his arguments appear suspiciously subtle and sophistical.

We do not know why Demosthenes undertook the case. It may be that Androtion was a supporter of Aristophon, and that Demosthenes was trying his hand first on the side of the Opposition. (Aristophon had certainly himself proposed a similar commission to enquire into cases of debt to the sacred and secular funds of the State[2]; and it is therefore probable that Androtion's decree had his approval.) Or he may have been particularly interested in the case on account of the alleged failure of the Council to build the proper number of ships. That his interest in all that affected the navy was already active had been shown by the Speech on the Trierarchic Crown, and by his own repeated service in person as trierarch; and it was to be still more plainly proved in the following year. The passage in the Speech against Androtion[3] in which he emphasises

---

[1] It is very probable that he had some technical justification, in point of law; but he had none in equity.

[2] Dem., *in Timocr.*, § 11.   [3] §§ 12–16.

and illustrates from history the dependence of the prosperity of Athens upon the efficiency of the navy is thoroughly characteristic of him. Besides this, he may well have been moved to indignation, as he often was later, by what seemed to him to be rascality masquerading in the guise of service to the State; and it is at least of interest that he claimed now, as later, to try the conduct of politicians even in small things by the standard of the highest traditions of the city. Androtion professed to have increased the value of certain golden crowns, which had been awarded as marks of honour and dedicated in the temples, by recasting them into the form of golden cups,—mere signs of wealth.

And [says Demosthenes] he did not even observe that never to this day has this People been eager for the acquisition of money; but for honour it has been eager, as for nothing else in the world. It is a sign of this, that when Athens had money in greater abundance than any other Hellenic people, she spent it all in the cause of honour; her citizens contributed from their private resources; and she never shrank from danger when glory was to be won. Therefore she has those eternal and abiding possessions—the memory of her actions, and the beauty of the offerings dedicated in honour of them—the porticoes which you see, the Parthenon, the Colonnades, the Dockyards—no mere pair of vases these, no paltry cups of gold, three or four in number, weighing a mina apiece, to be melted down again whenever you choose to propose it.

For the rest, the Speech is vigorous and the tone of virtuous indignation well-sustained, expressing itself in irony, in rhetorical questions, in short pungent sentences and strongly worded phrases.

The second speech which Demosthenes must have composed at about the time when the Social War was drawing to an end (or perhaps shortly after peace had been made) was that against the law of Leptines. Leptines had proposed, with the approval of Aristophon, to abolish—retrospectively as well as for the future—those grants of immunity from certain burdens[1] imposed by the State, which had frequently been made as the reward of distinguished public services. The proposal doubtless arose out of the prevailing agitation of mind in regard to the resources of the State; and was probably suggested by recent real or supposed abuses of the practice of granting such immunity. Demosthenes himself a few years later[2] protested against the recklessness with which these grants were made; and the opponents of the law desired not to retain the existing practice, but to amend it in a better manner than Leptines' proposals would have.[3]

The law was carried in the Assembly, probably

---

[1] The chief of the burdens in question were the choregia— the duty of providing choruses for the Dionysiac and some other festivals; and the gymnasiarchy, or stewardship of the games celebrated at the Panathenæa, etc. The giving of tribal banquets and some other duties were also included. But no such permanent immunity was given from the trierarchy or the war-tax.

[2] *In Aristocr.*, § 201.   [3] Note 2.

in 356; but the mover was at once indicted for the illegality of his proposal by one Bathippus. Bathippus however died, and more than a year elapsed before his son Apsephion took up the case. It was now only possible to attack the law, not the mover[1]; and in accordance with custom, the People, who by passing the law had made it their own, appointed speakers to defend it—Leptines himself, Aristophon, Leodamas, and Cephisodotus (all distinguished orators), and a highly respected citizen named Deinias. Apsephion was represented by Phormio, and Demosthenes supported his case, acting nominally in the interest of Ctesippus, the son of Chabrias, who had been slain in battle at Chios and had left his immunity to his son.[2] The main grounds of the charge of illegality were doubtless set forth by Phormio, who addressed the court first. Demosthenes, though he pays some attention to the legal aspect of the case, lays special stress on the bad moral effect of such a law—on the unwisdom of abolishing one of the incentives to public-spirited action, and so causing the city to appear ungrateful for good service done to it; and, above all, on the breach

---

[1] See Note 1.

[2] It is not certain whether Ctesippus was actually a party to the prosecution; or whether Demosthenes was merely persuaded or engaged to speak by Ctesippus or his mother (towards whom, Plutarch tells us, he was said to have felt an attraction, though he did not go so far as to marry her). I can see no sufficient reason for supposing (as Blass does) that Demosthenes did not deliver this speech himself.

of faith, so contrary to the traditions of Athens, involved in taking away privileges which had been granted, merely because some few of the recipients had proved unworthy of them. He further points out that neither the State nor any of its citizens would gain much by the law. So far there can be little doubt that Demosthenes was right; and the tone which he adopts is dignified and statesmanlike. On the other hand, many of the arguments which he uses are almost transparently sophistical[1] and give the impression not only that he must have calculated out all the possible arguments for and against the measure, and the ways of meeting the former and urging the latter, but also that he could equally well have argued on the other side; and this cool and calculating unfairness alienates the reader's sympathy (in spite of the generally pleasing style and high moral tone of the Speech) more than the injustice which appears in later speeches as the result of passionate indignation in a good cause. The result of the trial is not certainly known.[2] But we hear very little of grants of immunity after this; and it is at least probable that the law was allowed to stand.

The Speeches against Androtion and against

---

[1] In particular he takes cases which Leptines' law was evidently not intended to cover—if it seemed to cover them, it was at most a matter of bad drafting—and treats them as typical.

[2] The point is a disputed one, and no piece of evidence has been produced which cannot be interpreted consistently with either theory of the issue.

Leptines are mainly of interest because they show us Demosthenes at a time when he was little more than a political lawyer, and not yet a statesman fired by strong conviction. His convictions gathered strength slowly; and though the qualities which appear in his later work are already seen in certain parts of these speeches, the contrast between them and the Third Philippic or the Speech on the Crown indicates how much he had yet to develop both as a statesman and as an orator. But even as a statesman he makes a very favourable appearance in 354, in the Speech on the Symmories or Naval Boards—the first of his extant speeches before the Assembly.

The debate in which the Speech was delivered was occasioned by reports circulated in Athens of the vast preparations for war which Artaxerxes was making, and which the Athenians, alarmed by the attitude which the King had adopted towards their allies, and uneasy owing to the help which Chares had given to Artabazus,[1] viewed with apprehension, fancying that the King might be intending to make an attack upon themselves. (His preparations were really directed against his own rebellious subjects in Egypt and Asia Minor.) A number of speakers urged the Assembly to forestall the supposed intentions of Artaxerxes by declaring war upon the Persian Empire; and they appealed to the traditions of the past, the glories of Marathon and Salamis, in favour · of their

[1] See above, p. 110.

proposal.[1] It is plain that the proposal itself was little short of madness. Even if the danger to the possessions of Athens from Philip of Macedon had not been growing more and more pressing (as will be shown in the next chapter), it would have been a hopeless task for her to attack Persia single-handed; and to attempt to persuade the other Greek States to join her would have been equally hopeless, even if the King's preparations had been aimed at her. The Greeks were altogether disunited, and Athens had no funds with which to enter upon such a campaign. Demosthenes therefore opposed the project, urging the reasons just given, and making them palatable to his audience by dovetailing into them the conventional contrasts between Persian and Athenian honour, by referring to the championship of Athens against Persia—still to be maintained, but not by action at inopportune moments,—and by expressing his confidence that if any real danger from Persia did arise, men and money would be forthcoming readily enough; though at the same time he argues that it would not be to the interest of the King himself to attack Greece. The latter argument is less convincing; but the main purport of the Speech is sound and statesmanlike.

But while deprecating the rash proposal to

[1] The idea of war with Persia had also perhaps been rendered attractive to many by the writings of Isocrates, and particularly by the *Panegyricus*.

THE STATUE OF DEMOSTHENES IN KNOLE PARK

REPRODUCED BY PERMISSION OF LORD SACKVILLE

FRONT VIEW

declare war, Demosthenes took advantage of the interest aroused by the debate to propose a practical reform, with a view to increasing the efficiency of the navy. The political situation obviously required Athens to be ready for action, if not against Persia, at least against other enemies; and the system introduced in 357 by the law of Periander had not proved satisfactory in every respect. It has already been mentioned[1] that the richer members of the Naval Boards instituted by that law found ways of evading their proper share of the burden—they would, for instance, arrange that certain work should be done by a contractor for a talent, and would then exact the whole of the talent from their poorer colleagues.[2] They spent little or nothing themselves, and yet obtained the immunity which was granted to a trierarch from all other burdens[3] for the current year, and also from the liability to the trierarchy itself until after the lapse of another year.[4] It would also appear that the duties of the several Boards and of their members were distributed in an unbusinesslike manner, so that in case of default it was not certain who was responsible; and besides this, the Twelve Hundred, who were liable to the burden under the law, were twelve hundred only in name, owing to the number of special exemptions which were allowed. Demosthenes proposed to increase the Twelve Hundred to a

[1] p. 96.   [2] Dem., *in Meid.*, § 155.
[3] Not, however, from the war-tax.   [4] Dem., *de Cor.*, §§ 102 ff.

nominal two thousand, in order that when all exemptions had been allowed for, there might actually be twelve hundred persons available; and to make so minute a subdivision of the members of the Boards, the taxable property, and the vessels to be equipped, and so detailed an assignment of definite duties to definite groups of persons, in regard to collection and equipment, that evasion should be impossible, and that the duties should be properly carried out. The thoroughness of the proposed reform is very characteristic of Demosthenes. As in his earlier speeches he had considered every possible argument that could be adduced on either side, so in proposing a practical measure, he leaves no detail unprovided for, and tacitly anticipates every objection, while at the same time he appeals to the People to display that unselfish readiness to perform any duty that might be laid upon them, without which the best-planned scheme must fail.

The proposed reform was not accepted; but it was a significant declaration of policy; and the main object of the Speech was achieved, for war was not declared against Persia. That this result was mainly due to Demosthenes is almost certain, for scarcely any other speaker, he tells us,[1] supported him; and if it seems strange that he should have carried such weight, when he had only been a regular speaker in the Assembly for about a year, it must be remembered not only that his case was

[1] *Pro Rhod.*, § 6.

THE STATUE OF DEMOSTHENES IN KNOLE PARK

SIDE VIEW

really unanswerable, though it might require some courage to state it in face of the misplaced patriotic appeals of the other side, but also that he himself had probably attracted attention by now, both by his obvious oratorical gifts, and by his public-spirited performance of the duties of the trierarchy and the other liturgies which he had discharged.

The position which Demosthenes intended to take up towards the leading statesmen or parties of the day is not expressly defined in the Speech, because it was not the custom to mention living statesmen by name in the Assembly. But it is probable that Aristophon, discredited by the failure of his policy in the Social War, had retired in the interval between the attack upon the law of Leptines and the debate on the Persian question; or, if not, that the proposal of war with Persia was the last effort of his supporters. Eubulus, whose policy was mainly one of peace and retrenchment, was taking his place as leader, and receiving support particularly from the richer classes—the leaders of commerce and the principal tax-payers—to whom the avoidance of war (except so far as it was necessary for purely defensive purposes or for the protection of trade) was of great importance. In the Speech against Leptines Demosthenes had spoken in opposition to Aristophon; and in the Speech on the Naval Boards he was on the side of Eubulus, in so far as he deprecated a rash military venture and laid stress upon the exhaustion of the financial resources of Athens.

But Demosthenes was certainly not an advocate' of the interests of the well-to-do classes,[1] for the reform of the Naval Boards which he proposed was designed to make it impossible for the rich to evade their duties; and he wished to carry on in a more satisfactory manner the preparations for a crisis which might arise at any moment. Before long his antagonism to the policy of Eubulus is more clearly defined; and our next task will be to attempt to realise more completely what that policy was.

The aims and methods of Eubulus are still a subject of controversy among historians of Greece. It is admitted, on all hands, that he was an upright and incorruptible statesman—no small distinction for a politician of those times—and that he was a master of finance. It is disputed whether his policy was wise and patriotic or merely narrowly prudent.

We have seen how greatly the city had suffered in consequence of the Social War. There were indeed some who minimised her losses and her exhaustion[2]—she had still in fact a considerable fleet, though little money for its upkeep; there were even (as we have seen) those who were not afraid of provoking the hostility of Persia; and there must already have been some who cried for

---

[1] Even in attacking the law of Leptines, he was not supporting the granting of immunities to rich men in any indiscriminate fashion. [2] See Isocr., *Areopag.*, §§ 1, 2.

vengeance upon Philip.[1]   Yet there can be no real
doubt that the first need for the moment was a
breathing space, in which the city could replenish
her treasury, repair her navy and her defences,
and enable her trading-vessels once more to ply
along the great trade-routes without fear.   It was
under such circumstances that Eubulus began to
take control of affairs.   In 354 he became a
member of the Theoric Board,[2] and owing to the
confidence reposed in him, the chief elective offices
in the administration came to be held by members
of that Board.[3]   Under his direction the number
of triremes was greatly increased, the dockyards
were repaired and enlarged, and a very considerable sum of money collected, without recourse
being had to extraordinary taxation.   It appears
that the success of Eubulus' finance was partly
due to the provident construction of the annual
Budget—for the fact that the Theoric Board
was appointed for four years, and the tenure of
the chief financial offices by its members, must
have made it more possible than before to construct
plans on a large scale—and partly to his encouragement of trade, which, among other advantages,
increased the sums received by means of indirect taxation.   Thus Eubulus not only instituted
large operations, which must have been "good for

---

[1] Comp. Dem., Phil. I, § 43 (spoken in 351–0).

[2] It is disputed whether he held any other specific office, and
as there is no evidence either way, the question is insoluble.

[3] See above, p. 98.

trade," in connection with the docks and fortifications, but he greatly improved the roads and the
water-supply of the city itself—useful measures,
at which Demosthenes scoffs unjustly,[1] but which
conferred benefits upon the masses as well as upon
the trading classes. By the institution of a new
and more expeditious procedure for the settlement
of mercantile disputes, he rendered an undoubted
service to Athenian commerce.[2] At the same time
he kept a strict eye upon officials, and prosecuted
them remorselessly if any sign of corruption or
irregularity appeared.[3] Recognising the actual
weakness of the city, and her inability at the
moment to pursue an imperialistic policy with
any success, he would not be drawn into war,
though he took steps, as we shall see, to secure the
interests of Athens in the Thracian region, and so to
protect the corn-supply, and, while refusing to enter upon a campaign against Philip, took proper
measures of defence when Philip seemed likely to
threaten Attica. The apparently incurable disunion of the Greek States was an obstacle to any
attempt to form a lasting coalition against the rising Macedonian power, and he recognised the fact.

On the other hand there can be no doubt that
he confirmed and gave new security to the system

[1] Olynth. III, § 29.
[2] Heges., *de Hal.*, § 12; Pollux, viii., 63, 101; Harpocr., *s. v.*
ἔμμηνοι δίκαι: comp. Xenophon's treatise *On the Revenues*, ch. iii.
(from which Eubulus may possibly have derived the idea).
[3] See Dem., *de Fals. Leg.*, §§ 290–294.

by which theoric money was distributed; and he
may even have extended the distributions. In
what way he did this cannot be determined with
absolute certainty; but that there was a law which
in some way forbade the application of the theoric
money to military purposes, and that in 349 it was
a recent law, and therefore in all probability was
proposed by Eubulus and his party, is proved by
the demand made by Demosthenes in that year[1]
that its repeal should be facilitated by those who
had proposed it. The statement of a scholiast
that Eubulus enacted that any proposal to repeal
this law should be punished with death is due to
a misunderstanding of some words of Demosthenes.[2] It is most likely that the law put an end
to the assignment of unallocated funds (whether
for military or other purposes) by means of decrees
of the People, and that it did so simply by enacting
that all funds not allocated in the annual Budget[3]
should become theoric money; for no decree might
contravene a law, on pain of penalties which
might be very heavy, and in order to pass any
special vote of money out of the surplus it would
be necessary to repeal the law of Eubulus. That
is why, when in 349 Demosthenes desired to convert the theoric money to military purposes, he
demanded the appointment of Nomothetæ; for
only through Nomothetæ could laws be repealed
or passed.[4]

[1] Olynth. III, § 12. [2] *Ibid.*
[3] See above, p. 125. [4] See above, p. 91, and Note 3.

The meaning of Eubulus' policy now becomes clearer. So long as large sums could be voted by decrees of the People, suddenly inflamed by fiery oratory and encouraged to declare war, there was no security for his plan of rehabilitating the fleet and the defences, and so making effective provision against attack. Little harm could be done by the prohibition of such votes, so long as he and his friends occupied all the financial offices, and took care in the annual Budget to provide sufficiently for these measures of defence and for the public improvements which he wished to carry out, thus including all the military expenditure which they contemplated within the Budget, instead of leaving it to fall on the surplus. By such careful budgeting Eubulus was able to provide for all the needs of the State (assuming that actual war could be avoided), and to satisfy the People by the distribution of the surplus which remained when all other requirements had been covered. For obviously he was forced to do something to reconcile the masses to the abandonment of an imperialistic policy. To abandon such a policy was contrary to their natural sentiment; and orators who flattered their pride by reference to the glories of the past, and kept their ambition in a state of activity, increased the force of this sentiment. But the distributions of theoric money could be utilised as a kind of premium of insurance[1]

---

[1] The metaphor is borrowed from Beloch, *Attische Politik*, p. 178.

against interference with his plans of retrenchment and repair of the defences. It was not without reason that Demades spoke of these distributions as the "cement of the democracy."

The policy of Eubulus is thus quite intelligible; its aim was in itself a good one, and the ability which he displayed in carrying it out was remarkable. Yet its weakness is also clear. In the first place, he assumed too readily that it would be possible to avoid war for a considerable time; and he was so reluctant to abandon the delusion that, as we shall see, he postponed taking action, when war was forced upon him, until it was too late. [2] In the second place, no argumentation can get over the fact that sums which might have gone to constitute a strong reserve were thrown away upon amusements which had acquired a disproportionate importance in the life of the people. Lastly, a policy which might be justifiable and advantageous when controlled by strong and able hands, might become disastrous under a weaker leader, or through popular pressure. The temptation for the People to demand, and for the demagogue to grant, increased sums for such distributions, and so to starve the administration, might become irresistible; and we cannot entirely refuse to listen to the contemporary writers who re-

---

[1] With the same end in view, Eubulus increased the attractions of some of the festivals, and there with his own popularity; comp. Dem., Olynth. III, § 31, where the grant of special processions at the Boëdromia is mentioned.　　　　[2] See below, Ch. VI.

garded Eubulus as encouraging the People in idleness and pleasure, to an extent which rendered them unready for courageous and patriotic service when it was most needed. "Eubulus," says Theopompus,[1] "was a demagogue conspicuous for his care and industry; he provided a great amount of money, and distributed it to the Athenians, with the result that under his leadership the city became thoroughly cowardly and idle"; and Aristotle's strictures[2] upon the practice of distributing surplus funds to the People have obvious reference to Eubulus. "The multitude receives the money to-day, and is as badly off as ever to-morrow; and to support the poor in this way is like pouring water into a broken pitcher."

It may be argued in reply that the People were already so far enervated and demoralised that the action of Eubulus was the effect rather than the cause of their moral weakness; and that in recognising the fact as it was, he was doing the best thing that the circumstances permitted. Yet (apart from the question whether the People were by this time so hopelessly demoralised as this implies) it is difficult not to feel that his policy was somewhat cynical; it was certainly destitute of any such high ideal as Demosthenes constructed for himself on a foundation of Athenian traditions, hoping as he did that he would be able to persuade his countrymen not merely to applaud patriotic sentiments when they fell from the lips of their

[1] Fr. 91 (Oxford Text).   [2] Ar., *Pol.*, VI (VII), p. 1320a.

orators, but also to face the hard work and self-sacrifice which were necessary if sentiment was to be translated into action. The success, however short-lived, of Demosthenes in this aim shows that the idea was not a chimerical one.

But at the moment when he first came into power, Eubulus was almost certainly right. Retrenchment and repair of the defences and the fleet were absolutely necessary, whether they were accompanied by distributions of money or not. It was very desirable to avoid war, if possible; and the proposals which Demosthenes made in his next two public speeches, high-spirited and patriotic though his intentions were, were almost certainly mistaken. It will be convenient to consider these at once, though they fall rather later in time than some of the events which must be narrated in the next chapter.

The first arose out of affairs in the Peloponnese. Here for the last ten years, Sparta had been waiting quietly for an opportunity to recover her power; and in 353 such an opportunity seemed to have occurred. Since 355 the Thebans, who had previously supported the enemies of Sparta in the Peloponnese, had been engaged in the Sacred War (of which more is to be said hereafter) against the Phocians. They were thus less able to help their friends in South Greece. The latter therefore turned towards Athens for support and (probably in the last year of Aristophon's leadership) were received favourably. The Messenians in particular received a solemn promise of Athenian aid, in event of any attempt on the part of Sparta to violate their independence.[1] In 353 the Spartans, with no little ingenuity, made a proposal to the other Greek States that there should be a restoration of territory to its original owners. The proposal was bound to meet with some support in Athens, since its acceptance would secure the recovery of Oropus, which had been held by Thebes since 366, and the restoration of the towns friendly to Athens in Bœotia—Thespiæ, Platææ, and Orchomenus. Of the Peloponnesian States, Elis would be attracted by the prospect of recovering Triphylia from the Arcadians, Phleius by that of the restoration to them of Tricaranum, which was now occupied by the Argives. Sparta herself would then obviously claim to recover her dominion over Arcadia and Messenia, and would expect the support of the other States who had benefited by the restoration to them of their own former possessions.

When the discussion in the Assembly took place, and embassies both from Sparta and from Megalopolis had been heard, the question was very warmly debated. In favour of the Spartan proposal were the bitter feeling of most of the Athenians towards Thebes, the desire to recover Oropus, and the reluctance to break with the Spartans, who had fought side by side with the Athenians at Mantineia and elsewhere. Demosthenes, though he

[1] Paus. IV, xxviii., §§ 1, 2.

professed to be impartial in comparison with previous speakers, supported the Arcadian appeal,
on the ground that the interest of Athens required
that a balance of power should be maintained
between Sparta and Thebes, and that the Spartans
would gain too great a preponderance, if they
were permitted once more to be overlords of
Messenia and Arcadia. Besides this, Athens was
already pledged to support the Messenians; and
to accede to the Arcadian appeal would be in effect
to prevent the Spartans from committing aggressions in either quarter. At the same time, the
alliance with the Arcadians must be frank on both
sides, and the Arcadians on their part must formally renounce their alliance with Thebes. It
was not likely, Demosthenes argued, that Sparta
would actually go to war; and even without yield-
ing to the requests of Sparta it would be possible—
and that, even with the help of Sparta herself—
to recover Oropus and to demand from Thebes the
restoration of the suppressed towns. On these latter
points, Demosthenes' argument is very unconvincing, resting as it does on the assumption that Sparta
was interested, not in the recovery of her Empire, but
in giving effect to general principles of justice—the
very thing which he himself denied, in denouncing
the unscrupulous part which Sparta was playing.[1]

[1] Both in this Speech and in the next, Demosthenes shows that
he has not yet fully grasped the importance of distinguishing an
abstractly possible argument from a good one. Increased
knowledge of affairs remedied this defect.

As regards the main question, there can be little doubt that to make alliance with the Arcadians would really have involved serious risk of war with Sparta, and probably also with Thebes. Even if Sparta had recovered her dominion in the Peloponnese, it would not have harmed Athens, since in case of war the Peloponnesian subject-States would have been certain to turn against Sparta once more. From the point of view of Athenian interests, in the existing circumstances, Eubulus' policy of non-intervention was undoubtedly the safer. On the other hand, it is impossible not to appreciate the higher grounds upon which Demosthenes rested his case—fidelity to the promise given to the Messenians, and the traditional attitude of Athens towards the victims of others' aggressions; and in a sense, future events afforded a certain justification of his policy. For when the Athenians had rejected the Arcadian alliance, a temporary relief from the pressure of the Sacred War enabled Thebes to send help to the Arcadians, who became more closely connected with Thebes than ever, and, a few years later, like the Thebans, became allies of Philip, all the efforts which the Athenians then made to obtain their support proving unsuccessful. Hostilities were carried on inconclusively between Sparta and the Arcadians for two or three years, until in 350 a Peace was made, by which the Arcadians retained their independence. The conception which Demosthenes had put forward of the duty of Athens

towards the injured appears again in his Speech
in defence of the Liberty of the Rhodians. At
the end of the Social War in 355, Rhodes, which
had been one of the leading cities in the revolt,
fell into the hands of Mausolus, King of Caria—a
vassal of Persia, who had assisted the allies against
Athens. He fostered an oligarchical conspiracy
in the city. The democratic party were driven
into exile, and the oligarchs, who acted with
cynical brutality,[1] maintained their position by
means of the Carian garrison. Similar events
took place in Cos; and Athens thought it necessary,
as a precaution, to strengthen the band of Athenians resident in Samos.[2] In 351 (or possibly a
year or two earlier)[3] the Rhodian exiles sent a
deputation to Athens, asking for help and restoration—in other words for the liberation of the island
at once from the oligarchy in possession and
from the power of Artemisia, who had succeeded
(probably in 353) to the throne of her brother
and husband Mausolus. The Athenians were
little inclined to accede to the request. This
same democratic party had led the revolt against
Athens in 358, and popular feeling rejoiced over
their misfortune. Demosthenes, however, urged
the Athenians to forget their grudge, to take up
their traditional rôle as protectors of democracies
everywhere, and to remember the risk to which
Athens herself would be exposed, if oligarchies

[1] Theopomp., fr. 118 (Oxford Text).
[2] Dionysius, *de Dein.*, ch. xiii.   [3] Note 4.

were established in all the States of Greece, and the Athenian democracy were left alone. The recent disasters suffered by Artaxerxes in Egypt, he argued, made it unlikely that either he or Artemisia would seriously oppose the re-establishment of Athenian influence in the island.

There can, however, be little doubt that Demosthenes underrated the danger of war with Caria or Persia, if Athens interfered in Rhodes. In any case, such interference was directly contrary to the policy of Eubulus, with whom on this occasion the People as a whole was in sympathy. The generous, though probably impolitic, appeal of Demosthenes failed; and several years later he speaks[1] of Cos and Rhodes as still subject to Caria. Artemisia herself died shortly afterwards, of grief (so it is said) for the death of Mausolus.[2]

The air of impartiality which Demosthenes studiously affects in the three speeches to the Assembly which have now been considered makes them appear comparatively tame and in places academic in tone. But now and then, as we have seen, the idealist in him breaks out, and he demands that Athens shall play a part worthy of her past. He parts company, however, with the vulgar jingoism of the popular orators of the day, in his insistence that such a policy involves personal work for each individual citizen, and that patriotic sentiment without personal self-sacrifice is useless.

[1] *De Pace*, § 25.
[2] Theopomp., fr. 275 (Oxford Text), etc.

In the last of the three speeches[1] he emphasises strongly both the breach with Athenian tradition made by his opponents, and the difficulty of rousing his audience to act upon the principles which they professed. It is true that in dealing both with the Arcadian and with the Rhodian appeal, he advocated the policy which was probably unwise at the moment; it would have been very ill-advised to divert into other channels the forces and the funds which were certain to be needed before long against Philip. Demosthenes had still much to learn as a politician. But the significance of these early speeches in relation to his career as a whole lies (in spite of one or two touches of almost cynical opportunism,[2] which may have been designed to commend him to the Assembly as a man of the world) in the growing sense of national duty which they reveal; in the plain enunciation of certain important principles, such as the doctrine of the Balance of Power, and the assertion of the necessary hostility of monarchies and oligarchies to a democracy like the Athenian; and in the appeals which he makes to the lessons of the past. In these points these speeches form the first of a long series in which the same ideas can be traced.

The trial of Timocrates, the colleague of Androtion in the Commission for recovery of arrears of

---

[1] *Pro Rhod.*, §§ 25-33; comp. Isocr., *de Pace*, § 30.
[2] *E. g., pro Megal.*, § 10; *pro Rhod.*, § 28.

taxation, whose proceedings have already been described, requires a brief notice, if only because it illustrates certain remarkable features of Athenian public life. As in the trial of Androtion—of which the case may be considered a sequel—the speech of the prosecutor Diodorus was written by Demosthenes.

In 355 the Athenians sent an embassy to Mausolus, King of Caria, perhaps to protest against his action in assisting the rebellious allies of Athens or in interfering in the affairs of Rhodes. The ambassadors were Androtion, Melanopus, and Glaucetes; the ship on which they sailed was commanded by Archebius and Lysitheides. On the way they captured an Egyptian merchant-vessel, which they brought to Athens. The Assembly decided that as Athens was on friendly terms with the King of Persia,[1] and Egypt was in revolt against him, the Egyptians were enemies of Athens (though in fact they had but recently been assisted by Athenian generals and soldiers), and the vessel was therefore a lawful prize. Accordingly the prize-money ought to have gone to the State, and the two trierarchs were legally responsible for paying it over. After some time Euctemon denounced them to the Commission recently appointed on the motion of Aristophon to enquire into debts to the State, for their failure to account for the sum, which amounted to nine and a half

[1] The recall of Chares in the previous year was nominally based on the same assumption.

talents; and subsequently proposed a decree that payment should be required from them, but that as the money was admittedly in the hands of Androtion, Melanopus, and Glaucetes, the trierarchs should be allowed to argue before a court the question, whether they or the three ambassadors were liable. Androtion failed to convict Euctemon's decree of illegality; and the three tried various devices for evading payment, but in vain. At last, in 353, they found themselves in the position of having to pay the debt at once, or to be condemned by a court to pay a sum which would amount to about treble the original debt; in the latter alternative they would be imprisoned till the sum was paid. They therefore got Timocrates to propose a law that any debtor to the State who had been sentenced to imprisonment (as well as to repayment) should be permitted to give bail by himself or his friends for the amount of the debt, and allowed until a month before the end of the current year to discharge it; after that period his bail should be escheated, and himself imprisoned. In order to smuggle the law through, a certain Epicrates was induced to propose in an Assembly in the middle of July, 353, a decree that the Nomothetæ should be summoned next day, on the pretext that insufficient funds had been voted for the Panathenæa. The Nomothetæ met; nothing was done in regard to the Panathenæa; but Timocrates' law was somehow passed. Diodorus and Euctemon prosecuted Timocrates for the alleged illegality of the law; and the trial probably took place early in 352. There can be no doubt that the law was illegal, and was merely a device to enable Androtion and his colleagues to postpone the evil day. The relevant arguments of Demosthenes on this point are conclusive. It is therefore all the more pity that he should in this Speech (as in that against Leptines) have used other arguments directed against consequences which no one would have dreamed of expecting from the law, and which could only be inferred from it (if at all) because it had been hastily and overwidely drafted.[1] He strains every point against Timocrates and Androtion in a way which is at least disingenuous, and which certainly makes a bad impression.[2] At the same time, the knowledge of law and the sureness of touch which he shows are remarkable, and here and there a striking and vivid piece of writing foreshadows some of the best of his later work.[3]

We do not know what the result of the trial was. If Timocrates was condemned to a fine, it is probable that it was not so heavy as to force him to go into exile; as he is generally supposed to be the Timocrates who supported Meidias against Demos-

[1] Esp. §§ 79–101.

[2] The text of the Speech as it stands appears to be a conflation of two speeches, or of two recensions of the same Speech; but its exact history cannot be certainly reconstructed. Part of the Speech consists of a repetition of a considerable section of the Speech against Androtion, with very slight alterations.

[3] *E. g.*, § 208, much admired by Longinus.

thenes some years later. Androtion and his colleagues had actually paid the sum due from them before the trial of Timocrates began[1]; and though this would not purge Timocrates' guilt in proposing the law, it might mollify the jury when the penalty had to be fixed. Androtion himself was still active in Athens in 346.[2]

NOTES ON CHAPTER IV

1. No proposal might be made in the Assembly which was inconsistent with the existing laws. The proposer of any such motion was personally liable to prosecution (though only within the year), and the law might be repealed at any time after a trial before a jury. The rule was a safeguard against inconsistencies in the law, and against the risk which the People ran of being misled by an able orator into passing measures contrary to their own will, which was assumed to be embodied in the existing law.

2. The ultimate object of the law of Leptines is not very clear. It can hardly have been an important measure of finance. It is true that the preamble stated that it was enacted in order that the richest men might have to undertake the burdens; and that some of those who enjoyed immunity must have been more or less wealthy men. But they were comparatively few in all; the relief given to the rest by the distribution of the burden among a slightly increased number would be slight; and the general revenues of the State would gain nothing. Nor can the law be accounted for by a dislike on the part of the democracy for hereditary privileges. Most of the grants of immunity were indeed made to a man's descendants as well as to himself; but there is no evidence to show that the Athenians thought of the extension of a compliment to the descendants of a distinguished servant of the State as inconsistent with democracy. It is much more likely that there were notorious cases of the privilege being enjoyed by the undeserving; or that it had been much granted

[1] §§ 187 ff.
[2] *C. I. A.*, iv., 109b (Dittenb. Syll. Ed., ii., No. 129).

of late to persons (such as powerful generals) of whom the democracy was suspicious.

3. See Francotte, *Les Finances des Cités Grecques*. Francotte's account of the law and policy of Eubulus is the most satisfactory that I have seen. He notes that the law was occasionally evaded by passing, not decrees, but special laws, dealing with small necessary expenses, grants of crowns, etc., and that it might be evaded in small matters in various other ways. But the proposal of a large vote for purposes of war would have certainly been followed by prosecution.

4. Dionysius places the Speech for the Rhodians in 351. Butcher and others would date it a year or two earlier, on account of the comparatively slight mention of Philip, which they suppose to be too casual for the year of the First Philippic. But the allusion to Philip shows that in the speaker's opinion, though not in that of his opponents, Philip is a very formidable foe. The other arguments for an earlier date are even less convincing.

CHAPTER V

THE RISE OF PHILIP

BEFORE some of the events narrated in the last chapter had taken place, the great struggle between Athens and the royal house of Macedonia had begun.

The Macedonians of antiquity were a mixed race, and the degree of kinship between them and the Hellenic peoples is a matter upon which no agreement between scholars has been attained. The Macedonians proper lived on the low lands watered by the Axius and the Haliacmon, between the mountains and the sea, with Pella for their capital, though the more ancient centre, and the burial place of their kings, was Ægæ or Edessa.[1] They were a more or less settled agricultural people, whose lands provided for them the necessities of life, and who engaged comparatively little in foreign trade. They were the subjects of an absolute monarchy of an almost Homeric pattern, holding their lands at the pleasure of the King, giving him military service at his command, and in every way bound to do his bidding, except

[1] Now Vodhena.

that in matters of life and death the assembly of
fighting men appears to have had a right to give
the final decision, and the will of the same body
was at least as influential as the right of birth in
determining the succession. But in the upper
valleys, and among the mountains, there dwelt a
number of tribes—Lyncestæ, Orestæ, Elimiotæ,
and others—governed by princes of their own,
nominally indeed subordinate to the King of
Macedonia, but restless and always liable to rebel.
These were probably nearly akin to the Illyrians
who lived to the westward of them (between them
and the Adriatic), and to the Pæonians on the
north of Macedonia. There is also some evidence
of the existence of Thracian stocks within Macedonia itself.

That the royal house of Macedonia was at least
partly Hellenic by descent had been admitted in
the fifth century B.C., by the officials of Olympia,[1]
who allowed the Macedonian prince, Alexander,
to compete in the Olympian games—a privilege
strictly confined to Hellenes. But with regard
to their subjects there was always a doubt. On
the one hand, there was a tradition that they, or
some of them, had migrated from Greek lands into
Macedonia. On the other, they were often spoken
of as barbarians, because they were backward in
culture, and their dialect was difficult to understand. (There was the same doubt about the
peoples of Epirus and inner Ætolia, and for similar

[1] Herod., v., 22.

reasons.) The remains of the Macedonian dialect are too meagre, and the extent of its borrowings from the vocabulary of the Greeks proper too uncertain, to justify any conclusion as to the nationality of those who spoke it; and we have to be contented at present with the probability that they were in some degree akin to the Hellenes on the one side and the Illyrians on the other, and that the two stocks (and perhaps others with them) were blended in varying proportions in different localities. [1]

In one respect the Macedonians afforded a strong contrast to all but the least advanced Greek peoples, namely, in the fact that their organisation was a tribal and quasi-feudal one, and did not, as with the Greeks, centre in city-states. [2] The Macedonians proper, as distinct from the hill-tribes, appear to have been organised primarily for military purposes. The greater number of the able-bodied land-holders made up the infantry or "foot-guards" [3]; and a smaller body of wealthier and more honourable men composed the cavalry, or "Companions" of the King. [4] At the time of Philip's accession the Companions may have numbered some six hundred. Of these a specially selected group—probably under a hundred—were "Companions of the King's person" [5]; and the highest ambition of the Macedonian was to attain a position in this group. But in this organisation the hill-tribes had no part.

---

[1] Note 1 at the end of the Chapter. [2] The unit was the ἔθνος, not the πόλις. [3] πεζέταιροι. [4] ἑταῖροι. [5] οἱ ἀμφ' αὐτὸν ἑταῖροι.

On the sea-coast the freedom of action of the Macedonians was held in check by the Greek colonies planted there. In the time of the Peloponnesian War the King, Perdiccas II., had failed, in spite of his political ingenuity, to shake off these fetters. His successor, Archelaus, had made efforts to modernise his kingdom, building roads and chains of forts, and probably attempting to unite the unordered elements in his kingdom by combining all in one national army. He was an admirer of Greek culture, and encouraged the literary men of Greece to frequent his Court. Euripides and Agathon ended their days there; Timotheus the lyric poet and Zeuxis the painter also visited Pella; Socrates was invited thither, but declined to go. But the efforts of Archelaus had little permanent success, and in the confusion which followed his death in 399, the advance which had been made towards a higher civilisation was neutralised. The coastward towns, Olynthus, Acanthus, and Amphipolis, increased in power, and in spite of a temporary set-back, owing to the intervention of Sparta in 379,[1] the Olynthian League grew powerful and continued to act as a barrier in the way of Macedonian ambition.

Amyntas III., whose reign lasted (though not without interruptions)from 393 to 369, was generally on terms of friendship with Athens, and, as we have seen,[2] acknowledged her title to Amphipolis. He married the Lyncestian princess Eurydice,

[1] See above, p. 48. [2] p. 53.

who bore him three sons—Alexander, Perdiccas, and Philip, who was born in 382. Alexander, who succeeded Amyntas in 369, was murdered after a reign of a year; and the young Perdiccas only secured the throne from the pretender Pausanias by the intervention of Iphicrates, who was invoked by Eurydice. At the beginning of the reign of Perdiccas III., Ptolemy of Alorus, the son-in-law and paramour of Eurydice, acted as regent; and when (in 367) the Theban general Pelopidas advanced from Thessaly to Pella, Ptolemy made an agreement with him, and was obliged to give Philip, then fifteen years old, with other hostages as a security for its fulfilment. Philip was taken to Thebes, and lived there in the house of Pammenes until 364, when he was released and returned to Macedonia. Perdiccas, like Archelaus, was inclined towards literature and philosophy, and Euphræus, a pupil of Plato, was for a time his principal adviser.[1] But in spite of the help given to him by Iphicrates, and of a short-lived alliance with Athens which Timotheus persuaded him to make, he gave his support to Amphipolis in her struggle to hold out against Athens. In 359 he was killed in a rising of the hill-tribes, perhaps instigated by Eurydice herself, in revenge for the murder of Ptolemy by the King's orders.[2]

[1] Comp. Athen., xi., p. 508e. οὕτω ψυχρῶς συνέταξε τὴν ἑταιρίαν τοῦ βασιλέως ὥστε οὐκ ἐξῆν τοῦ συσσιτίου μετασχεῖν, εἰ μή τις ἐπισταῖτο τὸ γεωμετρεῖν ἢ τὸ φιλοσοφεῖν. For Euphræus, see Phil., III, § 59, and below, p. 325.

[2] So Justin, VII, v.

The Macedonians first proclaimed his infant son King, with Philip as regent; but very soon, in view of the need of a strong hand, they transferred the kingship to Philip himself, who accepted it, we are told, under compulsion.[1]

Philip was still only twenty-three years of age; but his early life had taught him lessons by which he had profited to the full. He had learned that success could only be achieved by a strong hand, and that if he was to reign over Macedonia in security he must not be over-scrupulous as to means. His sojourn in Thebes had given him an opportunity for observing the successes and methods of Epameinondas and Pelopidas—the one a unique embodiment of commanding military genius and high culture, the other the most reckless and daring soldier of his age. He had learned to appreciate the almost unbounded opportunities which lay open to a strong man in the Hellenic world, as it then was; and he had become familiar with the recent improvements upon the traditional organisation of Greek armies. He had learned that the leader of a strong army, who could attach his men to himself by sentiment as well as by interest, and could not only hold his force together by discipline, but could develop methods of fighting which would give it an immediate advantage over those who followed more conventional lines, was practically certain of success.

Moreover he was the man for his task. Fear-

[1] *Compulsus a populo* (Justin, VII, v.).

less and resolute; not to be turned aside by a defeat here and there, or by any misfortune to his own person; discerning and clever in dealing with different kinds of men and States; never eager to secure in haste what might be better secured by patience, or to use force where fraud would serve, he was entirely fitted for the execution of an ambitious and far-reaching policy in that age. Besides this, he was personally attractive, not only to the rough Macedonian soldiers, with whom he mingled freely on familiar terms, but also to the cultured representatives of the Greek States, who were sent to treat with him. He had learned at Thebes, among other lessons, to appreciate Hellenic literature and refinement; he encouraged dramatic artists to visit his Court at Pella; and, when the time came, he engaged Aristotle himself as the tutor of his young son Alexander. He was an able and persuasive speaker, and the orators of Athens themselves felt the power of his adroit eloquence.[1] Though he indulged freely in the coarser vices, he confined his indulgence for the most part to seasons when it could not interfere with his plans; and it in no way affected either his own hardiness—his constitution was of iron—or his requirement of similar hardiness from his soldiers. He used money no less skilfully than other means of persuasion to effect his purposes; his generosity was lavish, and it was believed by later generations that his victories were won with

[1] Æsch., *de F. L.*, §§ 42, 43, etc.

gold as often as arms. That he employed deception to achieve his ends cannot be doubted, though
his faithlessness on certain occasions was certainly
exaggerated by Demosthenes. The rectitude of
ancient and modern critics may deplore some of
the methods which Philip used, and the licenses
which he permitted himself in his private life.[1]
But deceit and corruption are not so entirely
unknown in modern political warfare that we can
afford, on account of his use of them, to refuse all
admiration to a strong man, who, with every
instrument thoroughly at his command, played
his great game with skill, precision, and courage,
and seldom mistook either the men with whom he
had to deal, or the surest method of dealing with
them.

How soon Philip conceived the policy which it
was his life's work to carry out, we do not know.
Doubtless the necessity of reorganising the army
and improving its methods of fighting presented
itself first. Before long he may have determined
upon the conquest of the Hellenic world; and in
any case he must have been aware from the first
that Macedonia could not be perfectly independent,
so long as she was hemmed in by Hellenic colonies
out of his control, and by warlike and restless
tribes, not yet subdued. The idea of the conquest
of the Nearer East probably grew in his mind
later, when his army had reached its full efficiency,
and his lordship over Greece was as good as

[1] Note 2.

achieved. It may even have been suggested by Isocrates.

However this may be, the organisation of the army was his first task. By the formation of regiments on a territorial basis, bound together by a local patriotism which was to lead to a more comprehensive national spirit; by offering new prospects of promotion from one rank in the army to another, and so appealing to the ambition of the individual soldier; by attaching the higher ranks above all, but all ranks in ascending degrees, to his own person; he created a united national force, which he drilled into efficiency by relentless practice as well as by experience in actual warfare. The introduction of a longer spear for the use of the infantry gave his phalanx a great advantage when meeting the enemy: his cavalry, brought to the highest pitch of mobility, were frequently so employed, under his skilful generalship, as to determine the issue of battle by their action at critical moments, and were given an importance which cavalry had seldom possessed in Greek warfare; he further availed himself of the great improvements in siege-instruments which the engineers of the day devised; and his cavalry and infantry were supplemented by archers and light troops of other descriptions, so as to be prepared for every contingency.[1]

Above all, Philip's army was kept together as

[1] On Philip's army, see Hogarth, *Philip and Alexander of Macedonia*, pp. 50–64, etc.

a standing force. At first this may well have caused some discontent, and there may be some truth in the account which Demosthenes gives in the Second Olynthiac of the state of feeling in Macedonia.

You must not imagine [he says], men of Athens, that Philip and his subjects delight in the same things. Philip has a passion for glory—that is his ambition; and he has deliberately chosen to risk the consequences of a life of action and danger, preferring the glory of achieving more than any King of Macedonia before him to a life of security. But his subjects have no share in the honour and glory. Constantly battered about by all these expeditions, up and down, they are vexed with incessant hardships; they are not suffered to pursue their occupations or attend to their own affairs; and for the little that they produce, as best they can, they can find no market, because the trading stations are closed on account of the war.

In the same Speech, Demosthenes speaks of Philip's jealousy of any credit ascribed to his subordinates; and Polyænus[1] relates that Philip professed to prefer victories won by diplomatic conversations to those secured by arms, because the glory of the latter had to be shared with others, while that of the former was all his own. But we know that Philip in fact recognised to the full the qualities of Antipater and Parmenio, his principal generals; there is no other evidence,

[1] Polyæn. IV, ii., § 9.

apart from Demosthenes' statements, to suggest any disunion of spirit between Philip and
his men; and it would seem to be one of Philip's
greatest distinctions, that before long he did
make his subjects feel that they had a share
in the honour and glory, and that their interest
was not at strife with their loyalty to himself.
In any case, the possible inconveniences of a
standing army, equipped with every kind of
force, were more than counterbalanced by the
immense advantage which it gave him over his
enemies. "It is not," says Demosthenes, "as
commander of a column of heavy infantry that
Philip can march wherever he chooses, but because
he has attached to himself a force of light infantry,
cavalry, archers, mercenaries, and a miscellaneous
camp. . . . Summer and winter are alike to him,
and there is no close season during which he sus-
pends operations."[1] And again, "with a standing
force always about him, and knowing beforehand
what he intends to do, he suddenly falls upon whom-
soever he pleases; while we wait until we learn that
something is happening, and only then, in a turmoil,
make our preparations."[2] His own position of
absolute command was an even greater element
in his success; and upon this also Demosthenes
lays some stress.[3] In short, it must soon have
been plain, both to his admirers and to those who

[1] Phil. III, § 49.
[2] *De Chers.*, § 11; comp. *de Cor.*, § 235.
[3] *E. g.*, Olynth. I, § 4; *de Cor.*, § 235.

dreaded him, that any who would resist him had to deal with a man of extraordinary genius, who had won for himself a position of extraordinary advantage.

At the beginning of his reign it was necessary for him to move with caution. His claim to the throne was disputed by more than one pretender. But he had the support of the Macedonian army, which he had won over by eloquent language, and he rid himself of his rivals without serious difficulty. One of them, Argæus, had been assisted by Athenian troops. It was not, however, a convenient moment for Philip to enter upon a quarrel with Athens. His own forces were not yet in order—the Athenians had shown signs of reviving strength in this very year, in the recovery of their supremacy over the Chersonese, and he himself had to face an immediate struggle with the hill-tribes of Pæonia and Illyria. He therefore assumed an attitude of generosity, and sent back to Athens, without demanding any ransom, the Athenian citizens whom he had taken among the defeated supporters of Argæus. At the same time he sent an embassy to Athens,[1] asking for peace; and since the Athenians had given their aid to Argæus on the understanding that Argæus

---

[1] Dem., *in Aristocr.*, § 121; Diod. XVI, iii., § 4; Justin, VII, vi. [Diodorus and Justin are the principal continuous authorities for the remainder of this chapter; but many statements rest on passages of Demosthenes (esp. in the Olynthiacs and Philippic I) and other orators, and on allusions in various writers. The more important references to these are given.]

would restore Amphipolis to them, he found it
convenient to recognise the Athenian claim to the
town, in order to obtain for the moment a Peace
which he had no intention of keeping. It was
fortunate for him that the Athenians failed to
take the obvious step of garrisoning Amphipolis
without delay, and that within a few months they
became involved in war with their allies, and so
had little opportunity for attending to their
interests elsewhere.

Accordingly, after a campaign against the
Pæonians and Illyrians, in which the new tactics
were employed with complete success, and a large
district was added to his kingdom, Philip returned
to the coast (late in 358), appeared before Amphipolis, which had given him some provocation,[1]
and demanded its surrender. The Amphipolitans
at once despatched Hierax and Stratocles to
Athens to ask for help. To counteract their
appeal, Philip wrote a letter to Athens, explaining
that he was attacking the town with the intention
of placing it in the hands of Athens. In reply to
this the Athenians sent Antiphon and Charidemus
to negotiate with him; and it was arranged that if
he gave up Amphipolis to Athens, he should receive Pydna from Athens in its stead. This
arrangement was very discreditable to the Athenian representatives. Pydna, though it had been
a Macedonian possession until Timotheus won it
over for Athens about the year 364, was an ally

[1] Diod. XVI, viii., § 2.

of Athens, and might well claim to be consulted before being surrendered to Philip; and so the nature of the bargain was kept secret, lest it should become known at Pydna; the Athenian People were only informed in vague terms that an understanding had been arrived at. Philip had now secured the support of a party in Amphipolis; and it was by their treachery, as well as by means of his engines, that he took the town, probably in the autumn of 357.[1] A scholiast says that after its capture he at once put the traitors to death, on the ground that they were not likely to be more faithful to him than they had been to their own fellow-citizens. He then banished all who were hostile to him in the town.

So confidently did the Athenians expect to receive Amphipolis, that when the Olynthians, alarmed at Philip's success, appealed to them for aid against him, they would not listen. In consequence of this, the Olynthians tried to secure themselves by making an agreement with Philip himself; and it was quite in accordance with his plans to accede to their overtures, and to make a Peace which was destined to last until it should be convenient to him to crush them in their turn. It was provided in the agreement that the Olynthians should not make terms with Athens apart from himself.[2]

---

[1] Dem., Olynth. I, § 5.

[2] Dem., *in Aristocr.*, § 108; Olynth. II, § 14; Phil. II, § 20, etc.

THE TEMPLE OF HERA, AT OLYMPIA

PHOTO BY ALINARI

How the Athenians expected to be able to give Pydna to Philip was never disclosed; for Philip, instead of waiting for the fulfilment of their promise, himself took possession of Pydna by force (assisted by treachery from within) and refused to give up Amphipolis. He next joined the Olynthians in an attack upon Poteidæa. This was one of the most important towns of the Chalcidic peninsula; it had long been a rival of Olynthus; and a large body of Athenian colonists was established there. Its capture was rendered easy by treachery from within; and the Olynthians received from Philip both it and also Anthemus, and profited greatly by the cultivation of the territory which he added to their own, and by the increase in their trade.

The Athenians had, in spite of the Social War, resolved to send an expedition to relieve Poteidæa, but it did not start in time.[1] Philip, nevertheless, allowed the Athenians whom he captured in the town to depart without ransom. He was not yet ready to take measures which might exasperate Athens; even in besieging Poteidæa he was nominally acting as the ally of the Olynthians; and, as we have seen, he gave up the town to them. It was just at this time that he received three messengers with good tidings. The first told him of a victory of his general Parmenio over the Illyrians; the second of the success of his force in the Olympian games; the third of the birth of his son Alexander.[2]

[1] Phil., I, § 35, etc.   [2] Plut. *Alex.*, iii.

At about the same time Philip was enabled to satisfy the want of money which was pressing heavily upon him. His occupation of Amphipolis opened the way to the gold-mines of Mount Pangæus, east of the Strymon, which were being worked at the time by settlers from Thasos: and he took advantage of an appeal made to him by these settlers, when hard pressed by Thracian assailants, to occupy their town, Crenides, and to enlarge it into a city which he named, after himself, Philippi. He at once began to work the mines, and from this time onward they provided him with a large and steady income, which before long amounted to as much as one thousand talents a year. The Athenians, hampered by the Social War, were unable to take any active steps to check his advance. They made an alliance, indeed, in 356,[1] with the Pæonian Lyppeius, the Illyrian Grabus, and the Odrysian prince Cetriporis, the eldest son of Berisades, to whom (in the division of his father's share of the Odrysian kingdom which took place on his father's death) there fell the western portion, including the district in which Amphipolis and Crenides lay. But Cetriporis could not retain the district against Philip, and in 355 Philip made a victorious campaign against the Pæonians and Illyrians. Moreover, his conquest of the district east of the Strymon enabled him to take advantage of its luxuriant forests to provide himself with timber, with which

[1] *C. I. A.*, II., 66.

to build a fleet—an absolute necessity if he was to maintain his hold on the coast, and to resist the Athenians on their own element. His occupation of the coast-town Datum, which Callistratus had re-founded (in conjunction with settlers from Thasos) when he was expelled from Athens, gave him a convenient naval station. He was now able to interfere with Athenian trade, and also to occupy convenient islands, which had hitherto been infested by pirates. Before the end of 355 he had rid himself for the time of all danger from the newly-made allies of Athens, and was in a position to renew direct operations against Athenian interests on the coast of the Thermaic gulf; and he could now dispense with the pretence of acting as the ally of Olynthus.

He accordingly laid siege to Methone, which was the last important Athenian town on the gulf, and was used by the Athenians as a naval base. (It had been brought within the Athenian alliance by Timotheus about ten years before.) The siege probably began in the last months of 355.[1] The town made a brave resistance, but was at last forced to surrender. In the course of the siege an arrow deprived Philip of the sight of his right eye. The citizens were allowed to depart free, but with only one garment apiece, and their territory was divided among Philip's followers.

Philip was now master of the whole coastline of the Thermaic gulf, as well as of the seaboard from

[1] Note 3.

the east side of the Chalcidic peninsula to a point perhaps fifty miles or so beyond Amphipolis. He had ample supplies of money and ships; and his army had so far proved irresistible. Athens, on the other hand, had lost all the stations which she had possessed on the coasts of Macedonia and Chalcidice, and had been unable to give any effective help to her allies in those regions. Even Methone had been suffered to fall unaided; and the policy of Eubulus was to avoid so far as possible all active measures of hostility. In the period which we have now to consider, we shall see Philip pushing his conquests far along the Thracian coast, and also securing a foothold in Thessaly; until finally, there being no longer any reason for allowing the Olynthian confederacy to interrupt the continuity of his empire, he turns upon Olynthus itself. The chronology of the years 354–351 has been the subject of prolonged controversy, and the precise order of some of the events remains uncertain; but there is no doubt about the course of events as a whole.

It was probably in 353 that Philip made his next move along the Thracian coast. We have seen how in 359 the Thracian kingdom had been divided between Cersobleptes, Berisades, and Amadocus, and how, not long afterwards the Chersonese, with the exception of Cardia, had been definitely handed over to Athens by Cersobleptes, in consequence of the activity of Chares. Soon after this Berisades had died, and his share of the kingdom had been divided between his sons, of whom Cetriporis, as has been narrated, had made alliance with Athens, but had not succeeded in keeping Philip out of the western part of his dominions. Amadocus and the sons of Berisades seem to have remained on friendly terms with Athens, but Cersobleptes was naturally anxious to get rid of them, and to reign once more over the whole Odrysian kingdom. Hostilities had, it seems, already begun, the sons of Berisades entrusting their cause to the generals Simon, Bianor, and Athenodorus.

At the same time Cersobleptes desired to effect his end without opposition from the Athenians, who just about this time (in 353), to confirm their occupation of the Chersonese, had sent a body of colonists to Sestos.[1] It is possible that at this time Cersobleptes thought of an alliance with Athens as his best resource against the probable advance of Philip. Accordingly (probably in 353) he sent Aristomachus as his representative to Athens, to emphasise the friendly sentiments of himself and his general Charidemus towards the city. Aristomachus further asserted that Charidemus and no one else would be able to recover Amphipolis from Philip, and urged the Athenians to elect him general. The suggestion was taken

---

[1] Chares established them in the town by force, killing and enslaving the inhabitants who resisted. Diod., XVI, xxxiv. For the chronology, see Foucart, *Les Athéniens dans la Chersonèse*, p. 28 ff., where a satisfactory solution of the difficulties is given.

up by one Aristocrates, who further proposed that
the person of Charidemus should be declared
inviolable, and that any one who killed him should
be liable to summary arrest in any territory belonging to Athens or her allies. The proposal
was cleverly contrived in the interests of Cersobleptes; for had it been passed, its effect would
have been that Simon, Bianor, and Athenodorus
would be afraid to act against Cersobleptes'
forces, commanded by Charidemus, for fear of incurring the ill-will of Athens. The decree, however, was at once indicted as illegal by Euthycles,
who engaged Demosthenes to compose his speech
for him. But the trial did not take place until
the summer of 352; and before that time Philip
had once more made his appearance on the
Thracian coast, and had seized the towns of
Abdera and Maroneia.

Upon this, Cersobleptes, instead of looking any
more (if he had done so previously) to Athens to
help him against Philip, appears to have thought
it better to come to terms with Philip himself, and
so to resume his former attitude of hostility towards Athens. Accordingly he sent Apollonides
of Cardia, a town which had remained hostile to
Athens, to negotiate for him with Philip at Maroneia, and gave Philip securities for his fidelity.
At the same time he probably hoped that Philip
would espouse his cause against Amadocus; but
in this he was disappointed; for Philip, finding
that Amadocus intended to offer resistance, ap-

pears to have thought it better not to lose time in conquering an enemy who could be conquered at any time, but to return to Greece, where a great opportunity for extending his influence was now opened to him, in the form of an invitation to interfere in the Sacred War. (Demosthenes says[1] that, had it not been for the resistance of Amadocus, there would have been nothing to save the Athenians from having to fight without delay against the Cardians and Cersobleptes. But it is difficult to think that Philip regarded the resistance of Amadocus as important, except in so far as time would have been required to crush it.)

In the negotiations between Philip and Cersobleptes at Maroneia the Theban general Pammenes also appears to have taken some part; for Cersobleptes (so Demosthenes tells us) gave pledges "to Philip and Pammenes." Pammenes had been sent by the Thebans to support Artabazus in his revolt against the Persian King, at some time after the Athenians had compelled Chares to withdraw his assistance from him.[2] On his way either to or from Asia Minor, Pammenes met Philip at Maroneia. They were old friends, for Philip had lived in Pammenes' house while a hostage in Thebes; and perhaps Pammenes with his army gave Philip his support during the nego-

[1] *In Aristocr.*, § 183. (This Speech is, as before, our principal authority for Thracian affairs.)

[2] See above, p. 110.

tiations, at least so far as to increase the formidable appearance of Philip's host.[1]

Philip now began to return homewards[2]; but on his way back he had to pass Neapolis, where Chares was waiting with twenty ships. (Neapolis was a member of the Athenian confederacy, situated on the coast not far from Datum, in the district already conquered by Philip; but the town seems so far to have remained independent of him. In 355 it had appealed to Athens for help,[3] and Chares may have been sent in answer to this appeal.) Philip contrived to get past by a clever ruse. He sent four of his swiftest vessels in advance; Chares went in pursuit of them into the open sea, and while he was thus employed, Philip got past Neapolis in safety with the rest of his force. The four ships also escaped. (It was possibly about this time that Chares defeated the mercenaries of Philip under the command of Adæus, a general who was surnamed "the Cock." Theopompus[4] tells us that in celebration of this victory Chares feasted the Athenians with funds given him out of the temple treasures of Delphi by Onomarchus, the Phocian general in the Sacred War, of whom more is to be said hereafter. The event must therefore be placed between Onomarchus' seizure of the treasures in 354 and his death in 352.)

The trial of Aristocrates took place in 352, and the speech which Demosthenes composed against him is by far the most remarkable which we have yet considered. Apart from the exhaustive treatment of the Athenian law of homicide, which displays the thoroughness generally characteristic of Demosthenes' legal arguments, and proves conclusively the illegality of Aristocrates' decree, the manner in which he handles the question of Athenian policy in regard to Thracian affairs as most masterly. Demosthenes argues strongly that the right policy for Athens is to prevent the absorption of power over the whole of Thrace by one man—in other words, to keep Cersobleptes in check by strengthening the rival princes and confirming them in their reliance upon Athens[1]; while the effect of such a decree as Aristocrates had proposed would be to make these princes believe that Athens was veering round to the side of Cersobleptes, if she could accord such unparalleled honours to his chief minister and general. He shows also by a spirited narrative of Charidemus' career that the man himself was quite unworthy of such an honour, and that his allegiance could not be counted upon, whatever Athens might do for him. Towards the end of the Speech, he makes an onslaught upon the statesmen who were influential at the time, the party of Eubulus, denouncing them for enriching themselves while

---

[1] It is the same doctrine of the Balance of Power as he had applied to Peloponnesian affairs and to the case of Sparta and Thebes in the previous year, in the Speech for the Megalopolitans. (See above, pp. 132–33.)

impoverishing the State, and for degrading the democracy by accustoming it to obey their own dictates in a servile and unworthy manner.[1] The Speech has a trenchant vigour and a breadth of outlook which are far in advance of the qualities displayed in Demosthenes' earlier work; and its nobility of tone and the absence from it of all personal rancour have been generally recognised.

It has, however, been doubted whether the policy recommended by Demosthenes was the best under the circumstances. There seem to have been two alternatives open to the Athenian people at this time. The one, upheld by Eubulus and his party, was to preserve peace for the present at all costs, or at least to take no more active steps against Philip than were absolutely necessitated either by imminent danger or by the imperialistic tendency of the multitude, who were likely to insist upon some kind of retaliation against Philip's aggressions. (It was probably in view of some such pressure that Chares had been sent to Neapolis.) The possibility of avoiding war, and at the same time of holding Philip in check, might seem to be offered by an alliance with Cersobleptes. If that prince were permitted to unite all Thrace under his own sway, he would be a powerful buffer between Philip and the Chersonese, the retention of which

[1] Considerable portions of §§ 207–210 are repeated in Olynth. III, §§ 25–31. Probably Eubulus' supporters were influenced by the desire to save their wealth in supporting a peace-policy. But if some grew rich, we have no proof that they did so by illegitimate means.

was essential to Athens, since without it her corn-supply was menaced; and there was the chance that Cersobleptes would do the main part of the fighting, with the able general Charidemus to lead his forces, while Athens could continue to recruit her strength, sending only a small squadron to his support. From this point of view, the policy advocated by Demosthenes—that of rejecting the overtures of Cersobleptes—must have seemed a mistaken one.

But the alternative policy which evidently was in Demosthenes' mind had at least as much to recommend it,—the policy of keeping Cersobleptes weak by maintaining rival princes by his side in Thrace, and of preventing Philip from extending his influence in that direction, by taking such active measures against him as would keep him fully occupied nearer home. The difficulty of Eubulus' policy lay in the fact, which Demosthenes emphasises strongly,[1] that past experience had shown that Cersobleptes and Charidemus were not to be relied upon, and that no alliance with them would be certain to fulfil its object. Moreover, Athens already had engagements with the other princes. The weakness of Demosthenes' policy was that (in all probability) Athens was not yet in a condition to prosecute war against Philip with sufficient vigour to ensure success. In fact, Athens was in a position of danger, whichever plan she followed; and the difference between

[1] §§ 123–137.

Demosthenes and his opponents was a phase
of the more fundamental difference in regard
to the policy to be pursued towards Philip,
the one side appealing to national traditions
and ideals, the other to motives of prudence
and to the unwillingness of the People to go
out and fight in person, however excited the
crowd might be at each new aggression of their
enemy.

Neither policy was free from danger; neither
could be certain of success; and whether we sym-
pathise more with Demosthenes or with Eubulus,
each of whom viewed the situation from one point
of view, and neither of whom, perhaps, saw it
whole, is a question of temperament rather than
a matter to be settled by argument. The same
problem recurs repeatedly in the history of the
next few years.[1]

We do not know whether Aristocrates was condemned for the illegality of his proposal. The
decree itself, having been brought before the Council only, and not before the Assembly, would have
ceased to have any force (even apart from the
suspensory effect of Euthycles' indictment) at
the end of the archonship in which it was passed,
—in other words, even before the trial took place.
But in 351 we find Charidemus among the generals of Athens, and (either late in 353, or in
352) alliance was made between Athens and
Cersobleptes.

[1] Note 6.

COIN OF COTYS

COIN OF CETRIPORIS

COIN OF PHILIP (SILVER)

COIN OF PHILIP (GOLD)

COIN OF ALEXANDER (SILVER)

COIN OF ALEXANDER (GOLD)

COIN OF LYSIMACHUS (SILVER)

COINS OF MACEDONIAN AND THRACIAN KINGS

NOTES ON CHAPTER V

1. The best recent discussion of the subject is that by G. Kazarow, "Observations sur la nationalité des anciens Macédoniens" (*Bull. corr. Hell.*, xxiii., p. 243 ff.); in which the writer combats successfully the arguments used by Hoffmann (*Die Makedonen und ihre Sprache*) and Beloch to prove the close relationship of the Macedonians to the Greeks, and agrees with those who connect them more closely with the Illyrians. See also Cavaignac, *Histoire de l'Antiquité*, vol. ii., bk. iii., ch. iv., for an account of Macedonia. A more thorough examination of Macedonian personal and local names may some day throw light upon the ethnological problem; and it is possible that the course of political events may render Macedonia more accessible to the exploring scholar.

2. Theopompus insists (in many of the extant fragments) upon the drunkenness and immoralities of Philip and his companions. We cannot say how far he is telling the truth; but we may suspect that he was not free from the desire to draw sensational pictures with a view to edification. Polyænus, IV., ii., gives a number of anecdotes in illustration of Philip's resourcefulness and unconventionality in military matters.

3. An inscription (*C. I. A.*, ii., 70), dated about Dec. 26, 355 B.C., commends Lachares of Apollonia for bringing something into Methone; and it is not easy to explain the special merit of such an action unless the town was already beleaguered. Diodorus narrates the siege and fall of Methone twice (XVI., xxxi and xxxiv.), under the years 354–3 and 353–2 respectively. See also Kahrstedt, *Forschungen*, p. 42.

4. The circumstances of the mission of Pammenes are very obscure. The Thebans had previously been on good terms with the Persian King, and they were on good terms with him again in 351, when he sent them a present of money. Demosthenes perhaps had some inkling of the temporary alteration of their policy in 354 (Speech on the Naval Boards, §§ 33, 34). Pammenes seems soon to have been suspected by Artabazus of negotiating with the King's supporters (Polyænus, VII., xxxiii., § 2).

5. The chronology of Philip's Thracian campaign is very uncertain. Demosthenes, *in Aristocr.*, § 183, records Philip's presence at Maroneia, and the mission to him of Apollonides,

bringing securities from Cersobleptes to Philip and Pammenes; and as far as Demosthenes is concerned the date may be any time between 355 and 352, when the trial of Aristocrates took place. (Demosthenes also records Amadocus' opposition to Philip.) Diodorus apparently places Pammenes' expedition in 353–2, but does not mention his meeting with Philip. Diodorus' dates, however, are very unreliable, and the attempts to extract certainty from his history by tracing out the different authorities whose works he is supposed to have clumsily combined are very inconclusive. It is nowhere stated whether Philip's meeting with Pammenes took place on the latter's outward or homeward journey. If on the former, Philip must have made an expedition to Thrace in 354 or (more probably) 353, and the events here discussed must have occurred then, as is assumed in this chapter; if on the latter, one expedition to Thrace, in 352, after the check at Thermopylæ (see, below p. 178) will suffice; and the events in question will then be part of the same campaign as the siege of Heræon Teichos in November, 352. But the fact that Polyænus, IV., ii., § 22, speaks of Philip returning (ἐπανῄει) after taking Abdera and Maroneia suggests that the latter alternative is the less likely of the two. The schol. on Æsch., *F. L.*, § 81, states that Philip helped the Byzantines and Perinthians and Amadocus against Cersobleptes in a dispute for the possession of territory, and made him surrender the disputed ground to them, and give his son as a hostage to himself. As Demosthenes does not mention these events, they probably fell late in 352 (after the trial of Aristocrates). Indeed the πίστεις mentioned in § 183 as given by Philip to Cersobleptes at Maroneia could hardly have included his son without Demosthenes noticing the fact: and these events therefore were probably part of the campaign which included the siege of Heræon Teichos (see below). On the former expedition in 353 Amadocus had resisted Philip; in 352 he fought on the same side. Possibly the Amadocus who appears in 352 was in fact the son of the opponent of Philip in 353: *cf.* Harpocr., *s.v.* Ἀμάδοκος ... δύο γεγόνασιν οὗτοι, πατὴρ καὶ υἱός, ὃς καὶ Φιλίππῳ συμμαχήσων ἦλθεν εἰς τὸν πρὸς Κερσοβλέπτην πόλεμον.

6. Kahrstedt (*Forschungen*) has attempted to prove that Demosthenes was animated throughout the years 355–351 by a desire to forward the interests of Persia; but the arguments used to prove this are very far-fetched and inconclusive.

CHAPTER VI

THE OLYNTHIAN WAR

WE have seen that after taking Abdera and Maroneia and granting terms to Cersobleptes, Philip returned homewards. He did so in response to an invitation which he had received from the princes of the ruling dynasty of Larissa to assist them against the princes of Pheræ and their allies the Phocians, and so to take part in the Sacred War. In order to understand the situation it is necessary to go back a few years.

The battle of Leuctra in 371 had given Thebes the supremacy over her neighbours the Phocians; but the latter were not content to be subjects of Thebes, and in 362 they had refused to join in the last campaign of Epameinondas in the Peloponnese; for they were still, as they had been before the battle of Leuctra, on friendly terms with Sparta. Before long the Thebans found a pretext for attempting to punish them, which would give to the attempt the colour of religious sanction.

The temple and oracle at Delphi were under the control of the Amphictyonic Council, representing a very ancient confederacy of twelve Greek tribes, which no doubt were originally more or less equal in power, but in the course of history had come to differ widely in importance. The twelve tribes included not only the Thessalians, Bœotians, Dorians, and Ionians, and such tribes of secondary importance as the Achæans, Phocians, and Locrians, but also the comparatively insignificant Malians, Perrhæbi, Magnetes, Dolopes, and Œnianes (or Œtæans). Each of these tribes had two votes in the Council. Athens appears to have exercised one of the Ionian votes, Thebes one of the Bœotian, Sparta one of the Dorian. The geographical position of the smaller tribes was such as to make it likely that the Thebans and Thessalians (at any rate if united) could command a majority of votes in the Council; and since the battle of Leuctra the Thebans had begun to use the Council to further their political ends. Thus they caused it to impose a heavy fine upon Sparta for the seizure of the Cadmeia in 383, perhaps treating this act as a violation of the oath which bound the members of the League together; and in 356 the Council was led to mulct the Phocians in a very large sum for some offence, the nature of which is variously reported,[1] but which was probably the encroachment upon land dedicated to Apollo, the god of Delphi. They further proposed to dedicate the Phocians' own territory to the god. At the same

[1] Diod., XVI, xxiii.; Justin, VIII, i.; Paus., X, ii., 1; and Athen., XIII, p. 560 (quoting Duris). The principal authority for the history of the Sacred War is Diodorus' XVIth book.

THE THEATRE AND TEMPLE OF APOLLO AT DELPHI

PHOTO BY ALINARI

time they increased the penalty previously imposed upon the Spartans; for of course it had not been paid. Whether Sparta and Athens, which were both traditionally friendly to the Phocians, were represented at the meeting of the Council is unknown; if they were, they must have been outvoted.

The Phocians, led by Philomelus, refused to pay the fine; and after obtaining some financial aid from Archidamus, King of Sparta, proceeded in 355 to seize the temple of Delphi, and erase the record of the sentence against them. (The temple was in the hands of the Delphians, who were originally a branch of the Phocian race. There was a standing dispute between the Delphians and the Phocians as to the control of the temple, and Philomelus' action was not without some show of justification.) The Phocians also defeated the forces of the Locrians, their neighbours, who attacked them at the instigation of Thebes; and Philomelus secured (though not without threats of violence) the approval of the Pythia, the priestess of the oracle, for his designs. The Thebans and Thessalians (most of whom were traditionally hostile to their restless Phocian neighbours) now induced the Amphictyonic Council to declare a "Sacred War" against the Phocians, and summoned the Greek peoples to join in punishing them for their sacrilege. The response seems to have been fairly general on the part of the tribes situated to the north of Bœotia; Byzantium also, which had for several years been friendly to Thebes, sent supplies of money.[1] The Spartans sent one thousand men to the assistance of the Phocians[2]; and to procure mercenaries, Philomelus made use of part of the treasures of the Delphian temple, probably intending at the time to repay them.

What was the attitude adopted by Athens? It is impossible to give a certain answer. Aristophon and Eubulus were alike disposed towards friendship with Thebes as a general policy,[3] though on the other hand, there was a long history of friendship between Athens and the Phocians, and the People as a whole detested the Thebans. (Demosthenes himself was generally friendly to Thebes.)[4] It is possible that at first the political leaders in Athens took the Theban side, and the record of a treaty between Athens and the Locrians,[5] which seems to fall in the early years of the war, lends some colour to this view. In any case, though they appear to have returned a friendly answer to the Phocian appeal, they at first gave the Phocians no active help; and the popular mind seems to have been divided between a strong disapproval of the

[1] Dittenb., *Syll.* (ed. 2), i., 120.

[2] *Cf.* Æsch., *de F. L.*, § 133 ff.

[3] Dem., *de Cor.*, § 162.

[4] *Cf.* Æsch., *de F. L.*, § 106. καὶ γὰρ πρὸς τοῖς ἄλλοις κακοῖς βοιωτιάζει. Demosthenes' Speech for the Megalopolitans was much more favourable to Thebes than to Sparta, though he used the conventional phrases of dislike for the Thebans to disarm suspicion.

[5] *C. I. A.* ii., 90. See Schwartz, *Demosthenes' Erste Philippika* (Festschr. für Th. Mommsen), p. 17.

sacrilegious acts of the Phocians, and a sentimental anxiety lest they should be exterminated.[1]

The war was waged with great ferocity from the first. Philomelus gained some striking successes, but in 354 was defeated by the Thebans near Neon and killed himself. He was succeeded by Onomarchus, who made an unscrupulous use of the temple-treasures, not only to pay mercenaries, but also to give presents to powerful persons in many cities, no doubt in order to obtain through them the support of their countrymen.[2] Among others who joined him was Lycophron, prince or "tyrant" of Pheræ, who was desirous of restoring the domination of his house over the Thessalians; for since the death of Alexander, a few years before, the house of Pheræ had lost its supremacy, and the Aleuadæ of Larissa had come to the front. In 354 and the greater part of 353 Onomarchus appears to have been in the main successful. He defeated the Locrians, and also restored Orchomenus and liberated it from the power of Thebes. He also obtained command of the all-important pass of Thermopylæ; and though he sustained a check from the Thebans at Chæroneia, this does not seem to have greatly injured his cause. Before the end of 353, the princes of Larissa, Eudicus and Simus, invoked the aid of Philip against the rival house of Pheræ; Philip, as we have seen, obeyed the call; and Lycophron thereupon sent in haste for Onomarchus and his army.

[1] Dem., *de Cor.*, § 18.   [2] Theopomp., fr. 240, 241 (Oxford Text).

Onomarchus first sent his brother Phayllus, who was soon driven off by Philip. He then went to the rescue himself, and defeated Philip severely in two battles. Philip was little daunted; encouraging his downcast troops, he withdrew from Thessaly for a time, but only, as he said, "like a ram, in order to butt the harder next time." For the moment Lycophron was master of Thessaly, and Onomarchus pursued his successes farther south, and captured Coroneia. But early in 352 Philip reappeared, and, crowning his men with laurel to proclaim their championship of the cause of Apollo and so to give them confidence, he obtained a complete victory over Onomarchus and Lycophron near the coast of Magnesia. Onomarchus lost his life, and Philip put to death a very large number of prisoners as guilty of sacrilege; some, however, of the fugitives were picked up by Chares, who happened to be sailing by the Magnesian coast at the time. Philip now besieged and took Pheræ, deposed Lycophron and put an end to the despotic régime, and became master of practically the whole of Thessaly.

Whatever had been the attitude of Athens earlier in the war, it was now evident that she could no longer ignore the growing power of Philip. It has been suggested that Chares may have been sent to Magnesia in order to co-operate with Onomarchus; though the only evidence is that of Diodorus, who treats his presence there as accidental. But when, after taking Pheræ, Philip pro-

ceeded to attack Pagasæ, the most important sea-
port of Thessaly,[1] the Athenians resolved to send an
expedition to the aid of the town. Unfortunately,
like the expedition to Methone, it arrived too late,
when Philip had already become master of the port.
Philip now arranged the affairs of Thessaly, acting
on the whole in a lenient and conciliatory fashion,
but taking for himself the harbour-dues and retaining Magnesia in his own occupation. Then,
before July, 352, he moved towards Thermopylæ.

On this occasion the Athenians were in time.
There can be no doubt that Eubulus, no less than
the war-party, now realised the necessity of
measures of defence. The only alternative would
have been to make peace with Philip and come to a
definite arrangement as to territory, both in Greece
and in Thrace; but this would certainly have
meant the renunciation of Amphipolis by Athens;
and to this the majority of the Assembly would
not yet have consented. Nothing remained then
but to oppose Philip, and the measures taken were
proposed by a supporter of Eubulus, Diophantus
of Sphettus. The citizens were thoroughly roused
and volunteered for service; and five thousand
infantry and four hundred cavalry were sent by
sea to Thermopylæ under Nausicles at a cost of
two hundred talents (including the private expenditure of the soldiers). At Thermopylæ, Phayllus,
the successor of Onomarchus in the command,
already waited on land with a powerful army, in

[1] It lay close to the site of the modern Volo.

12

which the Phocians, whom he had rallied once
more, were supported by large contingents of
Spartans and Achæans, and by the mercenaries
who had previously fought for Lycophron. On
hearing of the arrival of the Athenian squadron,
Philip abandoned the attempt to cross the Pass;
and Demosthenes more than once[1] refers to this
occasion as one of the few on which, in recent
years, the Athenians had acted worthily of their
traditions, and so had entirely succeeded in their
object. Apart from the danger of an advance,
Philip's willingness to retire is not hard to explain.
He had already gained immensely in prestige
in this campaign, not only by the mere fact of
his victory, but by the rôle he had been able to
assume, of champion of the god of Delphi, whose
sanctuary had been violated by Onomarchus and
the Phocians in a way which shocked the religious
sentiments of the Greeks generally, whatever might
be the political interests of each State. To create
a favourable feeling towards himself in this way
was no slight gain; and he may well have been
content for the moment to enjoy the advantage
of this, without endangering it by attempting to
push his conquests further. It is also probable
that with Thessaly in his power (though not yet
perfectly subdued) to the north of the Pass, and
with the Thebans, his allies, farther south, and
presumably able to hold the defeated Phocians in
check, he saw that less was to be gained by trying

[1] *E. g.*, Phil. I, § 13; *de F. L.*, §§ 84, 86; *de Cor.*, § 32.

to cross the Pass in face of strong opposition, than
by pursuing and consolidating his conquests to the
east of Macedonia.

So we find him before the end of 352 once more
in Thrace. It has already been narrated that
about a year before this, he had taken securities
from Cersobleptes and had been opposed by
Amadocus, but had refrained from retaliating.
On the present occasion, he appears to have aided
Amadocus against Cersobleptes. "The peoples of
Byzantium and Perinthus," so a scholiast states,[1]
"and Amadocus the Thracian, made war upon
Cersobleptes, king of a portion of Thrace, on
account of some disputed territory. Philip assisted them and defeated Cersobleptes, and forced
him to yield the territory to those who claimed it.
He further took Cersobleptes' son as a hostage,
and carried him off to Macedonia." (Æschines
saw Cersobleptes' son at Pella, where he was still
kept in captivity, when he went there as ambassador six years afterwards.) Philip seems in fact to
have been following the very policy which Demosthenes had recommended to Athens in the Speech
against Aristocrates—that of dividing the power
over Thrace among a number of persons or States;
and his alliance with Byzantium appears natural
enough when we remember that the Byzantines,
like himself, had supported the Theban side in
the Sacred War. He further made alliance with
Cardia, and so secured for himself a stronghold

[1] On Æsch., *de F. L.*, § 81.

overlooking the Chersonese—a very serious menace to the power of Athens. In November of the same year he laid siege to Heræon Teichos. The exact position of this fortress is not known, but it was probably so near either to the Chersonese or to the coast along which the Athenian corn-ships passed that the Athenians could not contemplate Philip's action with equanimity; and they were once more roused to a fit of energy. Demosthenes' own words best describe the sequel[1]:

Amidst all the discussion and the commotion which took place in the Assembly, you passed a resolution that forty warships should be launched, that men under forty-five years of age should embark in person, and that we should pay a war-tax of sixty talents. That was in the month of November. That year came to an end.[2] There followed July, August, September.[3] In September, after the Mysteries, and with reluctance, you despatched Charidemus with ten ships, carrying no soldiers, and five talents of silver. For so soon as news had come that Philip was sick or dead—both reports were brought—you dismissed the armament, men of Athens, thinking that there was no longer any occasion for the expedition. But it was the very occasion; for had we then gone to the scene of action with the same enthusiasm which marked our resolution to do so, Philip would not have been preserved to trouble us to-day.

---

[1] Olynth. III, § 4.
[2] The Athenian year ran, roughly speaking, from July to July.
[3] *I.e.*, of 351 B.C.

The account which Demosthenes gives can easily
be filled out. We can imagine that the militant
instincts of the democracy were so keenly aroused
by the alarm raised by the war party, that Eubulus thought it necessary to yield so far as to send
an expedition to Heræon Teichos. Then came the
news of Philip's illness, which enabled Eubulus
once more to advocate inaction, the wealthier
citizens to seek to avoid the expenditure, and the
rest to relapse into their customary unwillingness
to do their own fighting.[1] (It is noteworthy that
we now find Charidemus in the service of Athens.
Probably Philip's activity in Thrace had convinced
him that the cause of Cersobleptes was destined
to be lost, and the Athenians were doubtless better
pleased to have him as a supporter than as an
opponent.)

We have seen that about this time the proposal
of Demosthenes to help the exiled Rhodian democrats was made and defeated,—no doubt by the
influence of Eubulus, who in this matter acted
wisely, since it would have been very imprudent
to risk offending Persia, when there were other
enemies to be reckoned with. Artaxerxes was
just now engaged in the attempt to reduce his
rebellious subjects in Egypt to obedience, and was
doubtless anxious to be free from troubles elsewhere. The refusal of Athens to take part in the

---

[1] In the Speech for the Rhodians (delivered, probably, early
in 351), Demosthenes had upbraided the Athenians in passing
for thinking of Philip as a foe not worth reckoning with.

Rhodian quarrel was therefore convenient to him; and at the same time he apparently tried to secure the inactivity of the Thebans by sending them a large present of money in answer to the appeal which they made to him, when they were hard pressed for funds with which to carry on the Sacred War. For the war was dragging on inconclusively. Phayllus had achieved some successes, but had died before the end of 352, and had been succeeded by Phalæcus; but the war continued to be waged in Bœotia and Phocis for some years, without any decisive action taking place; though at times the Phocian territory suffered severely from the incursions of the enemy.

When Philip recovered from the illness which forced him to raise the siege of Heræon Teichos, he appears to have turned his thoughts at once to Olynthus. He had suffered that city to remain at the head of the Chalcidic League, and to retain Poteidæa, Anthemus, and other territories; but it must have become more and more plain to all that he was not likely to refrain from requiring the submission of the league, and so consolidating his dominions, so soon as it should be convenient to him. Already in 352 Olynthus had taken advantage of Philip's absence in Thrace to make overtures to Athens, and had thus broken her compact with him, under which peace was only to be made by her with Athens in conjunction with himself; and shortly afterwards Philip's step-brother Arrhidæus, who had opposed Philip's accession to the throne, took refuge in Olynthus and was welcomed there.[1] Early in 351—this at least is the probable date—Philip made his appearance within the territory of Olynthus.[2] It may be that he was only led to cross the borders of the Chalcidic League in the course of making good his conquest of the neighbouring territory of the Bisaltæ, on his way back from Heræon Teichos[3]; he certainly took no hostile steps against the cities of the League, and even protested his friendship towards them. But it was probably now that, in response to an embassy from the Chalcidic cities, he quoted to them a fable about War and Violence, which he represented as supernatural powers whom they seemed likely to bring down upon themselves.[4]

During the years 351 and 350 Philip left the Olynthians unmolested. It is possible that he suffered from a recurrence of his illness,[5] and that during part of the time he was occupied in the fortification of strongholds in Illyria, and in hostilities against Arybbas, King of the Molossi.[6] But there can be no doubt that he was all this time fostering in Olynthus a party favourable to himself, and secretly intriguing in Eubœa, with a view to creating such occupation there for the Athenian

[1] Dem., *in Aristocr.*, §§ 107–9, and schol. in Olynth. I, § 5.
[2] Phil. I, § 17; Olynth. I, § 13.
[3] See Schäfer, ii., p. 122.
[4] Theopomp., fr. 124 (Oxford Text); comp. Babrius, Fab. 70.
[5] Dem., *Procæm.*, xxi., § 2.
[6] Dem., Phil. I, § 48; Olynth. I, § 13.

forces as would render them unable to come to the aid of Olynthus, when he chose to fall upon it.

It is most probable that it was early in 351 that his ships began to make those raids upon Athenian territory which are mentioned both by Demosthenes and by Æschines. They not only descended upon Lemnos and Imbros, and carried off Athenian citizens as prisoners of war; but they also seized a fleet of Athenian corn-ships off Geræstus (the southernmost point of Eubœa), and actually landed troops at Marathon, and carried off the Athenian state-galley, which was conveying a deputation to a religious festival at Delos.[1] The alarm which these acts occasioned is described by Æschines, who says that the special meetings of the Assembly which were called in the midst of the alarm and turmoil caused by the news outnumbered the regular meetings. Yet no active steps were taken, except that of sending Charidemus—probably to the Hellespont—as described in the passage already quoted from the Third Olynthiac, with ten ships and five talents, and leaving him to find mercenaries for himself; and it must have been at one of the meetings of the Assembly in this year (probably in the autumn, after the despatch of Charidemus)[2] that Demosthenes delivered his First Philippic Oration.

[1] Dem. Phil. I, § 34; *in Neær.*, § 3; *Prœm.*, xxi., § 2; Æsch., *de F. L.*, § 72.

[2] This is more likely than the view that the sending of Charidemus was due to the speech. The sending of Charidemus is probably referred to in § 43.

It was the first occasion on which Demosthenes had opened the debate, and it required some courage on the part of a man only thirty years of age to rise without waiting for older men (in accordance with the custom of the Assembly) to give their opinions first. "But," he said, "since we find ourselves once more considering a question upon which they have often spoken, I think I may reasonably be pardoned for rising first of all. For if their advice to you in the past had been what it ought to have been, you would have had no occasion for the present debate." He then proceeded at once to the attack. The unfortunate position of affairs was entirely due to the refusal of the Athenians to take a personal part in the defence of their country. It was the reliance upon mercenaries, the failure to support them and their generals with funds, and the intermittent character of their military operations, that placed the interests of Athens at the mercy of Philip. In a few strokes he depicted the Athenian people of his day—their excitability, their love of sensational gossip, their inability to sustain any impulse which they might feel for the moment, and to follow it out into effective action.

What? [he asked]—do you want to go round asking one another: "Is there any news?" Could there be any stranger news than that a man of Macedonia is defeating Athenians in war, and ordering the affairs of the Hellenes? "Is Philip dead?" "No, but he is sick." And what difference does it make to you?

For if anything should happen to him, you will soon raise up for yourselves a second Philip, if it is thus that you attend to your interests. Indeed, Philip himself has not risen to this excessive height through his own strength, so much as through our neglect. I go even further. If anything happened to Philip— if the operation of Fortune, who always cares for us better than we care for ourselves, were to effect this too for us—you could descend upon the general confusion and order everything as you wished; but in your present condition, even if circumstances offered you Amphipolis, you could not take it; for your forces and your minds alike are far away.

Besides this, the whole military system of Athens was at fault. The delay in organising a force even when it had been resolved upon was fatal in dealing with an adversary like Philip, and offered a strong contrast to the promptitude with which all arrangements in connection with the popular festivals were carried out. Nor could anything be done by isolated expeditions to the places attacked.

The method of your warfare is just that of barbarians in a boxing-match. Hit one of them, and he hugs the place; hit him on the other side, and there go his hands; but as for guarding or looking his opponent in the face, he neither can nor will do it. It is the same with you. If you hear that Philip is in the Chersonese, you resolve to make an expedition there; if he is at Thermopylæ, you send one there; and wherever else he may be, you run up and down in his steps. It is he that leads your forces.

It was therefore absolutely necessary, Demosthenes insisted, that there should be a standing force, kept permanently at the seat of war. Moreover, this force should consist in a large measure of citizens, whose presence would at least act as a check upon the independence of the generals, and make them less likely to desert the war to which Athens had sent them and go off upon some more profitable expedition. Further, Demosthenes reminded his hearers, these generals, receiving no support from home, plundered the very allies of Athens, and obtained acquittal when brought to trial, by pleading the difficulties of their position. This could only be remedied by providing both funds and citizen-soldiers liberally.

At the same time, Demosthenes was careful to distinguish his attitude from that of the noisy orators, who clamoured for war and proposed measures of a magnitude which was absurd under existing circumstances—with the result that nothing was done at all. He had thought out carefully what, in his opinion, the situation required, and had worked out the details after his manner. The force ultimately to be created was one of fifty ships, carrying citizen-troops, with transports for half the cavalry of the city; and this was to be kept ready for immediate action in case of any emergency. But since this armament could not be organised at once, he proposed that a smaller force should be prepared for immediate service, consisting of two thousand soldiers, of whom five hundred were to be citizens, and two hundred cavalry, including fifty citizens. The citizens should serve in relays, and ten warships would be required. This force was not to fight any pitched battle, but to harry Philip's coasts, to keep him in check, and, above all, to prevent him from plundering the allies and territory of Athens. It was to receive bare rations—the amount was exactly calculated—and for the rest was to support itself. (Demosthenes accompanied the proposal with a detailed exposition of the sources from which he expected to be able to draw the necessary funds, but the schedule was unfortunately not published with the Speech, and has not come down to us.) The general in command, he said, would determine the particular operations to be undertaken, as circumstances required; the force would winter in the islands subject to Athens, and whenever the opportunity occurred, would lie close to the Macedonian coast, and block the mouths of the ports.

In order to rouse his countrymen to the pitch of enthusiasm which would induce them to take the steps which he urged upon them, Demosthenes appealed to every motive that could influence them—pride in the past, shame at the present, trust in the help given by Heaven to those who help themselves, alarm for the future if the danger were not averted by vigorous action. Beside the eloquence of this Speech the earlier orations—with the exception of parts of the Speech against Aristocrates—seem cold.

The proposals of Demosthenes have often been criticised. Of their practicability in detail we have no means of judging. But it is perfectly clear that if Philip was to be opposed at all—and it is really upon that fundamental question that his critics differ from Demosthenes—it could only be by neutralising the advantages which Philip possessed, through a change in Athenian methods of warfare, of the kind which Demosthenes proposed. Whether the Athenians would face the necessity of personal service and of a standing army was (just as he represented it) a question of character and resolution; and he believed in them enough to think them capable of the necessary sacrifices. That he was mistaken is perhaps small blame to him. The suggestion (which, of all that he makes in the Speech, sounds most strange to modern readers), that the presence of citizen-soldiers in the army was required in order to be a check upon the generals' independence, was probably sensible enough in the circumstances of the time. If, as it was, a general was to a great extent in the hands of his mercenaries, and had to lead them where they wanted to go, their influence would at least be partially counteracted by the presence of a large body of citizens, whose claim to the general's services on their country's behalf could make itself felt on the spot.

But so far as we know, Demosthenes' Speech bore no fruit. At least we know of no operations against Philip which can be assigned to the year

350. Instead of this we hear of trivial quarrels of the Athenians with their nearer neighbours, the Megareans and Corinthians. The Megareans appear to have trespassed upon land sacred to the two goddesses of Eleusis, Demeter and Persephone, whom the Athenians held in the deepest veneration; and an Athenian force, led by the general Ephialtes, invaded Megara, and forced the Megareans to recognise a delimitation of the sacred territory by the officials of the Eleusinian mysteries.[1] An armed force was also sent into the territory of Corinth to attend the Isthmian Games, because the Corinthians, for some reason unknown to us, had omitted to send the Athenians the customary official invitation to the Games. To these quarrels Demosthenes not unjustifiably refers[2] with contempt, since in pursuing them the People was neglecting its more vital interests.

It is probably to the same year that we must refer the friendly communications[3] between Athens and Orontas, satrap of Mysia, who was in revolt against the King of Persia, and had helped the Athenian generals with supplies of corn. These communications showed a different attitude on the part of the Athenians towards Persia from that which had led them in 356 to recall Chares when he was helping Artabazus. Moreover, the rebellious subjects of the King in Egypt were being assisted by the Athenian Diophantus, and owed much of

[1] See Didym., *Schol. in Dem.*, Col. 13, for details.
[2] Olynth. III, § 20.   [3] *C. I. A.*, ii., 108.

their success to his generalship. (On the other hand, Phocion, of whom much more will be said in the sequel, is found in 350 helping the King's forces at the siege of Salamis, where Euagoras had revolted. Perhaps by this time Orontas had been subdued, and the King may have threatened the supporters of the rebel satrap, and caused them to veer round once more.) There is much that is obscure in the relations of Athens to the King at this time, but the hostile attitude which she appears to have adopted for a time may possibly be explained by recent communications between Philip and Artaxerxes. It is at least probable that Philip had thought it well, before turning his attention to conquests nearer home, to come to a temporary understanding with Artaxerxes which would secure him against Persian interference with his own recently acquired power in Thrace and on the Hellespont.[1]

In the meantime Philip was encouraging the party favourable to himself in Olynthus, the leaders of which were Euthycrates and Lasthenes, assuring them that he meant their city no harm, and inducing them to persuade their fellow-citizens to dismiss his opponents from their confidence.

---

[1] Demosthenes (Phil. I, § 48) alludes to a rumour that Philip had sent ambassadors to the King; and Arrian, II, xiv., quotes a letter of Darius to Alexander the Great, reminding the latter of his father's friendship and alliance with Artaxerxes Ochus. There is no indication in Arrian of the date of the alliance, and some would place it about 343; but I think the year 351–0 is more likely to be the right date.

Thus persuaded, the Olynthians exiled Apollonides, the leader of the anti-Macedonian party, and
before long took what proved to be the fatal step
of appointing Lasthenes to command their cavalry.

And so [says Demosthenes[1]], when some of them
began to take bribes, and the People as a whole were
foolish enough, or rather, unfortunate enough, to re-
pose greater confidence in these men than in those
who spoke for their own good; when Lasthenes roofed
his house with the timber which came from Macedonia, and Euthycrates was keeping a large herd of
cattle for which he had paid no one anything, when a
third returned with sheep, and a fourth with horses;
while the People, to whose detriment all this was being done, so far from showing any anger or any disposition to chastise men who acted thus, actually
gazed on them with envy, and paid them honour, and
regarded them as heroes—when, I say, such practices
were thus gaining ground, and corruption had been
victorious, then, though they possessed one thousand
cavalry, and numbered more than ten thousand men,
though all the surrounding peoples were their allies,
though you went to their assistance with ten thousand
mercenaries and fifty ships, and with four thousand
citizen-soldiers as well, none of these things could
save them. Before a year of the war had expired
they had lost all the cities in Chalcidice, while Philip
could no longer keep pace with the invitations of the
traitors, and did not know which place to occupy first.

The history of the years 349 and 348 affords a

[1] *De F. L.*, § 265 ; *cf.* Phil., III, §§ 56, 63, 64, 66, and *de Chers.*,
§ 59.

striking proof of the demoralisation of the political leaders in these cities, and of the ruthlessness with which Philip removed out of the way, by foul means no less than by fair, any obstacle that barred his progress. He virtually declared war on Olynthus, despite his renewed professions of good-will, early in 349, when he demanded the surrender of his step-brother. This demand the Olynthians refused. Probably they recognised that they would now in any case have to fight to the death; and they renewed their appeal to Athens, asking once more for the alliance which had been talked of three years earlier, and for practical assistance against Philip.[1] In the meantime they declined to make any agreement with him, though he appears to have made proposals to them.

The First Olynthiac Oration of Demosthenes formed part of the debate upon the Olynthian request. It has indeed been disputed whether it was actually the first of the three Olynthiacs to be delivered, but expressions used in it leave no doubt that the alliance, or at least the nature of the help to be given to the Olynthians, had not yet been determined upon, and that at the time of its delivery Olynthus itself had not been attacked, and none of the Chalcidic cities had been actually taken; nor can Philip's expedition to Thessaly (which occurred later in 349) have taken place. The traditional order of the Speeches is in fact the most probable, and the character of the

[1] Philochorus ap. Dion. Hal. ad Ammæum, I., ix.

13

several Speeches, in this order, admits of easy explanation.

Demosthenes began by congratulating his hearers on the happy fortune which had offered so desirable an alliance to Athens, and by laying stress upon the certainty (as he regarded it) that Philip, unless checked at a distance, would make his way to Attica itself; and that if he did this, the country, and above all the farmers, would be ruined. He entreated his countrymen to fling aside their short-sighted indifference, and to exchange their love of ease for a strenuous activity on behalf of the Olyn-thians and of their own interests. He reminded them of Philip's restless energy, and his skill in using his opportunities, and contrasted it with the dilatoriness of the Athenians, who were al-ways too late to effect their object. He further urged that the present moment was a peculiarly opportune one; for not only had Philip been dis-appointed at not carrying all before him without having to strike a blow, but the Thessalians were growing restive and were likely to revolt against his supremacy.

The Speech was not confined to generalities. Demosthenes had, as usual, a definite plan of action in view, and did not shrink from the re-sponsibility and the risk of proposing it. One force must go to Chalcidice to save the towns of the League; another to the Macedonian coast, to inflict damage upon Philip's own country. As regards funds, he hinted, not obscurely, that the only right course was to divert the festival-money to military uses; but as it was obvious that the People were not prepared for this, he suggested a general war-tax as the best means of raising money.

The proposals of Demosthenes were strongly opposed, and among others, Demades[1] (a brilliant extempore orator who afterwards played a considerable part in the history of Athens) spoke against them. But the alliance with Olynthus was made; Chares was sent with two thousand mercenaries and the thirty ships which were already under his command; and in addition, eight ships were to be sent when they could be got ready.[2] The mission of Chares, however, proved fruitless—for what reasons we do not know. His enemies in Athens (the party adverse to war) renewed their campaign of accusations against him,[3] and apparently he was inadequately supplied with funds; for it seems most likely that at the time when the Second Olynthiac was delivered, no war-tax had yet been levied; and it is not improbable that the People, in deciding upon an expedition, had abstained from voting money to maintain it. Besides this, the same orators appear to have represented Philip in the most formidable light, as a power with whom it was useless to contend.

Under some such circumstances the Second

---

[1] Suid., *s. v.* Δημάδης.   [2] Philochorus ap. Dion. Hal., *l. c.*
[3] The accusations may very likely have been true enough. See Dem., Olynth. II, §§ 27–29.

Olynthiac was delivered, not long after the First.
Demosthenes insists briefly upon the shamefulness
of his countrymen's inaction, and then devotes a
large section of the Speech to the argument that
Philip's power, being based upon selfishness and
treachery, could not last, and that there were
already signs of its approaching collapse. The
argument does more credit perhaps to the orator's
faith in moral principles than to his insight into
the situation of the moment. Possibly it was
adopted merely as a convenient method of persuading the multitude that Philip was not so
formidable as he was said to be. Yet there is a
ring of sincerity about it, which perhaps justifies
us in thinking that Demosthenes' experience had
not yet been long enough to show him that the
triumph of righteousness in mundane affairs is
often long postponed, and cannot be reckoned
upon at any given moment.

When power [he says] is cemented by good-will,
and the interest of all who join in a war is the same,
then men are willing to share the labour, to endure
the misfortunes, and to stand fast. But when a man
has become strong, as Philip has done, by a grasping
and wicked policy, the first excuse, the least stumble,
throws him from his seat and dissolves the alliance.
It is impossible, men of Athens, utterly impossible, to
acquire power that will last, by unrighteousness, by
perjury, and by falsehood. Such power holds out
for a moment or for a brief hour; it blossoms brightly,
perhaps, with fair hopes; but time detects the fraud,

and the flower falls withered about its stem. In a house or a ship or any other structure it is the foundations that must be strongest; and no less, I believe, must the principles which are the foundation of men's actions be those of truth and righteousness. Such qualities are not to be seen in the acts of Philip to-day.

In the later speeches against Philip we find little remaining of this fine faith.

But the orator's application of these principles was not a happy one. For the picture which follows of the disaffection of Philip's followers, and of the incompetence of the warriors who surrounded him (if not of their dissoluteness), must be greatly overdrawn, even though it purports to be based on first-hand evidence. There can also be little doubt that the representation which he gave of Philip's condition was ill-judged, for it is never wise to set too low a value on an enemy, and Demosthenes may even have contributed to the failure of his own object, by encouraging the People (contrary to his custom) to think too lightly of their danger. They were not at all unlikely to seize on this part of his Speech and neglect the rest.

Demosthenes next turns upon the Athenians themselves the blame for the misconduct of their generals, whom they would not supply with the means to carry on the war, and who therefore resorted to actions which roused the virtuous indignation of the citizens who sat at home at

ease. He demands once more (as the only solution of the difficulty) that the citizens shall go on
active service in person, and shall contribute
funds in proportion to their wealth; and further
that they shall reform their behaviour in the
Assembly and listen impartially to the various
counsels given to them, in order that they may
choose the best. "You used, men of Athens, to
pay taxes by Boards; to-day you conduct your
politics by Boards. On either side there is an
orator as leader, and a general under him,"—the
reference is probably to Chares and Charidemus,
who were respectively patronised by rival groups,
—"and for the Three Hundred,[1] there are those
who come to shout. This system you must give
up; you must even now become your own masters;
you must give to all their share in discussion, in
speech and action." The Second Olynthiac goes
beyond the First in the hint which it contains of
a reform of the taxation-system, by which all,
without exception, should be obliged to contribute
in proportion to their income; in the proposal
(repeated from the First Philippic) that the citizens
should serve in the army in relays, until all had
served; and in the suggestion that an embassy
should be sent to make common cause with the
discontented Thessalians. But none of these suggestions was carried out; there was little or no
improvement in the attitude either of the dominant
party or of the People towards the war; and about

[1] See above, p. 51.

this time Chares was recalled to take his trial upon the charges preferred by his enemies, and was not, it would seem, immediately replaced.

Philip now began a series of attacks upon the towns of the Chalcidic League. Among the first to suffer was Stageira, the birthplace of Aristotle, which was razed to the ground.[1] (Its restoration was permitted many years later upon the intercession of the philosopher.) His operations, however, seem to have been interrupted by the necessity of reducing the Thessalians to order. They had grown restive, as we have already seen. Peitholaus, one of the dynasty expelled from Pheræ had returned[2]; the fortification of Magnesia by Philip's generals had been interfered with; and the Pheræans had resolved to demand from Philip the restoration of Pagasæ, and to refuse him the enjoyment for the future of their harbour and market dues. In consequence of this, Philip once more expelled Peitholaus, and took steps to quell any tendency to insubordination, whether by force or by those friendly assurances which he knew so well how to give and to break.

In the course of the summer, probably as soon as Philip's operations in Chalcidice began, the Olynthians again appealed to Athens for help. In response to the appeal Charidemus was transferred from the Hellespont to Chalcidice, with eighteen ships and a mercenary force consisting of four thousand light infantry and 150 cavalry.

---

[1] Diod., XVI, lii. [2] *Ibid.*

At first his conduct of the war appeared to promise success. He overran Pallene (one of the three promontories of the Chalcidic peninsula, already invaded by Philip), and devastated Bottiæa, a district of Macedonia south of the river Lydias. But the promise came to nothing, through Charidemus' own fault; for instead of prosecuting the campaign further he gave himself up to the grossest debauchery, and even demanded from the Olynthian Council the means to satisfy his lusts.[1]

Nevertheless the temporary success of Charidemus may have caused some elation in Athens, and in the debate in which Demosthenes' Third Olynthiac oration was delivered most of the speakers appear to have talked light-heartedly of wreaking vengeance upon Philip. It is probable that the special subject of the debate was the financial provision to be made for the operations in aid of Olynthus; the date which seems most likely is the autumn of 349. Though the orator repeats briefly some of the points of the earlier Speeches (emphasising the discredit attaching to Athens, and the danger of allowing the war to be carried into Attica), his main object is now to urge the necessity of setting free the money which at present passed into the festival-fund, and of using it for the purposes of the war. The probable nature of the difficulty has already been explained.[2] Demosthenes' words leave no doubt that Eubulus and

---

[1] Philochorus *ap.* Dion. Hal., *l. c.;* Theopomp., fr. 139 (Oxford Text).   [2] See above, p. 127.

his party had succeeded, by means of a comparatively recent law, in giving fresh security to the
distributions of festival-money. No motion to
use that money for the war would be legal, until
the law in question had been repealed; and the
repeal of the law could only be effected by the
Nomothetæ, the Legislative Commission appointed
out of the jurors for the year, to which the making
and unmaking of laws was entrusted.

The danger of attempting to secure the desired
end by any more direct means was illustrated by
the fate of Apollodorus, who about this time
proposed a resolution in the Council (and subsequently brought it before the Assembly) that
the Assembly should decide whether the surplus
funds at the disposal of the administration should
go to the festival-fund or to the military chest.
According to the account given in the Speech
against Neæra[1] (the work of an unknown contemporary of Demosthenes), no one in the Assembly voted against the proposal; and though
this is probably an exaggeration, the Assembly
doubtless approved warmly of the proposal. But
Apollodorus was indicted by Stephanus for the
illegality of his decree, and was fined a talent. We
do not know what the precise relations between
Demosthenes and Apollodorus at this time were.[2]
It is clear, however, that their policy in regard to
the festival-money was identical,[3] but that Demos-

[1] § 5.   [2] See Appendix to this chapter.
[3] On this policy in general, see above, pp. 96–98.

thenes was more careful than Apollodorus to go to work in a legal manner.

In the Third Olynthiac he demands the appointment of a Legislative Commission, and further requests that the first step shall be taken by those who were responsible for the mischievous law. He also demands the repeal of certain laws with regard to military service, which gave encouragement to malingerers, and took the heart out of patriotic citizens. He goes on to insist with greater emphasis than ever upon the need of personal service, and of such a reorganisation of the financial system as would require every citizen to render his duty to the State, according to his age and capacity, before becoming entitled to any share in the public funds. We do not know if this proposal was embodied in any formal motion; if it was, it was not carried; and certainly no Legislative Commission was appointed. But the words in which Demosthenes outlines the kind of reorganisation which he has in view are sufficiently remarkable.

"What?" some one will ask, "do you suggest that we should *work* for our money?" I do, men of Athens; and I propose a system, for immediate enforcement, which will embrace all alike; so that each, while receiving his share of the public funds, may supply whatever service the State requires of him. If we can remain at peace, then a man will do better to stay at home, free from the necessity of doing anything discreditable through poverty. But if a situation like the present occurs, then, supported by these same sums, he will serve loyally in person, in defence of his country. If he is beyond the age for military service, then let him take, in his place among the rest, that which he now receives irregularly and without doing any service, and let him act as an overseer and manager of business that must be done. In short, without adding or subtracting more than a small sum, and only removing the want of system, my plan reduces the State to order, making your receipt of payment, your service in the army or the courts, and your performance of any duty which the age of each of you allows, and the occasion requires, all part of one and the same system. But it has been no part of my proposal that we should assign the due of those who act to those who do nothing; that we should be idle ourselves and enjoy our leisure helplessly, listening to tales of victories won by somebody's mercenaries[1]; for that is what happens now. Not that I blame one who is doing some part of your duty for you; but I require you to do for yourselves the things for which you honour others, and not to abandon the position which your fathers won through many a glorious peril, and bequeathed to you.

It may be that such a proposal had no chance of success; and modern critics have spoken contemptuously of Demosthenes' unpractical and fanciful schemes of reform. Yet we cannot but feel that the history of Athens would have been the poorer, if no one had set forth a policy worthy of the great traditions of the city. It is true that

[1] An obvious reference to Charidemus.

idealism is easier for the Opposition than for those who are responsible for the detailed working out of practical measures. Yet it is plain that it required no small courage in Demosthenes to speak in this tone. Those who associate him with vulgar demagogues need to remember that on this occasion Demosthenes was opposing not merely the dominant party, but the whole force of popular desire; for, so far as the festival-money was concerned, Eubulus and the People were entirely at one. Consequently, he tried to make the People realise the wrong done to them by the politicians who spoke to please them, and effected their own ends by flattering the desires of the multitude; and he repeats with little alteration some of the passages which he had already used in composing the Speech against Aristocrates. The contrast between the spirit of the great statesmen of Athens in old days and that of his own opponents is drawn in a passage[1] which is too long for quotation, but is one of the most impressive in all his speeches.

In 348 Philip made his appearance again in Chalcidice with a large army, and continued the work of conquest. One after another the towns fell into his hands; corruption and treachery did his work even more effectively than force.[2] Mecyberna, the port of Olynthus itself, distant less than three miles from the city, and Torone, the chief

[1] §§ 24–31.　　　　[2] Diod., XVI, liii.

town of the Sithonian peninsula, were betrayed, and he took them without having to strike a blow. At last he threw off all pretence. Hitherto he had continued to profess friendly intentions towards Olynthus; but when he was within five miles of the city, he suddenly told the Olynthians that there were only two alternatives—either they must cease to live in Olynthus, or he to live in Macedonia.[1] Once more the Olynthians appealed to Athens, begging for a force, not of mercenaries, but of citizens. The Athenians were at last roused; but they were in great difficulties; for, owing to the intrigues of Philip in Eubœa, they found themselves involved in hostilities with their former allies in that island. It was, however, determined that Chares should go to the relief of Olynthus with a citizen force of two thousand heavy infantry and three hundred cavalry.[2] But Chares had not yet passed the public examination of his conduct in his former expedition to Olynthus, in reference to which a trial upon charges brought by Cephisodotus hung over his head; and he demanded that the matter should be settled before he went. Cephisodotus complained that Chares was making the demand with his hand on the throat of the People; but it may be taken as certain that no accusation was allowed to stand in the way of his departure, and he sailed.[3] Unhappily he was hindered by the stormy wind which blows for some

---

[1] Dem., Phil. III, § 11.   [2] Philochorus *ap.* Dion. Hal., *l. c.*
[3] Ar., *Rhet.*, III, x., 1411a.

weeks in the summer from the north over the
Ægean; and before he could arrive at Olynthus,
the city had fallen by treachery.[1] It had held out
bravely against repeated assaults by Philip's army,
and had inflicted heavy losses upon it. But in the
end Lasthenes, who had been given the command
of the Olynthian cavalry, betrayed them on the
field, in conjunction with Euthycrates; and with
their betrayal all was lost.[2]

About the month of August, 348, Philip entered
Olynthus. By his orders the inhabitants (among
whom a number of Athenian citizens were captured) were sold as slaves[3]; and with cruel cynicism
the traitor Euthycrates was appointed to determine the price to be paid for each.[4] Philip's step-
brothers Arrhidæus and Menelaus were taken and
put to death.[5] The conqueror made large presents
of captives and spoil to his friends and supporters;
and not long afterwards Æschines described how
he had met the Arcadian Atrestidas travelling
home from Macedonia with a large body of women
and children given to him by Philip.[6] The Olynthian territory was given principally to Macedonian chieftains, and large parts of Chalcidice were

[1] Suid., *v. s. κάρανος.*

[2] Dem., Phil. III, §§ 56, 66; *de F. L.,* § 267; Diod., *l. c.,* etc.

[3] Æsch., *de F. L.,* § 15; Dem., Phil. II., § 21; Diod., *l. c.,* etc.

[4] Hypereides, fr. 76 (Oxfd. Text). The truth of the story that
Aristotle the philosopher pointed out to Philip the wealthiest of
the citizens happily rests on very doubtful authority. (See
Grote, Pt. II, ch. lxxxviii).

[5] Justin, VIII, iii.   [6] Dem., *de F. L.,* §§ 305, 306.

probably worked by their former inhabitants as slaves, for the benefit of Philip and his retainers.[1] Among the friends of Philip who profited by his distribution of the lands taken from the allies of Athens were (according to Demosthenes)[2] both Æschines and Philocrates, of whom much more will be heard shortly. By the time that Philip's work was finished, thirty-two Chalcidic towns had been annihilated, and that (Demosthenes tells us[3]) with such savagery that a few years afterwards no one could have told that their sites had ever been inhabited. Most of them were never restored; and Appian,[4] writing in the second century after Christ, says that no trace remained of them except the foundations of the temples. Even if, as some modern writers[5] assert, Demosthenes somewhat exaggerated the calamity for rhetorical effect, there can still be no real doubt of the sweeping nature of the destruction inflicted by the conqueror upon this unhappy region.[6] Those who could derived some satisfaction from the fact that when the traitors had done their work, they were cast aside by Philip, who knew them too well to trust them.[7]

The Athenians gave a home and the privileges of citizenship to those fugitives from Olynthus who

---

[1] Æsch., *de F. L.*, § 156, and Dittenb., *Syll. Inscr.* (ed. 2), No. 178.   [2] Dem., *de F. L.*, §§ 145, 146.   [3] Phil. III, § 26.

[4] *Bell. Civ.*, IV, 102.   [5] *E.g.* Beloch, *Gr. Gesch.*, ii., p. 505 n.

[6] Pliny (*Nat. Hist.*, ii,, 27) spoke of the blood-red meteor, which fell to earth in 349, as a message of the sanguinary cruelties which accompanied the fall of Olynthus.   [7] Dem., *de Chers.*, § 40.

had made good their escape, and tried to quiet their own consciences by passing resolutions of strong condemnation against the traitors.[1] But the prospect of the final loss of all hope of recovering Amphipolis (for this was a necessary consequence of Philip's victory) cannot have been easy to face. Philip, on the other hand, celebrated his victory by holding a festival in honour of the Olympian Zeus, with dramatic performances to which he summoned all the most celebrated actors of Greece, feasting his friends and making presents to them with lavish generosity.[2]

We must now recur to the unexpected crisis in Eubœa, which was at least a partial cause of the failure of the Athenians to render effective aid to Olynthus.[3] We saw that the influence of Athens in Eubœa had been restored by the brilliant campaign of Timotheus about the year 357, when the Athenians liberated the people of Eubœa at their own request from the domination of Thebes; and in 352 Demosthenes[4] mentioned Menestratus of Eretria as a ruler friendly to Athens. But very soon after this Philip had begun to feel his way in the island. In the First Philippic Demosthenes quoted a letter which Philip had sent to the Eubœans, though its purport has not

---

[1] Dem., *de F. L.*, § 267; Suid., *s. v.* κάρανος; Harpocr., *s. v.* ἰσοτελής etc.

[2] Demosthenes (*de F. L.*, § 192 ff.) tells a touching story of the favour asked, in response to Philip's invitation, by the comic actor Satyrus.   [3] Above, p. 183.   [4] *In Aristocr.*, § 124.

come down to us. It appears probable, however, that he went to work by encouraging the establishment of tyrants in the important cities of the island, and by supporting them with money and men. In Eretria, in 348, the ruler, who was favourable to Athens, was Plutarchus; and a rising against him was led by Cleitarchus,[1] who was probably now (as he was later) in close touch with Philip. Plutarchus accordingly sent to Athens to ask for aid. Demosthenes strongly opposed the granting of this request, desiring doubtless that the undivided forces of the city should be employed to save Olynthus from Philip. His action in so doing has been much criticised, on the ground that Eubœa was far nearer to Athens than Olynthus, and that a hostile power there could be a very dangerous foe. But it is quite possible that he was right. The only chance of defeating Philip was to strain every nerve, and to let no other call stand in the way. Experience had shown that a short and sharp campaign[2] might suffice to reduce Eubœa; and this might, without inordinate risk, be postponed until the Olynthian crisis was over.

However this may be, Plutarchus had a powerful helper in Athens in the wealthy Meidias, the friend of Eubulus and the enemy of Demosthenes, whom he actually accused of fomenting trouble in Eubœa in order to injure Plutarchus, the friend of Athens.[3] Owing to the influence of Eubulus and

---

[1] Schol. on Dem., *de Pace.*, p. 161.
[2] Like that of Timotheus; see p. 68.   [3] Dem., *in Meid.*, §110.

14

Meidias, it was resolved to send assistance to Plutarchus; Phocion, a brave soldier and a member of Eubulus' party, but trusted by all alike for his blunt and outspoken honesty, crossed with a force of infantry and cavalry about the month of February, 348,[1] and Meidias went with him as a cavalry officer.

The detailed history of the expedition is not very certain. But it appears that some of the cavalry were transferred to Olynthus,[2] and that Phocion unwisely sent home the rest of them, thinking that they were not wanted.[3] With the remainder of the force Phocion took up a disadvantageous position near Tamynæ, while Plutarchus encamped in the neighbourhood. Here Phocion was beleaguered by Callias and Taurosthenes, two brothers who held sway over Chalcis, and of whom the former had obtained aid from Philip (probably in the form of troops serving under Philip's generals in Thessaly), and the latter had hired mercenaries who had previously been engaged in Phocis.[4] Phocion was hardly pressed, and though he affected to think little of the desertions of the more frivolous of his soldiers, he sent to Athens for reinforcements. The Council at once ordered back the

---

[1] Dem., *in Bœot. de nom.*, § 16. Demosthenes described Phocion as "the pruner of his periods" (ἡ τῶν ἐμῶν λόγων κοπίς).

[2] Dem., *in Meid.*, § 197.

[3] Meidias on his return home denounced the way in which the expedition had been conducted; *ibid.*, § 132.

[4] Æsch., *in Ctes.*, §§ 86, 87; Plut., *Phocion*, xii., xiii.; Dem., *in Meid.*, § 161 sqq. See also Note 1 at the end of the Chapter.

cavalry who had been sent home, and called for rich men to volunteer to be trierarchs, so heavy was the expenditure demanded at this time. Among the volunteers was Meidias himself.[1] Before the reinforcements could leave Athens, an engagement had been forced upon Phocion at Tamynæ by the action of Plutarchus, who marched out of camp to meet an attack of the enemy without waiting for Phocion. The Athenian cavalry, also too impatient to wait for Phocion, followed Plutarchus in some disorder. After very little fighting Plutarchus fled; and it was only by hard fighting that Phocion, having appeared on the field of battle, was able to win the day. Among those who were specially distinguished in the fight was Æschines, who was sent to take home the news of the victory.[2] The conduct of Plutarchus was set down to treachery, and Phocion proceeded to expel him from Eretria, and to occupy the commanding fortress of Zaretra, while Callias took refuge with Philip.

On hearing of Phocion's victory, the Athenians had countermanded the reinforcements which they had voted; and Phocion was obliged to send a second message to ask that they should be despatched. Before they could leave Athens, the Dionysiac festival took place (in March, 348)[3],

---

[1] Demosthenes ungenerously suggests that he volunteered to be trierarch only to avoid fighting with the cavalry, of which he was an officer.   [2] Plut., *Phoc.*, xiii.; Æsch., *de F. L.*, § 169.

[3] Note 2. The Speech of Demosthenes against Meidias is the chief authority for this affair and the events connected with it.

and Demosthenes acted as choregus on behalf of the Pandionid tribe, having volunteered to undertake the expenditure and returned from the army in Eubœa, where he had been serving, in order to fulfil the duties of his office. In the midst of the festival, to which a certain religious sanctity was attached, Meidias entered the theatre in a violent manner, and struck him a number of blows on the head with his fist. This outrageous act was only the last of a series of attempts to interfere with Demosthenes in the discharge of his duties. For Meidias had already tried to prevent the members of the chorus which Demosthenes furnished from obtaining the usual exemption from military service; he had broken into the house of the goldsmith whom Demosthenes employed, and had damaged the gold crowns and gold-embroidered robes which were being made for the chorus; he had corrupted the chorus-trainer and even the archon who presided at the Dionysia; he had tried to induce the judges at the festival to promise to vote against Demosthenes' chorus; and he had blocked up the entrances by which the chorus was to march into the theatre. It is not surprising that though Demosthenes had secured the services of the best flute-player in Athens, Telephanes by name, and Telephanes had done his best to replace the chorus-trainer, the prize went to another.

On the day following the Dionysia, the Assembly met in the theatre, to consider (as was customary) any matters that arose out of the festival. Demosthenes laid a formal complaint against Meidias, and the Assembly passed a vote condemning the latter's act, and so strengthened Demosthenes' hands with a view to his intended prosecution of Meidias before a law-court. We shall see later on what the issue of this affair was. The prosecution of Demosthenes by Euctemon, the friend of Meidias, for desertion in returning from Eubœa was not persisted in. It was indeed too absurd to have a chance of success.

After the Dionysia the troops which Phocion had asked for were sent, and the cavalry encamped (as before) at Argura. (Meidias however stayed with his ship.) In the course of the summer Phocion was succeeded in the command by Molossus. The recall of Phocion is possibly explained by the fact which Plutarch mentions immediately before it, that Phocion, after occupying Zaretra, had set free all the prisoners who were of Hellenic nationality, fearing the orators at Athens, lest they should force the People in anger to take some cruel action against the prisoners—an action at once creditable to Phocion's good feeling, and significant of his well-known contempt for the People and their leaders. However this may be, his successor mismanaged the war, and was himself taken prisoner. Before the summer was over, peace was made upon terms disadvantageous to Athens. The Eubœan towns obtained their independence, and the Athenians cherished some ill-feeling against them for several years. Carystus alone remained a member of the Athenian alliance. A particular cause of annoyance lay in the fact that Plutarchus, when pressed for payment by some of his mercenaries, had given them some Athenian soldiers as security,[1] and these the Athenians had actually been obliged to ransom at heavy cost.

The Eubœan war may temporarily have cast a shadow over the popularity of Eubulus. His cousin Hegesileos, who had been second in command to Phocion and was accused of abetting the proceedings of Plutarchus, was tried and condemned, and Eubulus did not venture to appear in his defence.[2]

The events of the year 348 were thus disastrous for Athens. Not only was Philip's power now consolidated down to the southern borders of Thessaly, but Athens herself was practically isolated. The Eubœans, her most powerful allies, were lost to her; her settlers in Lemnos, Imbros, and other islands were exposed to the attacks of Philip's captains; and if Philip made his way to the Hellespont, it was doubtful whether she could oppose him with any chance of success.[3]

To assign the responsibility for the course which events had been allowed to take is no easy task. There can be little doubt that Demosthenes was right in seeing signs of grave moral decay in the

[1] Schol. on Dem., *de Pace*.   [2] Dem., *de F. L.*, § 290.
[3] Note 3.

Athenian People as a whole. Their love of pleasure and their indifference (except in sentiment) to the national honour, so long as the festival-money was not interfered with, did not exist only in his imagination; and when all allowance is made for the excuse—it was hardly more—afforded by the religious character of the festivals, we cannot but feel that the People had primarily themselves to thank for their disasters. It was the same moral causes, reinforced by the unwillingness of many to leave their business, that accounted in a great measure for the refusal of personal service in the army. The professional soldier might be a more efficient fighter, but professional soldiers were ruinously expensive; and the better morale of the citizen-soldier fighting for his own country probably went some way towards compensating for his technical deficiences; the hard-won success of Phocion's citizen-hoplites at Tamynæ showed that such a force was not to be despised. Now and then, in a moment of excitement, the citizens would rise and take the field; but their enthusiasm was short-lived, and they would not face a fully-considered system of regular service in relays, such as Demosthenes advocated.

It is not worth while to attempt to apportion the blame more precisely between the People and their leaders. Eubulus' policy came to shipwreck over foreign and military affairs, largely because funds were not forthcoming for active warfare, however well he had provided for defensive measures; and funds were not forthcoming because he either would not or dared not curtail the festival-fund, nor would he draw, as he might have done by means of a war-tax, upon the wealth of the richer classes who were his principal supporters. A few volunteer trierarchs were a poor substitute for the contributions which the considerable private wealth of the citizens of Athens might have provided. But the measures of a political leader necessarily depend to a great extent upon what he can expect his followers to consent to; and the defects of the policy of Eubulus largely arose out of those of both the richer and the poorer classes; for the one would not make great sacrifices, and the other would not give up the distributions; and it was doubtless his misfortune that he was given no time to carry out his policy of retrenchment and the gradual building up of a navy, but was confronted by a combination of circumstances which proved too strong for him and for Athens. The conjunction of the Eubœan difficulty with the Olynthian crisis was cunningly contrived by Philip, and rendered the efforts of the Athenians ineffectual just at the moment when they were preparing to throw some real energy into the assistance which they gave to the beleaguered town. The strain upon them was great[1]; and though it might probably have been met by means which they did

---

[1] In the early part of 348 there was not enough money to pay the juries, so that the courts had to be suspended (Dem., *in Bœot. de nom.*, § 16).

not see fit to adopt, neither politicians nor people proved equal to dealing with the situation. It is to the credit of Demosthenes that throughout these years he represented fearlessly the higher side of the national spirit as he understood it, and attempted to revive in his countrymen what, in spite of themselves, he believed to be their true character.

Before closing this account of the first period of the war with Philip, it will be convenient to narrate the sequel to an incident which has already been described, the assault of Meidias upon Demosthenes at the Dionysia of 348. Demosthenes, as we have seen, encouraged by the vote which the Assembly passed in condemnation of Meidias' misconduct, gave notice that he would prosecute him before a jury. Even after this, Meidias proceeded to commit further acts of annoyance against Demosthenes, and opposed (though unsuccessfully) his selection as a Councillor for the year 347–6, by bringing false accusations against him at the scrutiny to which, like all other candidates for office, Demosthenes had to submit. At the meeting of the Assembly at which Meidias' conduct at the Dionysia had been considered, Eubulus, in spite of Meidias' entreaties, had refused to rise and speak in his defence. But it became known later that he intended to support Meidias at the trial; and it also became apparent that no public speaker would give his aid to

Demosthenes. That the influence of Eubulus
with an Athenian jury was very great is proved
by the pains which Demosthenes took to counteract it both in the Speech against Meidias and in his
prosecution of Æschines.[1] Meidias himself was
also a person of no small influence, and held a
number of offices which carried with them some
importance and dignity, however reprehensible he
might have been in his performance of the duties
attached to them. Demosthenes therefore may
have felt that his chances of winning his case, in
the existing condition of public feeling, were small,
for the popular indignation at the insult to a
choregus had doubtless soon worn off; and Meidias'
friends appear to have intimated that Meidias
was ready to pay adequate compensation, if the
prosecution were dropped. Accordingly, before the
case was actually brought into court, Demosthenes,
after repeatedly rejecting all overtures, at last
came to terms with Meidias (probably late in the
year 347), and accepted half a talent from him in
settlement of his grievance.[2] It is possible that
he was partly influenced by political considerations;
for we shall see shortly that in the year 347–6
Demosthenes acted in harmony with Eubulus and
his party in forwarding the negotiations for the
Peace with Philip, which had now become necessary; and he may have been glad, by abandoning

[1] Dem., *de F. L.*, §§ 290 ff.

[2] Half a talent was by no means a contemptible sum, though
Æschines and others scoff at Demosthenes for accepting it.

his suit against Meidias, to avoid creating difficulties, and also, it might be, imperilling his own position in Athens.

The speech which Demosthenes composed for the prosecution of Meidias survives, though there are indications that it did not receive a final revision, and it was probably not published by Demosthenes himself. It is a vigorous attack upon the whole life and career of Meidias (including unhappily some of those fictions about the parentage of the accused which seem to have appealed to Athenian juries). The orator repeatedly insists that the insult was less to himself than to the People (who had already expressed their indignation), and recalls, one after another, the acts of violence and outrage of which he alleges Meidias to have been guilty. He deals with parallel cases in the past—both those from which Meidias might hope to draw some arguments in his defence, and those which formed precedents for his condemnation. He disparages the vaunted public services of Meidias, and compares them with his own. After employing every argument which can blacken the guilt of Meidias himself, he attacks Eubulus and the other supporters of the accused, and calls upon the jury to vindicate the laws, and to make Meidias an example to all other offenders.

The Speech follows the obvious lines, but is powerfully written in a tone of warm indignation, varied here and there by pathos, when he recounts the calamities of Meidias' former victims,[1] and even by a touch of something like humour, as when he imitates Meidias' own manner of addressing the People,[2] or when he sums up his consideration of the services of Meidias to the State.[3]

Where then is his brilliant record? What do his services to the State and his magnificent outlay amount to? I cannot see, unless we are to think of the house that he has built at Eleusis—so tall that it darkens the whole neighbourhood; or the pair of white horses from Sicyon which takes his wife to the Mysteries or wherever she pleases; or the three or four footmen who accompany him as he sweeps through the market-place, talking about his bowls and drinking-horns and wine-cups in a loud voice, so that the passers-by may hear.

The attitude which Demosthenes takes up—that of a champion of the rights of the democracy against the vulgar and insolent rich—is perhaps a little overdone; but the portrait of Meidias is vigorously drawn, and takes its place worthily beside those of other villains depicted in Greek and Roman oratory.

APPENDIX TO CHAPTER VI

(*On the Affair of Phormio and Apollodorus*)

The action of Demosthenes in connection with the dispute between Phormio and Apollodorus is so much disputed, and the questions raised are of such importance, owing to their bearing upon the estimate to be formed of his character, that they demand special consideration.

---

[1] *E.g.*, §§ 95 ff.   [2] § 203.   [3] § 158.

Phormio was first the slave and then the confidential freedman of Pasion, the great Athenian banker. Pasion died in 370, leaving two sons, Apollodorus and Pasicles. In his will he provided that Phormio should marry his widow (receiving with her a considerable dowry) and should be one of the guardians of his younger son Pasicles; and that until Pasicles came of age, Phormio should rent the business, which included a shield-factory as well as the bank, paying a fixed rent to the estate, and making what profit he could for himself. It was intended that the property should remain undivided until Pasicles came of age, and should then be apportioned equally between him and his elder brother, Apollodorus. But the conduct of Apollodorus made this impossible. He appears to have been a man of some public spirit, and to have served more than once as trierarch with distinction. (We have already seen how he claimed the "Trierarchic Crown" offered in 360.[1]) But his ambition to serve the State was more than compensated by his careless and extravagant habits, and he was at the same time extremely litigious. No less than eight of the speeches included, rightly or wrongly, among those of Demosthenes were written by or for Apollodorus, and we know that he appeared in many other lawsuits, and was ready to prosecute any one, relation or stranger, upon any provocation.

The result of Apollodorus' conduct was to imperil the security of the joint estate by the liabilities which he was always incurring: and in consequence of this, the guardians of Pasicles resolved to make a division of the property, without waiting for Pasicles to come of age, in order to save their ward's share. It was, however, arranged that Phormio was to retain the lease of the business, paying half the rent to Apollodorus, and keeping half for the benefit of Pasicles. In 362 Pasicles came of age, and Phormio's lease determined; he set up business as a banker on his own account, and was granted the citizenship of Athens, in recognition of his high qualities, as his master Pasion had been granted it before him. In the course of the negotiations which followed the termination of the lease, and again after certain legal proceedings which took place on the death of Apollodorus' mother in 360, Apollodorus gave Phormio a formal release from all claims. In spite of this, about the year 350, he entered a claim against

---

[1] See pp. 31–32.

Phormio for twenty talents. Phormio thereupon resorted to the procedure by *paragraphé*,[1] pleading that (whatever the merits of the case) the action brought was illegal, because Apollodorus had already given a discharge from all claims, and because the Statute of Limitations forbade such claims to be made after the expiration of five years from the winding-up of the trust.

A litigant who pleaded a *paragraphé* had the right to be heard first, and Phormio, who, owing to his foreign descent and his unfamiliarity with the courts, did not speak in person, was represented by his friends, one of whom delivered the speech composed for him by Demosthenes. This speech not only made good the technical plea, but also dealt in a manner which seems almost mercilessly conclusive, with the original case. It further attempted to meet the jealous attitude adopted by Apollodorus towards Phormio—once his father's slave, but now his stepfather—and emphasised the services rendered by Phormio not only to Apollodorus and his family, by the preservation of their property for them, but also to the State. Above all the speaker insists on the value of honesty in business, in contrast to the spendthrift life and dishonest litigiousness of persons like Apollodorus. The moral force of the speech proved irresistible. Apollodorus did not receive one fifth of the votes of the jury, and therefore incurred a very heavy fine, in addition to the loss of his case.

But Apollodorus would not accept his defeat without a struggle. As Aphobus had prosecuted one of Demosthenes' witnesses, so Apollodorus prosecuted one of the witnesses who had supported Phormio. As in the former case, so in the latter, the witness was one whose evidence was unimportant; Phormio's justification of the *paragraphé* would have been conclusive without it. Nevertheless any conviction for false-witness would almost certainly have led to a new trial of the original case, and a new trial instituted under such circumstances would not have been likely to terminate in favour of Phormio.

Now among the speeches of Demosthenes there have descended to us two written for Apollodorus in prosecution of this very witness, Stephanus; and it has naturally been felt that if, after his impassioned oration for Phormio, Demosthenes changed sides, and assisted Apollodorus in the attempt to overthrow a verdict

---

[1] See above, p. 33.

which he himself had done most to secure and to justify, he did not act like an honourable man.   Nor would this be his most serious deflection from a high standard of honour in the matter.   For the manner in which the First Speech against Stephanus treats the case is even more discreditable, if it is the work of Demosthenes. He argues that the very documents on which he had relied to prove Phormio's plea in the previous trial are either non-existent or are forgeries by Phormio himself; and whereas he had in the former speech paid an eloquent tribute to Phormio's high charac- ter and distinguished services, he now attacks him in a scurrilous and ungentlemanly manner, coupling the attack with the gross- est insinuations with regard to Apollodorus' own mother and brother.   Apollodorus himself might conceivably have spoken thus; but if Demosthenes carried the art of writing in the character of his client so far as this, we can only say that it proves his ability more conclusively than his honour.   The case against Stephanus was in fact a very bad one; to most of the conten- tions of the speaker the reply is either actually contained in the Speech for Phormio, or is such as suggests itself immediately; and the skill of the advocate is not sufficient to conceal their weakness.

Unfortunately no final decision as to the authorship of the Speeches against Stephanus is possible.   The Second Speech, indeed, which is weak both in argument and in style, no one now believes to be the work of Demosthenes; possibly it is a sub- sequently written version of a reply made by Apollodorus on the spur of the moment.   But in regard to the First Speech the arguments for and against Demosthenes' authorship are almost equally divided.   As regards the internal evidence there is, on the one hand, little in the style or the argument which would have suggested that it was not his work, had it not been for the incon- sistency of the attitude adopted in this speech with that assumed in the Speech for Phormio; and one striking passage is almost identical with a passage in the Speech for Pantænetus, which is usually admitted to be Demosthenes' work.   On the other hand, there are a few phrases and passages which do not read as if they were his, and which at least leave room for the possibility that the Speech was composed by another.   A certain monotony of expression—particularly in the use of connecting particles and pronouns—has been thought to be unlike Demosthenes, and the parallelism with the "Pantænetus" does not prove identity of authorship, since identical passages sometimes occur in different orators.[1]

But the question is further complicated by external evidence. It is clear that Demosthenes was thought to have done something dishonourable in connection with Apollodorus and Phormio; but what he was originally accused of was not the composition of speeches for both sides. "What idea," asks Æschines, "are we to have of a born traitor? Is he not a man who treats those who have to do with him and trust him, as you have treated them?— a man who writes speeches for money, to be used in court, and shows them to the other side? You wrote a speech for Phormio the banker, and got your fee; and you showed it to Apollodorus, who had prosecuted Phormio on a capital charge."[2] This can only mean that Demosthenes showed Apollodorus his Speech for Phormio in the original trial. (The charge is called a capital one by a slight exaggeration, not unparalleled in Greek oratory, because the sum involved was so great that Phormio, if condemned, would be obliged to go into exile.) It is possible that the explanation which certain scholars[3] propose is the true one— that Demosthenes tried to reconcile Apollodorus to Phormio, and showed him the Speech to prove to him the hopelessness of his case, but in vain. It would be easy for Æschines to misrepresent this as an act of treachery to Phormio, while it is very difficult to suppose that if Demosthenes had actually treated Phormio as the writer of the First Speech against Stephanus treats him, Æschines and Deinarchus, who raked up every possible scandal against him, would not have made full use of the fact.

But if this is so, how are we to explain the fact that Plutarch[4] and other late writers definitely state that Demosthenes wrote for both Apollodorus and Phormio? Plutarch says that it was like selling swords to both sides from the same factory. (This does not in itself seem to be a very grave offence; but the point perhaps lies in the reference to the occupation of Demosthenes' father.) Probably the statement is due simply to the fact that speeches for both were found in the Corpus of Demosthenic speeches, compiled in the first instance at Alexandria. A

---

[1] See above, p. 27.　　　　　　[2] Æsch., *de F. L.*, §§ 165, 173.
[3] Note 4.　　　　　　　　　　　[4] Plut., *Dem.*, xv.

later writer, Zosimus (c. 500 A.D.), still further exaggerates the supposed iniquity of Demosthenes; and it may be that the whole story is based on a misunderstanding, which, when once started, went on enlarging itself.

Those who believe that Demosthenes did write the First Speech against Stephanus usually ascribe his conduct to political motives. We have seen[1] that just about this time, Apollodorus proposed a decree in the Assembly that the People should decide whether the surplus revenues should be used for military purposes, instead of passing automatically into the festival-fund. This was precisely in accordance with the policy which Demosthenes earnestly advocated in the very year of the trial of Stephanus, with a view to war against Philip of Macedon. But it is very doubtful whether such considerations could really have weighed with Demosthenes. Apollodorus' proposal was probably made in the same headstrong spirit as his many prosecutions; it was illegal; he was heavily fined for it; and it is probable that it did more harm than good to the cause which Demosthenes desired to forward. It is, moreover, difficult to suppose that any advocate who had triumphantly succeeded in a good case would take up a bad one against his former client in reference to the very same matter, whatever the political situation.

There is, therefore, at least good reason to hope that Demosthenes was not guilty of the atrocious conduct ascribed to him. If he was, there is little that can be said in extenuation of it. The plea that the relations of a speech-writer and his client were not so close as those of a modern lawyer with those whom he represents cannot help him much; and it does not even touch the real point of the gravamen—the utter heartlessness and want of good feeling shown by an attack upon Phormio's character as scurrilous as his previous eulogy had been noble. The eulogy, no less than the attack, viewed in this light, would be no more than a piece of cold-blooded trickery. All that can be said is that if Demosthenes did act thus, there is nothing in all the rest of his career—for his fierce attacks upon his own enemies are a very different matter—which is even remotely parallel to this action; and though this is no exculpation, it at least enables us to deny that such conduct was characteristic of him.

---

[1] Above, p. 201.

15

NOTES

1. Some historians assume that these mercenaries were sent by the Phocian leader Phalæcus. But this is nowhere stated in our authorities, and the Phocians were in alliance with Athens. It is at least equally likely that Taurosthenes induced some of the mercenaries hitherto employed by Phalæcus to come over to Eubœa by offering higher pay. If, however, Phalæcus deliberately sent them to oppose the Athenians, it must have been because the dissensions in the Phocian ranks had already reached a point at which, because the party opposed to Phalæcus was friendly to Athens, he himself chose to take the opposite line. This happened towards the end of 347 (see below, p. 238); but we have no evidence that early in 348 it was already so.

2. The date of the Eubœan expedition has been much disputed, and some historians place it in 350 or 349 rather than in 348. The following are the principal considerations which appear to determine 348 as the true date:

(1) Demosthenes was choregus in the year of the expedition and the Speech against Meidias was written for delivery in the archonship of the second archon after the one in whose year the choregia fell (τρίτον ἔτος τουτί, § 13). Further (§ 111) Demosthenes was a member of the Council in the year of the Speech. Now supposing that his choregia fell in March, 348 (in the archonship of Callimachus, who held office from July, 349, to July, 348), the Speech must have been composed for the archonship of Themistocles, *i.e.*, for a date after July, 347; and in the archonship of Themistocles, 347–46, we know that Demosthenes was in fact a Councillor. Those who date the expedition and the Speech earlier suppose that he was also a Councillor in 350–49 or 349–8. This would have been legally possible; but as the Councillors were chosen by lot, it is hardly likely; and there is absolutely no independent evidence of his having been a Councillor in either of those years.

(2) The Olynthiac Orations, probably delivered in the summer and autumn of 349, know nothing of the Eubœan trouble.

(3) The Speech against Neæra, § 3, and the Speech against Meidias, § 197, make it certain that the citizen-expedition to help Olynthus fell in the same year as the Eubœan expedition.

(4)   According to Æschines, *de F. L.*, § 12, the Eubœan envoys came before the Assembly to discuss terms of peace shortly before the capture of Phrynon by privateers, which took place during the Olympian truce.   The truce fell in July, 348.

3.   Grote is very probably right in assigning to the weeks immediately following the fall of Olynthus the disappearance of Chares from view.   Antiochus was sent to look for him, and to tell him that the people of Athens failed to understand why, when Philip was on his way to the Chersonese, the Athenians did not even know where to find their general or the force which they had sent out; and Æschines (*de F. L.*, § 71) speaks of 1500 talents spent in the course of the war upon runaway generals, of whom he names Deiares, Deipyrus, and Polyphontes—men otherwise unknown to us.   Grote connects the mission of Antiochus with a panic on the part of the settlers in the Chersonese, and it is very likely that rumours of Philip's alleged intention to proceed thither may have been circulated at this time.   Schäfer (ii., p. 178) even thinks that Philip's generals were actually sent thither.

4.   Schäfer in particular takes this view.   The whole question is well summed up in Paley and Sandys' *Select Private Orations of Demosthenes*, ii., pp. xxxix ff.   It should be added that it is very improbable that the Speech was composed either by Apollodorus himself, or by the writer who composed most of the extant speeches delivered by him.

CHAPTER VII

THE FIRST EMBASSY TO PHILIP

EVEN before the actual fall of Olynthus it must have become plain to most clear-sighted politicians that Athens was not in a position to carry on the war against Philip with success. She had let slip the opportunity which she might have taken in 349, of throwing herself with vigour into the defence of Olynthus, and in 348, when the Athenians realised somewhat more clearly the gravity of the situation, it was too late; for the movements in Eubœa led them to divide their forces, and neither their energy, nor the funds which they chose to consider available, were sufficient for the double task. The successful continuance of the struggle with Philip being thus impossible, the only course which sensible men could take was to come to terms with him.

Philip also was anxious for a suspension of hostilities. Athens was not indeed, from his point of view, so serious a foe as the Athenians liked to believe, and he could well afford to have patience before he proceeded to bring his rivalry with her to an issue. At the same time she was strong enough at sea to make the carrying out of his more immediate objects much more difficult than it would otherwise have been. Her action at Thermopylæ in 352, and the determination which she had shown, even under the leadership of Eubulus, to maintain her position on the shore of the Hellespont, were sufficient evidence of this; and it would be easier for him both to advance his power in Greece itself and to confirm and extend his sway in Thrace, if he could come to some such arrangement with Athens as would get rid of, or at least delay and hamper, her interference with his movements. Further, he was suffering from the closing of his ports by Athenian ships, and the raids which Athenian commanders made upon his coasts.[1] Some have even thought that he had already in view the project of uniting all Hellas under his sway, in order to proceed to the conquest of the East; and that for this purpose he desired the co-operation of the Athenian fleet, which was as superior to his own, as his land forces were to those of Athens. However this may be (and there is no evidence upon the point), in the summer of 348, when the envoys from the Eubœan towns went to Athens to discuss the terms of the Peace to be made between Athens and the Eubœans, Philip authorised them to say that he too desired to come to an understanding.[2]

[1] Dem., *de F. L.*, § 315.
[2] Æsch., *de F. L.*, § 12. The last Athenian expedition to Olynthus had doubtless already departed, but owing to bad weather had not reached its destination.

Shortly afterwards an Athenian named Phrynon was captured by Philip's ships in the course of a raid, during the time (so he asserted) of the Olympian Truce,[1] when, according to Greek custom, hostilities should have been suspended. He was ransomed, and on his return to Athens requested the Athenians to appoint an envoy to go on his behalf to Philip, and to ask for the restoration of the sum paid for his freedom. Ctesiphon was sent, and returned with a message from Philip stating that he had entered upon the war with Athens against his will, and would still be glad if it could be terminated. He added other friendly expressions; the message was welcomed by the People with enthusiasm, and a vote of thanks to Ctesiphon was passed.

Immediately afterwards, Philocrates carried a decree that permission should be given to Philip to send envoys to Athens to discuss terms of peace. Thereupon Lycinus (representing, according to Æschines, certain interested persons, who had stood in the way of a similar proposal of Philocrates before the return of Ctesiphon) impeached Philocrates for the alleged illegality of the decree,[2] and demanded the infliction of a fine of one

[1] *I.e.*, about the month of July. The object of the Truce was to allow all who desired to do so to travel to Olympia for the games without fear.

[2] Philocrates' decree may have run counter to a resolution to receive no envoys from Philip, forming part of the terms of alliance with the Olynthians (Schäfer, vol. ii., pp. 23, 166); but there seems to be no definite evidence as to the nature of the illegality alleged.

hundred talents. Philocrates, who was ill at the time of the trial, was defended by Demosthenes, "in a speech which lasted all day," and was acquitted. Lycinus failed to obtain a fifth part of the votes of the jury, and so became himself liable to a heavy penalty.[1]

The action of Demosthenes in defending Philocrates may be explained in one of two ways, according as the trial of Philocrates is supposed to have taken place before or after the fall of Olynthus. If Demosthenes defended the proposer of negotiations for peace even before Olynthus had fallen, we can only suppose that he had already seen the hopelessness of continuing the struggle for the present, and had had the courage to act upon his changed conviction. On the other hand, it is improbable that he would really have consented to abandon Olynthus in the hour of her greatest need; and it is much more likely that the trial of Philocrates did not take place until some time after Olynthus had been taken.[2] For Phrynon can hardly have returned to Athens before the end of July, 348; some time must have elapsed between his return and that of Ctesiphon; and also between the proposal of Philocrates and his trial. It is probable therefore that the trial did not take place until some weeks at least—possibly months—after the fall of Olynthus, and by this time, as we shall see, Demosthenes was certainly

[1] Æsch., *de F. L.*, § 14; *in Ctes.*, § 62.
[2] Note 1 at the end of the Chapter.

convinced of the necessity of peace, and could defend Philocrates without inconsistency.

The capture of Olynthus and Philip's treatment of the inhabitants and (together with them) of the Athenians whom he found in the city, caused a momentary revulsion of feeling in Athens against the proposed arrangement with Philip; and even Eubulus himself and his supporters were carried away by it. Eubulus addressed the Assembly in very strong terms in regard to Philip, praying (Demosthenes tells us[1]) that perdition might seize him, and proposed to send embassies throughout the Greek world and "almost to the Red Sea,"[2] with the object of uniting all the Hellenes in opposition to Philip, and of summoning a congress for the purpose. These proposals were supported in speeches of a highly patriotic tone, and among those who spoke in their favour was Æschines—a man of somewhat humble birth, who had been first a schoolmaster, then an actor, and then a clerk in government offices, until he came into prominence as a supporter of Eubulus. He was a man of great talent, and a ready extempore speaker; and the magnificent voice with which nature had endowed him gave him a great advantage when addressing a people so impressionable as the Athenians. On the present occasion, Demosthenes tells us, Æschines quoted the decrees of Miltiades and Themistocles—the heroes of the

[1] *De F. L.*, § 291.   [2] *Ibid.*, § 304.

Persian wars—and the oath of allegiance taken
by the young Athenian soldier on assuming his
armour.[1] He doubtless pictured Athens as once
more taking the leadership of a Panhellenic
confederacy, as she had done in the Persian wars.

The embassies were sent.[2] Æschines himself
went to Arcadia, where Philip had been intriguing
with some of the leading politicians, and had
evidently found favour; for the Athenian party
among the Arcadians had already sent representatives to Athens through Ischander.[3] On his
return, Demosthenes says,[4] Æschines

reported to the Assembly the long and noble
speeches, which, he said, he had delivered on your
behalf before the Ten Thousand at Megalopolis,
in reply to Philip's spokesman, Hieronymus; and he
described at length the criminal wrong that was done
not only to their own several countries, but to all
Hellas, by men who took bribes and received money
from Philip. Many a time in the course of his speech
he called Philip 'barbarian' and 'devil' and he reported the delight of the Arcadians at the thought
that Athens was now waking up and attending to
affairs.[5]

He also gave an indignant account of the fate
of the captured Olynthians, illustrating it by that

[1] *De F. L.*, § 303.

[2] As to the date of the embassies, there can be little doubt that
they took place in the late autumn and winter of 348–7, though
there is no direct evidence. Diod., XVI, liv., has obviously no
chronological value. [3] *Ibid.*, § 303. [4] *Ibid.*, § 11.

[5] *Ibid.*, § 305.

of the women and children carried off to Arcadia by Atrestidas,[1] and narrating how he had been moved to tears by the sight, and by the thought of the unhappy condition of the Greek world, in which such cruelties could go unpunished.[2]

The embassies, however, entirely failed to secure their object. None of the southern Greek States seem to have imagined at present that Philip's growing power involved any danger to themselves; and none of them had reason to be so much interested in the welfare of Athens as to join in a league for her benefit. It has indeed been suggested that Eubulus did not expect any result from these missions to the Greek States; that they were only sent in order to convince the People, who were momentarily in a militant mood, of the hopelessness of continuing the war, by demonstrating the isolation of Athens; and that the speeches of himself and Æschines (both at Athens; and at Megalopolis) were nothing but a piece of elaborate acting. Fortunately it is not necessary to ascribe such motives in order to explain their action. It is far more probable that the state of public feeling immediately after the fall of Olynthus was such that Eubulus resolved to make a desperate effort to bring about the Panhellenic coalition, which alone could offer to Athens the least chance of defeating Philip at that time. When this attempt failed, all parties alike must have seen the inevitableness of a Peace; and Demosthenes himself

[1] See above, p. 206. [2] Dem., *l. c.*, § 306.

acted in concert with Philocrates in forwarding the negotiations, though, in the light of his subsequent conduct, we can have little doubt that he regarded the Peace only as an armistice, during which Athens might recover her strength and prepare herself to return to the struggle with renewed vigour.

Among the Athenians who had been taken prisoners in Olynthus were Iatrocles and Eucratus. (The latter is otherwise unknown; the former appears again as an ambassador to Philip.) The relatives of these men supplicated the Assembly in solemn form, laying an olive-branch upon the altar and beseeching the People to take steps to obtain the liberation of the captives; and they were supported by Philocrates and Demosthenes. In answer to their appeal, with which many others whose friends had been captured must have sympathised, the actor Aristodemus, who was on familiar terms with Philip in consequence of his professional visits to the Macedonian court, was sent to negotiate for their release.[1] Another actor, Neoptolemus, appears to have accompanied him, or at least to have travelled to Macedonia about the same time.[2] Iatrocles was set at liberty without

---

[1] Æsch., *de F. L.*, §§ 15 ff.

[2] Dem., *de F. L.*, §§ 12, 315. It is possible that Neoptolemus had been for some time bringing messages of good-will from Philip, even before Demosthenes had been convinced of the necessity of peace. For Demosthenes (*de Pace*, §§ 6, 7) describes how he had warned the People against Neoptolemus (though in vain), and this can hardly have happened after the fall of Olynthus.

ransom, and, on arriving at Athens, spoke of Philip's good-will towards the city. Aristodemus did not return for some time, owing (as Æschines tells us) to some matter of business, though others have supposed (less probably) that he was detained by Philip as a kind of hostage, when he heard of the embassies sent from Athens to the other Greek States. The Athenians became impatient at his absence, and at last—probably late in the summer of 347—the Council passed a resolution ordering him to return. He obeyed, and in his report to the Assembly again declared Philip's good-will to Athens, and added that Philip would gladly form an alliance with her. Demosthenes, who was a member of the Council for the year 347–6, and apparently an influential member,[1] proposed that the Council should not only pass the vote of thanks which was customarily given by the Council to a returning ambassador, but should also award him a crown.[2]

It was about this time that a fresh crisis occurred in the Sacred War, in consequence of which a serious complication was introduced into the relations between Athens and Philip. The war

[1] This is shown by the fact that on the entry of the Council into office, he was chosen to perform the solemn inaugural sacrifices on its behalf, and was appointed to other posts of dignity—among them those of leader of the mission sent to represent the city at the Nemean Games, and of priest to the Awful Goddesses, whose shrine lay in a cave beneath the Areopagus (*in Meid.*, § 114). See Note 2. [2] Æsch., *de F. L.*, § 17.

had been dragging on indecisively. The Phocians retained possession of the important Bœotian towns of Orchomenus, Coroneia, and Corsiæ, as well as of the places which gave them command of the Pass of Thermopylæ—Alponus, Thronium, and Nicæa. But the Delphian treasury was exhausted by the expenses of the war; and it was found that some of the Phocian leaders had been enriching themselves out of the temple treasures. Phalæcus was deprived of his command, and replaced by Democrates, Callias, and Sophanes; but since his deposition only divided the forces, and the mercenaries still remained faithful to him, he was restored to the generalship, though the strife of the factions was not healed. At this point the Thebans and Thessalians, still unable to conquer their enemy, applied for help to Philip, in the name of the Amphictyonic Council. Philip appears either to have postponed giving an answer, or at most to have sent a few soldiers, wishing to reduce the Thebans to a lower depth of humiliation before coming to terms with them—so at least Diodorus says.[1] The Phocians appealed to Athens, and the Athenians promised to help them.[2] (The promise must have been made before Philip had definitely given his adhesion to the Thebans; it would hardly have been possible to give it afterwards without

[1] Diod., XVI, lviii.
[2] Their readiness is doubtless explained by the attractive bait which the Phocians dangled before them—the control of Thermopylæ.

breaking off the negotiations for peace with Philip.) The Phocian envoys offered to place the strongholds commanding Thermopylæ in the hands of the Athenians, if they would send a force to take them over; and Proxenus, the Athenian admiral, was ordered to proceed to Thermopylæ at once. At the same time it was resolved to equip a fleet of fifty ships, and to call upon all citizens under thirty years of age, who were liable to service, to join the expedition.

But when Proxenus appeared at Thermopylæ, Phalæcus dismissed him in an insulting manner; and Archidamus, who came from Sparta in response to an appeal from the Phocian authorities, was similarly treated. For so strong was the dissension in the Phocian ranks that Phalæcus refused to acknowledge the acts of the rival faction (by which, it seems, the messages to Athens and Sparta had been sent); and he also insulted the heralds who came from Athens, in accordance with custom, to announce the religious truce at the season of the Eleusinian mysteries (September, 347), and imprisoned the envoys who had carried the appeal for help to Athens. Proxenus appears to have returned to his former station at Oreus, and the fifty ships which had been voted were of course not sent, though they lay ready in harbour in case of need.[1] For the Phocian people as a whole, the

---

[1] Dem., *de F. L.*, § 322. On the chronological difficulty see Note 3.

conduct of Phalæcus proved fatal, as will appear
hereafter.

Philip seems not to have committed himself for
some time to any definite step; for as late as the
spring of the next year, all the parties interested
appear to have been quite uncertain of his intentions.[1] He did, however, send his general Parmenio into Thessaly, to intervene in a dispute
between the towns of Pharsalus and Halus in the
interest of the former; and the treatment of Halus,
as well as that of the Phocians, became a disputed
question in connection with the peace-negotiations,
to which we may now return.

Not long after the beginning of 346, Philocrates
proposed a decree in the Assembly, that ten
ambassadors should be sent to Philip to discuss the
question of peace, as well as other matters that
were of interest to both parties, and to request
him to send plenipotentiaries to Athens, with
whom peace might be finally concluded. Demosthenes was nominated one of the ten by
Philocrates, Æschines by Nausicles[2]; and as the
assistance of Aristodemus upon the embassy was
desirable, owing to his previous friendly relations
with Philip, Demosthenes moved a resolution
in the Council that messengers should be sent to
the towns in which Aristodemus had professional

---

[1] See below, pp. 268, 274.

[2] See above, p. 177. Nausicles was probably a member of
Eubulus' party.

engagements, asking that he might be excused from fulfilling them.[1] The other members of the embassy were Iatrocles, Ctesiphon, and Phrynon (all of whom had, like Aristodemus, experienced Philip's favour), Philocrates himself, Nausicles, Dercylus, and Cimon. With them went Aglaocreon of Tenedos, as the representative of the allies of Athens.

Up to this point there is no serious doubt as to the facts (for although within a year or two, when the Peace had come to be regarded with disgust at Athens, both Demosthenes and Æschines were eager to disclaim all connection with the inception of the negotiations,[2] there can be no question that both were in fact prominently concerned in it). But from this point onwards the two orators—and they are virtually our only authorities—give quite different accounts of the facts at every stage; and neither of them scrupled to distort the truth when it suited their purpose, each being anxious to appear to have had nothing to do with Philocrates or with the steps which led to results so unwelcome to the Athenians as those which followed the Peace proved to be. Much therefore remains uncertain.

The discrepancy between the two accounts of the embassies begins even before the departure of the ambassadors from Athens. According to Demosthenes' story[3]—told in 343, when he wished

---

[1] Æsch., *de F. L.*, §§ 18, 19.   [2] Note 4.
[3] Dem., *de F. L.*, § 13.

to convict Æschines of corruption, by proving
that, having once been opposed to Philocrates, he
had inexplicably altered his mind—Æschines
came to him and suggested that they should act
in concert during their mission, and should particularly keep an eye upon "that abominable
and shameless man, Philocrates." To this story
Æschines replied, with justice, that such a proposal
would have been absurd and even impossible,
when he knew that Demosthenes had been supporting Philocrates from the outset and had been
nominated a member of the embassy by him.[1]
Æschines adds that Demosthenes (who especially
associated with Aglaocreon and Iatrocles) made
himself intolerable to his colleagues on the journey;
and that when the ambassadors were discussing
what they should say to Philip, and Cimon expressed his apprehension lest Philip should get the
better of them in argument, Demosthenes boasted
that he had an inexhaustible stream of arguments;
and that what he had to say about the Athenian
claim to Amphipolis and the origin of the war was
so convincing that he would be able to "sew up
Philip's mouth with an unsoaked rush,"—to persuade Philip to restore Amphipolis, and to induce
the Athenians to permit the return of Leosthenes,
who had been banished from Athens for his misconduct of the war.[2]

Whether this tale was true or not, the ambassadors lost no time on the journey. They did not

[1] Æsch., *de F. L.*, § 20.   [2] *Ibid.*, § 21.

16

even wait at Oreus for the herald who had been
sent in advance to procure a safe-conduct, and
who should have returned to meet them there;
instead of doing so, they sailed at once and came
to Halus, which was being besieged by Parmenio,
Philip's general; passing thence through the
Macedonian camp, they came to Pagasæ, and did
not meet the herald till they reached Larissa. On
their arrival at Pella, they were granted an interview by Philip, and addressed him in order of age,
the last place being assigned to Demosthenes, as
the youngest member of the mission.[1]

Æschines (from whom we get our only report of
the interview) describes his own speech at length,
and tells how he recounted the services rendered
by Athens in the past to Philip's house and to
Philip himself, the earlier history of the struggle for
Amphipolis, the legendary grounds for the Athenian claim to that town, and the acknowledgment of
that claim by Philip's father Amyntas. If, he
concluded, Philip based his own claim upon his
capture of the town in war, it could be justified
only if the war was a war against Athens—which
Philip had never admitted; for if it was not, he
had taken from the Amphipolitans a town which
belonged not to them, but to Athens. We can
imagine that Philip must have smiled inwardly at
this academic harangue, which Æschines retails
without any consciousness of the futility of addressing legendary and historical arguments to one

[1] Æsch., *l. c.*, §§ 22, 25.

so little likely to be swayed by such considerations.[1] We do not know what the other envoys said; but at last it came to the turn of Demosthenes, and his colleagues, Æschines tells us, expected a grand fulfilment of his boasted intentions. But instead of rewarding their expectations, he broke down hopelessly from nervousness, forgot his notes, and lost the thread of his argument; and in spite of the kindly encouragement of Philip, who bade him not take his misfortune to heart as though he had broken down on the stage, he was utterly unable to proceed, and the interview was suspended.[2]

When the ambassadors had retired, Demosthenes attacked Æschines angrily—we have still only Æschines' word for the story—and declared that he had ruined the city and her allies; and, when he was asked for an explanation, demanded if Æschines had forgotten the exhaustion of the People and their intense desire for peace. "Or is it," he asked, "those fifty ships which have been voted,[3] but will never be manned, that have made you so confident? For you have irritated Philip to such an extent by what you have said, that the result of the embassy is likely to be, not peace, but an interminable war."[4] The meaning of this scene, if it ever took place, must be that Demos-

---

[1] Such arguments however were conventional in Greek diplomacy, and Isocrates uses them, even to Philip, almost *ad nauseam*.

[2] Æsch., *l. c.* §§ 34, 35. See Note 5.

[3] The reference is to the ships which were to have been sent to Thermopylæ to join Proxenus. (See p. 238.)

[4] Æsch., *l. c.*, §§ 36, 37.

thenes was himself intensely anxious for peace, in view of the helpless condition of Athens at the moment, and thought that, by opening the question of Amphipolis, Æschines had spoiled all chance of it. (It may even have been this fear which led him to break down before Philip.) Æschines had no time to answer this attack before the herald recalled them to Philip's presence to hear his decision. Philip proceeded to reply to each of the ambassadors in order, referring with special emphasis to the arguments of Æschines—Æschines himself tells the story—but making no allusion to anything that had been said by Demosthenes. His friendly tone disproved the truth of Demosthenes' apprehensions, and Demosthenes was so mortified at being proved in the wrong that he lost control of himself, and even behaved badly at the complimentary feast to which Philip had invited the ambassadors.[1] As to the substance of Philip's answer, we learn[2] that Philip undertook not to attack the Chersonese before the Athenians had come to a decision in regard to the Peace; and the ambassadors took with them a letter from him, promising in general terms to confer great benefits on Athens if he were granted alliance as well as peace.[3]

Demosthenes, according to Æschines' story, appears soon to have regretted his unfortunate conduct; and lest it should become known at Athens, he did his best on the way home to ingratiate himself with his colleagues, promising to

[1] Æsch., *l. c.*, §§ 38, 39. [2] *Ibid.*, § 82. [3] Dem., *de F. L.*, § 40.

assist them individually in their private needs and
their public career, and lavishing fulsome praises
upon the address of Æschines to Philip; and while
they were all dining together at Larissa, he even
laughed at himself for his breakdown, and spoke
with admiration of Philip's ability. Æschines expressed his agreement, and Ctesiphon went so far
as to say that he had never seen so charming a man
as Philip. "Ah!" cried Demosthenes,"neither of
you would dare to speak of Philip in such terms
to the People!" They declared that they would
do so; and Demosthenes in turn declared that he
would hold them to their promise, while at the same
time he entreated Æschines to tell the People that
"Demosthenes also had spoken in defence of the
claim of Athens to Amphipolis."[1] (It is clear that
the People had not yet realised that the recovery
of Amphipolis, however nearly it might touch their
pride, was not practically possible; and though
the ambassadors must have known it well enough,
none of them was anxious to admit it publicly.)

The ambassadors must have re-entered Athens
about the end of March, 346. They first announced the result of their mission to the Council;
and the Council, on the motion of Demosthenes,
who spoke in laudatory terms of his colleagues, and
of Æschines in particular, decided to propose to the
People that a crown of olive should be awarded to
each of them, and that they should be invited (in

[1] Æsch., *l. c.*, §§ 40–43.

accordance with custom) to a complimentary banquet in the Prytaneum—the Guildhall of Athens.[1]

They next came before the Assembly, and spoke as had been arranged. Æschines and Ctesiphon used the language which Demosthenes had declared they would not dare to use, in praise of Philip's charm, his good memory, and his talents as a speaker; and Æschines described Philip as a thorough Hellene, and anything but a barbarian, as some called him.[2] Æschines also tells us that he remembered Demosthenes' request, and told the Assembly that he had left it to Demosthenes to say anything that might have been passed over in regard to Amphipolis. But when last of all Demosthenes rose, he turned upon his colleagues (says Æschines), and rubbing his head and making his usual fantastic gestures, rallied them upon their garrulity and their compliments to Philip. "I will show you," he said, "how to report the result of an embassy. Read the resolution under which we were sent." The clerk read it. "Well," he said, "these were our instructions, and we have fulfilled them. Here is Philip's answer, and it is for you to discuss it." This businesslike brevity met with some applause, though some (Æschines says) exclaimed at its maliciousness. Demosthenes proceeded:

Æschines thought Philip an able speaker; I did not. Any one else in the same position could have done nearly as well. Ctesiphon thought he had a

[1] Æsch., *l. c.*, §§ 45, 46.　　　　[2] Dem., *de F. L.*, § 308.

THE STATUE OF AESCHINES IN THE NAPLES MUSEUM

glorious face; to me Aristodemus the actor is just as handsome. He was, they say, a good companion to drink wine with. Our colleague Philocrates was better. It is stated that an opportunity was left me of speaking about Amphipolis; but Æschines would rather have given me a share in his life-blood than in his argument.[1] All this, in fact, is beside the point, and I propose simply that a safe-conduct be given to the herald who has come from Philip, and to the envoys who are about to proceed hither; that, when they have arrived, meetings of the Assembly be summoned for two days, to discuss the question of alliance as well as that of peace; and that, if you think we deserve it, a vote of thanks be passed to us for our services, and that we be invited to a banquet in the Prytaneum to-morrow.

Demosthenes' mockery of his colleagues, if the scene really took place, was very unworthy of him; but he can hardly be blamed for proposing to carry out the ordinary formalities of Greek diplomacy, or for asking for the conventional expressions of approval from the Assembly; and his further motion, to give Philip's envoys seats of honour at the forthcoming Dionysiac festival was (like the banquet which he gave them) a natural civility, which his enemies afterwards misconstrued as evidence of disloyalty to his country.[2]

The two meetings of the Assembly were fixed, on Demosthenes' motion, for the 18th and 19th

---

[1] See Dem., *de F. L.*, § 254.

[2] Æsch., *de F. L.*, §§ 46–55; *in Ctes.*, § 63. For Demosthenes' reply, see *de Cor.*, § 28, and *de F. L.*, §§ 234–236.

of Elaphebolion—April 15th and 16th; and it was necessary, before any treaty could be made, that the situation should be discussed by the Synod representative of the allies of Athens, which was then meeting in the city.[1] The Synod, according to Æschines, resolved to agree to peace upon such terms as the Assembly should decide; they said nothing of an alliance with Philip; but added a proposal that it should be lawful for any Greek State to become a party to the Peace within three months. The effect of the acceptance of this proposal would clearly have been to give the Phocians a chance of securing themselves against Philip and the Thebans, by joining in the Peace. They also suggested that the decision of the Assembly should be postponed until the envoys sent in the winter by Athens to the Greek States had returned; probably because they wished to discover whether the other States would be likely to favour such a general Peace; and at a later time Æschines accused Demosthenes of having hurried on the meetings of the Assembly, without waiting for the return of those envoys, and so having ruined the chance of a universal Peace. It is very probable that Demosthenes did not desire to risk the chance of any change of feeling in Athens, and that, seeing peace to be necessary, he thought it best to conclude it as soon as possible.[2]

[1] See Marshall, *The Second Athenian Confederacy*, p. 334.

[2] The evidence, which is very perplexing, is discussed in Note 7. The view given in the text seems to be the most probable.

It appears to have been resolved on the motion of Demosthenes that the discussion in the Assembly should take place on the 18th of Elaphebolion, and the voting on the proposals made (but no speeches) on the 19th.[1] At the first meeting, Philocrates proposed that alliance as well as peace should be made with Philip, but that the Phocians and Halus should be excluded from it. (The envoys sent by Philip—Antipater, Parmenio, and, probably, Eurylochus—may already have made it plain to Philocrates that Philip would not admit the Phocians, and no doubt the terms proposed were virtually dictated by Philip.) This proposal Æschines denounced in very vigorous language, declaring that he could not support it so long as a single Athenian remained alive.[2] Instead of it, he upheld the proposal of the Synod of the allies, which would have given the Phocians and the people of Halus an opportunity of participating in the Peace, since it allowed three months during which any State might declare its adhesion to the treaty.[3] Demosthenes also supported the allies' proposal, and the Assembly broke up under the impression that peace would certainly be made, but that for the alliance it would be better to wait for three months or so, in case a general arrangement should then seem desirable.[4] On the

---

[1] Æsch., *de F. L.*, § 65.
[2] Dem., *de F. L.*, § 14; Æsch., *de F. L.*, § 63.
[3] Æsch., *in Ctes.*, § 71.
[4] *Ibid.* See Note 8.

next day, despite the motion which Demosthenes had carried in regard to the procedure, there was clearly considerable discussion as well as voting.[1] But the two accounts of the proceedings are entirely different. Demosthenes claims to have spoken in favour of the resolution of the allies, and implies that he was opposed to the making of an alliance with Philip; he declares that the People would not even listen to Philocrates, who had proposed alliance as well as peace; but that Æschines rose and supported Philocrates, denouncing those who reminded the Athenians of the deeds of their forefathers in ancient days, and expressing his intention of proposing a law that the Athenians should assist no Hellenic people by whom they had not previously been assisted— meaning that in the present case they should not support the Phocians.[2] Æschines, on the contrary, declares that he did not speak on the second day at all[3]; and that the sentiments imputed to him by Demosthenes were a distortion of those which he uttered on the first day, in reply to inflammatory speeches by certain orators, who tried to prevent the making of peace at all, and pointed to the Propylæa and the Acropolis, and appealed to the memory of Salamis and the tombs and trophies of the Athenians of old. In answer to such fire-

---

[1] Æsch., *de F. L.*, §§ 65–67, denies that there was any discussion; but in the *in Ctes.*, §§ 71 ff., he himself gives an account of the discussion on the second day of the debate.

[2] Dem., *de F. L.*, §§ 15, 16, 311.   [3] Æsch., *de F. L.*, §§ 66.

brands, Æschines declared, he had urged that while
it was well to bear these great traditions in mind, it
would also be well if the People were to imitate
the wisdom of their forefathers, without falling
into their errors and their unseasonable passion
for strife; he had held up to them as a warning
the disasters brought about by the rash policy of
Cleophon in the latter part of the Peloponnesian
War, and as an example the battles of Platææ,
Salamis, and Marathon.[1]   But as to the second
day, he states that Demosthenes himself supported
Philocrates, and showed to a certain Amyntor
(who was ready to give evidence of the fact) a
resolution to the same effect as that of Philocrates
—proposing alliance as well as peace with Philip—
which he had himself drafted and was ready, if
necessary, to hand in to the chairman.[2]   In the
Speech against Ctesiphon[3] he goes farther, and
declares that Demosthenes rose without leaving
time for any one to anticipate him, and said that
the proposals of the previous day were idle, unless
Philip's ambassadors agreed to them; that it was
wrong, however much they disliked the mover and
the name of an alliance, to "snap off the alliance
from the peace"; and that instead of waiting for
the tardy adhesion of the other States before
making the alliance, they should settle the question of peace or war for themselves.[4]   Demos-

[1] Æsch., *de F. L.* §§ 74–77.   [2] *Ibid.*, §§ 67, 68.

[3] *In Ctes.*, §§ 71, 72.

[4] Almost the very opinion which Dem., *de F. L.*, § 307, attributes to Æschines!

thenes then (so Æschines says) called Antipater
and asked him directly whether he would accept
the Peace without the alliance, and received a
negative answer. This of course meant that
any one who desired the Peace must give way on
the question of the alliance.

Thus Æschines and Demosthenes each accused
the other of supporting the resolution of Philocrates as against the proposal of the allies, and of
thus becoming responsible for the exclusion and
subsequent overthrow of the Phocians. (It must
be borne in mind that the accusations were made at
a time when they had become declared enemies,
when the overthrow of the Phocians had caused
the Athenians to regard the Peace with detestation,
and when each of the orators desired to prove to the
jury that he had supported the side which had since
become the popular one.) Can we form any reasonable opinion as to their real attitude at the
time? What seems clear is that on the 18th of
Elaphebolion it appeared likely that a Peace would
be made which would leave the door open to the
Phocians and the people of Halus, and to other
Greek States, if they decided within three months
to join in an alliance; and this proposition both
Æschines and Demosthenes supported. It is also
tolerably clear that between the debates of the
18th and the 19th something happened which
convinced certain of the politicians that such a
Peace was impossible—Philocrates had probably
known this before—and this can only have been

the discovery that Philip was absolutely resolved not to agree to such terms. This must have been intimated to them by Philip's envoys. That being so, what course was open to one who, like Demosthenes, believed peace to be necessary for the time? What but to attempt to convince the People that they must give up the proposal of the allies, and accept peace on Philip's own terms, viz., the making of a Peace and an alliance at once, without waiting three months? The most obvious way of doing this was that which, according to Æschines' account, Demosthenes adopted, viz., putting the question publicly to Antipater in the Assembly; and it is highly probable that, as Amyntor told Æschines, Demosthenes had a consequential motion drafted and ready. But even when they heard Antipater's reply, the Assembly were not ready to give up the plan which they had approved of on the previous day; and it is probable that before they consented they were led in some way or other to believe that they were not really sacrificing the Phocians to Philip and the Thebans by making the alliance at once. How was this managed? The Phocians and Halus were passed over in silence; Philocrates' motion was introduced, but they were not mentioned by name; and the explanation was given, so Demosthenes says,[1] by Æschines and his friends that Philip could not receive the Phocians openly as allies, owing to his

[1] Dem., *de F. L.*, § 321; comp. Phil. II, §§ 12, 28, and see Note 9.

own existing relations with the Thessalians and Thebans; but that when the Peace was made he would act in such a way as to satisfy the Athenians. If this was so, Æschines also had changed his mind in the night, and that is perhaps the most probable account of the matter; though Æschines may have sincerely believed that Philip would act in the manner described. Nor do we find any statement that Demosthenes on this occasion expressed any other belief.

But even with these assurances before them, the People were not induced to agree to the proposal of Philocrates, until Eubulus told them bluntly that unless they accepted it (of course in its new form, without any express mention of the Phocians or Halus) they must prepare for immediate war, pay a war-tax, and devote the festival-fund to military purposes.[1] This of course was the plain truth. Philip held all the cards; and unless peace were made on his terms, there must be a war, and the People must make those very sacrifices which they had so steadily refused to make. The threat was sufficient. It was resolved that the Athenian People and their allies should make peace and alliance with Philip and his allies, and none were specially mentioned or excluded. Further, it was agreed that each of the two parties to the Peace should retain what it possessed at the time when the Peace was made[2]; and the treaty also contained various provisions in reference to freedom of trad-

[1] Dem., *de F. L.*, § 291.   [2] Hegesippus, *de Hal.*, §§ 18, 26.

ing and the suppression of piracy.[1] The same ten ambassadors were appointed to receive the oaths of Philip and his allies in confirmation of the treaty.

But who were the "allies" on either side? The advocates of peace, in order to get their proposal carried at all, had left this point indefinite; and it was this that was a principal cause of the troubles and misunderstandings of the next few years. The politicians themselves can hardly have misunderstood the situation. The allies and possessions of Philip included all whom he had conquered, and his possession of Amphipolis and Poteidæa could not be questioned. The allies of Athens were those who were actually members of her confederacy, and were represented in the Synod of the confederacy. Philip evidently did not intend, and could not be expected, to recognise her right to make peace in the name of any others. It was no small thing that the possession of the Chersonese, with the exception of Cardia, was now guaranteed to her.[2]

But obviously a less precise interpretation of the term "allies" was also current in popular language, and there was no science of international law to lay down definitions. Consequently not only orators at Athens, but even diplomatists sent to Philip's court, could make a show of arguing

[1] "Philip's Letter," § 2; comp. Hegesippus, *l. c.*, §§ 12–15.
[2] Dem., *de F. L.*, § 78.

that the allies of Athens included any people or persons with whom she had a treaty of friendship, or to whom she had promised support—the Phocians, Halus, and even Cersobleptes.[1] (This prince, though he had been forced to give hostages to Philip, was no doubt still formally on terms of friendship with Athens[2]). It was even argued at a later date that Amphipolis still belonged to Athens by right.[3]

Difficulties arose from this cause almost immediately. For, a few days after the decision had been made, the Athenians and the allies represented in the Synod, in pursuance of a motion proposed by Philocrates, took the oath to maintain the Peace, in the presence of Philip's envoys. No representative either of the Phocians or of Cersobleptes took the oath[4]; but a representative of Cersobleptes claimed to do so; and at a later time, Demosthenes and Æschines each tried to blame the other for his exclusion. Probably both were agreed at the time that Cersobleptes' envoy could not legitimately be included, and it fell to Demosthenes, as president of the Assembly held on the 25th of Elaphebolion, to give a formal ruling to that effect.[5]

When the tangled evidence is carefully studied, there can be little doubt that up to the point at

---

[1] Dem., *de Cor.*, § 27.

[2] Æsch., *de F. L.*, § 9; *in Ctes.*, § 61, describes him as the "friend and ally of the city."

[3] See below, p. 312. [4] Æsch., *in Ctes.*, §§ 73–75. [5] See Note 10.

which the Athenians swore to the treaty, Demosthenes had not changed his mind as to the necessity of making peace, and although on the first day of the debate he had made an effort to confine the treaty to a Peace, without an immediate alliance, and so to save the Phocians and Halus, he had immediately seen the necessity of giving way upon these points, and had acted accordingly. If this is so, it is impossible to relieve him of the responsibility (which he shared with his colleagues) for the consequences of the Peace, however vehemently he may have wished to repudiate it afterwards. Not that the responsibility really involves any blame, for he was fully justified in carrying into effect his conviction of the necessity of peace at the time; he was acting as the interests of his country demanded; and there is no sign, up to this point, of any serious division of opinion among the leading politicians in Athens. It is only in their respective records or falsifications of the facts, and in their comments upon them in the light of their subsequent dissensions, that differences appear. If Demosthenes is to be blamed, it is not so much for helping to make the Peace, as for trying afterwards to disown his action.

For from this point onwards the friction, which seems to have arisen from comparatively trivial and personal causes, between Demosthenes and the other ambassadors, became rapidly transformed into definite opposition, accompanied by ill-will which neither he nor they took any pains to conceal. To him, the Peace was no more than an armistice, rendered absolutely necessary by circumstances, but only tolerable because it might be turned to good account, if the opportunity were taken of preparing for a resumption of the struggle. They, on the other hand, desired a lasting Peace, such as was inconsistent with Demosthenes' ideal of national honour. No sooner, therefore, was the Peace made, than he began to think about the means of preventing Philip from gaining fresh power or extending his influence farther southward. From this point of view, every action of his colleagues which seemed to further Philip's plans, or to offer any prospect of permanence to the Peace, presented itself to his mind as treason; and this attitude of mind developed so rapidly, that (if what he declared three years later was true) he was very unwilling to serve upon the Second Embassy, and would not have done so, but for the fact that, on his previous visit to Macedonia, he had promised to take ransom-money to some of the Athenian prisoners there.

NOTES TO CHAPTER VII

1. Æsch., *de F. L.*, § 15, says simply ὑπὸ δὲ τοὺς αὐτοὺς χρόνους Ὄλυνθος ἑάλω. In the Speech against Ctesiphon, § 62, he places the acquittal of Philocrates before the beginning of Themistocles' archonship (July, 347), but does not give any nearer indication of date.

2. At a time when both Æschines and Demosthenes were anxious to disown all connection with the Peace, Æschines (*in Ctes.*, § 62) accused Demosthenes of having obtained his place in the Council by corrupt means for the express purpose of support-

ing Philocrates. But there is no doubt that this story was an invention on the part of Æschines. He made a similar assertion about Timarchus (*in Tim.*, § 106); and, as Schäfer remarks, he had not thought of this calumny against Demosthenes at the time of the Speeches on the Embassy.

3. Æsch., *de F. L.*, § 134, says that the letter of Proxenus, giving an account of the treatment he had received, and the report of the heralds of the Mysteries were read at the same meeting of the Assembly as that at which the Peace was discussed. This has caused much difficulty; for the resolution of Philocrates, constituting the First Embassy, can hardly have been proposed for some months after the rebuff by the Phocians. Consequently Schäfer and others have thought that the Mysteries referred to were the "Lesser Mysteries," held in March and therefore (according to Schäfer) announced in February. But was there any solemn announcement of these to all the Greek states, as there was of the Eleusinian Truce in September? Grote is probably right in saying that there must have been many discussions of the peace-negotiations before Philocrates' resolution was proposed, and that the news from Thermopylæ was brought during one of these.

4. Æschines disclaims connection with the early negotiations in the *de F. L.*, § 20, and the passage in the Speech against Timarchus, § 174 (delivered in 345), does not prove that he claimed any credit for the Peace then (as is sometimes supposed), but only that he expected Demosthenes to charge him with responsibility for it, along with Philocrates—in other words, that by the time of the trial of Timarchus, Demosthenes wished to disavow his own share in the matter. In the *de Cor.*, §§ 20-24, Demosthenes disclaims all share in it very insistently, but none the less falsely.

5. Schäfer, ii., p. 204, thinks that Æschines is exaggerating Demosthenes' breakdown, and that Demosthenes, as the last speaker, naturally had not much to say, but summed up briefly. This is only conjecture, though we have no means of testing the truth of Æschines' story. Plutarch's statement (Dem., xvi.) that Philip paid special attention to Demosthenes' arguments may refer to the Second Embassy, or may quite possibly be unhistorical.

6. Æschines (*in Ctes.*, § 67) says that Demosthenes at first

proposed that the Assembly should meet on the 8th of Elaphe-bolion, April 5th, without waiting for the arrival of Philip's envoys. It is of course conceivable that he proposed a preliminary discussion on that day, though it is inconceivable that any one should have suggested the giving of a final decision without hearing what Philip had to say. Æschines treats the proposal as sacrilegious, since the 8th of Elaphebolion was a feast of Asclepius and the day appointed for the Proagon, a ceremony preliminary to the Dionysiac festival. For whatever reason, the 18th and 19th, when the festival would be over, were actually chosen.

7. The testimony as regards the allies' proposal and the en-voys mentioned in it is found in Æschines, *de F. L.*, §§ 57–62, *in Ctes.*, §§ 64–70, Dem., *de F. L.*, § 16, *in Ctes.*, §§ 22, 23. The chief points are as follows:

(1) Demosthenes (*de F. L.*, § 16) is indignant with Æschi-nes for making certain remarks on the 19th of Elaphebolion, in the presence of the envoys who had come from the Greek States in response to the embassies sent from Athens, on the advice of Æschines, in the vain hope of getting up a united war against Philip. This must refer to the embassies sent out late in 347 (above, pp. 232–33).

(2) To this Æschines replies (*de F. L.*, §§ 57 ff., and *in Ctes.*, §§ 67, 70) that there were no envoys present from any Greek States, and that the Athenian ambassadors sent to the States had not returned; but he seems to suggest that it was still worth while to wait for their return, and states that the Synod of the allies wished to delay the decision of the Assembly until their arrival; and he attacks Demosthenes for having forced on the meetings of the Assembly, without waiting for the envoys, and for having thus spoiled the chance of making a universal Peace and so saving the Phocians.

(3) To this Demosthenes answers (*de Cor.*, §§ 22, 23) that there were no Athenian envoys out on a mission to the Greek States at the time, for the Greeks had all long ago been tried and found wanting.

There are thus two points (often confused with one another by modern writers) upon which the orators contradict one another:

(1) Demosthenes states that there were *envoys from the Greek States* present in Athens on the 19th of Elaphebolion, who

had come in response to the Athenian embassies sent in the previous winter. Æschines denies this; and Demosthenes himself (*de Cor.*, § 23) implies that the Greek States had generally failed to respond to those embassies. If therefore any States at all had sent envoys to Athens, it is probable that very few had done so (see below).

(2) Æschines states that certain *envoys sent from Athens to the Greek States* had not yet returned, but were still out on their mission on the 19th of Elaphebolion. (As a matter of fact some of those sent in the winter had certainly returned—he himself, for instance.) Demosthenes replies that there were *no* Athenian envoys then out on a mission to the Greek States. It is strongly in favour of Æschines' statement, that in the *de F. L.*, § 60, he quoted the actual decree of the Synod of the allies, expressly asking that the Assembly should meet "when the envoys had returned to Athens and reported the result of their mission." It is difficult to avoid concluding that there must have been *some* Athenian envoys out on a mission at the time, and they must have been either some of the envoys sent in the winter of 347–6 to get up a united war against Philip (in which case Æschines is misrepresenting the facts—in the *de F. L.*, § 57, though not in the *in Ctes.*, § 64—in describing the object of their mission as a united war *or a united peace*); *or else* envoys sent after the mission of the ten ambassadors to Philip, to invite the Greek States to join in a general Peace. Kahrstedt (*Forschungen*, p. 67) adopts the latter alternative; but there is no real evidence of the sending of such envoys, and it is highly improbable that so soon after the sending of envoys to propose a united war, the Athenians would have sent others to propose a united peace. The first alternative therefore is the more probable—that some of the envoys sent in the winter had not yet returned, and that the allies thought it desirable to wait and ascertain from them what was the feeling of the other Greek peoples before finally concluding peace. (Although the embassies had on the whole proved a failure, some of the Greek peoples may actually have sent envoys to Athens in response, as Dem., *de F. L.*, § 16, implies, and if so Æschines was telling a falsehood in denying it; though it seems almost more likely, in view of his confident challenge to Demosthenes, that he was speaking the truth, and that Demosthenes was telling a false-

hood in order to exaggerate the shockingness of Æschines' language by stating it to have been used in the very presence of the envoys. Demosthenes is also probably wrong—*de Cor.*, § 23—in saying that *no* Athenian envoys were still out on a mission.) Demosthenes probably did not wish, for the reason given in the text, to delay the conclusion of peace by waiting for the return of the envoys.

8. Demosthenes' account of the proceedings of the 18th of Elaphebolion is probably less accurate than that of Æschines. He says (*de F. L.*, § 144) that the Assembly on that day ratified the proposal of the allies, and was on the point of summoning Philip's envoys to inform them of the decision, when Æschines forced an adjournment of the question until the next day. But by his own motion, no voting could take place on the first day; the only possible "ratification" on that day can have been in the form of applause; and the adjournment of the decision to the next day was the result of his motion, not of any action of Æschines. (The procedure laid down in his motion was not followed on the second day; but there was clearly some good reason for setting it aside, and this must have commanded the assent of the Assembly. No such reason can have been suggested on the first day, upon which there seems to have been no excitement or difficulty.)

9. Demosthenes implies that the statements of Æschines and his friends as to Philip's promises and intentions were made on this occasion as well as later, in July, not only in his speech in 343 at the trial of Æschines (§ 321), but also in 344 in addressing the Assembly itself, which it would be less easy, perhaps, to mislead as to what had taken place in its presence, viz., Phil. II, §§ 12, 28, —where references are made to the promises on the strength of which Philip *obtained the Peace*. This could only apply to April, and not to July, when the Peace had already been made. Whether the statements were really made by Æschines himself, and not rather by Philocrates, may be doubted; but if they were made by Æschines, it can hardly be doubted that he believed them; for, as we shall see, he was really anxious to save the Phocians, and Demosthenes' account of Æschines' attitude towards them is the grossest perversion of the truth. It was Demosthenes himself who was prepared, if necessary, to sacrifice the Phocians, in order to obtain peace for the time.

10. According to Æschines, *de F. L.*, §§ 82–86, the Assembly met on the 25th of Elaphebolion, and Demosthenes was in the chair. At this meeting Critobulus of Lampsacus appeared, and demanded in the name of Cersobleptes (who had not been mentioned in the debates of the 18th and 19th) to be allowed to swear to the Peace among the allies of Athens. Aleximachus proposed that he should be permitted to do so; but Demosthenes refused to put the motion—the passing of which he said, would mean the breaking off of the Peace—until he was practically forced to do so. (Æschines does not say that the motion was carried.) On the other hand Æschines (*in Ctes.*, § 73–5) says that Philocrates proposed, and Demosthenes put to the vote, a resolution that the oath should be taken that day by the allies represented in the Synod then sitting; and that as there was no representative of Cersobleptes present in the Synod, Cersobleptes came to be excluded. It is obvious that these two accounts are not consistent with each other. Both speeches, however, agree that Cersobleptes was in fact excluded; for in the *de F. L.*, § 86, Æschines states that Demosthenes had charged *him* with driving Cersobleptes' representative away, when the oaths were taken, immediately after the Assembly had been broken up. Plainly the exclusion of Cersobleptes was a thing which the Athenians came afterwards to view with disfavour, and both orators try to disclaim responsibility for it. (Grote, Pt. II., ch. 89, and Hogarth, *Philip of Macedon*, p. 91, both assert that Cersobleptes' representative *was* allowed to take the oath. This seems to be contrary to the evidence. The "Letter of Philip" appears to preserve a tradition of his exclusion, though it is there ascribed to the generals of Athens, doubtless because the oaths were taken in the generals' office.)

CHAPTER VIII

THE SECOND EMBASSY AND THE PEACE OF PHILOCRATES

THE ten ambassadors, upon their appointment to serve on the Second Embassy to Philip, were instructed to administer the oath of fidelity to the treaty just negotiated, both to Philip, and also to the magistrates of the peoples allied with him, in their several cities.[1] They were further ordered to negotiate for the ransom of the Athenian prisoners who were in the hands of Philip and his subjects, and to do all that they could to serve the interests of Athens in regard to the general situation.[2] Demosthenes states also that it was forbidden that any of them should have a private interview with Philip; but it is very doubtful whether an instruction implying so strong a mistrust of them and so overtly insulting both to them and Philip was really ever given them; though it was obvious, and it may have been stated, that only their collective action would be binding upon Athens.

As soon as Philip's envoys had left the city,

[1] Dem., *de F. L.*, § 278. [2] Æsch., *de F. L.*, §§ 103, 104.

264

Demosthenes urged his colleagues to sail as quickly as possible to the Hellespont, where Philip was now operating, in order to prevent him from making conquests in that region before taking the oath, and then excusing himself on the ground that he had not yet sworn to a Peace. He knew, he said, that the Athenians would not go to war afresh on account of places so conquered, when they had once agreed to peace on general grounds. His colleagues, however, displayed no haste; and since no regular meeting of the Assembly was due for some time, he procured a decree of the Council (which had been given authority on the matter), ordering the ambassadors to depart at once, and to join Proxenus, who was still lying off the north coast of Eubœa with his ship; Proxenus was then to convey them without delay to Philip, wherever he might be. The ambassadors left Athens and met Proxenus at Oreus; but instead of sailing, delayed there in order to enable Æschines to obtain an appointment as representative or consul of Oreus at Athens.[1] At last they went, not to the Hellespontine region by sea, but by land to Pella, and arrived there twenty-three days after leaving Athens. All the time Demosthenes protested against their dilatoriness with increasing emphasis.[2]

[1] He is mentioned as holding this office in 343–2 by Dem., *de Cor.*, § 82.

[2] Dem., *de F. L.*, § 156. (Most of our information about the Second Embassy comes from §§ 150–178 of this Speech.)

After their arrival at Pella, they had still to wait twenty-seven days before Philip himself appeared. The interval was spent by Demosthenes in making arrangements for the ransom of all the Athenian prisoners he could find; and for this purpose he had taken with him a talent of his own money.[1] In the meantime Philip had captured a number of strongholds in Thrace,—Doriscus, Serrhium, the Sacred Mountain, Myrtenum, and Ergiske,[2]—and had taken Cersobleptes prisoner. Cersobleptes' kingdom thus passed into Philip's power, though he did not remain in captivity— his son being already a hostage—but was allowed to remain nominally in possession of his dominions, though no doubt under conditions.

When, at a later date, the Athenian Eucleides was instructed to ask Philip for an explanation of his action in Thrace, Philip answered that he was within his rights, since he had conquered these places before he met the ambassadors or took the oath.[3] Demosthenes lays great stress on these conquests, as evidence of the faithlessness of Philip, and of the injury done to Athens through the dilatoriness of his colleagues. But in reality Philip's defence was a good one; and the fact that in 341 Demosthenes[4] thought it worth while to

[1] The attempt of Æschines, *de F. L.*, §§ 99, 100, to cast discredit upon Demosthenes' charitable work is unconvincing.

[2] Some of these places were probably unimportant, and Æschines scoffs at Demosthenes for his lamentation over places which no one had ever heard of before.

[3] Schol. on Dem., *de F. L.*, § 162.   [4] Phil. III, § 15.

invent the certainly false statement that Philip
had already taken the oath when he captured
these places, shows that he was conscious of the
soundness of Philip's case when the facts were
truly stated. Indeed, according to Æschines'
account[1] of the matter, Philip had captured Cersobleptes and the Sacred Mountain on the day
before the Athenians themselves took the oath,
and therefore before the ambassadors left Athens;
and as evidence of this, he produced a letter from
Chares. We cannot then tell whether the delay
of the ambassadors really injured the interests of
Athens at all. But, however this may have been,
Philip was within his rights in acting as he had
done: for these strongholds did not belong to
Athens at all, but to Cersobleptes; and though
Chares was defending them, it was for Cersobleptes,
who was at war with Philip, that he was doing so;
and Philip kept his word faithfully in not attacking the Chersonese. Further, it may be doubted
whether Philip would really have brought to an
end his conquests in Thrace (as Demosthenes
said he would have), even if the ambassadors had
proceeded directly thither and received his oath.
He would have been under no obligation to do so;
but the Athenians were so accustomed to regard
that region as within their own sphere of influence,
that Demosthenes found no difficulty (in 343) in
speaking of the loss of it as a loss to Athens, and
as due to the disobedience of the ambassadors to

[1] Æsch., *de F. L.*, § 89–92.

their instructions. No doubt the conquest of Cersobleptes' kingdom brought Philip nearer to the Chersonese, and this is what Demosthenes had sought to prevent; but he had no right to complain that Philip was playing Athens false. Nor is there any proof that the delay of the ambassadors was due to their corruption by Philip or his agents, though, if Demosthenes was telling the truth, they did contravene their instructions.

When Philip returned to Pella, he found there representatives of many Greek States, each hoping to persuade him to fall in with their wishes. He made himself agreeable to all, and seems to have led all alike to imagine that they were certain of success. Besides the Athenian ambassadors, there were envoys from Thebes, bent upon urging Philip to cross the Pass of Thermopylæ and terminate the Sacred War in their interest; there were Spartans, who hoped for the commission of the Delphian temple to the care of their kinsmen, the Dorians of Mount Parnassus, and also doubtless wished to deprecate Philip's intrigues with their enemies in the Peloponnese; there were Phocians, who had every reason to attempt to agree with the adversary quickly; and there were Eubœans, who in all probability were not well disposed towards Athens, and desired to retain Philip's support.

Philip appears to have courted the good-will of the Athenian representatives by lavish generosity. Demosthenes states that offers of large

sums of money were first made privately to each
of them; that when one of them refused—he coyly
abstains from mentioning his own name—Philip
sent a large sum to them all in common; and that
when he himself prevented the acceptance of it
in this form, his colleagues divided the sum among
themselves, in addition to what they had already
received. For his own part, he tells us, he asked
Philip to use the money, which he was offering the
ambassadors, to redeem the captive Athenians
from those of his subjects who had come into
possession of them, and that Philip, not liking to
reply that Demosthenes' colleagues had taken the
money, consented to do this, but postponed the
fulfilment of his undertaking, promising to send
the prisoners back in time for the Panathenæa.[1]
How much truth there is in this story, apart from
Philip's promise to send home the prisoners, we
cannot tell. Æschines declared that the other
ambassadors, having learned wisdom from the
trick played on them by Demosthenes on their
previous journey,[2] kept aloof from him,[3] and this
may have helped to make him unduly suspicious
of them. But that Philip tried to secure friends
for himself in Athens by lavishing presents upon
the ambassadors is more than probable, when we
know the use which he made of Macedonian gold
elsewhere; the pretext of hospitality to his guests
was a convenient one, and may have served to

[1] Dem., *de F. L.*, §§ 166–171.   [2] See above, p. 245.
[3] Æsch., *de F. L.*, § 97.

quiet their consciences. That scrupulous absten-
tion from all appearance of evil, which is demanded
of public servants at the present day, was not
expected, or at least was rarely found, in ancient
Greece.

The Theban envoys, Demosthenes tells us,
proved absolutely incorruptible; though it may be
doubted whether he is right in concluding that
the success of the Thebans was due to the impression made upon Philip by the conduct of their
ambassadors. Philip's perception of his interest
was hardly likely to be affected by such edifying
examples.[1]

It is evident that there was considerable dissension between Demosthenes and his colleagues
as to the way in which they were to carry out their
instructions.[2] They first read their instructions
aloud; and for some time the discussion turned
on points of minor importance. At last, Æschines
says, fearing that matters of greater weight would
be overlooked entirely, he reminded his colleagues
that while, of course, they were bound to receive
the oaths of Philip and his allies, and to negotiate
for the ransom of the prisoners, the real difficulty
lay in the execution of the injunction to do their
best for the interest of Athens in general. He
himself interpreted this instruction as having
reference to the advance of Philip to Thermopylæ,

[1] Dem., *de F. L.*, §§ 139–142.
[2] We are here dependent on Æschines (*de F. L.*, §§ 108–117)
for our information.

which every one assumed to be about to take place,
as it was evidently Philip's intention to bring the
Sacred War to an end; and he understood the wish
of the Athenian People to be that they should try
to persuade Philip to humble the Thebans, ard
to set up the walls of those cities of Bœotia which
the Thebans had destroyed. This had not been
expressed in the decree of the Assembly, only
because, if they failed in their object, it would be
better that the intention of the People should not
be generally known. It would be wrong, he declared, for the ambassadors of Athens to shrink
from coming to the point, for fear of incurring
the hostility of the Thebans. But Demosthenes
(Æschines declared) loudly protested against this
proposal, asserting that it was not the business
of the ambassadors to set up strife between Athens
and Thebes. "Let Philip go to Thermopylæ,"
said he; "no one will prosecute me for any movements of Philip with his army; but only for any
words or actions that are not covered by our
instructions." The result of the discussion was
that it was arranged that each of the ambassadors
should say to Philip what he thought it desirable to
say.

When the time for their interview with Philip
came, Demosthenes, though the youngest of the
ambassadors, insisted on speaking first, in order
that everything might not be said by others, before
his turn came. He began his address to Philip
by hinting that the ambassadors were not all

there with the same object, and proceeded to recount and emphasise his own services in forwarding the peace-negotiations, and the attentions which he had paid to Philip's envoys (upon which he laid such stress that his colleagues were thoroughly ashamed); he concluded with some very tasteless remarks about Philip himself, alluding sarcastically to the complimentary language that his colleagues had used. "I have not called you beautiful, for woman is the most beautiful thing on earth; nor a good drinker, for that, I conclude, is the way to praise a sponge; nor have I praised your memory; for such adulation is a task for a hireling sophist"; and he concluded amid the laughter of the assembled envoys of all the Greek States. Then Æschines rose, he tells us; and after remarking that the ambassadors had not been sent by the Athenians to defend their own actions, but had been chosen on account of their personal character, he spoke briefly of the ratification of the treaty, which they had come to obtain, and the other points definitely contained in their instructions; and then passed on to Philip's intended march to Thermopylæ. He begged Philip, if possible, to settle the questions in which the Amphictyonic powers were interested not by force of arms, but by a vote of the Council, after a regular trial of the case; but if that were impossible (as he supposed it was, since Philip's army was assembled and ready to start), he begged to put before Philip certain considerations arising out of the constitution of the Amphictyonic League, and the oath which bound its members together. This oath the Thebans had transgressed in destroying the Bœotian cities; and although it was right to punish the sacrilege committed against the temple at Delphi, it was those who had committed it that should be punished, and not their countries. Finally, he called upon Philip not to ratify by force the wrong-doing of the Thebans; and warned him, if he supported Thebes, to expect no gratitude from her.

It is not very difficult to gather from this account what policy Æschines and Demosthenes respectively had in view. Æschines seems to have made an honest attempt to save the Phocians, and to turn Philip's forces against Thebes by a recital of the misdeeds of the Thebans and a discussion of constitutional questions, though these could hardly be expected to influence Philip. This was certainly the policy which the majority of the People of Athens would have approved, as the debates upon the Peace had shown; and Æschines was probably right in his interpretation of the rather vague instructions given to the ambassadors.

Demosthenes looked somewhat farther ahead. He saw that if Philip were to possess himself of the Pass of Thermopylæ, and so to obtain the power to march farther southward, when he chose, the best chance of averting the submission of Athens to him would be in a combination between Athens and Thebes; and he did not want to cut off

18

all hope of this by taking a line hostile to Thebes
at Philip's Court. Accordingly he desired to confine the action of the ambassadors to the receiving
of the oaths and the ransoming of the captives.
His colleagues were probably aware of his object;
but the prevailing dislike of the Thebans was so
great that they could have no sympathy with him.
"To crown all his faults," Æschines declared,[1]
"he is a pro-Theban." But assuming—as Demosthenes assumed and his colleagues did not—that
the Peace was to be only an armistice, and that
the war against Philip was to be renewed so soon
as Athens was in a condition to renew it, Demosthenes' caution was probably wise.

Philip's own aim was doubtless by this time
tolerably well-defined. He intended, sooner or
later, to conquer both Thebes and Athens, or to
make satisfactory terms with them, but he was in
no hurry, and for the time it was quite convenient
to him to support Thebes, and so keep Athens
powerless. He must have seen, as clearly as Demosthenes saw, that the one thing which might
thwart him would be an alliance between Athens
and Thebes. Besides this, his prestige would suffer if he at once threw over the Thebans, with
whom he was supposed to be on friendly terms.
He therefore went his way as he had planned, but
played with the envoys of the various States until
the time came for him to make the decisive move;
and there is no reason to doubt that he led some

[1] Æsch., *de F. L.*, § 106.

at least of the Athenians (of course without making
any official intimation) to believe that he really
intended to march against Thebes, just as he led
the Spartans to believe that he would fulfil their
particular wishes. (So certain of this did the
Spartans feel, that they ventured to use threatening language to the Thebans present.[1]) He may
even have led the Phocians themselves to hope
for his favour.[2]

Philip declared his acceptance of the Peace at
Pella[3]; and the ambassadors remained there until
he was ready to proceed southwards. They then
accompanied him and his army as far as Pheræ;
and there the oaths were taken, Demosthenes
says,[4] in an insulting manner, in an inn; and the
ambassadors, instead of visiting Philip's allies in
their several cities and administering the oath to
their respective magistrates, were content to receive it at Pheræ from the persons introduced by
Philip as the representatives of his allies. Demosthenes perhaps exaggerates the importance to
Philip of preventing the Athenian ambassadors
from making a tour of the States allied to himself;
but Philip may well have thought that they might
cause mischief. That they disobeyed their instructions in not making such a tour seems certain;
but they probably attached little importance to
the manner of the ratification, so long as the

---

[1] Æsch., *de F. L.*, § 136.   [2] Dem., Phil. III, § 11.
[3] Dem., *de Cor.*, § 32. See Note 1 at the end of the Chapter.
[4] Dem., *de F. L.*, § 158.

ratification itself was secured. The Phocians, the people of Halus, and Cersobleptes had already been tacitly excluded from participation in the Peace, and it is probable that Philip expressly declared, before taking the oath, that they were not covered by the treaty to which he swore.[1] The representatives of Cardia took the oath among the allies of Philip; and though Demosthenes afterwards[2] blamed his colleagues for permitting this, he was not justified in doing so; for Cardia had been specially excepted from the towns in the Chersonese given up to Athens by Cersobleptes, and had made alliance with Philip in 352.

The ambassadors had now finished their work, and had only to make their report. Demosthenes (who had already tried to go home in advance of his colleagues, in order to denounce their alleged misconduct, and had chartered a vessel for the purpose, but had been prevented) drew up a draft-report, which his colleagues naturally rejected. They sent instead a letter drawn up by themselves, announcing the accomplishment of their mission.[3] They then proceeded homewards, bearing with them a letter from Philip, which Demosthenes afterwards asserted (no doubt falsely) to have been composed by Æschines at a private interview with Philip on the river Lydias in Macedonia,

[1] Dem., *de F. L.*, § 44.

[2] *Ibid.*, § 174; comp. *de Pace*, § 25; *de Chers.*, § 66.

[3] Dem., *de F. L.*, § 174.

before they started for Pheræ.[1] At the same time Philip marched towards Thermopylæ, and arrived there before the ambassadors reached Athens. They re-entered the city on the 13th of Scirophorion, or about July 6th.

The ambassadors had now to meet the Council, the Assembly, and the Board of Auditors or Logistæ, whose approval was required in the case of every public official on the termination of his office. In the Council, Demosthenes immediately denounced his colleagues as guilty of misconduct upon the embassy, and recounted the history of the negotiations from the beginning. Doubtless the charges which he made against them in the first instance were based on their delay at the outset, their failure to go direct to Philip in Thrace, and the manner in which they had allowed Philip's allies to take the oath. (He can hardly at this stage have charged them, as he did afterwards, with injuring the prospects of the Phocians.) The Council were convinced by his statement, and withheld from the ambassadors the compliments which were almost invariably paid to such persons—the vote of thanks, and the invitation to a banquet in the Prytaneum.[2]

Demosthenes further states[3] that he entreated

---

[1] Dem., *de F. L.*, § 36; Æsch., *de F. L.*, § 124. The gross insinuations which Demosthenes (*de F. L.*, § 175) makes against Æschines, who left Pheræ twenty-four hours later than his colleagues, are doubtless malicious inventions.

[2] Dem., *de F. L.*, §§ 18, 31, 32.   [3] *Ibid.*, § 18.

the Council that Proxenus, who was still lying with his squadron off the north coast of Eubœa, should be instructed to go to Thermopylæ, and prevent Philip from crossing the Pass. This statement it is very difficult to believe; it may well have been manufactured after the overthrow of the Phocians, when he was very anxious that the People should imagine that he had tried his hardest to prevent that calamity, and that his colleagues had deliberately helped Philip to accomplish it. It is most improbable that he wished to break the Peace at once, when the object for which he had desired it was unachieved; and the interference of Proxenus would have rendered the prospect of the alliance with Thebes, for which he ultimately hoped, more remote. Nor do we hear anything about the bringing of such a proposal before the People.

The Assembly met on the 16th of Scirophorion (July 10th). According to Demosthenes' account of the proceedings, Æschines rose without waiting for the resolution drafted by the Council to be read,[1] and announced that he had persuaded Philip to grant all the desires of the Athenians, and that there was no occasion for the alarm which

[1] This resolution should have contained the proposal about Proxenus, had any such been made. It is very doubtful whether Æschines would have been allowed to anticipate the promulgation of a resolution of the Council; and probably Demosthenes was trying to account for the fact that no one had ever heard of his proposal about Proxenus, by saying that Æschines prevented them from doing so by rising first.

THERMOPYLAE, THE PASS

PHOTO BY DR. G. B. GRUNDY

his arrival at Thermopylæ had occasioned; for if the Athenians would only wait for two or three days, they would hear that Thebes was being besieged, that Thespiæ and Platææ were being restored, and that the money due to the temple of Delphi was being exacted, not from the Phocians, but from the Thebans, who had themselves planned the seizure of the temple; for he had persuaded Philip, he said, that to plan such a deed was as impious as to commit it; and on this account the Thebans had set a price on his own head. He also gave the Assembly to understand that Philip would restore Athens to her old position in Eubœa —that was at least what the Eubœans themselves expected—and he added that there was yet another matter which he had arranged with Philip, but he did not wish to mention it yet, since even now some of his colleagues were jealous of him. This, Demosthenes says, was intended as a hint at the restoration of Oropus to Athens. Philip's letter was also read to the Assembly. In it Philip explained the fact that the ambassadors had not visited his allies severally by saying that he had himself retained them to help him effect a reconciliation between the two hostile Thessalian towns, Pharsalus and Halus. (Whether they really attempted to forward such a reconciliation we do not know. In any case Halus capitulated to Philip not long afterwards, and the inhabitants were banished or enslaved.[1]) He

[1] Dem., *de F. L.*, §§ 36–39.

also offered to do anything to gratify the Athenians that was consistent with his honour; but no specific promises were mentioned. This last fact made Demosthenes suspect that the promises made by Æschines were not genuine, and were made through the mouth of Æschines in order that no one might be able afterwards to accuse Philip himself of breaking his word. He therefore rose and denied all knowledge of any such intention on Philip's part, and tried to give his reasons for disbelieving in them; but being refused a hearing, owing to the insulting interruptions of Æschines and Philocrates, and the unwillingness of the People to disbelieve such good news, he contented himself with solemnly asserting his own disbelief in the promises, and disclaiming all credit, if they should be realised; while Philocrates remarked insolently, "No wonder that Demosthenes and I cannot agree! for he drinks water and I drink wine"; at which the audience laughed.

Such is Demosthenes' account of the debate,[1] and Æschines' attempt[2] to disprove its substantial truth is on the whole unconvincing. He denies that he made any promises: he admits that he had told Philip that in his own opinion Thebes ought to be a part of Bœotia, and not Bœotia a depend-

---

[1] Dem., *de F. L.*, §§ 19–26, 34–41, 44–46, 68, 102, 220; *de Cor.*, 35. Substantially the same account is found in the Speech on the Peace, §§ 9, 10, delivered very soon after the events and therefore more reliable; comp. also Phil. II, §§ 29, 30.

[2] Æsch., *de F. L.*, §§ 119–123.

ency of Thebes; and this, he says, was the only basis for Demosthenes' description of his speech. He also gives a slightly different version of the alleged conversation between himself and the Eubœan representatives. But when he admits so much, we can hardly fail to discern that he and his supporters did lead the Assembly to believe that Philip meant no ill to the Phocians. The result of the debate was the passing of a decree proposed by Philocrates, thanking Philip for his promised acts of justice, extending the Peace and alliance with Philip to posterity, and declaring that if the Phocians refused to surrender the temple of Delphi to the Amphictyons, Athens would take steps against those responsible for the refusal.[1] It is inconceivable that the Assembly should have passed this resolution, and recommended the Phocians to lay down their arms, had they thought that the Phocians would be treated as they afterwards were treated. Some one must either have caused them or allowed them to think that Philip would act generously towards them, and would not give way to the wishes of the Thebans. Æschines stated[2] at his trial in 343 that every one expected this, since no one believed that Philip would wish to render Thebes more powerful, and so more dangerous to himself; and that the ambassadors received the same impression from what they had seen and heard in Philip's camp. It may be taken

---

[1] Dem., *de F. L.*, §§ 47, 48; comp. §§ 55, 310.

[2] Æsch., *de F L.*, § 136.

as certain, therefore, that Æschines' own speech
on the 16th of Scirophorion confidently expressed
that view, though it was probably expressed with
perfect sincerity; and it is a confirmation of this,
that in 345, at the trial of Timarchus, Æschines
still spoke in sanguine terms of Philip's promises
to Athens, and of his hope of their fulfilment.[1]

Very shortly after the return of the ambassadors
from the Second Embassy, Philip sent two letters,
inviting the Athenians, now his allies, to send a
force to join his own army at Thermopylæ, and to
help in the decision of the questions in which the
Amphictyons were interested. Now this was
just what, if Æschines' account of Philip's intentions was correct, Philip might have been expected
to do; and it is very probable that he desired to
have an Athenian force at his side, to counteract
the influence of the Thebans in case the latter
should pursue an extreme policy, or attempt to
aggrandise themselves to an inconvenient extent,
Moreover, if the Phocians were to be helped at all,
it might well seem that the Athenians had now an
opportunity of using their influence to help them.
The invitation, however, was declined, on the
advice of Demosthenes and on the motion of
Hegesippus. Different reasons are given for the
refusal. On the one hand, the fear was suggested
by the anti-Macedonian party that Philip would

[1] Æsch., *in Tim.*, § 169. See Note 2.

THE VIEW FROM THERMOPYLAE

FROM A DRAWING BY H. M. PICKARD-CAMBRIDGE

keep the Athenian soldiers as hostages[1]; and on the other, the People may have been influenced, as Demosthenes asserts,[2] by the idea that the invitation showed that Philip meant no harm to the Phocians, and that therefore no action was necessary—a conclusion which they were always ready to adopt, and which was almost, if not quite, as much to Philip's advantage as their acceptance of his invitation would have been. Whether Demosthenes really feared treachery on Philip's part, or whether he was convinced that the Phocian cause was hopeless, and desired to avoid a fruitless collision with Thebes, there is no direct evidence to show. Æschines[3] attributes Demosthenes' action expressly to his leaning towards Thebes, and he is very likely right.

The Assembly had appointed ten ambassadors to convey to Philip the resolution of the 16th of Scirophorion. Demosthenes had been nominated as one of the ten, but in spite of much pressure, had refused to serve, and had entered a sworn excuse.[4] Æschines had also been elected, but either declined the office, or else failed to start at the same time as his colleagues, on account of illness.[5] But when the ambassadors had travelled no further than Chalcis in Eubœa, they were met with the news that Phalæcus and the Phocian mercenary army had surrendered to Philip on the

---

[1] Æsch., *de F. L.*, § 137.
[2] Dem., *de F. L.*, §§ 51, 52.
[3] Æsch., *de F. L.*, § 141.
[4] Dem., *de F. L.*, § 122.
[5] Note 3.

23d of Scirophorion (July 17th). There can be little doubt that treachery had been at work here; possibly Phalæcus, whose dissensions with the rival party among the Phocians have already been mentioned,[1] had had an understanding with Philip for some time; and certainly the terms of surrender permitted him and his eight thousand mercenaries to go to the Peloponnese unmolested, and thus left the Phocian people entirely at the mercy of Philip and his Theban and Thessalian allies; for the Spartan force, which had marched under Archidamus to help them, had returned home when they saw the position of affairs.

Demosthenes represents the surrender of the Phocians as the consequence of the resolution of Philocrates which the Assembly had passed on the 16th of Scirophorion, and therefore lays upon Philocrates and Æschines the whole responsibility for the fate of the Phocians. His argument, however, plausible as it is, must be pronounced quite unconvincing. Nothing could have saved the Phocians. Financial exhaustion, internal division, and treachery were the cause of their overthrow; and it is extremely doubtful whether their surrender was in any way hastened by the news of the debate in Athens, or by the impression conveyed by the speeches of Æschines and his colleagues, that Philip intended to deal generously with the Phocians.[2] Æschines was quite justified in replying that it was not his speeches, but the

[1] See above, p. 226.   [2] Note 4.

presence of Philip's army, that brought about the capitulation; but that if any action on the part of Athens had aggravated the disaster, it was the refusal of the Athenians, on Demosthenes' advice, to join Philip and use their influence to save the Phocians.

On hearing of the capitulation of Phalæcus, the Athenian ambassadors at once returned home. The first to reach Athens was Dercylus, who gave the news to the Assembly during a meeting which was held at the Peiræus in reference to the dock-yards, on the 27th of Scirophorion (July 21st). The intelligence was received with the utmost horror and alarm by the People, who had evidently been relieved of all apprehension for their Phocian allies, but were now panic-stricken lest Philip should intend to march into Attica itself. On the motion of Callisthenes, the Assembly resolved to bring in the women and children and movable property from the country, to strengthen the frontier garrisons, to fortify the Peiræus, and to hold the rural festival of Heracles within the city walls. They also instructed the ambassadors to depart once more for Philip's camp, and to do what they could to ameliorate the situation. Æschines now went with his colleagues, and found Philip engaged, along with the Thebans, in celebrating the success of his plans with high festivities, in which (according to Demosthenes[1]) they heartily joined. It was not, in fact, a time to make a de-

[1] Dem., *de F. L.*, §§ 128-130.

monstration of hostility to Philip by refusing his
hospitality, and Æschines probably acted with
tact, though by doing so he gave an opportunity
to his enemies to misrepresent his motives.[1]

Philip naturally made his mastery of the Phocian
territory complete, garrisoning those towns which
surrendered to him, and storming and destroying
those which did not. At the same time, he sent
a letter to Athens, announcing what he had done,
and expressing his astonishment at the hostile
attitude which the People had adopted, seeing
that the Phocians were not included in the Peace.[2]
He next summoned the Amphictyonic Council,
as Æschines had previously urged him to do.[3]
The representatives of the Bœotians and the
Thessalian tribes were doubtless in a majority,
the Thessalians having of course recovered their
Amphictyonic rights, of which the Phocians had
deprived them. The Œtæans proposed that all
the adult males of the Phocians should be executed
as guilty of sacrilege. Such savagery as this was
not approved by the Council; but it was decided
that the Phocian towns should be destroyed and
the inhabitants settled in hamlets of not more than

[1] Demosthenes' argument (*de F. L.*, §§ 126, 127) that it was
remarkable that Æschines should go to the Theban camp, if the
Thebans had set a price on his head, is also misleading; for, as
an ambassador, he would be safe in any case.

[2] The "Letter of Philip" cited in Dem., *de Cor.*, § 39, is probably not genuine; and Grote appears to be right in thinking that
the real letter must have been more conciliatory in tone.

[3] See above, p. 272.

fifty houses each—the hamlets to be at least two hundred yards apart; that the Phocians should be permitted to own the land, but should repay to the temple, by annual instalments of sixty talents, the value of the stolen treasure, and should not be allowed to possess horses or arms until the repayment had been completed; and that those who had fled should be liable to arrest anywhere, as being under a curse for their sacrilege.[1] The destruction of the towns was carried out by the Thebans, and the country was garrisoned with Macedonian troops.[2]

Æschines claims to have saved the Phocians from a worse fate by his efforts at the meeting,[3] and in fact, when the customs of Greek warfare are considered, it is doubtful whether they were harshly dealt with. The wholesale enslavement and the executions which generally followed a capitulation were conspicuously absent; and the life in villages, and those very near to one another,[4] was no serious hardship to an agricultural people. No doubt the condition to which they were reduced was painful enough. The Thebans probably went beyond the letter of the sentence, or at least spared no cruelty in carrying it out[5]; and most of those of the inhabitants who had the courage or the means withdrew into exile, in preference to submitting

---

[1] Diod., XVI, ix. [2] Dem., *de F. L.*, § 81.
[3] Æsch., *de F. L.*, §§ 142, 143.
[4] Not, of course, near enough for the formation of large strongholds by uniting the villages. [5] Justin, VIII, v.

to the new conditions.[1]   The pathetic picture
which Demosthenes afterwards drew of the state
of Phocis may not be greatly exaggerated.

Men of Athens [he says[2]], the horror and the im-
mensity of this calamity have never been surpassed
in our day in the Hellenic world, nor even, I believe,
in the time before us. . . .   The nature of the ruin
which the unhappy Phocians have suffered may be
seen, not only from these decrees, but also from the
actual results of the action taken; and an awful and
piteous sight it is, men of Athens.   For when recently
we were on our way to Delphi, we could not help
seeing it all—houses razed to the ground, cities
stripped of their walls, the land destitute of men in
their prime—only a few poor women and children left,
and some old men in misery.   Indeed no words can
describe the distress now prevailing there.

But it is doubtful whether, according to Greek
ideas, the guilt of sacrilege was not lightly
atoned for.   For Orchomenus and Coroneia, the
Bœotian cities which had helped the Phocians,
there was no mercy.   These the Thebans destroyed
utterly, and sold the inhabitants as slaves; and
the supremacy of Thebes over Bœotia was once
more complete.

The Amphictyonic Council transferred to Philip
the two votes which the Phocians had possessed
at their meetings; and in order to punish the States
which had given or promised assistance to the

---

[1] Dem., *de F. L.*, § 80.   [2] *Ibid.*, §§ 64, 65.

THE STADIUM AT DELPHI (SCENE OF THE PYTHIAN GAMES)

PHOTO BY ALINARI

Phocians, the Council took from Athens the right to precedence in consulting the oracle, which they had hitherto enjoyed, and gave this also to Philip. The Spartans were forbidden to enter the temple at all. Finally, it was resolved that Philip should preside over the Pythian games at Delphi in September, 346.

The news of these decrees of the Council was received at Athens with great indignation, and was followed by a strong revulsion of feeling against the Peace and its advocates. Both Sparta and Athens refused to send their usual official deputations to attend the Pythian games, though Æschines appears to have been present as Philip's guest.[1] This omission the Amphictyonic Councillors were not disposed to pass over, and they sent an embassy to Athens, bearing a letter from Philip, and demanding that the Athenians should recognise him as an Amphictyonic Power in place of the Phocians. Æschines supported the request, pleading that Philip's action had been dictated by the Thebans and Thessalians, in whose hands he had been.[2] But so strong was the feeling against him and against Philip, that the Assembly would not hear him; and so, says Demosthenes, "he stepped down from the platform, and showing off before the envoys who had come from Philip, told them that there were plenty of men who made a clamour, but few who took the field when it was required of them."

[1] Dem., *de F. L.*, § 128.　　[2] Dem., *de Pace*, § 22; Phil. II, § 14.

It would, however, have been the height of folly to have brought down upon Athens at this moment the united strength of Philip and the Thebans and Thessalians; and Demosthenes himself intervened to prevent this, and for this purpose delivered the Speech on the Peace, which has come down to us. Athens therefore gave the required recognition, and the Peace remained for the time undisturbed.

The result of the events of the two years between the autumn of 348 and that of 346 was that Philip had gained all that he had set out to gain, with no loss to himself, by the skilful handling of men and circumstances. He had secured a foothold to the south of Thermopylæ; his soldiers or allies held the Pass and the neighbouring town of Nicæa. (Nicæa itself was committed to the Thessalians, and they were also given control of Magnesia.) Phocis was held by Macedonian garrisons; and if he desired to march farther south there was nothing to hinder him. His recognition as an Amphictyonic Power had given him a definite position as the head of a Hellenic State, and the part which he had played as the champion of the god was one which brought with it a certain prestige.

Just after the Peace had been concluded at Athens in April, and before the surrender of the Phocians in July, the aged Isocrates addressed a letter to Philip, urging him to put himself at the head of the forces of the Greek States and lead a great expedition to the conquest of the East.

This union in a great enterprise, the old man argued, would heal the discords of the States with one another, and would enable them to rid themselves of the mercenary armies which were the curse of the time; for when the conquest of Asia was accomplished, the mercenaries could be settled in cities to be planted in these new dominions. In spite of the garrulity, the almost pathetic self-consciousness, and the want of all sense of proportion which the letter displays, there was something prophetic in the aged writer's advice. Philip may indeed have already conceived the great design which Alexander was destined to carry out; but it is at least possible that it was first suggested by Isocrates; though his fancy that the Greek States would take part in it voluntarily, before they were decisively conquered, and that their discords would vanish in the enthusiasm of a worthy common aim, was sadly out of date, and was never destined to be realised. Even if Philip was not inspired by Isocrates, the writings of Isocrates were widely read, and may have prepared men's minds for the announcement of the great design when the time came. Philip, however, was not yet ready. He at least had no misunderstanding as to the temper of the Greek States; and the hill-tribes on the northern and western frontiers of Macedonia claimed his attention. In the meantime he could feel tolerably secure against the fear of any hostile movement south of Thermopylæ.

The position of Athens was a far less enviable one than that of Philip. It was long before the People recovered from their remorse at the fate of their allies, the Phocians, for whose preservation they had done nothing; and Demosthenes took full advantage of this feeling to renew by degrees a more active hostility to Philip, whom he regarded with implacable determination as the enemy of his country's freedom.

The question of the responsibility of the several Athenian statesmen for the events of the years 348 to 346 is a very vexed one. But if the view which we have so far taken is correct, Demosthenes deserves no serious blame, however unattractive his behaviour on certain occasions may have been. He had plainly worked for the Peace from the time of the fall of Olynthus, until the Athenians swore to the treaty. But regarding the Peace simply as a breathing-space, to be spent in preparation for war, he had been anxious that the alliance with Philip should not be given too intimate or too permanent a character; and he had therefore strongly opposed Philocrates' motion to extend it to posterity, and he had attempted to secure the repulse of any friendly overtures which Philip made. Above all, he had looked forward to the future, and saw that the day would come when the Thebans might be ready and even glad to make alliance with Athens; and that whenever hostilities with Philip were renewed, the prime need of

Athens, herself a sea-power, would be that of a
land army to co-operate with her. For this he
could not look to Sparta, though Athens was on
friendly terms with the Spartans. For not only
was the day of the greatness of Sparta over, but the
freedom of action of the Spartans would always be
held in check by the other Peloponnesian peoples.
He could look only to Thebes. And so, although
it was impossible, in the existing state of feeling
in Athens, to advocate this policy openly, he had
opposed every step which might deepen the enmity
between the Athenians and the Thebans; and had
taken little or no part (so far as we can gather) in
advocating the sending of assistance to the Phocians, although when their ruin was accomplished,
he made it his main argument in his attacks upon
his opponents—a proceeding which it is impossible
to view without a certain disgust, and which can
only be justified in a very slight degree by the
patriotic ideal, the realisation of which he hoped
to advance by such unhappy means.

But what is to be said of the part played by
Philocrates and Æschines? Were they, as Demosthenes urged, the corrupt hirelings of Philip, working deliberately against what they knew to be the
interest of their country? It is very difficult to
prove this. With regard to the making of the
Peace in the first instance, there need be no question that they acted in perfect good faith; and
Æschines' change of mind between the two debates
on the 18th and 19th of Elaphebolion—the time

from which many writers are inclined to date his corruption by Philip's envoys—was probably made with perfect honesty, when he found that Philip was prepared to allow the Athenians less latitude than they had hoped. The delay of the ambassadors in carrying out some of their instructions and their failure to fulfil others to the letter must be admitted to have been grave faults in men placed in such a position of reponsibility. Yet it is extremely doubtful whether these faults had in fact any very serious consequences. It is very uncertain whether the ambassadors could have succeeded in preventing Philip from making good his conquests in Thrace; and even more uncertain whether any injury—beyond, at most, a trifling loss of prestige—was inflicted on Athens by the manner in which Philip's allies took their oath.

The most serious question was whether it was their doing that Philip was able to pass through Thermopylæ unopposed, and whether the doom of the Phocians had been brought upon them owing to the predictions which Æschines made to the Assembly in Athens: and the more carefully the facts are considered, the more certain it appears that it was not their doing. Nothing could, under the circumstances, have prevented the surrender of the Phocians; it is more than doubtful whether it was hastened by a single day owing to the decision of the Athenian Assembly; and if an Athenian contributed at all to the mitigation of their calamity, it was Æschines.

The strength of Demosthenes' charges against Æschines lay in the fact that Æschines' predictions had proved false. Was that Æschines' fault? Should he have realised beforehand that no reliance was to be placed upon the rumours which Philip had caused to be disseminated about the camp, or even upon the promises made by Philip himself? It was in his failure to realise this that his true weakness probably came out; and it is because, in spite of all that he should have learned from the conduct of Philip towards Athens in the matter of Amphipolis and Pydna, he was not on his guard, but was carried off his feet by the attitude of apparent friendliness and generosity which Philip adopted towards Athens, and also (it must probably be added) by the unconscious influence of Philip's lavish generosity towards himself and his colleagues, that he forfeits the claim to the highest character as a statesman. That he was definitely bribed to perform particular services and to deceive the People, in the manner alleged by Demosthenes, there is nothing to show. That he, and Philocrates to an even greater extent, benefited by Philip's munificence, and were influenced in their judgment of him accordingly, seems certain; and owing to this, they led the Athenians to believe much that was never destined to be realised. And although these promises and predictions were in all probability not the cause of the Phocian disaster, Demosthenes was right when he declared that all receipt of presents by an ambassador was criminal, and that when once there was money in one scale of the balance, it would always outweigh the reason in the other.

There is one other possible explanation of Æschines' conduct, though it seems a less probable one. It may be that he did not in fact place great reliance on the predictions which he made; but that he believed nevertheless that it was of vital importance to Athens that a lasting alliance with Philip should be made, and therefore thought himself justified in using these predictions and the promises contained in Philip's letter to gain that end, taking the risk of their being falsified. But this also, though it might be defended by a casuist, would not be a wise or proper course for a statesman.

Demosthenes certainly supposed that the conduct of Æschines was corrupt and traitorous throughout. His subsequent friendly relations with Philip, maintained in spite of the failure of his predictions, were, Demosthenes thought, a proof of this.[1] We know little of these friendly relations, apart from the fact that Æschines went to Philip's camp after the surrender of Phalæcus, and remained with him until after the Amphictyonic meeting and perhaps until after the Pythian games. But there is no reason to doubt that at this time he was exerting his influence, as a friend of Philip, on behalf of the unhappy Phocians; and the statements, which Demosthenes often makes,

[1] Dem., *de F. L.*, §§ 102 ff.

that Æschines shared Philip's joy at the success of his deception, instead of sharing the disappointment of the Athenians, rest on no evidence but Demosthenes' word, which in such a case is unfortunately worth nothing. Even if Æschines' friendship with Philip was as great as Demosthenes alleged, it would still have to be remembered that Philip was the accepted ally of Athens, that Æschines and his party believed the alliance to be the best thing for Athens as well as for Philip, that it was to be a permanent alliance, and that Philip's action in regard to the Phocians was no wrong to Athens under the terms of the treaty; and so it could hardly be a crime to be Philip's friend.

Our conclusion, therefore, is that Æschines deceived the People, only because he was himself deluded; that for his own delusion he was doubtless to blame; but that the consequences of the delusion and the deception were not in fact so serious as Demosthenes represented. Indeed the Athenians were perhaps prevented by them from going to war with Philip, when they were not well prepared to do so, in a fit of alarm at his arrival at Thermopylæ: and their worst result was the cruel disappointment of the People at their non-fulfilment—a disappointment the consequences of which were to no one more serious than to Philocrates and Æschines themselves.

For the rest, we have before us here, as in the rest of this history, two irreconcilably different ideals of national policy. Demosthenes is filled with the passion for national freedom. Æschines and his party aim at a solid and lasting peace. Both ideals are defensible; and it was not yet certain that the former, any more than the latter, was impracticable. According as the one or the other appeals to us most strongly, we shall side with Demosthenes or Æschines; for, as has already been stated, it is upon the temperament of the critic rather than upon argument that the decision will depend. In the following chapters we shall trace the gradual rise of Demosthenes to a position in which he became as powerful as if he had been formally elected Prime Minister. His ascendancy was not attained all at once, and he had to suffer more than one rebuff; but in the end he succeeded in causing the People to realise that his ideal for Athens was also their own, and to face a decisive struggle in the cause of freedom.

NOTES TO CHAPTER VIII

1. It is disputed whether Philip actually took the oath at Pella or at Pheræ. Demosthenes, *de Cor.*, §32, only says that ὡμολόγησε τὴν εἰρήνην (which might signify an informal declaration of acceptance)—and his expression in the *de F. L.*, §44, τοὺς ὅρκους ἔμελλεν ὀμνύναι, if taken literally, implies that Philip, like the allies, took the oath at Pheræ. But Demosthenes, *de Cor.*, §32, certainly means it to be understood that Philip had sworn to the Peace in Macedonia; otherwise he could have no ground for saying that the ambassadors ought to have left Philip, instead of accompanying his march southward. (He adds that they were bribed to remain with Philip.) Demosthenes may however be misrepresenting the facts; and the am-

bassadors may really have remained at Philip's side because they could not get him to take the oath till he reached Pheræ.

2. The passage (Æsch., *de F. L.*, § 121) which some have interpreted as an assertion by Æschines that Demosthenes himself expressed his commendation of Æschines' address to Philip on the Phocian question, is seen, when properly interpreted, to record only a sarcastic reply to Æschines (Schäfer, ii., 269 n.; Goodwin's edition of the *de Corona*, p. 262). Rohrmoser (*Ueber den philokrateischen Frieden*, p. 809) tries to save Æschines' credit by supposing that the promises of Philip were only made on condition that the Athenians joined Philip's forces and helped him to settle the Phocian difficulty; but there is really no evidence of this.

3. Demosthenes' suggestion that Æschines stayed behind in order to counteract any possible change of feeling on the part of the People during his colleagues' absence is probably quite groundless. Demosthenes further states that Æschines entered a sworn excuse, and sent his brother, with a physician to testify to his illness. To this Æschines replies (probably without truth) that the laws did not allow any one to decline an office to which he had been elected; and that he had only sent his brother to apologise for his failure to set out with his colleagues.

4. Demosthenes' argument in the *de F. L.*, § 123, that Philip could not have remained at Thermopylæ or in Phocis, if the Athenians had not abstained from helping the Phocians and so left them powerless to resist, is at first sight plausible. "It was absolutely impossible for Philip to stay where he was, unless you were misled. There was no corn in the country, for, owing to the war, the land had not been sown, and to import corn was impossible so long as your ships were in command of the sea; while the Phocian towns were many in number, and difficult to take except by a prolonged siege. Even assuming that he were taking a town a day, there are two and twenty of them." But the argument depends on the assumption that Phalæcus would not have surrendered anyhow—an assumption not likely, when we consider that he had no money, that the Phocians were divided, and that he probably had an understanding with Philip. (Philip would otherwise hardly have given him such easy terms.) Nor is it likely that Philip's commissariat was so imperfectly organised as Demosthenes implies; and we do not know what powers of

resistance the Phocians could have offered without Phalæcus and his troops. Further, the calculation of dates by which Demosthenes (*de F. L.*, §§ 52–61) tries to prove that the debate in Athens was the cause of Phalæcus' surrender, is highly ingenious; but it is no proof.

CHAPTER IX

THE NOMINAL PEACE AND THE RENEWAL OF
THE WAR

IN spite of the adverse judgment passed by the Council, Æschines had succeeded in persuading the Assembly to accept the motion of Philocrates, and to refuse to listen to Demosthenes' version of the proceedings of the embassy. There remained a third ordeal which he must face, before he could feel himself to be out of danger. The returning ambassadors had to undergo a scrutiny by the Board of Auditors or Logistæ; and any citizen could give notice that he intended to prosecute an official under an audit for misconduct in his office. Then the case must be tried by a jury, over which the Logistæ presided. If Demosthenes' statement[1] is true, Æschines made an attempt to evade this scrutiny; and Demosthenes alleged that he did so through consciousness of guilt, though his motive, when we consider the state of popular feeling immediately after the surrender of the Phocians, may well have been nothing worse than consciousness of danger. The attempt, however,

[1] Dem., *de F. L.*, §§ 211 ff.

failed, and when Æschines appeared before the Board, Demosthenes gave notice of his intention to prosecute him.

Demosthenes was supported by Timarchus, who had been, like himself, a councillor in the year 347-6, and had taken a somewhat active part in promoting the repair of the fortifications.[1] Timarchus had also proposed to the Council a measure forbidding any Athenian, on pain of death, to supply arms or fittings for ships of war to Philip.[2] But unfortunately Timarchus had in his youth been notorious for his gross immorality, and this gave Æschines an opportunity for delaying the attack upon himself and weakening its force. He prosecuted Timarchus himself for the sins of his past life, and demanded that he should be disfranchised as the law commanded. Despite the fact that Timarchus had filled many important offices, and that the offences alleged against him had been committed many years before, the record against him was too clear to be ignored; Demosthenes did not even venture to speak in his defence; and he was condemned and lost his citizenship. Some discredit was doubtless reflected upon Demosthenes owing to his association with Timarchus, and he waited for this to pass off before proceeding further with the prosecution of Æschines.[3]

---

[1] Æsch., *in Tim.*, § 80.   [2] Dem., *de F. L.*, § 28.

[3] In the course of that prosecution, he replied, with very strong feeling, to part of Æschines' speech against Timarchus.

The trial of Timarchus probably took place early in 345. During that year, while the Athenians were actively restoring their fortifications and dockyards and rehabilitating the fleet,[1] Philip was busily engaged upon the internal organisation of Macedonia. As a security against the less settled tribes upon his frontiers, he planted colonies among them, which he supplied partly by the transplantation of some of his Macedonian subjects —not without some hardships to them,[2]—and partly, in all probability, by the transference to those districts of the inhabitants of the Greek towns which he had conquered in Thrace and Chalcidice.[3] This policy had probably the double effect of introducing a civilising influence where it was much needed, and of breaking down, by the transference of inhabitants from place to place, the local subdivision of his kingdom, and so preparing his subjects for a more truly national unity.[4] At the same time he probably re-organised the financial arrangements of his kingdom, increased his store of arms, and enlarged his fleet; and a few years of comparative peace greatly increased his material prosperity.[5]

Peace, however, in the full sense, was not long

[1] By the year 343, they possessed 300 ships of war, fully equipped (Dem., *de F. L.*, § 89).   [2] Justin, VIII, 5.

[3] See Reichenbächer, *Die Gesch. der Athenischen und Makedonischen Politik*, pp. 8–10.

[4] A few years later he carried the same policy further by planting colonies among the "barbarians" of Thrace. See below, p. 330.   [5] Dem. *de F. L.*, § 89.

possible for him. Early in 344 we find him once more engaged in a campaign against the Illyrian tribes on his frontiers[1]; and it was probably in this campaign that he was wounded in the leg, while in pursuit of the Illyrian King Pleuratus.[2]

When this expedition was over, he carried out— probably in the late summer of 344—a re-organisation of Thessaly, setting a tetrarch (no doubt a partisan of his own) over each of the four divisions of the country,[3] and placing a Macedonian garrison in Thessaly. It was arranged that the public revenues of Thessaly should henceforth be paid to himself, and perhaps also that Thessalian troops should form a regular part of his army.[4] In the same year the Thessalians elected him archon or overlord of Thessaly for his life.[5] Philip accomplished these changes, it would seem, with great tact; the supersession of the local princes or "tyrants" was a popular step; and he appears everywhere to have turned the strife of factions to his own advantage. Isocrates, in a letter to Philip,[6] written probably just after the work in

[1] Diod., XVI, lxix.

[2] Didym., *schol. in Dem.*, Col. 12. Meyer (*Isokrates' zweiter Brief*, pp. 760, 761) is probably right in inferring from the name of Pleuratus that it was against a northern branch of the Illyrians that his campaign was directed, and that Philip may have penetrated almost to the Adriatic.   [3] Note 1 at the end of the Chapter.   [4] Dem., Phil. II, § 22; *de Chers.*, § 14.

[5] See E. Meyer, *l.c.*, p. 762, and his edition of Theopompus' *Hellenika*, p. 229, etc.

[6] Isocr., *Ep. ii.*, § 21. For the date of this letter, see E. Meyer, *l.c.*, pp. 762, 763.

Thessaly was accomplished, congratulated him upon it, adding that it was far harder to capture the good-will of a people than to take their walls. In the same letter he begged Philip, in view of his high vocation, not to expose himself rashly to personal dangers, and urged him to court the good-will of Athens, and not to believe all the evil that he heard spoken of her. "You will never," he declared, "find a State that can do better service either to the Hellenes or to your own interests."

Philip had in fact some reason to feel vexation with Athens. Public opinion in the city had set strongly against him since the overthrow of the Phocians, and Demosthenes had done his best to encourage this unfriendly feeling. The Athenians had sent Eucleides—probably late in 346—to remonstrate with Philip in regard to the Thracian towns which he had taken before returning to Pella to ratify the Peace, and to ask for their restoration to Cersobleptes, and for the extension to that prince of the advantages of the Peace.[1] This request he naturally refused. But he was by no means anxious to re-open hostilities with Athens, and his whole policy from this time onwards goes to prove that he really desired, at this period, not, as Demosthenes incessantly asserted, the conquest of Athens, but a good understanding with her, and an alliance on friendly terms; though

[1] Dem., *de F. L.*, § 181.

20

the fact that Philip was bound to be the predominant partner in any such alliance must in any case
have set Demosthenes against it. And so, while
rejecting a demand which was not reasonable,
Philip offered to cut a channel across the Chersonese at his own charges[1]—an operation which
would have provided the Athenian settlers in the
Chersonese with a good line of defence against the
incursions of the Thracians, and would probably
have conferred a great benefit upon Athenian
merchant-ships. The offer does not appear to
have been accepted; and in the autumn of 344—
probably about the time when Isocrates was composing his letter—envoys were sent, of whom
Demosthenes was the chief, to the Peloponnese,
to counteract the influence of Philip there.

The Peloponnesian peoples were no nearer con-
tentment than they had been for many years.
We have seen how the Arcadians—those at least
whose centre was at Megalopolis—had been
compelled by the rejection of their appeal to Athens in 353 to rely upon Thebes, and the growing
friendliness between Athens and Sparta had also
induced other Peloponnesian peoples who were
hostile to Sparta or afraid of her to enter into
relations with Philip. The embassies from Athens
after the fall of Olynthus had failed to arouse any
feeling against Philip in southern Greece; the

[1] Dem., Phil. II, § 30; cp. Heges., *de Hal.*, §§ 39, 40. The
exact date of Philip's offer is uncertain; but Schäfer (ii., p. 347)
must be approximately right in placing it at this point.

Arcadians, Messenians, and Argives were all under the domination of parties which had an understanding with him, and he had helped them by sending them supplies of money and mercenary soldiers, and by requiring the Spartans to leave Messenia undisturbed.[1] Demosthenes and the other envoys now attempted to persuade them that Philip's friendship was untrustworthy, and was only offered in order that he might the more easily rob them of their freedom. Demosthenes reminded them of the final issue of Philip's alliance with Olynthus, and of the steps by which he had acquired his complete dominion over Thessaly.[2] But in spite of the applause which his eloquence called forth, Demosthenes had to confess that he had failed to make any impression[3]; the Arcadians soon afterwards passed various complimentary decrees in honour of Philip, resolving to erect his statue in bronze, and to welcome him within their walls, if he came to the Peloponnese; the Argives did likewise[4]; and before long envoys came to Athens from Argos and Messene (doubtless with Philip's approval) to make a formal complaint against the interference of the Athenians with their efforts to maintain their independence of Sparta.

About the same time Philip himself sent to

[1] Dem., Phil. II, § 15.

[2] *Ibid.*, §§ 20–25. He misrepresented, however, the attitude of the Thessalians to Philip; they were probably quite contented under his sway.   [3] *Ibid.*, § 27.   [4] Dem., *de F. L.*, §§ 261, 262.

Athens a formal remonstrance against the assertions of the Athenian orators that he had broken
the Peace and had been false to his promises.   He
had, he declared, made no promises; and he demanded that the charges should be proved or
withdrawn.[1]   It is with this situation that Demosthenes dealt in the Second Philippic, a speech of
which the first object was to convince the Athenians that Philip's plans were all being organised
for the one purpose of subduing Athens; and that
it was with this intent that he was courting the
support of the Thebans and Peloponnesians, who
were not, like Athens, prevented by any considerations of righteousness from forwarding his cause.
In the latter part of the Speech he denounced the
corruption of the orators who had brought forward
the promises and predictions by which the People
had been induced to consent to the Peace; he
referred more than once to Philip's "breaches of
the Peace," and upbraided his audience for their
failure to take any steps to prevent the fulfilment
of Philip's designs.   The text of the answer which
he proposed to give to Philip's envoys has not
come down to us; nor do we know whether the
Assembly adopted it.

The Speech is an eloquent one; and it is therefore the greater pity that—in so far as it assumed that Philip had broken faith with Athens—
it should have been based upon a false hypothesis;
indeed Philip's own promises, as contrasted with

[1] Liban., *Hypoth. ad Dem. Phil. II.*

the predictions of Æschines, seem to have been of the vaguest possible character. But that Philip was scheming for the ultimate overthrow of Athens, and deceiving her with offers of friendship until the convenient moment came, was a perfectly possible inference from the facts before the orator, viewed in the light of Philip's past dealings with other peoples; and a partial explanation, though not a justification, of the stress laid in the Speech upon Philip's "promises" may be found in the fact that the orator was preparing to carry out his threatened prosecution of Æschines, and doubtless desired to take every opportunity of impressing upon the People beforehand the main points of his case, chief among which was the alleged falsity of the promises conveyed and the predictions uttered by Æschines. There is every reason to think that the unpopularity of Æschines and his friends was increasing; and two events, which probably occurred soon after the delivery of the Second Philippic, are very significant of this.

Late in 344 or early in 343 the inhabitants of Delos laid before the Amphictyonic Council a request that the Athenians should be deprived of the control of the famous temple of Apollo in that island. (Whether the Amphictyonic Council had any traditional jurisdiction over Delos we do not know; but to have denied the right of the Council to decide the question might have involved the risk of an Amphictyonic war against Athens.)

Æschines was appointed by the People to present the Athenian case—a good appointment in itself, for Æschines was more likely than any member of the opposite party to carry weight with a body of whom the majority were allies of Philip. But the Council of Areopagus, who, for some reason unknown to us, had been given power to revise the choice of the Assembly, cancelled the appointment of Æschines; and Hypereides, an energetic supporter of Demosthenes, was sent in his stead.[1] The Amphictyonic Council, after hearing Euthycrates, the betrayer of Olynthus, on the one side, and Hypereides on the other, decided in favour of Athens,—possibly at a hint from Philip, who clearly desired to avoid causes of offence for the present.

An even heavier blow to Philip's friends was the condemnation of Philocrates, in the first half of 343, upon an indictment preferred by Hypereides for corruption and for not having given the best advice to the People.[2] Whether Philocrates had really been guilty of corruption we do not know. Demosthenes subsequently spoke as if the fact were notorious, and had been admitted by Philocrates himself, who, he said, used even to make a parade of his guilt, "selling wheat,[3] building

---

[1] Dem., *de F. L.*, § 209; Hyper. in *Demadem*, fr. 76 (Oxford Text), etc.

[2] Hyper., *pro Euxenippo*, §§ 29, 30 (Oxford Text).

[3] *I.e.*, wheat received from Philip, or bought with Philip's money. Dem., *de F. L.*, § 114.

houses, saying that he was going to Philip whether you elected him or not, changing Macedonian gold openly at the bank." Like Æschines, we are told, he had received gifts of land from Philip; like Atrestidas, he had brought home women captured in Olynthus.[1] Whether all this was true or not, he discerned that he had no chance of acquittal, and left Athens. He was condemned to death in his absence. In the course of the trial, Demosthenes, who expressed his surprise that Philocrates alone was accused of bringing about results of such magnitude, challenged any of Philocrates' colleagues, who had had no share in his misconduct and disapproved of his actions, to come forward and say so,—offering to accept the word of any one who made such a disclaimer. No one responded; and Demosthenes made much of this in the subsequent trial of Æschines, who would not "accept acquittal even when it was offered him," even though he had none of the excuses which some of his colleagues might have pleaded.[2] About the same time Proxenus was tried and condemned—we do not know on what charge—through Demosthenes' influence.[3]

The reply of the Assembly, whatever it was, to Philip's protest did not prevent him from sending Python of Byzantium (a pupil of Isocrates and an

[1] Dem., *de F. L.*, §§ 145, 309.

[2] *Ibid.*, §§ 116–118; comp. Æsch., *in Ctes.*, §§ 79–81.

[3] Dem., *de F. L.*, § 280; Deinarch. *in Dem.*, § 63.   See Schäfer, ii., p. 369.

able speaker) to Athens early in 343, accompanied by envoys from his allies, to convey an offer to consider the amendment of anything that might be amiss in the terms of the Peace, and to express his regret that, when he was desirous of making the Athenians his friends, more than all the other Greeks, they were induced by self-interested orators to repel his overtures.[1] Æschines supported the representations of Python, while Demosthenes (as he tells us)[2]

would not give way before the torrent of insolent rhetoric which Python poured out upon the Assembly, but rose and contradicted him, and would not betray the city's rights, but proved the iniquity of Philip's actions so manifestly that even his own allies rose up and admitted it.

It was, however, decided to send Hegesippus as ambassador to Philip, to propose certain alterations in the terms of the Peace. Of these the most important was that the clause which ordained that "each party should retain *what they possessed*" at the time of making the Peace, should now be made to ordain that "each party should retain *what was their own*," an alteration which was intended, beyond all doubt, to reopen the question of the right to Amphipolis and Poteidæa. It was also resolved to propose the inclusion of all

[1] The mission of Python may have been in part the outcome of Isocrates' letter to Philip (see above, p. 290).

[2] *De Cor.*, § 136.

the Greek Peoples in the treaty, as well as the allies of the two contracting parties; to guarantee their autonomy and promise them aid against any aggressors; and to ask Philip once more to surrender the places taken from Cersobleptes in April, 346. It appears that the Athenians also laid claim to Cardia.

It is probable that the question of Halonnesus, which continued to be a matter of controversy in the next year, was already included among the subjects of negotiation between Philip and Athens.[1] Halonnesus was a small island near Sciathus. It was the stronghold of a pirate named Sostratus, who had probably been doing damage to Philip's ships. Philip had driven him out and taken possession of the island, and the Athenians, who claimed the ownership of the island, now requested Philip to restore it to them.

Hegesippus was a person devoid of tact and violent in speech, and gave great offence to Philip, who even went so far as to banish the poet Xenocleides, Hegesippus' host during his visit to Macedonia.[2] With regard to the proposals of the Athenians, Philip rejected at once the suggested alteration of the clause with regard to the possessions of the two parties, declaring that he had not

[1] The chief authority on this matter is the Speech of Hegesippus *de Halonneso*, which has descended to us among the speeches of Demosthenes. Hegesippus' authorship is denied by Beloch, *Gr. Gesch.*, ii., 539, but defended, more or less convincingly, by E. Meyer, *Isokrates' zweiter Brief*, p. 776.

[2] Dem., *de F. L.*, § 331.

offered, or authorised his envoys to offer, any such change. He was ready to include the other Greek peoples in the Peace; and to submit to arbitration both the question of the Thracian towns and the Athenian claim to Cardia—as he well might, his case being apparently a very strong one. He was also ready to go to arbitration in regard to Halonnesus, or to give the island to Athens as a free gift. On the advice of Demosthenes and Hegesippus, arbitration was refused, upon the ground that no impartial arbitrator could be found; and Philip was informed that the Athenians did not wish him to *give* them the island, but to *give it back*—a mere matter of syllables, at which Æschines and the comic poets of the time scoffed,[1] but one involving the whole question in dispute as to the ownership of the island. Philip naturally refused to do as he was bidden.

The Speech of Hegesippus which has come down to us was made in one of the debates about Halonnesus early in 342. It is thoroughly unreasonable in tone and argument, and in expression is sarcastic and violent; though the contention that it was beneath the dignity of the Athenians, to whom belonged the empire of the sea, to accept islands from Philip, or to go to arbitration with him, was calculated to win applause. On nearly every point raised in the Speech Philip could give a fair reply; and though it is uncertain whether modern international law would have admitted

[1] Æsch., *in Ctes.*, § 83; Antiphanes, fr. 169 (Kock).

Philip's right to the island (assuming that it had belonged to Athens before it was occupied by the pirate captain), it may also be doubted whether, seeing that the pirate had been suffered by Athens to remain undisturbed and to molest the traffic at his pleasure, the power who expelled him might not equitably claim to have taken the island from him and not from Athens.[1] At least Philip's offer to "give" it to Athens was a fair compromise; and the statement of Demosthenes, that no impartial arbitrator could be found, was little more than an intimation that he was working for a renewal of hostilities. Still Philip's patience was not exhausted; and though he retained Halonnesus, he as yet took no step which could give the Athenians an excuse for war.

At the same time as the mission of Python to Athens, early in 343, there arrived also an embassy from the King of Persia, asking for a renewal of ancient friendship between the Great King and the people of Athens.[2] The circumstances which led the King to send messages at this time to several of the Greek States are not precisely known, but it may be taken as certain that he was apprehensive of Philip's intentions with regard to Asia Minor. His viceroys in that region had displayed great independence while he was engaged in the reconquest of Egypt; and he may have been

[1] See Phillipson, *International Law of Greece and Rome*, vol. ii., pp. 132-151.
[2] Didym., *schol. in Dem.*, Col. 8. See Note 2.

desirous to obtain an alliance with some of the
Greek States which would act as a counterpoise
to the influence which Philip was likely to exert
in favour of the viceroys in Asia Minor, as his
intimacy with one of them, Hermeias of Atarneus,
had shown.   But the Athenians were in no mood
at present to abandon their traditional enmity
towards the King.   It is highly probable, in view
of his later policy,[1] that Demosthenes may have
urged them to do so, in the hope of obtaining a
powerful ally against Philip.   But if so, he failed.
The Athenians replied that their friendship would
remain, so long as the King abstained from attacking the Greek cities in Asia Minor.   This was of
course tantamount to a refusal of the King's proposition.   The Thebans and Argives, on the other
hand, sent him substantial aid against Egypt,
and it was largely this that enabled him to re-
conquer the rebellious province.

It was, in all probability, shortly after midsum-
mer, 343, that the accusations of Demosthenes
against Æschines came before a court of law,
consisting of 1501 jurors, under the presidency of
the Logistæ.   The speeches of Demosthenes and
Æschines have both come down to us, not indeed
in the exact form in which they were delivered,
but in that in which they were afterwards published, some alterations of the original text having
been made, and some arguments inserted in each,

[1] Note 3.

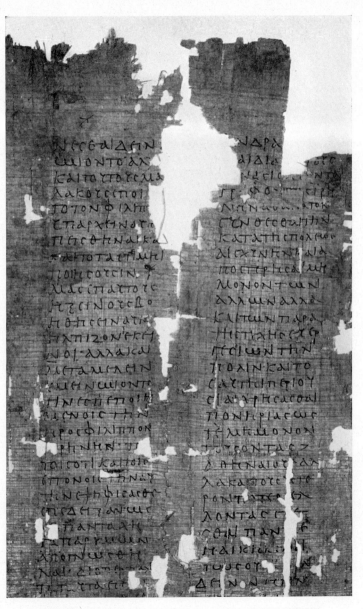

PAPYRUS FRAGMENT OF DEMOSTHENES' SPEECH ON THE EMBASSY

in order to meet the adversary's points, or to correct the unfavourable impression which certain passages had made upon the jury.

The Speech of Demosthenes opened with a brief statement of the duties of an ambassador, and an outline of his proof, to be given fully afterwards, that Æschines had failed to fulfil those duties in any particular. The first half of the Speech consists mainly of a narrative of the events upon which the case turned; and we have already seen reason to conclude that the version which Demosthenes gave of the facts was in many ways a distorted one. The ruin of the Phocians and the capture of the Thracian towns by Philip were represented as entirely due to the corruption of Æschines and his colleagues. The second part of the Speech lays especial stress on the mischief wrought in Greece by traitors, and upon the deceptive and ingenious character of Philip's policy, which Æschines—so Demosthenes argued—had furthered. It also contains passages of self-defence against the charge of participation in the peace-negotiations, and of vehement personal attack upon Æschines, his relations and supporters. The reply of Æschines was largely composed of narrative. It was a businesslike and detailed answer to the charges made against him, and although it does not show the same oratorical force and emotional power as the speech of Demosthenes, it remains one of the most striking orations of antiquity. Æschines was supported by Eubulus, whom we now see for the last time taking a conspicuous part in political controversy, and by Phocion, whose blunt honesty and courage always carried great weight. He was acquitted by thirty votes.[1]

To what causes is the acquittal of Æschines to be attributed? The support given to him by Eubulus and Phocion doubtless counted for something; for in spite of the growing popularity of Demosthenes and the feeling of irritation against the authors of the Peace, the People strongly sympathised with Eubulus in his desire to avoid war and to defend the theoric fund against possible encroachments; and there was in all probability some fear (since Demosthenes is at pains to dispel it),[2] that the condemnation of Æschines would lead to a renewal of war with Philip. Again, the part played by Demosthenes himself in the earlier negotiations for peace could not really be disguised or explained away; and Æschines pressed strongly the point that Demosthenes was accusing him on the ground of transactions for which he himself shared the responsibility. That Demosthenes was conscious of this weakness in his position is shown by the great care which he took to define the issue.[3] Æschines, he declared, was not being

[1] This was known to Plutarch (*Dem.*, xv) from Idomeneus of Lampsacus, a friend of Epicurus, and therefore almost a contemporary witness: comp. *Vit. X Orat.*, 840b, c; and see Note 4.

[2] *Ibid.*, §§ 134 ff., 341, 342.

[3] Dem., *de F. L.*, §§ 91–97, and 202 ff.

tried because the city made peace, but because she made peace on dishonourable terms and with disastrous results.

But, after all, the true reason for Æschines' acquittal was probably that Demosthenes could not prove him to be guilty. We have already seen that upon the most important points, Æschines had a good reply to the allegations brought against him; and more than once he turned the tables upon Demosthenes very effectively, and not only contrived to place his assailant's own conduct during the two embassies in a very unfavourable light, but also showed that Demosthenes had done less than he himself had done to help the Phocians, whose calamities, alleged to have been due to Æschines and Philocrates, were the starting-point of Demosthenes' most impressive argument. The fact that Æschines was actually supported by the testimony of some of the Phocian exiles must have told heavily in his favour. It is also probable that Demosthenes overshot the mark, even for the taste of an Athenian jury, in the grossness of the stories and suggestions which he produced in regard to Æschines and his friends. One story the jury actually refused to allow him to complete[1]—the story of the ill-treatment of an Olynthian woman by Æschines, which Æschines declared to have been invented by Demosthenes.[2]

[1] Dem., *de F. L.*, §196 ff.; *cf.* Æsch., *de F. L.*, §§ 4, 154–158.

[2] Æschines brought forward Aristophanes of Olynthus to

The Speech of Demosthenes contained indeed passages of magnificent oratory, such as might well prove irresistible; the general principles to which he appealed were sound and nobly enunciated, however unjustified his application of them in this particular case; his unique power of convincing narration was never more impressively exercised, however untrue some parts of the narrative may have been; the wide prevalence of treachery and corruption in the Greek States was beyond question; and these causes, coupled with the strong dislike which prevailed for the Peace of Philocrates and its real or supposed consequences, perhaps account for the smallness of the majority by which Æschines was acquitted. It must also be remembered that though Æschines could not be shown to be guilty of corruption, and though no modern jury could possibly have condemned him, he had almost certainly profited to a considerable extent by Philip's friendship; and that though he was probably as sincerely convinced of the advantages to be gained by Athens through alliance with Philip, as Demosthenes was convinced of the opposite, his increased prosperity might well make others suspicious. But we cannot doubt that he was rightly acquitted, and that Demosthenes, though passionately sure that the only sound or worthy policy for Athens was one

testify that Demosthenes had offered him money to vouch for the story, and to declare that the woman was his wife. (There were probably lies on both sides.)

of strenuous antagonism to Philip, was not justified in the construction which he placed on the
part taken by Æschines in opposition to that policy.
Indeed, an impartial historian can hardly avoid
going further than this: for Demosthenes' distortion of the truth at many points in his argument
(intended, as it was, to conceal his own part in
making the Peace), and above all the shameless
use which he made of the calamities of the Phocians
—calamities which he had done nothing to prevent,
whereas his opponent had at least attempted to
mitigate them; but which he nevertheless set
forth in tones of the deepest pathos and indignation—must remain a blot upon his character as
a man and an orator, which the worthiness of his
political aims and the nobility of much of his
subsequent career cannot wholly wipe out.

The effect of the verdict upon the current of
political life at the time is hard to estimate.
Probably in view of the narrowness of the majority,
it was that of a drawn battle, damaging to both
parties; but it is impossible, upon the evidence
before us, to judge whether the party of Æschines
benefited more by his acquittal than Demosthenes
gained by having so nearly secured a victory. It
is certain that from this time onwards Demosthenes' influence grew steadily: it was he and his
supporters who practically guided the action of
the city for the next five years; and this can only
mean that, whatever reasons the jury had for
acquitting Æschines of corruption, the sympathies

21

of the People were with the main principles of Demosthenes' policy.

An incident which probably occurred soon after the trial[1] of Æschines illustrates the exacerbation of feeling between the two orators. A certain Antiphon, who had been struck off the roll of citizens in a revision of the list which had taken place in 346, was found by Demosthenes concealed in the Peiræus, whither Demosthenes said he had come under a promise to Philip that he would burn the dockyards. (We do not know what evidence Demosthenes had of this; but, in view of Philip's evident desire to avoid a quarrel with Athens at this time, the story seems most unlikely.) Demosthenes arrested him and brought him before the Assembly; Æschines protested that the conduct of Demosthenes in arresting the man without authority was unconstitutional, and induced the Assembly to let him go. Demosthenes, however, informed the Council of Areopagus; and through their action, Antiphon was re-arrested, tried, tortured, and executed. "And so," adds Demosthenes, "ought you to have treated Æschines." Plutarch, who alludes to the story, speaks of Demosthenes' action as "very aristocratic"; and it can hardly be defended.

In the latter half of the year 343, Philip, while

---

[1] The date is not stated; but the incident is not mentioned in either of the speeches at the trial of Æschines. The only account of it is in Dem., *de Cor.*, §§ 132-134.

studiously avoiding any breach of the Peace with Athens, was extending his influence in many directions; and the Athenians took some steps to neutralise, if possible, the effect of his movements. In Epirus Philip took up the cause of Alexander, brother of his wife Olympias, against Arybbas (Alexander's uncle and former guardian), whom he compelled to surrender the Molossian kingdom to Alexander. He also increased the extent of that kingdom by bringing within it the district of Cassopia (in the south-west corner of Epirus), with its three towns, Pandosia, Boucheta, and Elateia[1]; and he proposed further to add to it Ambracia, and the island of Leucas, both colonies of Corinth. The Athenians thereupon sent embassies, in which Demosthenes, Hegesippus, and Polyeuctus[2] took part, to the Peloponnesian States, with the object of arousing feeling against Philip. It was perhaps in consequence of this that the Corinthians, whose colonies were menaced, applied to Athens for aid. The appeal was favourably received. The Athenians sent troops to Acarnania to defend Ambracia, and resolved, if an opportunity offered, to take up the cause of Arybbas, who, on seeking refuge in Athens, had been welcomed with honour and granted the citizenship.[3] The alliance of Athens was also

[1] Or Elatreia.

[2] And perhaps also Cleitomachus and Lycurgus.

[3] Justin, VIII, vi.; Diod., XVI, lxxii.; Dem., *in Olympiod.*, §§ 24–6; Phil. III, §§ 34, 72; *C. I. A.*, ii., 115. On the date see Beloch, *Gr. Gesch.*, ii., p. 543 n.

sought by the Achæans, whose colony at Naupactus on the Ætolian coast had been promised by Philip to the Ætolians, in order to gain the good-will of the latter. But, being still desirous of avoiding hostilities with Athens, Philip did not at present proceed further against either Ambracia or Naupactus, but returned to Macedonia through Thessaly. Here also the emissaries of Athens had been busy, attempting to undermine the loyalty of Philip's Thessalian and Magnesian subjects[1]; and it was perhaps for this reason that he now left Macedonian garrisons in Nicæa (which in 346 had been entrusted to Thessalian soldiers), and in Echinus, a Theban colony, but situated on the borders of the Thessalian territory on the north coast of the Maliac Gulf.[2]

At about the same time Philip's troops were engaged in Eubœa, and his agents in the Peloponnese. His adherents in Eretria had brought about the overthrow of the democracy in that town, and the establishment of an oligarchy, at the head of which stood Cleitarchus. The democrats took refuge in Porthmus, the port of Eretria, and were there besieged by Philip's soldiers. Shortly afterwards (perhaps early in 342) we find the Macedonian general Parmenio supporting Philistides, who headed a similar revolution in Oreus, and was similarly established as "tyrant." These events, though in no way a breach of the

[1] Schol. on Æsch., *in Ctes.*, § 83.

[2] Dem., Phil. III, § 34 and "Reply to Philip's Letter," § 4.

Peace, were undoubtedly grave disasters for Athens. Oreus would be a valuable base of operations for Philip against Sciathus, Peparethus, and the other islands of that group. Eretria became, by the change, a "fortress overlooking Attica." Moreover, the revolutions had been carried out with some cruelty, and Demosthenes describes in eloquent and pathetic language the fate of Euphræus, the democratic leader in Oreus, who had dared to expose and denounce the intrigues of Philistides and his friends.[1] The government of the "tyrants" thus established was, according to Demosthenes, cruel and despotic.

A noble recompense did the people in Oreus receive, for entrusting themselves to Philip's friends, and thrusting Euphræus aside! and a noble recompense the democracy of Eretria, for driving away your envoys and surrendering to Cleitarchus! They are slaves, scourged and butchered![2]

Philip appears to have attempted to effect a similar revolution in Geræstus.[3] The people of Chalcis, however, under the leadership of Callias and Taurosthenes, made overtures to Athens. Callias had formerly been on good terms with Philip and had spent some time in his company, but had in some way offended him; he had also been friendly with the Thebans, but now (in order to protect himself against Philip's friends,

[1] Dem., Phil. III, § § 59 ff.; comp. *de Chers.*, § § 18, 36.
[2] Dem., Phil. III, § § 65, 66.   [3] Dem., *de F. L.*, § 326.

Cleitarchus and Philistides) came over to the Athenian side.[1] It was probably about this time that Demosthenes and Callias began those communications which ended in the alliance of 341; and that (on Demosthenes' advice) a corps of soldiers under Chares was stationed in Thasos, to protect the islands.[2]

In the Peloponnesian States also Philip's friends were active. In 343 (before the trial of Æschines) two of Philip's adherents in Megara, Perillus and Ptœodorus, attempted a *coup d'état* with the aid of a mercenary force sent by Philip: but Phocion marched rapidly to the aid of the Athenian party with a force of Athenian soldiers, fortified Nisæa, the harbour of Megara, and connected it by long walls with the town[3]; while Demosthenes negotiated an alliance between Athens and Megara.[4] In Elis Philip's party got the upper hand, and terrible massacres occurred. Among those slain were the remnant of Phalæcus' mercenary force, which (after taking part in some fighting in Crete) had been hired by exiles from Elis to assist them against the Macedonian party and its allies, the Arcadians.[5] These movements in the Peloponnese could not fail to make a great impression upon the Athenian People, as they did

[1] See Æsch., *in Ctes.*, § 86 ff.　　[2] *Vit. X Orat.*, 845 e.

[3] Dem., *de F. L.*, § § 204, 295 ff., 326; *de Cor.*, § 71; Phil. III, § 27; Plut., *Phoc.*, xv. (Plutarch gives no date for Phocion's expedition, but this must almost certainly be the occasion).

[4] Dem., *de Cor.*, § § 234, 237; Phil. III, § 74.

[5] Diod., XVI, lxiii.; Dem., *de F. L.*, § 260, etc.

upon Demosthenes; it appears that in the year 343–2 the alliance between Athens and the Messenians was renewed[1]; and these events doubtless prepared the way by their effect upon Athenian public opinion for the alliance against Philip in 341, in which many Peloponnesian peoples joined.[2]

Early in 342 Philip went once more to Thrace, leaving the young Alexander to govern in Macedonia in his absence. His object was, in all probability, not merely to complete his conquest of Thrace itself, where Cersobleptes was once more active, but also to obtain control over the route by which the Athenian corn-supply passed, and therewith the power to force Athens to come to terms, if force proved necessary. If, as is likely, the design of the conquest of Asia Minor was already present to his mind, it would be essential to make sure of his ground on the nearer side of the Hellespont, before embarking upon an eastern campaign.

It was as important for Athens, if she desired to retain her independence, to keep the great corn-route open, as it was to Philip to obtain the power to close it. Athens had, in fact, only two alternatives. She might make an agreement with Philip, to be sincerely kept by her as well as by him, and arrange a precise delimitation of territories and spheres of influence. If she chose that alter-

[1] *C. I. A.*, iv., 2, 114 b; comp. *Vit. X Orat.*, 851a.
[2] Note 5.

native, the two powers could live in peace side by side (Athens retaining the Chersonese) and could fight side by side in the great campaign in the East which Isocrates had advocated. Or, if she would not do this, she might go to war with him, at the head of as many of the Greek States as would follow her lead. There were difficulties in connection with both alternatives. A power in alliance with Philip could never hope to be the predominant partner, and Athenian pride was not ready to take the second place. Besides this, there was a natural and genuine disbelief in the likelihood of the honest observance of any treaty by Philip; for though his attitude towards Athens throughout the last few years had not only been formally correct, but even forbearing, his past history had not been such as to inspire confidence, and even now he was spreading his net all round Attica, so that it seemed likely that before long she would be entirely isolated. Nor was there any sure guarantee, whatever agreement might be made with Philip, that the hostile neighbours of Athens would remain at peace with her. On the other hand, the disunion of the Greek States made it uncertain whether Athens would find any following against Philip that would be of much real advantage to her; and although Philip was not likely to be able to cut her off from the sea, there was no land-force which could be relied upon to hold him in check and prevent the ravaging of Attica. Moreover, the disinclination of the People for the sacrifices entailed by war was as great as ever, however much their pride might rebel at the idea of Philip's ascendancy.

But Demosthenes' choice had long been made: and the People, though not yet brought to the point at which they would take strong measures at any sacrifice, were disposed to follow his lead; and though he could not yet propose the one measure in which hope lay, an alliance with Thebes (since neither they nor the Thebans were yet ready for this), he took steps during the next few years to drive Philip to such hostile action as would convince the People that they must fight, if they were to remain true to that passion for autonomy and leadership which was one of the dominant elements in their national character. There can be little doubt that Demosthenes interpreted the collective feeling of the mass of his fellow-countrymen rightly; and his efforts were now all directed to forcing them to translate their feeling, which was apt to show itself only in spasmodic outbursts, into steady action, undertaken after thorough preparation.

Philip's campaign in Thrace was completely successful, though few details are known to us. He conquered the whole territory of the princes Cersobleptes and Teres. The latter, who died in the course of the war, had been given the citizenship of Athens (though he had joined Philip in his earlier campaign); and the Athenians had vainly sent protests to Philip, requesting him to allow

these princes to retain their kingdom, as allies of
Athens. Philip made the perfectly correct reply
that these princes had not participated in the
Peace of 346, and that he was under no obligation
to recognise them as allies.[1] The dominions thus
definitely added to his kingdom Philip proceeded
to secure by the foundation of military colonies,
of which the chief were Calybe (or Cabyle) and
Philippopolis (on the upper waters of the Hebrus), the former being nicknamed Poneropolis
—"Rogueborough"—on account of the alleged
character of the settlers planted there.[2] He
strengthened his position on the northern frontier
of Thrace by his friendly reception of Cothelas,
King of the Getæ, who lived between the Hebrus
and the Danube; and (since his principles did not
force monogamy upon him) he married Cothelas'
daughter.[3] He also made alliance with the Greek
colony of Apollonia on the Black Sea, and probably with Odessus (Varna) and other smaller Greek
settlements on the same coast.[4] Ænos at the
mouth of the Hebrus, the last ally of Athens in
Thrace, deserted her for Philip in 341.[5] In the
course of his campaign Philip captured a number

[1] *Ep. Phil.*, §§ 8, 9. See Note 6.

[2] Dem., *de Chers.*, § 44; Steph. Byz., *s. v.* Φιλίππου πόλις;
Theopomp., fr. 107 (Oxford Text), etc.

[3] Satyr. fr. 5; *ap.* Athen., xii., p. 557 d; Steph. Byz., *s.v.* Γέται.
The permission of polygamy sharply distinguishes the Macedonians from the Greeks.

[4] Justin, IX, ii.; Arr., VII, ix., 3, etc. (for full refs, see Schäfer,
vol. ii., pp. 446–450). [5] Dem., *in Theocr.*, § 37.

of strongholds, of which Drongilus and Masteira are particularly named, though their positions are not certainly known[1]; and he passed the winter of 342–1 in Thrace, enduring great hardships with his army.

The Athenian commander in the Chersonese in 342 was Diopeithes of Sunium. Either in that year, or shortly before, the Athenians had sent a fresh body of settlers to the Chersonese, and these were generally well received by the towns in the peninsula. But Cardia, which claimed to be the ally, not of Athens, but of Philip, naturally refused to admit them. Diopeithes was instructed to look after the interests of the settlers, and raised a body of mercenaries, for whom he provided pay by acts of piracy against the trading ships of smaller islands and maritime towns, or by exacting contributions from them, under the name of "benevolences," in return for which their ships were safely escorted by his squadron. (In acting thus, Demosthenes says, Diopeithes was following the regular practice of Athenian commanders.[2]) When he began to threaten the Cardians, the latter appealed to Philip for support, and a Macedonian garrison was sent to protect the town. Diopeithes now went further, and committed a direct act of hostility against Philip's dominions. For, while Philip was fighting in the interior of Thrace, Diopeithes made a raid into Thracian

[1] Dem., *de Chers.*, § 44, etc.   [2] *De Chers.*, §§ 24 ff.

territory and plundered the country about Crobyle
and Tiristasis, which lay near the entrance to the
Chersonese from the side of the Propontis; and
when Philip sent an envoy named Amphilochus
to negotiate for the return of prisoners, Diopeithes
seized him, and would not let him go until he had
paid a ransom of nine talents.[1]

Philip had already offered to submit to arbitration in regard to Cardia, and he now (early in 341)
despatched a strong protest to Athens, declaring
that he would take active measures to protect the
Cardians.[2] The matter was discussed at a meeting of the Assembly, and we learn from Demosthenes' speech on that occasion all that we know
of the debate. The peace-party attacked Diopeithes on account of his irregular and piratical
actions, which, they declared, were bound to end
in war with Philip; and they evidently succeeded
in rousing considerable feeling against the commander. They laid great stress on the blessings
of peace, and accused the anti-Macedonian politicians of designs upon the public funds—in other
words, upon the festival-money. Demosthenes
admitted (for the sake of argument) the unjusti-
fiability of Diopeithes' actions, though he spoke
of them under the name of "assistance to the
Thracians"; but he insisted that when Philip was
advancing his dominion in a manner most perilous
to Athenian interests, it was not the time to recall
or to attack the commander who was at least do-

[1] *Ep. Phil.*, § 3.   [2] *De Chers.*, § 16.

ing something to maintain the Athenian cause
—still less to send another commander and fleet
to bring him back, or keep guard over him, as his
opponents had proposed. To interfere with him
now would be to do the very thing that Philip
would wish. He further urged the seriousness of
the danger lest Philip should advance to Byzantium while the Etesian winds were blowing; for
then Athens could do nothing to hinder him,
unless she had a strong force in the Chersonese.
As to the risk of war with Philip, he replied that
it was only the misleading influence of Philip's
party that prevented the Athenians from seeing
that Philip, whatever professions he might make,
was already at war with them. In an impressive
passage[1] he imagines the other Hellenes interro-
gating the Athenians as to their policy:

" Is it true, men of Athens, that you send envoys
on every possible occasion, to tell us of Philip's designs
against ourselves and all the Hellenes, and of the duty
of keeping guard against the man, and to warn us in
every way?" We should have to confess that it was
true. "Then," they would proceed, "is it true, you
most contemptible of all men, that though the man
has been away for ten months, and has been cut off
from every possibility of returning home, by illness
and by winter and by wars, you have neither liberated
Eubœa nor recovered any of your own possessions?
Is it true that you have remained at home, unoccupied
and healthy—if such a word can be used of men who

[1] §§ 35-7.

behave thus—and have seen him set up two tyrants
in Eubœa, one to serve as a fortress directly menacing
Attica, the other to watch Sciathus; and that you have
not even rid yourselves of these dangers—granted that
you did not want to do anything more—but have let
them be? Obviously you have retired in his favour,
and have made it evident that if he dies ten times over,
you will not make any move the more. Why trouble
us then with your embassies and your accusations?"
If they speak thus to us, what will be our answer? I
do not see what we can say.

He then defines what he regards as the proper attitude for Athens to adopt[1]:

First, men of Athens, you must thoroughly make up
your minds to the fact that Philip is at war with
Athens, and has broken the Peace—you must cease
to lay the blame at one another's doors—and that he
is evilly-disposed and hostile to the whole city, down
to the very ground on which it is built. . . . But
his hostilities and intrigues are aimed at nothing so
much as at our constitution. . . . For he knows very
well that even if he becomes master of all the world,
he can retain nothing securely, so long as you are a
democracy; and that if he chances to stumble anywhere, as may often happen to a man, all the elements
which are now forced into union with him will come
and take refuge with you. . . . And so he would
not have Freedom, from her home in Athens, watch-
ing for every opportunity he may offer. . . . Secondly, you must realise clearly that all the plans
which he is now so busily contriving are in the nature

[1] § 39 ff.

of preparations against this country; and wherever any one resists him, there he resists him on our behalf. For surely no one is so simple as to imagine that when Philip is so covetous of the wretched hamlets of Thrace, and when to get these places he is enduring heavy labours, and the extremity of danger, the harbours and the dockyards and the ships of the Athenians, the produce of their silver-mines, and their huge revenue have no attraction for him; or that he will leave you in possession of these, while he winters in the very pit of destruction for the sake of the millet and the spelt in the silos of Thrace. No indeed! It is to get these into his power that he pursues both his operations in Thrace and all his other designs.

The only remedy, Demosthenes insisted, lay in the organisation and efficient maintenance of a standing force, to defend the liberties of the Hellenes. He then turned to attack his opponents, and their anxiety to prosecute the orators and generals of the war party, and upbraided the People vehemently for their readiness to listen to them:

Yours is the one city in the world where men are permitted to speak on behalf of the enemy without fear; a man may take bribes, and still address you with impunity, even when you have been robbed of your own. . . . Aye, and you know that of such speakers, some who were poor are rapidly growing rich; and some who were without name or fame are becoming famous and distinguished, while you, on the other hand, are becoming inglorious instead of famous, bankrupt instead of wealthy. For a city's wealth consists, I imagine, in allies, confidence, loyalty—and of all these you are bankrupt.[1]

After defending himself against the charge, which his opponents had brought against him, of lacking the courage of his opinions, and of abstaining from formally moving the measures which he recommended, he concluded with a proposal that Diopeithes' force should be maintained, and envoys sent in all directions to organise the movement against Philip.

Above all [he added], we must punish those who take bribes in connection with public affairs, and must everywhere display our abhorrence of them; in order that reasonable men, who offer their honest services, may find their policy justified in their own eyes and in those of others. If you treat the situation thus, and cease to ignore it altogether, there is a chance—a chance, I say, even now—that it may improve. If, however, you sit idle, with an interest that stops short at applause and acclamation, and retires into the background when any action is required, I can imagine no oratory, which, without action on your part, will be able to save your country.

The Speech glows with an enthusiasm which is obviously genuine, and was in every way calculated to commend to the People the policy which the speaker believed to be the only one consistent with the interest and honour of Athens. In fact, matters had now gone so far that war was practi-

[1] § 64 ff.

cally inevitable, and whether or not Demosthenes was to be blamed for having done his best to produce such a state of things, there could be no doubt of his duty when once it was brought about. Accordingly in this Speech and in the Third Philippic the tone of authority is more strongly marked than in most of his earlier orations; though he is still conscious of the strength of the opposition, and of the danger to himself which his policy involved.

We do not know whether the Speech on the Chersonese had any immediate result, beyond its effect on public opinion, though it is certain that Diopeithes was not recalled. It is also certain that within two or three months of the date of the Speech, the feeling of the Athenians had become much more positively militant, and the outbreak of war in Thrace much more imminent. It was in a debate upon a renewed application for supplies from the army in the Chersonese that the Third Philippic was delivered. In this Demosthenes' policy is even more fully declared. It was not now, he insisted, in any selfish interest of her own, but as the champion of the Hellenes against the enemy of their freedom, that the Athenians must take the field. He again declared that Philip was not only at war with Athens, but was obtaining all the advantages of an unopposed conqueror at her expense: and Philip could not be expected to make a formal declaration of war, when it was much more to his purpose to cause the Athenians to take no steps against him, on the ground of the existence of the Peace. He next traced rapidly and forcibly the growth of Philip's power until his influence had extended itself not only over Thessaly, but over Eubœa, Megara, Elis, and western Greece.

But [he continued [1]], though all of us, the Hellenes, see and hear these things, we send no representatives to one another to discuss the matter; we show no indignation; we are in so evil a mood, so deep have the lines been cut that sever city from city, that up to this day we are unable to act as either our interest or our duty require. We cannot unite; we can form no combination for mutual support or friendship, but we look on while the man grows greater, because every one has made up his mind (as it seems to me) to profit by the time during which his neighbour is being ruined, and no one cares or acts for the safety of the Hellenes. For we all know that Philip is like the recurrence or the attack of a fever or other illness, in his descent upon those who fancy themselves for the present well out of his reach. . . . What [he asks [1]] is the cause of these things? For as it was not without reason and just cause that the Hellenes in old days were so prompt for freedom, so it is not without reason or cause that they are now so prompt to be slaves. There was a spirit, men of Athens, a spirit in the minds of the People in those days, which is absent to-day—the spirit which vanquished the wealth of Persia, which led Hellas in the path of freedom, and never gave way in face of battle by sea or land; a spirit whose extinction to-day has brought universal

[1] §§ 28, 29.   [2] § 36 ff.

ruin and turned Hellas upside down. What was this spirit? It was nothing subtle or clever. It meant that men who took money from those who aimed at dominion or at the ruin of Hellas were execrated by all; that it was then a very grave thing to be convicted of bribery; that the punishment of the guilty man was the heaviest that could be inflicted, that for him there could be no plea for mercy, nor hope of pardon. No orator, no general, would then sell the critical opportunity whenever it arose—the opportunity so often offered to men by fortune, even when they are careless and their foes are on their guard. They did not barter away the harmony between people and people, nor their own mistrust of the tyrant and the foreigner, nor any of these high sentiments. Where are such sentiments now? They have been sold in the market and are gone; and those have been imported in their stead through which the nation lies ruined and plague-stricken—the envy of the man who has received his hire; the amusement which accompanies his avowal; the pardon granted to those whose guilt is proved; the hatred of one who censures the crime; and all the appurtenances of corruption. For as to ships, numerical strength, unstinting abundance of funds and all other material of war, and all the things by which the strength of cities is estimated, every people can command those in greater plenty and on a larger scale by far than in old days. But all those resources are rendered unserviceable, ineffectual, unprofitable, by those who traffic in them.

At the same time, Demosthenes was under no delusion as to Philip's power. Athens, in spite

of her recovery from the impoverished condition
in which she found herself some years before, was
not yet strong enough to risk a pitched battle
on land against Philip's modernised army. Her
policy was rather to hold him in check by perpetual operations, forming part of a lengthy campaign, and so to conduct operations at a distance
that he might be unable to draw nearer to Attica.
In the latter part of the Speech, he returned to
the attack upon his opponents, and upon the
People for their apathy in regard to his opponents'
disloyalty[1]; and cited instance after instance to
show the disasters brought about by Philip's
friends—in Olynthus, in Oreus, in Eretria. Finally he moved that preparations for war should
at once be begun, and that envoys should be sent
to the Peloponnesian States, to Chios and Rhodes,
and to the King of Persia himself (whose interests
in regard to Philip were the same as those of
Athens), to organise the world against Philip.
No one would do this, he declared, if Athens did
not. "The task is yours. It is the prerogative
that your fathers won, and through many a great
peril bequeathed to you."

A mere summary of this great Speech, and a few
quotations, can give but a poor impression of its
power. It is a stronger proof of it, that the policy
advocated in it was instantly adopted. Reinforcements and money were sent to Diopeithes;
within a month or two at most Chares also was

[1] See Ch. III., p. 82.

in the Chersonese,[1] and Athenian garrisons were
placed in Proconnesus and Tenedos.[2] The exertions made by Athens were such as, a short time
before, no one would have believed her capable
of making. Her envoys went in all directions.
Demosthenes himself travelled to Byzantium: by
his efforts the old alliance between Byzantium
and Athens was renewed; grudges on both sides
were forgotten; and the key of the Black Sea was
thus once more in friendly hands. (At a later
date Demosthenes recalled[3] with some pride that,
in consequence of this, Athens was kept supplied
during the war which followed with the necessaries
of life in greater plenty than during the years of
peace in Alexander's reign.) From Byzantium he
passed to Abydos, and succeeded in transform-
ing its long-standing ill-feeling against Athens into
friendship.[4] He also renewed friendly relations
with the Thracian princes, though whether with
those who had already been conquered by Philip,
or with others, who may have retained a nominal
independence, we do not know.[5] It may have
been on the same tour that he went to Illyria,
since he couples the Illyrians with the Thracian
princes in the enumeration of those with whom he
had negotiated. Hypereides travelled to Rhodes,
and probably to Chios also, and secured their
alliance.[6] Messengers were also perhaps sent to

[1] *C. I. A.*, ii., 116.
[3] *Ibid.*, § 89.
[5] *Ibid.*, § 244.
[2] Dem., *de Cor.*, § 302.
[4] *Ibid.*, § 302.
[6] *Vit. X Orat.*, 850a.

the King of Persia; and he certainly sent money to Diopeithes.[1]

It is, however, possible that the embassy to Persia was not sent at once. We hear,[2] it is true, of a certain Ephialtes who was sent to the King when Philip was besieging Byzantium, and who secretly brought back large sums of money from the King to induce the popular leaders in Athens to commence war. Demosthenes, it is said, received three thousand darics, and Hypereides also shared in the distribution. It is impossible to test the truth of this story, or to decide whether Ephialtes was sent as the result of Demosthenes' advice. But it is at least probable that the People did not immediately overcome their repugnance to a step so contrary to their traditions and inclinations as the appeal for help to the King; and if the Fourth Philippic is (as some suppose) a pamphlet issued by Demosthenes himself somewhat later than the delivery of the Third Philippic, it shows that the suggestion of an embassy to the King needed to be reinforced by further argument than he had given to the point in that Speech. There is, however, no evidence to show that (as some modern critics surmise) the action of the Athenians in seeking alliance with the King alien-

---

[1] Ar., *Rhet.*, II, viii., p. 1386a 13. The reply of the King to the Athenians quoted by Æsch., *in Ctes.*, § 235, cannot, as is generally stated, refer to this occasion, but must belong to the year 335, since it was given "shortly before Alexander crossed into Asia."

[2] *Vit. X Orat*, 847f., 848c. The authority is not very reliable.

ated from them the sympathies of the other Greeks. Thebes and Sparta at any rate could not throw stones at them, and many of the other States shortly afterwards joined in league with Athens. And though there is no doubt a formal inconsistency between Demosthenes' strong expressions in reference to the great traditions of Athens as the champion of the Greeks against Persia, and his advocacy of a Persian alliance against Philip, the latter policy was dictated by higher reasons than considerations of mere consistency. Indeed, to use the help of Persia to secure the freedom of Greece was scarcely even inconsistent with the principle underlying the traditional attitude of Athens, and was certainly no treason. The assertion that Demosthenes himself received money from the King occurs first in a very late and not always reliable authority, and may be false; but even if it is true, it is a gross exaggeration to state, as some modern historians do,[1] that from this time onwards Demosthenes was the chief agent of Persia in Greece. His later relations with Persia will be considered in their place.

It was not only by embassies that Demosthenes prepared for the struggle. On his proposal a definite alliance was made in the summer of 341 with Chalcis in Euboea; and the envoys sent to deprecate this by Cleitarchus and Philistides failed to obtain a favourable hearing at Athens.[2]

[1] Ed. Meyer, *Isokrates' zweiter Brief*, p. 778.
[2] Dem., *de Cor.*, § 82.

Before July was over the Athenian general Cephisophon had expelled Philistides from Oreus,
and in the following month Cephisophon was succeeded by Phocion, who besieged Eretria, drove
out Cleitarchus, and (as had been done in Oreus)
restored the democracy.[1] In conjunction with
Callias of Chalcis Demosthenes now proceeded
to organise a league against Philip, and the Athenians about the same time conferred the citizenship
of Athens upon Callias and his brother Taurosthenes. Callias and Demosthenes went to the
Peloponnese and obtained promises of large sums
of money and considerable contingents of soldiers
from Corinth and Megara, and from the Achæans.
(The Spartans, and, as was natural, the Peloponnesian States in which Philip had influence, stood
aloof.) Demosthenes also travelled to Acarnania,
and received the adhesion, not only of the Acarnanians, but of Ambracia, Leucas, and Corcyra
as well. Callias appeared before the Assembly
in person, probably in January or February, 340,
and reported the results of his tour; and (according
to Æschines' account) spoke of further advantages
gained, which must at present be kept secret.
Demosthenes confirmed this hint, and reported
the promises which he had himself received. He
further stated that arrangements had been made
for a congress at Athens, to be held in a very
short time, on the 14th of Anthesterion (March
7th), 340. The congress was probably held, since

[1] Didym., *schol. in Dem.*, Col. i.; Diod., XVI, lxxiv.

Plutarch[1] records the reply made by Hegesippus to the new allies, who desired their rates of contribution to be settled, that "war cannot be put upon rations"; and although Æschines[2] describes the announcements made by Demosthenes as a conspicuous illustration of Demosthenes' skill in making his falsehoods detailed and circumstantial, there is no reason to doubt that the promises were really given; for most of the States named did in fact give help to Athens in the campaigns of 339 and 338. Demosthenes claimed[3] that from these sources there came, besides citizen-troops, fifteen thousand mercenaries and two thousand cavalry.

In dealing with the Eubœans, as afterwards in making alliance with Thebes, Demosthenes sought to render the friendship stable by offering generous terms to the new allies. Instead of requiring the Eubœan States to contribute to the Athenian League, he persuaded the Assembly to permit—by a decree, Æschines says, "longer than the *Iliad*"—the formation of a separate Eubœan confederacy, and to authorise the peoples of Oreus and Eretria to contribute their funds to Callias instead of to the treasury of the Athenian allies. There can be little doubt that this was a wise as well as a generous step. It was well worth some sacrifice to establish a united Eubœa, and to convert the island, which Philip might have made his base of operations against Athens, into a

[1] Plut., *Dem.*, xvii.   [2] *In Ctes.*, § 99.
[3] *De Cor.*, § 237.

barrier against him.[1]   Æschines, however, eleven
years later,[2] attacked Demosthenes fiercely, for
thus depriving the Athenians of the contributions
from Euboea, and rendering Euboea independent
of Athens, except for the futile provision that the
citizens of Chalcis should come to the aid of Athens
if she were attacked.   He further alleged that
Demosthenes had been bribed to do this by the
gift of a talent apiece from Chalcis, Eretria, and
Oreus; and described how the people of Oreus
vainly tried to persuade Demosthenes to let them
off this payment, promising to erect a statue to
him; and how in the end they were obliged to
mortgage their public revenues to him, until the
talent was repaid with interest.   In the story as
told by Æschines there are some very improbable
statements,[3] and the whole tale may be fictitious,
even though Hypereides and Deinarchus also allege that Demosthenes made money out of the
negotiations with Callias; for when the morality
of Greek statesmen generally was such as it appears to have been at this period, it was a matter
of course that any statesman who gave advantageous terms to another State would be accused
of having done so for a bribe.[1]

However this may be, Callias proved himself

[1] *De Cor.*, § 301; *cf.* § 237 ff.   [2] *In Ctes.*, §§ 103-105.

[3] Such as that Cleitarchus, the expelled tyrant of Eretria, as
well as the son of a former tyrant of Oreus, took part in the
transaction.

[4] On the date of the Euboean alliance, see Reichenbächer,
Die Gesch. der athenischen u. makedonischen Politik, pp. 30-34.

an active partner; for, with ships lent to him by
Athens, he attacked the towns on the Gulf of
Pagasæ and took them all; and seizing any merchant-vessels that were sailing to Macedonia, sold
those on board as slaves. The Athenians passed
a vote of thanks to him for these achievements,
which, in the spirit if not in the letter, involved
a distinct breach of the Peace of Philocrates.[1]
About the same time (probably late in 341 or early
in 340) acts of direct hostility were committed.
The islanders of Peparethus (who belonged to
the Athenian alliance) seized Halonnesus and
expelled Philip's soldiers, who had occupied it
since the expulsion of the pirates; and when in
return Philip's ships made a raid upon Peparethus,
the Athenian admirals were ordered to make
reprisals.[2] Besides this, a Macedonian herald
named Nicias, carrying despatches, was seized on
Macedonian territory by the Athenians, and kept
in prison for ten months; and the despatches were
publicly read in the Assembly.[3] The Athenian
forces stationed in Thasos offered a refuge to
pirate ships, despite the clause in the treaty with
Philip by which both parties bound themselves to
suppress piracy.[4] At Athens itself, Demosthenes
caused the arrest of Anaxinus of Oreus, whom he
alleged to be a spy in Philip's interest, though

---

[1] *Ep. Phil.*, § 5. It may be that technically the acts of Callias,
even when he had borrowed ships from Athens, could not constitute a breach of the Peace by Athens.

[2] *Ibid.*, §§ 12–15.   [3] *Ibid.*, § 2.   [4] *Ibid.*

Æschines declares that he had come to Athens to make purchases for Philip's wife, Olympias; and, on Demosthenes' motion, Anaxinus was tortured and executed, despite the fact that he had once been Demosthenes' host at Oreus[1]—an unpleasant incident, but very significant of the strength of the prevalent feeling against Philip. At the Dionysia in March, 340, on the proposal of Aristonicus, Demosthenes was crowned with a wreath of gold before the assembled People, for his services to the city.[2]

In the meanwhile Philip had not been idle in Thrace. Before the end of 341 the whole country was in his power; and it became plain that (as Demosthenes had foreseen) the turn of his former allies, Byzantium and Perinthus, must shortly come. The Byzantines, as has already been narrated, had now made alliance with Athens, and when Philip called upon them to join in resisting the Athenians in the Chersonese, they replied that such action could not be required of them under the terms of their treaty with him.[3] About the end of July, 340,[4] his ships sailed up the Hel-

---

[1] Perhaps during the delay at Oreus on the Second Embassy. Demosthenes taunts Æschines with receiving Anaxinus, as well as the envoys of Cleitarchus and Philistides on a former occasion; but Æschines as Consul of Oreus at Athens would be bound to do this; see Dem., *de Cor.*, §§ 82, 137; Æsch., *in Ctes.*, § 224.

[2] Dem., *de Cor.*, § 83.   [3] *Ibid.*, § 8.7

[4] Philochorus, fr. 135; for the date see Kromayer, *Antike Schlachtfelder*, i., p. 178.

lespont; but the Athenian commander in the Chersonese showed such hostility, that Philip, to protect his ships, marched his army alongside of them through the Chersonese, while the Athenian commanders invoked the assistance of the Byzantines. (The opposition of the Athenians to the passage of Philip's ships had been enjoined upon them by a decree proposed in the Assembly by Polycrates, and was thus an act of open war.[1])

Philip now laid siege to Perinthus with the aid of all the devices that he and his engineer Polyeidus could contrive. The inhabitants made a magnificent resistance, but would probably have been forced to surrender, had not the Persian King ordered his satraps to render them all possible assistance. In consequence of this order, a large body of mercenaries crossed from Asia Minor, under the command of the Athenian Apollodorus and Aristomedes of Pheræ.[2] The Byzantines also helped the Perinthians both with men and supplies; and the resistance was so successful that Philip suddenly departed, leaving only part of his forces before the walls, and laid siege to Byzantium itself.

It was about this time (in the autumn of 340) that there occurred the event which led to the actual declaration of war between Athens and Philip. The Athenian merchant fleet had collected

[1] *Ep. Phil.*, § 16.

[2] Diod., XVI, lxxv.; Paus., I, xxix., § 7; "Reply to Philip's Letter," § 5.

at Hieron[1] (an island belonging to Chalcedon and situated near the Asiatic coast, at the entry of the Bosporus), in order that Chares might thence escort them safely homewards with his war-ships. But during the temporary absence of Chares at a conference with the commanders of the Persian force, Philip succeeded in getting possession of the merchant-ships, to the number of 230, and not only took from them seven hundred talents in money and the cargoes of corn and hides which he found there, but also used the timber of the vessels themselves for his siege-works.[2] The Athenians appear to have sent a protest to Philip, and in reply he despatched a letter (of which the substance is probably contained in the "Letter of Philip" included among the orations of Demosthenes) enumerating the acts of hostility which the Athenians had committed against him since 346, denouncing the orators of the war-party, and declaring his intention of retaliating.[3] In reply, on the advice of Demosthenes (though possibly the formal motion was not moved by him)[4], it was resolved to remove the column on which the treaty of peace and

[1] Its name was due to its containing a temple of Zeus Ourios See Arrian, *Peripl.*, §§ 12, 25; Boeckh. on C. I. G., ii., 3797; Weil on Dem. *in Lept.*, § 36.

[2] Didymus, *schol. in Dem.*, Col., x., xi. (quoting Philochorus). The sum of seven hundred talents seems enormous; and it may at least be questioned whether the numeral is not corrupt. See Note 7.

[3] See Foucart, *Les Athéniens dans la Chersonèse*, p. 38.

[4] Dem., *de Cor.*, § 76; comp. Didymus, *l.c.*, and Æsch., *in Ctes.*, § 55.

alliance with Philip was engraved, to man a fresh fleet, and to carry on the war by all possible means.[1]

In order to facilitate the execution of this determination, Demosthenes propounded a reform of the trierarchic system, somewhat different in detail from that which he had put forward in 354, but with the same object—that of preventing the rich from evading their responsibilities. Whereas under the existing system rich men had contributed only a fraction of the cost of a single trireme, contributions were now to be graduated in strict proportion to property; and so "a man came to be charged with two warships, who had previously been one of sixteen subscribers to a single one."[2] It is for this strict apportionment of liability to property that Demosthenes afterwards claimed special credit. The wealthier citizens vainly attempted, he tells us, to divert him from his purpose by the offer of huge bribes, and to hinder the passage of the law by prosecuting him for its alleged illegality; the prosecutor did not obtain a fifth part of the votes of the jury, and so himself incurred a fine. Æschines of course opposed the law vigorously, but it was carried, and so successful was its operation that throughout the war with Philip not a complaint was raised against it; there were no cases of default; the work of equipment was properly done; and no ship was left at home as unseaworthy, or abandoned at sea.[3] Demos-

[1] Philochorus, *ap.* Dion. Hal., *ad Amm.*, i., x.
[2] Dem., *de Cor.*, § 104.   [3] *Ibid.*, §§ 102–109.

thenes himself was appointed overseer of the fleet,[1] and thus himself supervised the execution of his law. At some time or other after the passage of the law, modifications appear to have been introduced into it, probably in consequence of a renewed attack by Æschines; but there can be little doubt that, for the time, Demosthenes had his own way.[2]

Philip had doubtless expected to surprise Byzantium while its defenders were assisting the Perinthians. In this he failed; but he laid siege to the city with vigour, and did not relax his efforts throughout the winter. The Athenians ordered Chares, with forty ships, to attempt to relieve the beleaguered city; but the inhabitants mistrusted him (perhaps with good reason) and would not admit him to the city.[3] At first the Athenians were inclined to resent this; but Phocion declared that the fault lay more with the general than with the Byzantines; and he was thereupon himself sent out (with Cephisophon) in place of Chares, late in 340 or early in 339.[4] Demosthenes and Hypereides were among those who voluntarily furnished ships for the war.[5] Phocion was warmly welcomed by the besieged, and conducted the defence of the city in conjunction with Leon, a Byzantine who had been his friend when both were pupils of Plato in the Academy. His ships

[1] This was probably an extraordinary office, created for the occasion. [2] Note 8. [3] Note 9. [4] *C. I. A.*, ii., 809. [5] *C. I. A.*, ii., 808, 809; *Vit. X Orat.*, 848f, 851a.

also protected the Athenian corn-convoy.[1] The
peoples of Perinthus and Byzantium passed resolutions of gratitude to Athens in glowing terms,
and sent crowns to her, as did also the colonists
in the Chersonese; and Demosthenes afterwards
claimed to be the only statesman for whose deserts
the city had received a crown.[2] The Byzantines
were also assisted by ships from Chios, Rhodes,
and Cos—once their allies against Athens, and
now (perhaps owing to anxiety for the safety of
their own commerce) allies of Athens itself once
more; a Persian force crossed once more from Asia
to help them[3]; and in spite of persistent attacks,
Philip could not take the town. At last, after a
well-planned attempt on a moonlight night, which
might have succeeded had not the defenders been
roused by the barking of dogs, he resolved to depart
(early in the spring of 339).[4] By concocting a
carefully devised letter to Antipater, and contriving that it should fall into the hands of the Athenian commanders, he caused the latter to leave the
passage of the Bosporus open, and so got his ships
away from the Black Sea, where they appear to
have been confined.[5] On his way he perhaps
plundered the Athenian colonies in the Chersonese,
and apparently his fleet passed through the Hellespont without difficulty, probably because, as

---

[1] Dem., *de Cor.*, § 89.   [2] *Ibid.*, § 90 ff.

[3] Arrian, *Anab.*, II, xiv., § 5.

[4] For the date, see Kromayer, *Antike Schlachtfelder*, pp. 181,
184.   [5] Front., I, iv., § 13.

before, he kept the colonists employed on shore; but Phocion afterwards overtook some of his ships, and recovered some of the Thracian coast towns which Philip had taken, making descents upon various points until he was wounded and forced to return home.[1]

Philip now took his army off upon a distant expedition against the warlike Scythian King Ateas, who had insulted him in the previous year.[2] From this raid, which took him as far as the Danube, he carried off a vast number of captives, as well as horses, flocks, and herds[3]; and his success no doubt refreshed the spirits of his men. But on his way homewards, he passed through the country of the Triballi, a fierce tribe living on Mount Hæmus, and in a sudden attack by the tribesmen he not only lost the booty taken from the Scythians but was himself severely wounded in the thigh.[4] He succeeded, however, in fighting his way through into Macedonia, where he must have arrived in the spring of 339.

Up to this point the result of the struggle had been favourable to Athens, and Philip's failure to take Byzantium, and his subsequent misfortunes, must have given great encouragement to the Athenians. But some months before Philip's

---

[1] Justin, IX, i.; Syncellus III, 692; Plut., *Phoc.*, **xiv.** See Note 10.

[2] For anecdotes about this King, see Schäfer, ii., p. **519.**

[3] Justin, IX, ii.; Strabo, p. 307; Æsch., *in Ctes.*, § **128.**

[4] Justin, IX, iii.; Didym., *schol. in Dem.*, Col. **13.**

return to Macedonia there had been sown the seeds of new troubles for Athens, and new opportunities for Philip. The nature of these, and the issue of the struggle, will be the subject of the next chapter.

NOTES TO CHAPTER IX

1. On the difficulty in the evidence as to the Thessalian tetrarchies (Dem., Phil. II, § 22, *de Chers.*, § 26, and Harpocr., *s. v.* δεκαδαρχία) see the note in my translation of Demosthenes' Public Orations, vol. ii., pp. 166, 167. It is disputed whether the tetrarchies were actually created in 344, or whether Philip at first established a decadarchy or Council of Ten, and replaced it by tetrarchies in 343. But I am now inclined to think that the decadarchy is a myth, and that there was only one constitutional change.

2. It is not certain whether Artaxerxes had or had not yet effected the reconquest of Egypt at the time of this mission to Athens in 343. See Meyer, *Isokr. zweiter Brief*, p. 777; Kahrstedt, *Forschungen*, pp. 15 ff., and *Klio*, vol. x., p. 508; Lehmann-Haupt in *Klio*, vol. x., pp. 391 ff., and in Gercke and Norden's *Einleitung in die Altertumswissenschaft*, iii., pp. 61, 119; and Cavaignac, *Hist. de l'Antiquité*, p. 401. Kahrstedt gives strong reasons for thinking that Egypt was not subdued until the following winter— that of 343–2. The King may have wanted the Greek States to give him help against Egypt, or at least to facilitate his obtaining Greek soldiers as mercenaries. But he probably had Philip also in his mind. Some think that he first tried to negotiate with Philip himself and obtained a nominal and short-lived alliance; but the passage of Arrian, II, xiv., on which this conjecture is based, probably refers to an earlier period. See above, Chap. VI., p. 191.

3. Comp. Phil. III, § 71, where Demosthenes recommends an embassy to the King (in 341). The proposal is still more strongly argued in Phil. IV, §§ 31–34, where the writer urges that the fact that the King had seized Philip's confidant Hermeias proved his interest in the war with Philip, and protests against the application of the names "barbarian" and "public enemy" to the

Great King. Whether the Fourth Philippic was issued by Demosthenes as a pamphlet in the early summer of 341 (as Körte, *Rhein. Mus.*, lx., p. 3, believes), or was compiled from Demosthenic material by Anaximenes for insertion in his history (as Nitsche and Wendland think), it was certainly the work of some one intimately acquainted with the events and position of affairs in the early part of 341 (just after Phil. III.), and can safely be used as an authority.

4. Plutarch himself doubts whether the trial really took place, and whether the speeches were ever delivered, on the inadequate ground that neither orator distinctly refers to the trial in his speech at the trial of Ctesiphon in 330. Why should they? It was not an occasion of which either could be proud; it was a defeat for one, and a very narrow escape for the other, and Æschines, the victor in the contest, had least reason of all to mention it, since he desired his connection with the Peace to be forgotten. The expression used by Dion. Hal. (*ad Amm.*, i., 10) when he says that Demosthenes "composed" this speech, while in other cases he used words distinctly implying delivery, may be purely accidental. That there were some differences between the spoken and the published speech of Demosthenes is certain, and some of the replies to "anticipated objections" of the adversary were probably not written until after the trial.

5. Beloch believes that an alliance against Philip was made in 343–2; but the arguments urged against this view by Reichenbächer, *Die Geschichte der athenischen u. makedonischen Politik*, pp. 30, 31, are very strong.

6. The Letter of Philip, included among the works of Demosthenes, is probably extracted from the History of Anaximenes (see Wendland, *Anaximenes von Lampsakos*, p. 13); but there is no reason to doubt that it accurately represents Philip's point of view, though it cannot be assumed that all the arguments contained in it were embodied in one letter; and it seems safe to use it as an authority. The so-called "Reply to Philip's Letter" is mainly a compilation of passages from works of Demosthenes, probably derived from the same source; but there is no reason to regard it as unreliable as to facts.

7. There is great difficulty as to the ships taken by Philip. The account given in the text is taken from the Scholia of Didymus;

comp. Dem., *de Cor.*, §§ 73 and 139. A quite different account is given in the two decrees and the letter of Philip quoted in Dem., *de Cor.*, §§ 73–77. According to these, twenty Athenian ships, sent under Leodamas to the Hellespont as an escort for corn-ships sailing from the Hellespont to Lemnos, were seized by Philip's admiral Amyntas, and detained, in the belief that they were really going to help Selymbria, which was being besieged by Philip; but upon the representations of envoys sent from Athens, they were restored. The same story is cited (evidently from the documents in the *de Cor.*, *l.c.*) by the scholiast on the "Reply to Philip's Letter." But (1) there is nowhere else any reference to a siege of Selymbria by Philip (Nitsche, *Demosthenes und Anaximenes*, pp. 82 ff., is not at all convincing); and (2) the documents quoted in the text of the *de Cor.* are certainly spurious (see Goodwin's edition, App. VIII.). They do not even go to prove the point which Demosthenes wishes to prove; for the capture of ships immediately afterwards restored can hardly have been the cause of war; and there are sundry mistakes in them. We are therefore probably justified in rejecting the whole story, as Grote does. But if Selymbria really was attacked by Philip, it was doubtless on his way from Perinthus to Byzantium; and if the seizure of Leodamas' ships really took place, it may have been neglected by the Greek historians through a confusion of it with the later seizure of the 230 ships at Hieron.

8. We do not know to what Æschines refers (*in Ctes.*, § 222), when he says that he "convicted Demosthenes of stealing from the State the trierarchs of sixty-five swift ships"; but the reference is doubtless to his criticism of some detail of the scheme. It is probable that the criticisms of others led Demosthenes afterwards to modify the details; and Deinarchus states, as a matter of course, that he did so for money (Dein., *in Dem.*, § 42). Demosthenes (*de Cor.*, § 312) speaks of a damaging attack upon his law by Æschines, acting as the hireling of the wealthy members of the Naval Boards. We do not know when this took place; but it was probably some time after the law had come into working; since we gather from Æschines, *l.c.*, that the attack was based on the effects of the law.

9. Plutarch (*Phoc.*, xiv.) says that Chares was obliged to wander about, getting money from allied cities and despised by the enemy. It is, however, possible that the real reason for his

withdrawal was the death of his wife, and there is some evidence that he contrived to operate effectively against Philip at sea. See Schäfer, ii., pp. 508, 509, and references there given.

10. Some writers believe (on the evidence of a statement in Diod., XVI, lxxvii., which in any case is far too sweeping) that Philip now made peace with the Byzantines and their Greek allies, with the exception of Athens; but the evidence is not sufficient to show whether any arrangement was really made. See Grote, pt. ii., ch. 90.

THE ATHENIAN TREASURY AND MUSEUM AT DELPHI

PHOTO BY ALINARI

CHAPTER X

CHÆRONEIA

WE must now go back a few months, to the
meeting of the Amphictyonic Council
which took place in October or November, 340.[1]
At this meeting, the representatives of the Locrians
of Amphissa, who in the Sacred War against the
Phocians had been on the same side as the Thebans
and Philip, proposed that a fine of fifty talents
should be inflicted upon Athens, because the
Athenians had hung in a new chapel or "treasury"
in the precincts of Apollo at Delphi certain shields
which they had taken in the Persian wars, without
waiting for the dedication of the chapel, and in
regilding the shields had inscribed upon them the
words, "The spoil of the Athenians, taken from
the Persians and the Thebans, when they fought
against the Greeks." (The words had doubtless
been inscribed upon them originally, but they
may have become obscure through age.)

The Athenian "Hieromnemon" or representative
on the Council was Diognetus; while the official
delegates, or Pylagori, sent by Athens were Æsch-

[1] Note 1 at the end of the Chapter.

ines, Meidias, and Thrasycles.[1] When the Locrian representative had spoken, Diognetus sent for Æschines, and asked him to reply on behalf of Athens. But when he had entered the Council-meeting and was beginning to speak, one of the Locrians present —an ill-mannered fellow, Æschines declared, and perhaps prompted by some evil power—rose and told the meeting that they ought not to have allowed the name of the Athenians to be mentioned during that holy season, but should have excluded them from the temple as accursed, on account of their alliance with the sacrilegious Phocians. Æschines tells us that at this he became more angry than he had ever been in his life, and retaliated upon the Amphisseans by denouncing their impiety in cultivating the plain of Cirrha, which had been devoted to Apollo for ever in the time of Solon, and in making money out of the sacred harbour. Pointing to the plain, which lay spread out below them, and recalling its history, he declared that he himself and the People of Athens were ready to defend the consecrated land "with hand and foot and voice," and by every possible means.

And so [he continued], do you take counsel for yourselves. The sacrifices stand ready to be offered, and you are about to ask the gods for their blessing upon yourselves and your country. With what words, with what conscience, with what faces, with what

[1] Note 2. We have only Demosthenes' word for the statement that Æschines was elected by the Assembly when hardly any one was present.

confidence, can you dare to make your supplications, if you have left this accursed people unpunished? In plain and unambiguous words the curse stands inscribed against those who have committed such misdeeds, and those who have condoned them; and in it is the prayer that those who have not come to the help of Apollo and the other gods of Delphi may not sacrifice aright, and that the gods may not receive their offerings.

Such was the impression made by the fiery eloquence of Æschines upon men who (as Demosthenes says[1]) were unused to oratory, that their anger was now turned against the Amphisseans; and the Council bade their herald summon the whole adult population of Delphi to meet the Council and the delegates at day-break with pick-axes and spades, on pain of falling under a curse. The crowd thus collected descended next morning to Cirrha, destroyed the harbour, and set fire to some of the houses. But the people of Amphissa, hearing what had been done, came down in force from their own town, attacked the Delphians, and did some violence to the sacred persons of the Amphictyonic Councillors, who with difficulty made their way back to Delphi. Next morning the president of the Council, Cottyphus of Pharsalus, convoked an assembly of all the worshippers of the god who were present in Delphi. The con-

---

[1] No doubt truly; for they were mostly representative of the northern Greek tribes, who were not nearly so civilised as the Athenians.

duct of the Amphisseans was censured in strong terms; and it was resolved that the Council should hold an extraordinary meeting at Thermopylæ, before their next regular meeting, and should prepare a decree inflicting proper punishment upon the Amphisseans for their impiety in encroaching on the sacred ground, and doing violence to the Amphictyons.

When Æschines made his report at Athens, the Assembly at first strongly commended his action, though Demosthenes declared that it must lead to an Amphictyonic war against Athens—a prophecy which many supposed to have been prompted merely by personal ill-will against Æschines.[1] When however the decision came to be taken whether the Athenian representatives should attend the special meeting which had been ordered, Demosthenes, having first persuaded the Council, carried a resolution in the Assembly forbidding them to do so. (Æschines alleged that this was only done by a snatch-vote taken in his own absence.) The extraordinary meeting took place early in 339,[2] when Philip was far off in Scythia. No representatives of Athens or Thebes were present. War was declared by the Amphictyonic Council against the Amphisseans, and Cottyphus was appointed to command the Amphictyonic troops.

[1] The prophecy was fulfilled, not indeed immediately or literally (for Æschines had in fact averted this), but in all practical effect, a few months afterwards.

[2] Probably in January or early in February. See Note 3.

THE GRAND ALTAR AT DELPHI

At this point there is a discrepancy between our two authorities. Æschines states that, as the result of the first campaign, the Locrians were ordered to pay a fine by a specified date, to banish those who were responsible for their impious acts, and to recall those who had opposed them. Demosthenes, on the other hand, says that Cottyphus could only obtain troops from the Amphictyonic powers, and these (in the absence of support from Athens, Thebes, Sparta, and Philip) were ineffective; some did not even answer his summons, and the campaign was a failure. Whether on this account, or on account of the failure of the Locrians to pay the fine and carry out the other requirements of the Amphictyons, the question of the conduct of the war was reconsidered at the regular meeting of the Council in May or June, at which Cottyphus declared that unless the Amphictyonic peoples would take the field, and contribute sufficient funds, and fine those who would not serve, the only chance of success was to appoint Philip their general. The Councillors (mostly representatives of tribes which were in alliance with Philip) took the easier course, and elected Philip. His wound had healed; he accepted the invitation, and marched southward.

Such was the course of the events which led to a struggle more momentous, perhaps, than any since the Persian wars. What was the meaning of them? Demosthenes asserts that Æschines

had been bribed by Philip to attack the Amphisseans, and so create a situation in which Philip
could again intervene. He denies that the Amphisseans had made any complaint against Athens,
since they could not have done so without giving the Athenians formal notice, and such notice
had never been given. But an argument based
upon such a technicality is inconclusive. The
speech of the Locrian representative may not have
been in order, and may yet have provoked a reply;
or it may rather have been a notice of motion than
a formal motion. Æschines cannot at least be
denied the excuse of having acted under provocation. But was his action in itself justifiable?
This too it is difficult to deny; it seems extremely
likely that he really prevented the declaration of
an Amphictyonic war against Athens; there is
not the least evidence that his action was prompted
by Philip; and he probably acted in good faith,
when confronted by a critical situation.

What then was the explanation of Demosthenes
action? Æschines asserts that Demosthenes was
in the pay of the Locrians of Amphissa, and had
not only been bribed by them, when he was
Pylagorus in 343, to say nothing of their impious
acts to the Amphictyonic Council, but was actually
receiving twenty minæ a year from them, on the
understanding that he would forward their interests at Athens in every way. But it is possible
to place a more honourable construction upon his
action. The attack upon Athens in the Amphic-

tyonic Council had been made by the Amphisseans
as friends of the Thebans, whose feelings had been
hurt (probably through pure thoughtlessness) by
the restoration of an inscription which might more
happily have been suffered to remain obsolete,
and the revival thereby of the record of an old
stain upon their history,—their abandonment of
the Hellenic cause at the time of the Persian
invasion of 480. Demosthenes saw that, if Athens
was to hold out against Philip, she must not quarrel
with Thebes, and therefore must not join in action
against the Amphisseans. He must also have
known that the Thebans were growing discontented with their condition as allies of Philip, as
they came to realise that they could only occupy
a position of secondary importance. Indeed they
had committed at least one definitely unfriendly
act against Philip: for while he was in Scythia,
they had expelled the Macedonian garrison which
he had placed in Nicæa, and had occupied the
place themselves[1]; his garrisoning of their colony
at Echinus had probably offended them; and it
could hardly please them that those Peloponnesian
peoples who had once relied upon them now looked
to him as their protector. The feelings of the
Thebans would naturally have been made known
to Demosthenes by visitors from that city, since
he was Proxenus or Consul of Thebes in Athens.
Further, though it was true that Æschines had
diverted the immediate attention of the Amphic-

[1] Philochorus, *ap.* Didym., *schol. in Dem.*, Col., xi.

tyons from Athens to the Amphisseans, it was also true, as Demosthenes declared, that to rouse the Amphictyons, and particularly to rouse them against the Amphisseans, who had been Philip's allies, was an action not unlikely to give Philip an opening for intervention, and to render it probable that Athens would suffer as much as Amphissa. Demosthenes was convinced that Philip was bound to take some action against Athens before long; for although after Phocion's retirement the Athenian admirals seem to have carried on hostilities against Philip with poor success, the trade of the Macedonian ports suffered greatly from the raids made by Athenian ships,[1] and he was certain to desire to retrieve his reputation after his failure before Perinthus and Byzantium. And so it was even more necessary than before to preserve the good-will of the Thebans, whose feelings and interests were now being brought by the force of circumstances into harmony with those of the Athenians.

From this point of view, Demosthenes' refusal to countenance the attack of the Amphictyons upon the Amphisseans, the friends of Thebes, was wise and far-sighted, and the event fully justified it. But public opinion at Athens was still too ill-disposed towards Thebes to allow Demosthenes to give to the Assembly, as the real reason for his policy, his desire to make friendship with the

[1] Dem., *de Cor.*, §§ 145, 146.

Thebans: and hence he doubtless used other arguments.[1]

Some writers indeed have reproached Demosthenes for not allowing Athens to join in the war against Amphissa, in the belief that the appeal to Philip would have been rendered unnecessary if the Athenians had taken part in the war with vigour. But the struggle with Philip was bound to come soon; and it was not a time to alienate the most powerful ally whom Demosthenes hoped to gain, on the chance of postponing the struggle for a little. Others have said that, by following Demosthenes' policy, Athens lost her chance of joining in a great national enterprise, first in vindication of the national god of Delphi, and then in a campaign with Philip against Persia, crushing Thebes if necessary on the way. But—leaving aside the question whether Philip's aims were national and Hellenic, or whether he was not primarily interested in the enlargement of the Macedonian Empire—was a "national" enterprise, in which Athens would probably have to take the second place, reconcilable with the Athenian ideal, as Demosthenes interpreted it, and as it was probably viewed by his fellow-countrymen? Was it to be expected that any alliance between an absolute monarch and the democracy of Athens would be secure? And how were the People to be

---

[1] Æschines probably shared the popular animosity against Thebes, much as he afterwards lamented her overthrow by Alexander.

led to make an alliance which could only appear to them a surrender of the brilliant prospect of success opened up by the history of the last year? It seems then that Demosthenes took the one path which was consistent both with prudence and with the national honour, as the Athenians generally conceived it.

To the question whether the original complaint of the Amphisseans against Athens had been prompted by Philip, in the hope of stirring up an Amphictyonic war against Athens, no answer can be given. (If it was so, Æschines accidentally traversed Philip's purpose.) It is not inconceivable that it was so, for Philip must have known, as well as Demosthenes, that a final struggle with Athens had to come, and that owing to the defeat of the Macedonian party in Athens by Demosthenes, the issue could not be decided by treachery or by diplomacy, but only by arms, and an Amphictyonic war would be a highly convenient method of action. There is however no evidence which can be brought to bear on the question. That Cottyphus was acting deliberately in Philip's interest is stated by Demosthenes and others, [1] and is the more likely, perhaps, because his native town, Pharsalus, had greatly benefited by Philip's favours.

Philip, with an army composed of Macedonian and Thessalian troops, marched southward, without delay, taking, probably, the direct road from Lamia to Cytinium in Doris, and avoiding Ther-

[1] *E. g.*, Schol. on *de Cor.*, § 151.

Pass from Doris
to Dalbahi 31/7/99.

From summit of Pass
from Melia = to
Doris

THE PASS OF GRAVIA AND SITE OF CYTINIUM

FROM A DRAWING BY DR. G. B. GRUNDY

mopylæ. He first occupied Cytinium, which commanded the road over the mountains (by the Pass of Gravia) to Amphissa, the nominal goal of his march; but instead of proceeding directly to Amphissa, he diverged into the high-road which led into the Phocian plain, and thence to Thebes and Athens, and (early in September, 339) seized Elateia, which commanded the road at a point only a few miles north of the Bœotian frontier. It is highly probable that he also secured the less important routes over the mountains from Thermopylæ into the plain, which they enter near the modern villages of Dernitsa and Turkochori. With regard to the force in Nicæa at this moment there is some doubt; probably it was still in the hands of the Thebans, who had seized it in the previous year, but soon after his occupation of Elateia Philip requested them to hand it over to the Locrians in whose district it stood[1]; and it is possible that he had previously been making friends with this branch of the Locrian stock, on finding that the Thebans were becoming disaffected towards him.[2] However that may be, by fortifying Elateia he placed himself in a very strong position: the main roads in his rear were absolutely secure, and the position also had other advantages.

[1] Didym., *schol.*, Col. xi.

[2] So Glotz argues (*Bull. Corr. Hell.*, 1909, pp. 526 ff.). But the evidence which Glotz offers in support of his conjecture that Philip had also been entering into friendship with the Phocians and that he occupied Elateia as the friend of the Phocians, in whose territory it lay, is far from conclusive.

It may be taken as certain that the occupation of Elateia was primarily intended by himself as a menace to Thebes, and a warning to her to renew her rapidly vanishing friendship towards himself; and it was convenient to convey this without actually entering Bœotian territory, for that would have thrown Thebes into the arms of Athens. It seems equally certain that Philip intended now to make an end, once for all, of the opposition to himself in Greece. But, as usual, he wished to have some plausible ground for his action. The pretext for his presence in Greece was the commission given him by the Amphictyons to destroy Amphissa; but had he executed this commission at once, the pretext would have disappeared; his ostensible purpose would have been fulfilled, and he would have had no specious excuse for remaining in Greece. Besides this, the Phocian plain doubtless offered his army a better supply of food than the mountains between Cytinium and Amphissa could have afforded. For all these reasons, he occupied Elateia.

The Athenians were at first paralysed by the news; for not having realised (as Demosthenes had) the growing estrangement between Philip and the Thebans, they assumed that he had come to join forces with the Thebans, and to march with them upon Attica. A very famous passage of the Speech on the Crown[1] describes the effect of the news.

[1] *De Cor.*, §§ 169 ff.

It was evening, and one had come to the Prytanes[1]
with the news that Elateia had been taken. Upon
this they rose up from supper without delay; some of
them drove the occupants out of the booths in the
market-place and set fire to the wickerwork,[2] others
sent for the generals and summoned the trumpeter,
and the city was full of commotion. On the morrow,
at break of day, the Prytanes summoned the Council
to the Council Chamber, while you made your way to
the Assembly, and before the Council had transacted
its business and passed its draft-resolution, the whole
People was seated on the hillside.[3] And now, when
the Council had arrived, and the Prytanes had reported the intelligence which they had received, and
had brought forward the messenger, and he had made
his statement, the herald proceeded to ask, "Who
wishes to speak?" But no one came forward; and
though the herald repeated the question many times,
still no one rose, though all the generals were present,
and all the orators, and the voice of their country was
calling for some one to speak for her deliverance.
For the voice of the herald, uttered in accordance
with the laws, is rightly to be regarded as the common
voice of our country. And yet, if it was for those to
come forward who wished for the deliverance of the
city, all of you and all the other Athenians would have
risen, and proceeded to the platform; for I am certain
that you all wished for her deliverance. If it was for
the wealthiest, the Three Hundred would have risen,
and if it was for those who had both these qualifica-

---

[1] The acting committee of the Council.

[2] Probably a bonfire was a method of summons to an extraordinary meeting of the Assembly.   [3] *I.e.*, on the Pnyx.

tions—loyalty to the city and wealth—then those would have risen who subsequently made those large donations; for it was loyalty and wealth that led them so to do. But that crisis and that day called, it seems, not merely for a man of loyalty and wealth, but for one who had also followed the course of events closely from the first, and had come to a true conclusion as to the motive and the aim with which Philip was acting as he was. The man who was needed was found that day in me.

Demosthenes then describes how he dispelled the belief that Philip had a satisfactory understanding with the Thebans, and that it was therefore too late to prevent him from marching, with them, into Attica. Had this been so, they would have heard of his being, not at Elateia, but on the borders of Attica. It was because the attitude of the Thebans was still uncertain that he had occupied Elateia, in the hope of encouraging his friends in Thebes, and intimidating his opponents, and so compelling them to join him, whether they would or no. This, Demosthenes declared, there was still time to prevent, if the Athenians would forget their grudges against the Thebans, and offer them an alliance on generous terms. At the same time they must show that they were in earnest, by immediately arming all the citizen-troops and cavalry, and ordering them to march to Eleusis (the first halting place on the most convenient road to Bœotia); and they must give the envoys to be sent to Thebes, with the generals, full power to decide the

steps to be taken next. His eloquence carried the
Assembly with it: the levy of troops was ordered,
and he himself, with others, was immediately
despatched to Thebes. "This," he says, "was
the first step towards our new relations with
Thebes: the danger had seemed likely to descend
upon the city like a torrent in winter"[1]; but "this
decree caused the peril that encompassed the city
to pass away like a cloud."[2]

On his arrival at Thebes, Demosthenes found
envoys from Philip and the Thessalians already
there.[3] Philip was represented by Amyntas and
Clearchus, his allies by Thrasydæus and Daochus.[4]
Though the Thebans had been the friends and
allies of the Amphisseans, against whom he was
ostensibly marching, Philip was prepared to treat
them as neutrals, if they would either join him
in marching into Attica, or would even allow him
and his army an unopposed passage through
Bœotia. The Theban Assembly first heard the
envoys of Philip and his allies, who recalled all
the deeds which the Athenians had ever done
against Thebes, and held out the prospect of the
enrichment of the Thebans with Attic plunder,
or, if they refused Philip's overtures, of the plunder of Bœotia itself by his forces.[5] Demosthenes

---

[1] *De Cor.*, § 153.   [2] *Ibid.*, § 188.   [3] *Ibid.*, § 211.

[4] Diodorus states that Python was one of Philip's envoys, but
the quotation which he gives from *de Cor.*, § 136, refers to another
occasion.   [5] Dem., *de Cor.*, §§ 213, 214.

does not record his own reply in full: but there can be little doubt that he urged that if the Thebans joined Philip, the only result would be that Philip would be enabled to subdue Athens and Thebes separately, whereas the two cities, if united, might hope to defeat his arms entirely; he doubtless appealed with his matchless eloquence to the sense of Hellenic patriotism, and the terms which he offered were extraordinarily generous, in view of the previous relations between the two States. Thebes was to be recognised as mistress of Bœotia, and the Athenians undertook to assist her against any city that refused obedience to her; the command of the forces at sea was to be shared; the Thebans were to command on land, and the Athenians were to pay two thirds of the cost of the campaign.

At a later day Æschines bitterly attacked Demosthenes for offering terms so favourable to Thebes, and (as he declared) so humiliating to Athens. Nor can it be denied that to abandon the cause of Thespiæ and Platææ, the independence of which she had always championed, was to abandon a very noble element in the traditional policy of Athens; and it must also have touched her pride to give up Oropus. But as regards the division of the expenditure, it must be remembered that, in consequence of her situation, Thebes would have to defray the greater part of the cost of maintaining the troops quartered in her territory; and, in the position in which the Athenians were placed, it would have been madness to quarrel over the precise apportionment of responsibility and privilege between the two parties in the alliance. There is no doubt that Demosthenes acted boldly, for a member of a democracy, in offering such terms on his own authority; but the stake was worth the cost to Athens and the risk to himself. There is no more characteristic passage in his speeches than his defence against Æschines' strictures upon this agreement with Thebes.[1]

If you refer, Æschines [he says], to what was fair as between ourselves and the Thebans or the Byzantines or the Eubœans—if at this time you talk to us of equal shares—you must be ignorant, in the first place, of the fact that in former days also, out of those ships of war, three hundred in all, which fought for the Hellenes, Athens provided two hundred, and did not think herself unfairly used, or let herself be seen arraigning those who had counselled her action, or taking offence at the arrangement. It would have been shameful. No! men saw her rendering thanks to Heaven, because when a common peril beset the Hellenes, she had provided double as much as all the rest to secure the deliverance of all. Moreover, it is but a hollow benefit that you are conferring upon your countrymen by your dishonest charges against me. Why do you tell them *now*, what course they ought to have taken? Why did you not propose such a course at the time (for you were in Athens and were present) if it was possible in the midst of those critical

[1] *De Cor.*, §§ 238 ff.

times, when we had to accept, not what we chose, but what circumstances allowed?

What, he asks, would his opponents have said, if he had haggled over the terms, and the Thebans had joined Philip?

The Thebans and Athenians, in pursuance of Demosthenes' proposals, now sent urgent embassies to the other Greek States in the hope of winning their support, while Philip himself, fully realising the gravity of the crisis, wrote to his own allies in the Peloponnese (who had for the most part been hitherto on friendly terms with Thebes), representing himself simply as the champion of the Amphictyons against Amphissa, and (if Demosthenes' account is to be trusted) dissimulating his further intentions.[1] The Arcadians, in spite of their alliance with Philip, determined to remain neutral. The Messenians and the people of Elis followed their example. The Spartans, though hostile to Philip, adhered to the policy which they had followed for some years, of eschewing all entanglement in foreign affairs. Those who supported the Athenian and Theban cause were the Eubœans, Achæans, Megareans, and Acarnanians, and the inhabitants of Corcyra and Leucas.

Those politicians in Athens who were opposed to war attempted to find support in the evil omens which were reported shortly after Demosthenes' decree had been carried and acted upon. The

[1] *Ibid.*, §§ 156, 218, 222.

Delphic oracle prophesied calamity, and old orac-
ular sayings were quoted to the same effect.[1]
At Thebes, statues were said to have dripped with
blood.[2] Worse still, on September 21st, when the
candidates for initiation in to the Eleusinian mysteries went down to the sea to purify themselves,
some of them were killed by a shark.[3] But when
it was proposed to consult the oracle once more,
Demosthenes declared that the priestess of Delphi
had "philippized," as she had "medized," or taken
the Persian side, in the Persian wars, and he
reminded both Athenians and Thebans how the
greatest statesmen of each city, Pericles and
Epameinondas, had scorned such pretexts for
cowardice as were now put forward.[4] Nor would
he permit the march of the troops from Athens to
be delayed by unfavourable omens at the sacrifices
offered on their behalf; and for the time, both in
Athens and in Thebes, his word was law.

The measures which Demosthenes proposed
could not be carried through without funds. To
provide these, Demosthenes urged once more,
and this time with success, that the surplus revenues which had been spent on festivals should be
applied to military purposes.[5] He also carried a
resolution suspending for the time the work of
repairing the docks and the arsenal, and so set

---

[1] Plut., *Dem.*, xix., xxi.   [2] Schol., Apoll., *Arg.*, iv., 1284.
[3] Æsch., *in Ctes.*, § 130, and schol.
[4] Æsch.; *l.c.*; Plut., *Dem.*, xx.
[5] Philochorus, *ap.* Dion. Hal., *ad Amm.*, I, xi.   See Note 4.

free a considerable sum. It is in this same year that we hear first of the "treasurer of the military fund," and it is highly probable that the office was now constituted for the first time. The office was held by Callias, the nephew of Lycurgus; and Lycurgus himself, an able and courageous financier, and an ardent supporter of Demosthenes, became a member of the Theoric Commission in 338, and for the next twelve years, either in virtue of his own official position, or through his friends in office, controlled the financial administration of Athens.[1]

At the earliest possible moment[2] the Athenian forces joined those of Thebes, and received, on their arrival at that city, a warm and friendly welcome.[3] Freely received into the houses of the Thebans, they in no way abused their privileges, and the official friendship between the two States was doubtless confirmed by the personal good feelings thus generated. The allied forces now fortified the passes[4] through which Philip's route into Bœotia would necessarily lie. The most important of these was the Pass of Parapotamii, through which the Cephissus flowed from the Phocian into the Bœotian plain; the minor passes which crossed the same range (such as that leading

[1] See Note 5.

[2] If any reliance is to be placed on Æsch., *in Ctes.*, §140, the troops did not even wait for the formal ratification of the alliance by vote of the Assembly.   [3] Dem., *de Cor.*, §§ 215, 216.

[4] I follow closely the account of the campaign given by Kromayer, *Antike Schlachtfelder in Griechenland*, vol. i., which has superseded all previous work on the subject.

to Daulis, and another at the eastern end of Mt. Hedyleium) were doubtless also occupied.[1] At the same time, at the request of the inhabitants of Amphissa, a force of ten thousand mercenaries under Chares was sent to guard the approach to that town from Cytinium (which Philip's troops had occupied) by the Pass of Gravia; and the chief command at this station seems to have been held by the Theban Proxenus.[2]

In the earliest engagements, which Demosthenes describes as "the winter battle," and "the battle by the river," the allies were successful. (It seems likely that these engagements resulted from attempts on the part of Philip to force a way through the Pass of Parapotamii.) The allies also fortified Ambrysus, and perhaps other Phocian towns, which had been destroyed by Philip during the Sacred War.[3] Their spirits rose; mutual congratulations passed between Athens and Thebes; sacrifices and processions were held at Athens in gratitude to the gods, and the city, Demosthenes tells us,[4] was "full of pride and joy and thanksgiving." Demosthenes himself, upon the motion of Demomeles, supported by Hypereides, was awarded a golden crown, which was publicly conferred on him at the Dionysiac festival in March, 338, and though Demomeles was prosecuted for the alleged illegality of the decree by

[1] See map.
[2] Æsch., *in Ctes.*, § 146; Deinarch., *in Dem.*, § 74.
[3] Paus., IV, xxxi., § 3.   See Note 6.   [4] *De Cor.*, § 216.

Diondas, he was acquitted, and the prosecutor failed to obtain even one fifth of the votes of the jury—the proportion necessary to save him from a heavy fine. Philip appears to have thought it best to wait for reinforcements,[1] before taking further active measures.

It has often been argued that, in spite of these early successes won by the allies, the purely defensive tactics adopted by them, and the division of their forces, in consequence of the despatch of one quarter of the army to guard Amphissa— nearly twenty miles away from the main body at Parapotamii—were serious strategical errors. The latter step was strongly opposed by Æschines at the time, when it was proposed in the Assembly by Demosthenes, and he made it a point in his attack upon Demosthenes at a later date.[2] As regards the defensive attitude of the allies, they should have seen, it is urged, that they would be no better off, even if they remained in occupation of the passes for an indefinite time: Philip would still be undefeated and a menace to Bœotia and Attica, and their troops would be growing impatient at the prolonged hardships of camp-life. In reply it has been pointed out[3] that the line of defence chosen—the series of passes from Mount Parnassus to Lake Copais—was a very good one, completely protecting Bœotia and therefore Attica

---

[1] Diod., XVI, lxxxv.   [2] *In Ctes.*, §§ 146, 147.
[3] By Kromayer, *op. cit.*

also; that it would have been difficult or impossible
for Philip to circumvent the defenders at either
end of the line; and that by the occupation of these
passes, as well as of the southern end of the Pass
of Gravia, Philip was cut off (as he could have been
cut off by no other method) from access to the
Gulf of Corinth and his Peloponnesian allies; while
the Pass of Gravia was itself easy to defend from
the south, as modern no less than ancient experience
has shown, owing to the nature of the country.
Besides this it was highly probable that Philip
would not be able to remain for an indefinite time
at Elateia, but would be forced to return by the
unsettled state both of his own frontiers and of
his recently acquired dominions in Thrace. If, on
the other hand, Philip attacked and succeeded in
forcing the passes, the allies could still fall back
on the plain of Chæroneia, and choose their ground
for battle.

The fact that in the end Philip defeated the
allies was due less to defects in their general plan
of campaign than to his astuteness and knowledge
of human nature. He was well aware that a mixed
force of citizens from two large and several small
States, combined with bodies of mercenary soldiers,
was not likely to be completely under the control
of a single authority, exercising equal caution
and foresight at all points. Taking advantage,
no doubt, of a favourable moment, and having
(we may surmise) prepared the way by spreading
rumours of his feigned intentions, he arranged that

a letter addressed to his general, Antipater, should fall into the hands of Proxenus and Chares, the commanders of the allied forces stationed near Amphissa, stating that he was compelled suddenly to return, in order to quell a revolt in Thrace.[1] To give colour to this statement, he withdrew his troops from Cytinium. Thereupon the mercenary force guarding Amphissa naturally became slack, and neglected to keep guard. Suddenly, by a forced march, Philip, with a large body of troops, swept through the Pass of Gravia by night, annihilated the defending force, descended upon Amphissa, and took it. The town was afterwards destroyed by order of the Amphictyonic Council.[2] He then, by a vigorous move, pushed on to Naupactus—at least two days' march—and took it, giving it, as he had promised,[3] to his allies the Ætolians, and returning to Amphissa before his enemies could take any steps against him.[4] He had thus opened for himself a way to the Corinthian gulf,[5] and further, by occupying Amphissa and the surrounding territory, he had gained command of the passes leading through the outlying ranges of Mt. Parnassus and Mt. Korphis into the plain of the Cephissus to the south of Chæroneia. His troops could now, if he desired, come round by these passes and harass the allied army

---

[1] Polyænus, IV, ii., 8.   [2] Strabo, ix., p. 427.
[3] Dem., Phil. III, § 34.   [4] See, however, Note 7.
[5] This is true, whether Naupactus was taken on this occasion or not.

at Parapotamii from the rear. Of this possibility he at once took advantage, sending flying corps which plundered the western plains of Bœotia. He himself returned to Elateia.

It was perhaps just after this that Philip once more attempted to achieve his ends by diplomacy, instead of by further fighting. He sent envoys both to Athens and Thebes. At Athens, though Phocion warned his countrymen to reflect upon the consequences of defeat, and to make terms with Philip, Demosthenes (so Æschines asserts) threatened to drag any one to prison by the hair who mentioned peace; and when the Bœotarchs at Thebes showed an inclination to listen to Philip, he denounced them in the Athenian Assembly as traitors, and proposed to send a herald to Thebes to ask for a free passage for the Athenian forces marching against Philip, with the result that the Thebans were shamed into abandoning all thought of peace. He urged upon the Athenians the importance of fighting at as great a distance as possible from the city, and his influence both in Athens and Thebes was sufficient to ensure the continuance of the struggle.[1]

The generals at Parapotamii, finding their communications with Thebes and Athens threatened by Philip's light troops, now withdrew from the passes into the plain of Chæroneia, where they could check the plundering forays, and choose an advantageous position for the decisive battle.

[1] See Note 8.

Upon this Philip recalled his light troops and re-united them with his main army, and so with all his forces marched through the Pass of Parapo-tamii into the plain, and confronted the allies.

The decisive battle took place on the 7th of Metageitnion (probably the 2nd of August, in our reckoning[1]), 338. The allies' line stretched across the plain of Chæroneia, the left wing resting against the rocky hill of Petrachos, on which the town was built, the right touching the Cephissus, where it runs close beneath the steep western end of the mountain spur called Acontium. The total length of their front was perhaps a little over a mile. The allied army contained between thirty thousand and forty thousand men, of whom Thebes supplied twelve thousand infantry (in-cluding the "Sacred Band," with whom it was a point of honour to stand by one another to the death) and eight hundred cavalry, Athens about ten thousand infantry and six hundred cavalry, and the smaller states perhaps nine thousand infantry; the mercenaries employed numbered about five thousand, and the cavalry were made up by various contingents to two thousand in all.[2] Behind the left wing lay the entrance of passes leading to Lebadeia and Coroneia, by which, in case of need, it would be possible to retire without

---

[1] See Kromayer, *op. cit.*, p. 185. The alternative date is September 1st.

[2] This is Kromayer's computation, based upon calculations as probable as our information allows.

being harassed by cavalry in pursuit. This wing was constituted by the Athenian army, commanded by Stratocles, Lysicles, and Chares; Demosthenes himself served among the infantry, the words "Good Luck"[1] inscribed upon his shield. In the centre were the mercenaries and the contingents of the small States. The right wing was the post of greatest danger and responsibility. If the enemy could force their way through the defenders' line here, there was no means of outflanking them,[1] the plain would be open to the victors, and they would be able to cut off the retreat to Coroneia. In this position the Thebans were stationed under Theagenes. The Macedonian army numbered about thirty thousand infantry and two thousand cavalry—a rather smaller force than that of their opponents, but for the most part drilled to act in unison, and all under the command of one master-mind.

At the Theban end of the line the battle was at first hotly contested; but the young Alexander, whom Philip had placed in command of the Macedonian left, through his personal bravery and the encouragement given by it to his men, at last succeeded in forcing a way through the Theban ranks. Philip, on the contrary, on the Macedonian right, withdrew step by step before the

---

[1] Ἀγαθῇ τύχῃ.

[2] They might possibly, though not easily, have been outflanked, after forcing their way through, from the side of Chæroneia on the other wing.

impetuous onset of the Athenians, who felt confident of victory. Stratocles even bade his men pursue the enemy to Macedonia itself.[1] "The Athenians do not know how to win a victory," Philip is said to have remarked, as he observed the violence of their attack, and proceeded to draw them yet farther from the favourable position, on somewhat higher ground than his own, which they had at first occupied. At length, when he had retired about half a mile, and the Athenians, already tired,[2] had behind them, not the entrance to the passes, but only the steep rocky hill of Petrachos, which made retreat impossible for them, Philip suddenly halted and bade his men return the Athenian attack.[3] His plan was entirely successful; the Athenian line was broken; and Alexander, having forced his way through on the other wing, now threatened the allies in the rear. The position was hopeless. Some who were nearer the centre were able to escape and make for the passes, but those on the extreme left wing, caught between the enemy and the rocks, could only surrender or perish.[4] A thousand Athenian citizens were killed and two

---

[1] Polyænus, IV, ii., 2.   [2] Polyæn., IV, ii., 7; Frontin., II, i., 9.

[3] Some ancient writers (*e. g.*, Diod., XVI, lxxxv.) ascribes Philip's sudden change of tactics to jealousy of Alexander, but it can scarcely be doubted that military considerations were really the determining motive.

[4] None of our authorities say anything about the action of cavalry in the battle; but probably Philip completed his work by bringing his cavalry round upon the Athenian wing.

thousand taken prisoners. All who could fled in headlong rout, and among them Demosthenes. On the other wing, the Sacred Band had been cut to pieces where they stood, and the general loss in the Theban ranks was very heavy. No serious pursuit was attempted; probably Philip's men were too much exhausted; and the fugitives collected at Lebadeia.

Demosthenes was perfectly justified in hinting[1] that bad generalship was the cause of the defeat. There was no one commander, directing the operations of the allies as a whole. Phocion, the greatest Athenian general then living, had perhaps been away with the fleet in the Ægean when the commanders were being elected,[2] or else was not appointed owing to his known disapproval of the campaign; and the Greek commanders were entirely outgeneralled by Philip, who had already proved in previous contests the effectiveness of a feigned retreat, and of tiring out the enemy before attacking them. Lysicles, who, like Chares, was among the fugitives, was condemned to death by a jury at Athens; Lycurgus, who prosecuted, demanded of him how, after a defeat which entailed the death and capture of so many of his fellow-citizens and the enslavement of all Greece, he could dare to walk the streets of Athens in open day, being, as he was, a living reminder to his country of her shame and reproach.[3]

[1] *De Cor.*, §§ 194, 245.   [2] Plut., *Phoc.*, xvi.
[3] Diod., XVI, lxxxviii.

Of Stratocles we hear no more. Chares perhaps did not return to Athens.

Thus the cause of Hellenic liberty, for which Demosthenes had striven for so many years, was finally lost. A few brief struggles had yet to be made, but the battle of Chæroneia was in effect a thoroughly decisive blow. "With the bodies of those who fell here was buried the freedom of the Hellenes."[1] Close to the battle-field, where the Theban dead were buried, a marble lion was erected in memory of those who had died for freedom. This monument has in recent times been restored from the ruin into which it had fallen, and re-erected on or near the spot on which it originally stood.

Eight years afterwards in the Speech on the Crown,[2] Demosthenes was called upon to defend the policy which had led to so disastrous a failure. Æschines had left no argument untried which could fasten the defeat of Chæroneia upon his rival. The defence which Demosthenes made was, in effect, that since the policy was the only right and worthy one for Athens and since all that an orator or a statesman could do to make it successful had been done, he was not to blame if, through bad generalship or the inscrutable will of Heaven, the struggle had ended in defeat.

In everything the issue falls out as Heaven wills, but the principle which he follows reveals the mind

[1] Lycurgus, *in Leocr.*, § 50.

[2] *De Cor.*, §§ 192, 193; comp. §§ 194, 195, and 245, 246.

THE LION OF CHAERONEIA, PARNASSUS IN THE BACKGROUND

PHOTO BY MAURICE S. THOMPSON

of the statesman. Do not therefore count it a crime
on my part that Philip proved victorious in the
battle. The issue of that event lay with God, not
with me. But show me that I did not adopt every
expedient that was possible, so far as human reason
could calculate; that I did not carry out my plan
honestly and diligently, with exertions greater than
my strength could bear; or that the policy which I
initiated was not honourable, and worthy and indeed
necessary; and than denounce me, but not before.

He claimed above all to have interpreted aright
the deepest instincts of his fellow-countrymen,[1]
and only those who believe that no attempt is
justifiable which fails can refuse to accept his plea.
For years he had striven to foster the love of liberty in the Athenian people, until at last they were
ready to sacrifice everything else for the one thing
which they counted best, as their fathers had done
before them. To have succeeded in this aim, to
have produced so great a moral reaction in a people who were tending more and more to yield to
the pleasure of the moment, and to sacrifice national to private considerations, was in itself, perhaps, a greater service to his country than any
success which a general might have won. That
he had not misinterpreted the feelings of his countrymen was shown by their steady support of him
in the ensuing years, in face of all the attacks
of time-serving enemies. Defeated undoubtedly
the Athenians were, but they had become them-

[1] *Ibid.*, §§ 199, 206. See pp. 329, 490.

selves once more, if only for a moment, they had
fought for the noblest cause known to the Hellenic world, and the consciousness of this must
at least have been some consolation to the nobler
spirits among them in the years which followed
the battle of Chæroneia.

NOTES ON CHAPTER X

1. The story is told by Æsch. *in Ctes.*, §§ 113-131, and Dem.,
de Cor., §§ 143-152, and from the two accounts the facts can be
reconstructed with fair probability. It has been disputed
whether the quarrel broke out at the autumn meeting of 340,
or the spring meeting of 339; but Kromayer, *Antike Schlachtfelder*,
i., pp. 181, 182, has shown conclusively that it was at the autumn
meeting, in October or November.

2. The Pylagori were not members of the Council, and had no
vote in it, but were official representatives of their several States,
sent to transact business with the Council. They were perhaps,
as a rule, persons of greater distinction than the Hieromnemon.
It was as Pylagorus that Demosthenes had attended the Council
in 343. (See Sundwall, *Epigraphische Beiträge*, pp. 50, 51.)

3. Kromayer (*l.c.*) shows that Philip must have been elected
general at the spring meeting, not the autumn meeting of 339,
since the latter only took place in October or possibly early in
November. The spring meeting was in May or June, and this
would be long enough after Philip's return to Macedonia to
justify Æschines' statement (*l.c.*, §129) that it was πολλῷ χρόνῳ
ὕστερον, if he returned late in February or in March.

4. Schäfer concludes from the order of Philochorus' statements that Demosthenes carried these measures before the capture of Elateia, but the inference does not seem to be necessary.
The measures were passed in the archonship of Lysimachides,
i.e., after July 9th, 339; and it does not appear that between that
date and the capture of Elateia in September any event occurred
of so threatening a character as to induce the Athenian People to
divert the theoric money from the festivals—a step to which they
had always been obstinately opposed.

5. On the official position of Lycurgus, see Francotte, *Les*

finances des cités grecques, pp. 231, 232. He was for four years a theoric commissioner, and probably held various special commissions during and after that time. The office which most historians suppose him to have held—that of "chief of the administration" (ὁ ἐπὶ τῇ διοικήσει)—does not appear to have been constituted until a later date. Francotte thinks that the office of military treasurer may have existed as early as 347, but his argument is not conclusive.

6. Glotz, *Bull. Corr. Hell.*, 1909, pp. 526–546, argues that the rebuilding of the Phocian towns (except for the fortification of Ambrysus by the allies for purely military purposes) was really the work of Philip, whom he supposes to have become friendly with the Phocians since his rupture with Thebes. This involves a very violent treatment of Pausanias' statements, and does not seem to be proved. It is true that the Phocians are not mentioned among Philip's opponents at Chæroneia. But were the Phocians in a condition to engage in active hostilities at all at this period?

7. The taking of Naupactus by Philip is recorded in Theopompus, fr. 42 (Oxford text), and is placed here by Beloch (who follows Schäfer) because no other date can be found for it, though it is fair to notice that Schäfer has to emend Suidas' statement that the fact is recorded by Θεόπομπος ἐν β' (Book II), to ἐν νβ' (Book LII), because Book LII of Theopompus seems to have dealt with this period. Possibly the taking of Naupactus ought really to be placed after Chæroneia. (The event may only have been mentioned in passing in Theopomp., II.). Beloch's argument that after Chæroneia no one resisted Philip is not conclusive. We have no evidence to show that the people of Naupactus may not have done so, and Theopompus seems to imply that they did.

8. The authorities for Philip's communications with Athens and Thebes are Plutarch, *Dem.*, xviii., *Phoc.*, xvi., and Æsch., *in Ctes.*, §§ 149–151. But Æschines' story is not very clear as to the date of these proceedings, and Plutarch gives no precise indication. It is possible that these proceedings really belong to an earlier stage, before the arrangement with Thebes was decisively concluded.

CHAPTER XI

AFTER CHÆRONEIA

THE night after the battle of Chæroneia was spent by Philip in drunken revelry. He mocked triumphantly at the failure of Demosthenes' plans, as he shouted out the opening words of the orator's decrees,[1] beating time with his foot to their half-metrical rhythm. In his intoxication he jeered at his prisoners, until he was suddenly sobered by the remark of one of them, the Athenian orator Demades—"O King, Fortune has bidden you play the part of Agamemnon. Are you not ashamed to behave like Thersites?" At this he tore off his garlands, put an end to the revel, and ordered Demades to be set free.[1] But when the fugitives, who had assembled at Lebadeia, asked leave to bury their dead, he refused their request, although by so doing he was violating one of the most sacred traditions of Greek warfare; and they were forced to return to their homes, leaving their solemn obligation to their comrades unfulfilled.

The news of the disaster reached Athens first

[1] Δημοσθένης Δημοσθένους Παιανιεὺς τάδ᾽ εἶπεν.

[2] Diod. XVI, lxxxvii.; Plut., *Dem.*, xx.

through a rumour from Œnoe[1]; but soon the
defeated soldiers began to arrive, and its full magnitude became known. Amidst all the anxiety
and lamentation of the friends of the soldiers,[2]
the leading statesmen in Athens did not lose their
heads for a moment. On the resolution of Hypereides the Assembly passed, without delay, a resolution ordering preparations to be made for the
defence of the city. That such a project was not
hopeless, even though the country-districts of
Attica might be devastated by Philip, was shown
by the King's failure to reduce Byzantium, in
consequence of his inability to cut off her access
to the sea; for in the case of Athens his difficulties
would have been far greater. The Council of
Five Hundred marched under arms to the Peiræus
to take measures for its defence.[3] It was resolved
to bring the women and children from the country
districts into the city, to arm all citizens who were
between fifty and sixty years of age as a garrison
for the walls,[4] to restore their civic rights to those
who had lost them owing to judicial sentences, to
give citizenship to any resident aliens, and freedom
to any slaves, who would serve in the forces,[5] and
to appoint Charidemus, Philip's implacable enemy,
commander-in-chief.[6] Demosthenes, on his re-

---

[1] Hyper., *in Aristog.*, fr. 31 (Oxford text).
[2] Vividly described by Lycurgus, *in Leocr.*, §§ 39 ff.
[3] Lycurgus, *l.c.*, § 37.　　　　　　　　[4] *Ibid.*, § 16.
[5] Hyper., *in Aristog.*, fr. 29; *Vit. X Orat.*, 851a, etc.
[6] Plut., *Phoc.*, xvi.

turn, provided by a series of decrees for the details of the defence—the disposition of the garrisons, the entrenchments, the funds for the fortifications[1]; and the confidence of the People in him remained unimpaired. Arms were taken from the temples in which they had been dedicated, and slabs from the tombstones, to meet the urgent need. Demosthenes was also appointed corn-commissioner, and sailed away to procure corn and money for the city's use, while the financial control at home remained in the hands of Lycurgus.

The departure of Demosthenes at this juncture has been criticised with undue harshness. It is said that he quitted Athens when he should have been there to face the consequences of his policy; and that he left Hypereides and Lycurgus to do the hard work, and to incur the subsequent humiliation of submission to Philip. It is at least an equally plausible hypothesis that he was especially selected for the work of collecting corn and money, because all his eloquence would be needed to persuade the allies and others to supply these necessities at such a moment; and it is highly probable that when he left Athens, he did so in the confidence that the work of defence was in good hands, and that the policy of continued resistance to Philip was securely accepted by the People.

[1] Dem., *de Cor.*, § 248. Æschines, *in Ctes.*, § 159, and Plut., *Dem.*, xxi., state that from motives of caution, Demosthenes got his friends (especially Nausicles) to propose these decrees formally.

But this policy was not destined to be carried out, and the line of action adopted by Philip was probably the reason for this. We cannot indeed be sure of the precise order of events during the days which followed the battle of Chæroneia; but it is certain that Philip at once took stern vengeance upon Thebes, and at the same time displayed an astonishing leniency, and even friendliness, towards Athens. He placed a Macedonian garrison in Thebes, and entrusted the government to three hundred of his own supporters, who punished the patriotic party mercilessly with exile, execution, and confiscation.[1] He further decreed the dissolution of the Bœotian league, and the restoration of Orchomenus, Platææ, and Thespiæ, which had been traditionally hostile to Thebes.[2] The Theban prisoners captured at Chæroneia were sold into slavery, and the Thebans had even to pay for the privilege of burying their dead. The obedience of northern Greece was still more firmly secured by the planting of Macedonian garrisons in Chalcis and Ambracia, and (now if not earlier[3]) by the transference of Naupactus from the Achæans to the Ætolians.

Yet towards Athens Philip took no hostile action. Various reasons for this have been suggested—the difficulty of reducing the city; his genuine admiration of Athens as the centre of Hellenic culture; and (possibly the most important

[1] Justin, IX, iv., etc.   [2] Pausan. IV, xxvii., § 5, IX, i., § 3.
[3] See above, pp. 382, 391.

consideration of all) his desire to obtain without
trouble her co-operation in his projected Eastern
campaign. In any case Athens was not, like
Thebes, a revolted ally of his own,[1] and he might
well feel free to be generous. Either Philip's
attitude, or a sense (which may have revived in
the absence of Demosthenes) of the inevitable
hardships which further resistance would entail,
brought about a change of feeling in Athens.
The appointment of Charidemus, who (as Plutarch
states) had been clamorously nominated by the
wilder spirits in Athens, was cancelled by the
Council of Areopagus, and Phocion was elected
in his place; and when Philip sent Demades to
Athens, to express his willingness to enter into
negotiations, it was resolved to send Phocion and
Æschines, with Demades himself, as ambassadors
to Philip. By the terms of the Peace of Demades,
Athens was permitted to retain possession not
only of Athens, but of Delos, Lemnos, Imbros,
Scyros, and Samos.[2] Oropus was restored to her,
and the King promised not to send any warship
into the Peiræus, or any land-force into Attica.
On the other hand, the Athenian alliance was
dissolved, and its members (with the exception of
the island peoples already mentioned) were declared independent; the Chersonese passed into

[1] The alliance had been formally dissolved by the declaration
of war in 340; see p. 350.
[2] Diod., XVIII, lvi.; Aristotle, *Ath. Pol.*, 61, 62; *C. I. A.*, ii.,
824.

Philip's power[1]; and Athens herself became the ally of Philip. The bones of the Athenians slain at Chæroneia, who had been burned on the battle-field by the victors, were conveyed back to Athens by Alexander himself, accompanied by Antipater and Alcimachus, two of Philip's ablest generals; and the two thousand prisoners were restored without ransom. The reaction of feeling in Athens produced by this unlooked-for generosity was great. On the proposal of Demades, the citizenship of Athens was voted to Philip and Alexander, it was resolved to erect a statue of Philip in the market-place, and other honours were offered to the two generals.[2]

For the moment the Macedonian party in Athens seemed to have triumphed; Philip's aim was not, after all, what Demosthenes had said it was—the destruction of Athens; and Æschines at least boasted openly of his friendship with Philip. But on the return of Demosthenes, it was soon seen that the popular confidence in him unshaken. The renewal of the fortifications was actively continued, as inscriptions of the time make plain.[3] Instead of hurried preparations for defence, systematic building and modernisa-

---

[1] It is not mentioned in the list of Athenian possessions in Aristotle, *Ath. Pol.*

[2] Justin, IX, iv., v.; Polyb., V, x.; Plut., *Dem.*, xxii.; Hyper., *in Demad.*, fr., 77; Paus. I, ix., § 4; Demades, fr., etc.

[3] See Frickenhaus, *Athens Mauern*, pp. 14–29; and Wilamo-witz-Moellendorf, *Arist. u. Athen*, i., pp. 194, 353, etc.

tion of the fortifications were carried on; Demosthenes was appointed (by the Pandionid tribe) to be one of the Ten Commissioners[1] entrusted with the superintendence of the work; and during his tenure of office, he contributed as much as a talent and a half from his own property for the service of the State.[2] It appears also that a system of drill and military discipline, much more regular than had hitherto been enforced in time of peace, was now instituted for those who were liable to service.

It was a far higher mark of public respect, that Demosthenes was chosen to deliver the Funeral Oration in honour of those who fell at Chæroneia, despite the bitter opposition of Æschines and other orators of the Macedonian party. "And the reason," he told Æschines, in the Speech on the Crown,[3]

you know well, but I will tell it you nevertheless. The People knew for themselves both the loyalty and zeal which inspired my conduct of affairs, and the iniquity of yourself and your friends. . . . And further, they thought that one who was to pronounce an oration over the dead, and to adorn their valour, should not have come beneath the same roof, nor shared the same libation, as those who were arrayed

---

[1] τειχοποιοί. Whether he was appointed in 338 or 337 is uncertain.

[2] Æsch., *in Ctes.*, §§ 17, 31; Dem., *de Cor.*, § 113.

[3] §§ 286–288. The extant Funeral Speech which purports to be the one delivered by Demosthenes on this occasion is a patent forgery.

against them; that he should not there join hands
with those who with their own hands had slain them,
in the revel and the triumph-song over the calamities
of the Hellenes, and then come home and receive
honour—that he should not play the mourner over
their fate with his voice, but should grieve for them
in his heart. What they required they saw in themselves and in me, but not in you; and this was why
they appointed me, and not any of you. Nor, when
the People acted thus, did the fathers and brothers
of the slain, who were then publicly appointed to
conduct the funeral, act otherwise. For since (in
accordance with the ordinary custom) they had to
hold the funeral feast in the house of the nearest of
kin, as it were, to the slain, they held it at my house,
and with reason; for though by birth each was more
nearly akin to his dead than I, yet none stood nearer
to them all in common. For he who had their life
and their success most at heart, had also, when they
had suffered what I would they had not, the greatest
share of sorrow for them all.

The enemies of Demosthenes continued to show
their hostility by attacking him on every conceivable ground.

All those who were interested in injuring me [he
says[1]] combined, and assailed me with indictments,
prosecutions after audit, impeachments, and all such
proceedings—not in their own names at first, but
through the agency of men behind whom, they
thought, they would best be screened against recognition. For you doubtless know and remember that

[1] *De Cor.*, §249.

during the early part of that period I was brought to trial every day, and neither the desperation of Sosicles, nor the dishonesty of Philocrates,[1] nor the frenzy of Diondas and Melantus, nor any other expedient, was left untried against me. And in all these trials, thanks to the gods above all, but secondarily to you and the rest of the Athenians, I was acquitted;

and he justly prided himself upon the public testimony thus given to his integrity and patriotism. Hypereides was assailed in the same way.[2] He was impeached by Aristogeiton for the illegality of the decree which he had moved immediately after the battle, and by which slaves were set free, aliens enfranchised, and those condemned by the law-courts restored to their privileges. The decree was in fact plainly illegal; but Aristogeiton's opposition had already had the effect of making it a dead letter,[3] and the People accepted Hypereides' defence. "It was the arms of the Macedonians," he said, "that darkened my eyes. It was not I that proposed the decree; it was the battle at Chæroneia." It was plain that the honours paid to Philip and Alexander had been but the expression of an immense feeling of relief at the moment, in consequence of Philip's generosity, and that the real sentiment of the People remained true to Demosthenes.

After settling Phocis and Eubœa, Philip went to Megara, and thence to Corinth and the Pelo-

---

[1] Not the proposer of the Peace of 346.　　[2] *Vit. X Orat.*, 849 a.
[3] See above, p. 168.

ACRO-CORINTHUS AND THE TEMPLE AT CORINTH

PHOTO BY ENGLISH PHOTO CO.

ponnese. The Megareans and Corinthians received him with honour; and a Macedonian force was left at Corinth to command the Isthmus. Most of the Peloponnesian peoples submitted to him readily, and some displayed an ignominious flattery. The Spartans, on the contrary, bluntly refused to acknowledge him, in spite of their military weakness at the time; and in consequence of this he overran Laconia, and gave considerable portions of it to the Argives and others of his allies, though he refrained from attacking Sparta itself. He next held a congress of representatives of the Greek States at Corinth, and announced his intentions with regard to the invasion of the Persian Empire. He was formally appointed commander of the Greeks against Persia; the contingents to be furnished by the several States for the campaign were settled; and a common synod of the Greeks was now established, with Corinth as its meeting place.[1] The Athenians were called upon to furnish a fleet and a troop of cavalry; and Demades proposed in the Assembly the fulfilment of this demand; but it needed the influence of Phocion to persuade the Athenians to agree to it, in spite of their obvious inability to refuse,—so strong was the sense of shame at the position in which they found themselves.[2]

[1] Note 1 at the end of the Chapter.
[2] Diod., XVI, lxxxix.; Justin, IX, v.; Polyb., XVI, xxxiii.; Plut., *Phoc.*, xvi.; Oxyrh., Pap., I, p. 25, col. iii., l. 3 ff.; Wilhelm, *Attische Urkunden*, p. 43.

26

It was probably at about this time that the aged Isocrates wrote his Third Letter to Philip, expressing his satisfaction that he had lived to see the dream of his youth on the point of realisation— the union of the Hellenes in a great expedition against Persia,—a satisfaction which was his sole consolation amid the trials of old age. Before the end of the year 338 he died.[1]

The attacks of the Macedonian party upon Demosthenes and Hypereides in the law-courts were met by counter-attacks, in which Lycurgus was especially prominent. The first of his more notable victims was Autolycus, a member of the Council of Areopagus; upon whom the death penalty was pronounced for his withdrawal from Athens with his family and his money, when the news of Chæroneia had arrived, and the city had need of all her men and their resources.[2] Another was Lysicles, who had been general at Chæroneia, and was also condemned to death.[3] So relentless and successful was Lycurgus in his political prosecutions, that one of his opponents said that he dipped his pen, not in ink, but in death, when he composed his speeches.[4] His high personal character, and his known patriotism and incorruptibility, as well as his proved ability in practical administration, gave him great power; and the

[1] Note 2.   [2] Lycurg., *in Leocr.*, § 53, etc.
[3] Diod., XVI, lxxxviii.   See above, p. 387.
[4] *Vit. X Orat.*, 841e.

moral earnestness and pathos of his oratory were sufficient to conceal his harshness towards his opponents and the exaggeration of his language. Hypereides also took part in the campaign of litigation. Demades had actually proposed to confer the citizenship of Athens, and the office of proxenus, or consul for Athens, upon Euthycrates, whose treachery had brought about the fall of Olynthus; and Hypereides indicted the proposal as illegal.[1] The result of the trial is not known; but it is difficult to suppose that Demades received the approval of the jury.

Early in the summer of 337 Demosthenes was chosen commissioner of the festival-fund for the four years beginning in July of that year. We do not know to what extent the distributions of festival-money were carried out during his term of office. It was a time of peace, and probably the surplus no longer went (as it had done during the war by his own enactment) into the war-chest, but was at least in part distributed as "theoric money." That Demosthenes should have agreed to this is not inconsistent with his insistence in earlier years upon the application of the surplus to defray the cost of war. He had never in fact condemned the distribution as bad in itself, but only as bad when it was treated as more important than the vital needs of the State; and he had admitted that if those needs could be met without suspending the distributions, they ought to be so

[1] Apsines, I, p. 388.

met.[1] That condition was now realised. The large expenditure of Lycurgus on public buildings shows that the financial condition of the city must have been tolerably prosperous; and we can be sure that popular opinion must have demanded the resumption of the distributions.

The popularity of Demosthenes and the general sense of his generosity and administrative ability were expressed by a decree proposed by Ctesiphon early in 336, that Demosthenes should be crowned with a golden crown in the theatre at the ensuing Dionysia, on the ground that he continuously spoke and acted for the best interests of the city. The decree ordered that the herald should proclaim before the assembled multitude (which would include strangers from all parts of Greece) that Demosthenes was crowned for his merit and his courage.[2] The decree was passed by the Council; but when it came before the Assembly, Æschines gave sworn notice that he intended to indict Ctesiphon for the illegality of his proposal. This declaration *ipso facto* suspended the operation of the decree, and Æschines instituted judicial proceedings; but before he could bring the case to an issue, events took a turn which made it very unlikely that the Macedonian party would win any success with the People or a popular jury for some time to come.

When Philip had made his arrangements at

[1] Olynth. III, § 19.
[2] Æsch., *in Ctes.*, §§ 49, 236, 246; Dem., *de Cor.*, § 244, etc.

Corinth for his projected invasion of Asia, he
returned to Macedonia; and shortly afterwards a
quarrel which had long been imminent came to a
head. Philip had grown tired of his wife Olympias,
the mother of Alexander, and in 337 he married
Cleopatra, the niece of Attalus, one of his generals.
At the wedding-feast an angry scene took place
between himself and Alexander; Alexander departed into Lyncestis, and his friends were banished. But early in 336 a formal reconciliation
took place; Olympias and Alexander returned to
court; and it was arranged that Alexander's
sister (also named Cleopatra) should marry
Olympias' brother (her own uncle), Alexander of
Epirus; while Attalus was sent to Asia in command
(with Parmenio) of a large division of the army.[1]
We may pass over certain other complications of
the situation. Philip determined to celebrate
the wedding of his daughter Cleopatra at Ægæ
with great splendour; all the Greek States and
neighbouring princes sent embassies bearing presents; and among them the Athenians sent a
golden crown, and announced a decree which they
had passed, undertaking to deliver up any one who
had conspired against Philip's life and escaped
to Athens.[2] But in the midst of the feast, Philip

---

[1] Plut., *Alex.*, ix., x.; Justin, IX, v.; Diod., XVI, xci., etc.

[2] Whether, as Beloch (*A. P.*, p. 239) supposes, this decree was
passed in response to a demand by Philip for some fresh proof of
the loyalty of Athens, in view of the strong anti-Macedonian
feeling recently manifested there, there is no evidence to show.

was stabbed in the theatre, where the festal performance was about to begin, by an injured favourite named Pausanias, and died immediately. (July, 336.)[1] That Olympias was in the background of the plot is more than probable; the satisfaction which she did not hesitate to show lent colour to the suspicion; and the fact that Cleopatra, her rival, had just borne a son to Philip, who might some day contest the succession against Alexander, may have impelled her to desire Philip's instant death.[2]

Demosthenes received private intelligence of Philip's death, before the news was generally known in Athens; and it would be pleasant if we could draw a veil over his behaviour. He came before the Council with a joyful face, declaring that he had had a dream, in which Zeus and Athena had appeared to him, promising some great blessing to Athens. This was in itself nothing more than a piece of rather childish acting; but it was far more reprehensible that when the news was made public, he appeared in a festal garment, and with a garland on his head, though it was but seven days since the death of his own daughter; and that the People (doubtless following his lead) offered sacrifice in gratitude for good news and voted a crown to Pausanias. Phocion, to his credit, protested against this ungenerous exultation over the dead, and reminded

[1] Diod., XVI, xci.–xciv.   [2] Justin, IX, vii.; Diod., XVII, ii.

his countrymen that the army which had defeated them at Chæroneia was only diminished by one man.[1] The plea that Demosthenes' conduct was intended as a political demonstration—an invitation to other States to throw off the Macedonian yoke—is no excuse for the want of restraint and generosity displayed both by himself and the People.

It soon became plain how illusory was the idea that the death of Philip afforded an opportunity for the recovery of independence. Any such hope was excluded by the promptitude with which Alexander, recognised as King by Antipater and the army, took steps to secure his position. His half-brother Arrhidæus he treated indeed with consideration, and gave him a military command, first in Thrace and then as captain of the Thessalian cavalry. But all actual or possible conspirators or claimants to the succession were at once put to death; Cleopatra and her infant son fell victims to the ferocity of Olympias, though Alexander was not privy to her design; Attalus, Cleopatra's uncle, was assassinated in Asia Minor by Alexander's own orders—his hostility to Alexander was proved by the fact that the Athenians had opened communication with him;—and though Demosthenes chose to mock at the young King and to call him Margites, after a foolish character in an old poem,[2] he showed himself

[1] Plut., *Dem.*, xxii., *Phoc.*, xvi.; Æsch., *in Ctes.*, §§ 77, 78; Diod., XVII, iii.   [2] Probably of the sixth century B.C.

entirely capable of managing his difficult inheritance. Within three months of Philip's death he
marched southwards into Greece at the head of a
large army. He first claimed the allegiance of
the Thessalians, who resolved to join him in
marching against Athens.[1] At Thermopylæ he
was acknowledged by the Amphictyonic Council,
and proclaimed commander-in-chief of the Greeks;
and he expressed himself in friendly language to
the Ambraciots and Acarnanians, who had seemed
likely to give him trouble. He then proceeded
on his way and encamped outside Thebes.

The Athenians now repented of their rashness,
and, on the proposal of Demades, sent a deputation to apologise for their tardy recognition of
him. At the same time they once more brought
in their families and property from the country
into the city.[2] Demosthenes himself was elected
to serve on this embassy, but returned home after
accompanying his colleagues only as far as Mt.
Cithæron.[3] Alexander at first addressed the
envoys severely, but afterwards returned a gracious
reply; and the People of Athens, relieved of their
terror, voted him even higher honours than they
had conferred upon Philip.[4] After this Alexander
convened a congress of representatives of the
Greek States at Corinth (the Spartans still holding

[1] Diod., XVII, iv.; Æsch., *in Ctes.*, § 161.

[2] Diod., XVII, iv.; Justin, XI, iii.; Demades, fr., etc.

[3] Diod., *l.c.*; Æsch., *in Ctes.*, § 161; Dein., *in Dem.*, § 82; Plut.,
Dem., xxiii.   [4] Diod., *l.c.;* Arrian, I, i., § 3.

aloof); his leadership of the Greek forces was formally recognised, and a convention was drawn up, by which it was agreed that the several States were to be autonomous, and all forms of interference by one State with another were forbidden; the congress was to meet periodically; and it is most probable that a Macedonian force remained at Corinth.[1]

In the spring and summer of 335 Alexander was occupied with campaigns in Thrace and Illyria, undertaken with a view to ensuring the obedience of the restless inhabitants of those countries during his expedition into Asia. These campaigns were completely successful. But his absence at so great a distance allowed the sentiment of independence to revive once more in Athens and Thebes; false reports of his death encouraged the patriotic movement, and may have been used as arguments for action by Demosthenes and Lycurgus.[2]

Demosthenes appears at this time to have hoped to secure his country's freedom by making common cause with Persia. The details of these negotiations are not clearly known to us. Rather earlier

[1] The authority is the speech "On the Treaty with Alexander," certainly not written by Demosthenes, but perhaps a genuine speech of one of the anti-Macedonian party, and later in date than 332, since in § 7 it mentions events in Lesbos in that year (Arrian, III, ii., § 6).

[2] So the fragment of Demades states; but the authority is bad, as the fragment is probably a late forgery (see Blass, *Att. Ber.*, III, ii., p. 272).

—just after Alexander's accession,—Demosthenes' overtures (which were perhaps made without the knowledge of the People) appear to have been rudely repulsed, and the King bluntly refused to send money to Athens.[1] But soon afterwards Darius, who had probably succeeded to the throne about the end of 336, seems to have realised the formidable character of Alexander's intentions, and to have sent a sum of three hundred talents, to be used against the Macedonian power.[2] This sum the People refused, as was correct; but it is stated to have remained in the hands of Demosthenes, to be employed for the object specified. That his enemies should afterwards accuse him of misappropriating it was a matter of course.[3]

It was with the connivance and aid of Demosthenes that the Thebans now received back some of their exiled fellow-citizens (who had been sojourning in Athens), and then killed two of Alexander's officers, restored the democratic constitution, and besieged the Macedonian garrison in the Cadmeia. On Demosthenes' proposal the Athenians resolved to send help to Thebes; an army and fleet were made ready, and an embassy was sent to Persia to propose a formal alliance.[4] Demosthenes also sent large supplies of arms,

[1] Æsch., *in Ctes.*, § 238.

[2] According to Plutarch, proofs of this were found by Alexander at Sardis in some letters written by Demosthenes, and in records by Persian generals of the amount sent.

[3] Æsch., *in Ctes.*, § 240; Dein., *in Dem.*, §§ 10, 18; Plut., *Dem.*, xx.   [4] Arrian, II, xv.

bought with Persian gold, to Thebes. But the forces of Athens made no move. The People had already experienced the consequences of hasty action, and were apparently waiting to learn the truth about Alexander himself, and to discover what direction events were likely to take. Some of the Peloponnesian peoples also signified their sympathy with the revolt of Thebes; and some were persuaded by Demosthenes [1] to reject Antipater's demand for their help against the Thebans; but only the Arcadians sent any troops, and these marched no farther than the Isthmus. Had energetic action been taken by their friends, it is not impossible that the Thebans might have been successful, and Æschines afterwards [2] accused Demosthenes himself of bringing about the overthrow of Thebes by his miserliness; he would not even, Æschines says, advance the five talents for which the Macedonian mercenaries in the Cadmeia offered to betray the fortress. Deinarchus also accused him of refusing ten talents to Astylus, the leader of the Arcadian forces, and stated that others paid Astylus the money on condition that he should return home instead of going to the assistance of Thebes. [3] These assertions are hardly credible. It is much more likely that it was the influence of Phocion, whose caution had more than once justified itself, that kept the Athenians from carrying their sympathy into action.

[1] Dein., *in Dem.*, § 19; *Vit. X Orat.*, p. 850.
[2] *In Ctes.*, § 240. [3] Dein., *in Dem.*, § 20.

But though it is conceivable that the Athenians might have enabled Thebes to free herself, it is not likely. With astonishing suddenness, Alexander himself appeared with his army outside the walls of Thebes. At first he attempted to win the Thebans by conciliatory overtures; but they had suffered much from the garrison in the Cadmeia, and were determined to resist to the last.[1] Within a few days the town was taken by storm, the forces of Thespiæ, Platææ, Orchomenus, and the Phocians taking part in the assault, and giving vent to the hatred of many generations. Six thousand Thebans were slain in the massacre which followed, and over thirty thousand were taken prisoners. Alexander entrusted the decision of the fate of the conquered to the Greek peoples who had taken part in the siege. In accordance with that decision Thebes was razed to the ground, the temples and the house of Pindar alone being spared; nearly all the captives were condemned to be sold as slaves, and the remaining survivors of the Thebans were declared outlaws, to whom no Hellenic city must give shelter. The territory of Thebes was divided between Orchomenus and Platææ, and a Macedonian garrison once more occupied the Cadmeia.[2]

The destruction of Thebes caused a paroxysm of horror and fear in the other Greek States.

[1] Arrian, I, vii.; Diod., XVII, ix.
[2] Arrian, I, ix.; Diod., XVII, xiv., etc.

Some of them sought to secure themselves by giving evidence of submission to the destroyer. The Arcadians put to death those who were responsible for the despatch of troops to the Isthmus; the people of Elis recalled from exile the banished partisans of the Macedonian domination; the Ætolians asked pardon of Alexander for the sympathy they had shown with the conquered; at Messene and at Pellene in Achaia tyrants were set up who favoured the Macedonians.[1] The Athenians were not slow to recognise their own special peril, owing to the part they had played in encouraging the revolt of Thebes. The news of the massacre reached them in the midst of the Eleusinian Mysteries. The feast was broken off, and the city was once more prepared for defence against the expected attack; large sums of money were contributed both by citizens and resident aliens[2]; and the fugitives from Thebes were warmly welcomed, in spite of the prohibition pronounced by the King and his allies.[3] But once more the spirit of resistance was overcome by that of caution and alarm. On the motion of Demades, ten ambassadors were sent to Alexander with a message of congratulation, not only upon his safe return from Illyria, but also (if the accounts which have come down to us are correct) upon his punishment

---

[1] Diod., XVII, viii.; Arrian, I, x.; Speech on Treaty with Alex., §§ 4 ff., 10, 11; Paus., VII, xxvii., § 1.

[2] Dem., *de Cor.*, § 312; *in Phorm.*, § 38.

[3] Plut., *Alex.*, xiii.

of the rebellious Thebans. It is not surprising
that, on receiving this shameful despatch, the King
threw it away and refused to speak to the envoys.[1]
Subsequently, however, he offered to pardon
Athens, if she would send away the Theban refu-
gees who had taken shelter with her, and would deliver up to him the leaders of the anti-Macedonian
party, among whom were named Demosthenes,
Lycurgus, Polyeuctus, Charidemus, Ephialtes, and
others.[2]

In the debate which ensued in the Assembly,
Phocion, after being repeatedly called upon for his
opinion, recommended that the demands of the
King should be obeyed, declaring that the leaders
whose surrender was in question had brought
enough trouble upon Athens already, and that
he himself would gladly sacrifice his dearest friend
for the public good, after the example of the heroes
of legend. It is said that the People shouted this
proposal down. Demosthenes himself warned
them that it was not well for the sheep to surrender
the sheep-dog to the wolves; and that if they sold
the orators to Alexander, they would be selling
themselves into slavery, like merchants, who only
display a few grains of corn as a sample, but
thereby sell their whole cargo. Hypereides and
Lycurgus also opposed Phocion's proposal.[3]   The

---

[1] Arrian, I, x.; Plut., *Phoc.*, xvii.   See Note 3.

[2] Arrian, *l.c.*; Plut., *l.c.*, and *Dem.*, xxiii.; Diod., XVII, xv. The
names are not the same in all the accounts.

[3] *Vit. X Orat.*, 838d; Plut., *Phoc.*, ix.

resolution which was finally adopted was moved by Demades. (Diodorus states—we do not know on what authority—that he had been bribed by Demosthenes with a gift of five talents). It was determined to send an embassy to Alexander to ask pardon for the orators and generals whose surrender he had demanded, on condition that judicial proceedings should be taken against any who were guilty of misconduct; and to beg that the Theban exiles should be permitted to remain in Athens.

The embassy was headed by Phocion and Demades. The eloquence of the latter, and the outspoken advice which the former gave to the King, proved successful. In fact the sack of Thebes and the extirpation of one of the greatest cities of Greece was an act which was condemned by the moral sense of the Greeks generally; Alexander's own conscience was not free from misgivings about it; and he may have been glad to retrieve his character by showing clemency towards Athens. Accordingly he gave ear to Phocion's advice that he should turn his army against barbarians, not against Greeks; and reduced his demands to the requirement that Charidemus, one of the most irreconcilable opponents of Macedonia, should be expelled from Athens. With this the Athenians complied. Charidemus went to Persia and took service under Darius; and his example was shortly afterwards followed by Ephialtes and other Athenian generals. Alexander returned to Macedonia with the knowledge that he had nothing to fear for the present from the Greeks.

A resolution of the Assembly entrusted the Council of Areopagus with the promised enquiry into the use made of gold from Persia for the assistance of Thebes, but the Council allowed the matter to drop[1]; and although the enemies of Demosthenes repeatedly accused him of enriching himself with the money sent by the Great King, there is no evidence which deserves the name to show that he really did so; and the reception given to his defence in the Speech on the Crown, in which he claims to have been incorruptible from first to last, is scarcely consistent with the insinuations made by his enemies to the effect that his acceptance of large presents from Persia was matter of common knowledge.[2]

When we review the course of events from the battle of Chæroneia to the departure of Alexander to Asia, it is not easy to find sufficient reason for the severity with which the part played by Demosthenes has been criticised. It is plain that his own policy was one of resistance to the uttermost. That alone he considered to be worthy of the traditions of Athens. Whatever concessions to circumstances his fellow-countrymen, less courageous than himself, might make, he lost no opportunity

---

[1] Dein., *in Dem.*, § 10.

[2] Æsch., *in Ctes.*, §§ 173, 209, 259; Dein., *in Dem.*, § 70; Hyper., *in Dem.*, Col. 25; Plut., *Dem.*, xiv., etc.

which seemed to offer a chance of throwing off the yoke, and worked steadily, with Lycurgus, for the improvement of the defences, the increase of the efficiency of the army, and the strengthening of the financial resources of the city. It is also plain that he had the confidence of the People; and, conscious of this, he did not shrink from taking measures, which his country's interest seemed to demand, upon his own responsibility, whatever risk to himself they involved. Chief of these measures were the communications which he kept up during this period with Persia, with whom it was natural to make common cause against a common foe. It is true that his correspondence with Persia was, from a narrowly democratic point of view, a violation of the spirit of the constitution. "The Council and the Assembly," Æschines protested, "are passed over: despatches and embassies come to private houses, and those not from insignificant persons, but from the greatest Powers in Asia and Europe." Besides this, the responsibility for the expenditure of the money remitted from Persia to be used against Alexander was one which, when refused by the People, placed him in a very invidious position. Yet here again he took the risk of the charges of malversation which any one could bring, and which, though no one could prove them, could not, in all probability, be disproved without disclosing facts as to the use of this secret service money which had better be kept secret; and he was not afraid of being denounced as an autocrat. There is no valid ground for believing that Demosthenes acted, during this period, otherwise than with a single eye to what he believed to be the interest and honour of his country.

But was his action wise, as well as patriotic? Was his statesmanship equal to his good intentions? Here there is more room for doubt. We cannot tell whether he did or did not rely too strongly upon the support of his countrymen,—whether he ought to have known that they would not really go to the help of Thebes. It was at least a generous error, if he attributed to them still the spirit which they had shown before the battle of Chæroneia. Nor can we now tell how far his belief that the moment was a favourable one for the revolt of Thebes was reasonable. Alexander, so far as any one knew, was in Illyria, and some said he was dead. His sudden appearance before Thebes was at least as great a surprise to every one else as to Demosthenes himself; and it does not seem right to blame him for falling into an error which no one else avoided. It is easy to find fault with him in the light of our later knowledge of Alexander's character, and his skill in making sudden movements with a rapidity paralysing to his enemies. But in 335 Alexander was not so well known, in spite of his prompt action in the previous year, as he became a few years later. On the whole, therefore, it does not seem just to denounce the course pursued by Demosthenes during these years either as dishonest or as unstatesmanlike;

and more credit is due to him than has always been given for the courage and consistency which he displayed.

NOTES TO CHAPTER XI

1. Wilhelm, *Attische Urkunden* (Sitzungsber. Akad. Wien., 1911), shows that the confederation formed at Corinth included far more States than has been generally supposed, and that it was much more minutely organised, especially as regards the representation (on a proportional basis) of the several peoples in the common synod. (He interprets in this sense *C. I. A.*, ii., 160, 184, and some other inscriptions.) It is disputed whether Philip intended only to free the Greek towns in Asia from Persian rule, or to conquer the whole or the greater part of Asia Minor, or to enter upon a series of campaigns comparable to those actually carried out by Alexander. There is no evidence on the point.

2. The picturesque story of Isocrates being so overcome with grief at the defeat of Chæroneia that he refused food, and so died a few days after the battle, must be taken to be disproved; and apart from this story there are no good grounds for disputing the genuineness of the Third Letter to Philip. (See Beloch, *Griech. Gesch.*, ii., p. 574 n.) The Letter is in keeping with Isocrates' known sentiments, and the style is also his.

3. Grote and others doubt the story of this embassy to Alexander; and it is not clear that Plutarch's statement can refer to any embassy before Alexander's demands were made. His language is very obscure (*e.g.*, it is not at all plain to what the words τὸ μὲν πρῶτον ψήφισμα refer). That he was much confused about this period is shown by the fact that in his Life of Demosthenes, chapter xxiii., he runs together events of which some took place before and some after the taking of Thebes. Arrian also may have transferred to an earlier stage in the proceedings a message really sent to Alexander *after* he had demanded the surrender of the orators. But it is only too probable that, whether before or after, some such message was sent.

CHAPTER XII

GREECE IN THE ABSENCE OF ALEXANDER

WE know little of the history of Athens during the first years of Alexander's absence in the East. But it can be gathered that it was Demades who took the lead in public affairs, sometimes holding financial, sometimes military offices, and receiving frequent presents from Antipater, whom Alexander had left in charge of Macedonia and Greece. The statue of Demades in bronze was even erected in the market-place in his lifetime, contrary to Athenian custom; and he was accorded the honour of perpetual maintenance in the Prytaneum at the expense of the state. He was supported by Phocion, who was continually re-elected general, and (unlike Demades) declined all presents from Antipater; and also by Æschines, though the activity of the latter appears to have been intermittent, and he lived for the most part the life of a prosperous landowner. Among his possessions were included estates which had once formed part of the territory of Thebes.[1] Demo-

[1] Dem., *de Cor.*, §§ 41 ff. 307 ff; Æsch., *in Ctes.*, §§ 216 ff.; Dein., *in Dem.*, §§ 101; Plut., *Phoc.*, xxx., etc.

sthenes seems to have given up for the time all
attempt to influence the course of affairs. "When
there happened," he says to Æschines,[1] "what I
would had never happened, when it was not statesmen that were called to the front, but those who
would do the bidding of a master, those who were
anxious to earn wages by injuring their country,
and to flatter a stranger—then, along with every
member of your party, you were found at your
post, the grand and resplendent owner of a stud—
while I was weak, I confess, yet more loyal to
my fellow-countrymen than you." Æschines and
Deinarchus of course attribute his quiescence to
cowardice.[2] If it is cowardice to recognise the
temporary hopelessness of a cause, then Demosthenes is open to the charge; but that is not the
ordinary meaning of cowardice; and when there
seemed to be hope once more, Demosthenes acted
energetically enough.

A modern historian[3] has suggested that the reason for Demosthenes' retirement is to be found
in a *rapprochement* between himself and Demades, as the result of which Demades in 335 proposed the motion which prevented the surrender
of Demosthenes and others, while Demosthenes
undertook not to attempt to disturb the Peace, or
to interfere with Demades' acts. But there is no
sufficient evidence of any such agreement, and the
subsequent association of the two orators in the

---

[1] *De Cor.*, § 320.   [2] Æsch., *in Ctes.*, §§ 163 ff.; Dein., *l.c.*
[3] Beloch, *Att. Politik.*, p. 243.

affair of Harpalus[1] does not prove it. It is more
likely that Demades' motion was a compromise
dictated by the strong popular feeling against
conceding Alexander's demands on the one hand,
and the danger of refusing compliance on the other;
and that Demosthenes' abstinence from public
affairs was no more than a wise concession to
circumstances. Indeed, even after the supposed
compact with Demades, Demosthenes joined
Hypereides in opposing the proposal to furnish a
contingent to Alexander (as the Athenians were
bound to do)—a fact which of itself almost proves
that the compact never existed.[2] On the motion
of Phocion, twenty ships and a small corps of
cavalry were sent to join Alexander's army[3]; but
a number of Athenian volunteers took service in
the cause of Persia. Whether there is any truth
in the assertions of Demosthenes' enemies that he
sought a reconciliation with Alexander through the
mediation of a youth named Aristion, and with
Olympias through Callias of Chalcis, is very doubtful.[4] The statements made by Æschines and
Hypereides when prosecuting him some years
later are certainly not reliable testimony; especially as Æschines at least was particularly anxious
to prove that Demosthenes had really taken the
Macedonian side—a paradox which only falsehoods could support.

---

[1] See below, p. 461.   [2] *Vit. X Orat.*, 847 c, 848 e.
[3] Plut., *Phoc.*, xxi.; Diod., XVII, xxii.
[4] Æsch., *in Ctes.*, § 162; Hyper., *in Dem.*, col. 20.

But though defeated, the anti-Macedonian party was not wholly inactive. In 334 Diotimus, one of the generals whose surrender Alexander had demanded, died; and Lycurgus proposed a decree in his honour.[1] In the same year when the Persian fleet appeared in the Ægean, it was permitted by the Athenians to revictual at Samos.[2] But Alexander could afford to overlook these pin-pricks, and it is clear that he desired to remain on good terms with Athens. He even went out of his way to pay her compliments. After his victory at the Granicus in 334, despite the fact that he had captured a number of Athenians among the enemy, he sent a present to Athens and three hundred suits of Persian armour to be dedicated in the Parthenon; with the inscription, "Dedicated by Alexander, son of Philip, and by the Greeks, except the Lacedæmonians, out of the spoils taken from the Barbarians of Asia."[3]

Until the battle of Issus in 333, Demosthenes, who continued to receive special intelligence from the seat of war, cherished hopes that Alexander would be defeated in Cilicia, and regarded with unconcealed satisfaction the apprehensions of Æschines and other friends of the King[4]; but after that victory, no room was left for such hopes.

In the spring of 331 the Athenians sent an embassy to Alexander, bearing him a golden crown in honour of his victories; and he then set free those

[1] *Vit. X Orat.*, 844 a. [2] Arrian, I, xix., § 8.
[3] Arrian, I, xvi., § 7. [4] Æsch. *in Ctes.*, § 164.

of their fellow-citizens whom he had taken prisoners at the Granicus, and had before refused to
release[1]; and in ordering the affairs of Greece,
whether by his own commands or through his
regent Antipater, he appears to have been careful
to avoid, so far as Athens was concerned, any
breach of the agreement between himself and the
Greek States.

Thus the course of events in Greece was comparatively uneventful until after Alexander's
crowning victory at Arbela in 331, and the death
of Darius in the following year. Sparta alone
acted in a manner which threatened trouble.
The Spartan King Agis entered into communication with Persia, and in 333, supported by funds
received from Persian admirals, made himself
master of Crete. Consequently in 331, Alexander
ordered a large fleet under Amphoterus to take
action against Sparta, and sent money to Antipater
to be used in reducing the Spartans to obedience.[2]
At last, in 330, Sparta declared war against Alexander. The moment seemed favourable. Antipater was engaged in Thrace, where a revolt had
broken out under the leadership of the Odrysian
King Seuthes; and Memnon, one of Alexander's
own commanders, seems for a time to have joined
in it.[3] Further, there was considerable discontent

---

[1] Arrian, I, xxix.; III, vi.; *C. I. A.*, ii., 741 f.

[2] Arrian, III, vi.; Diod., XVII, xlviii.

[3] In this year the Athenians passed a decree in honour of
Rhebulas, son of Seuthes (*C. I. A.*, ii., 175 b). This may mean

in Greece at the violation of the promises made by Alexander at Corinth in 336, through the arbitrary conduct of Macedonian commanders. Tyrants had been set up, favourable to the Macedonian domination, in Messene, Lesbos, and Pellene, though it had been promised that there should be no interference with the constitutions of the States. Macedonian captains had seized Athenian and other trading vessels and detained them at Tenedos, and the Athenians had actually equipped a fleet of one hundred ships under Menestheus, son of Iphicrates, to recover them; but (in accordance with Alexander's policy of conciliation towards Athens) they were released before active measures were taken. A Macedonian trireme had entered the Peiræus, nominally to demand permission for the building of small vessels there for the Macedonian fleet, but more probably in the hope of recruiting the fleet with Athenian sailors, though the request had been withdrawn when the Athenians objected.[1]

Agis at first gained some slight successes. He defeated a Macedonian corps under Corrhagus; the people of Elis, all the Arcadians except those of Megalopolis, and all the Achæans except those of Pellene joined him; and he laid siege to Megalo-

---

that Rhebulas came to Athens to renew the old friendship between the city and the Thracian princes, and that the Athenians wished to show sympathy with the revolt of Seuthes. See Schäfer, iii., p. 200.

[1] Speech on Treaty with Alexander.

polis.[1] He also appealed to Athens for support, and
the extant speech (wrongly ascribed to Demosthenes) "On the Treaty with Alexander" may have
been delivered in one of the consequent debates in
the Assembly, by a supporter of the Spartan King's
request. It is not easy to ascertain with any
certainty what part Demosthenes took in the
discussion. According to Plutarch,[2] he began by
asking the Athenians to assist Agis, but afterwards
shrank back, finding that the People were not
willing to join in the rising. It may be suspected
that this is substantially the truth. That he did
at first encourage the Spartans to hope for Athenian aid seems to be indicated by Æschines' statement[3] that Demosthenes had claimed (though
falsely) a share in instigating the Peloponnesian
revolt, as well as a revolt in Thessaly, of which we
know nothing more; though in the same speech—
so Æschines states—he complained in a series of
strained metaphors of the helpless condition into
which his old opponents had brought the State,
and so excused himself from carrying his support
of the movement further. In another place,[4]
Plutarch states that the Athenians resolved to give
the Peloponnesians the support of their fleet—
perhaps they were influenced by Demosthenes'
attitude at the outset—but that Demades cleverly
parried this resolution, by pointing out that the

---

[1] Æsch. *in Ctes.*, § 165, 166; Dein., *in Dem.*, § 34; Diod.,
XVII, c.   [2] Plut., *Dem.*, xxiv.

[3] *In Ctes.*, § 167.   [4] Plut., *Præc. Ger. Rep.*, 818 e, f.

SPARTA

FROM A DRAWING BY H. M. PICKARD-CAMBRIDGE

only funds available for the expenditure which this policy would entail were those which he, as Theoric Commissioner, had saved for distribution at an approaching festival; and that the Athenians, rather than forego this distribution or contribute from their private property, were content to do nothing. In that case, Demosthenes might well complain that the sinews of the State had been cut by his opponents; and his withdrawal from his first attitude was dictated by simple prudence. It was of no use to encourage Sparta to expect support which the People would not give; and it is to Demosthenes' credit that he was not afraid to face the humiliation which such a withdrawal from his original position brought with it. Certainly nothing can be more despicable than the insincerity of Æschines and Deinarchus[1] in blaming him afterwards for doing nothing to help the Spartans against Macedonia, while at the same time they tried (as will be seen shortly) to fasten upon him some of the responsibility for the rising, and declared that his behaviour had brought discredit upon the city.[2]

The siege of Megalopolis was raised upon the arrival of Antipater with an army considerably outnumbering that of the Spartans and their allies. Agis gave battle, but was completely defeated, and himself slain.[3] Antipater demanded

---

[1] Æsch., *l.c.*; Dein., *in Dem.*, § 35.   [2] Æsch., *in Ctes.*, § 254.
[3] Curtius, VI, i; Diod., XVII, lxii., lxiii.; Paus., I, xiii., § 6; Justin, XII, i.; Plut., *Agis*, iii., etc.

fifty noble Spartans as hostages, and entrusted the sentence on the rebellious States to the congress of the Greeks at Corinth. But the Spartans appealed to Alexander, to whom the hostages were sent; and he pardoned all but the chief movers in the revolt, only commanding the payment of 120 talents to Megalopolis as compensation for the inconvenience caused to them by the siege.[1] A proposal was made by the enemies of Demosthenes to hand him over for judgment to the Amphictyonic Council, which was to meet in the autumn of 330, as though he had been in some way responsible for the disturbances; but the People refused to sanction this,[2] and showed thereby that though they might be unwilling to take any action which involved danger or sacrifice, their sympathy with the attitude of Demosthenes towards the Macedonian conqueror had not substantially altered.

Moreover, a notable trial of this same year (330) showed that the patriotic party was still active. Lycurgus prosecuted a certain Leocrates for desertion after the battle of Chæroneia. When the first report of the battle came, Leocrates had departed with all his belongings to Rhodes, to escape the ruin which seemed to be coming upon Athens, and had even reported at Rhodes that Athens was actually taken. He had subsequently settled at Megara as a resident alien, and engaged

---

[1] Curtius, *l.c.*; Diod. XVII, lxxiii.
[2] Æsch., *in Ctes.*, §§ 161, 254; Dem., *de Cor.*, § 322.

in trade on a considerable scale. In the year 331–0 he ventured to return to Athens; and Lycurgus, true to the stern principles which had led him to prosecute Autolycus, charged him with treason and demanded the death-penalty. The Speech of Lycurgus may still be read. He justly prides himself on his avoidance of all attempt to bring odium upon the accused by the introduction of matter irrelevant to the charge, and of references to the life of the prisoner, apart from the time of his offence. He spends all his energy in proving the enormity of the offence itself, judged by the standard of Athenian tradition; and a considerable part of the Speech consists of narratives of episodes in Athenian history, with long quotations from the poets. Though the language is exaggerated, the tone of the Speech is earnest and patriotic; but nothing can quite justify the attempt to put Leocrates to death for an offence committed eight years before, by way of making a demonstration against the Macedonian supremacy. The votes of the jury were equally divided and Leocrates was acquitted. The trial illustrates the sharp division of political opinion in Athens, and the large amount of support upon which statesmen of the patriotic party could still reckon, at least when no sacrifice was entailed by their policy.

It was probably at about the same time[1] that a certain Euxenippus was impeached by Polyeuctus

[1] It was at any rate between 330 and 324 (Blass, *Att. Ber.*, III, ii., p. 64).

for giving bad advice to the People and receiving bribes from those who were acting against the interests of Athens. From the remains of Hypereides' speech for the defence, it is evident that of the arguments used by the prosecutor, one of the most formidable was derived from the prisoner's alleged flattery of the Macedonians, and of Olympias in particular. That such an argument should have been used is some indication of the state of popular feeling.

It may have been the failure of the Spartan revolt, with which Demosthenes was known to have sympathised, that led Æschines to renew the attack upon him, in the form of a prosecution of Ctesiphon, which he had allowed to drop six years before, when the news of Philip's death had revived the antipathy of the Athenians to Macedonian rule. It will be remembered that Ctesiphon had proposed in the Council, and the Council had resolved, that a golden crown should be bestowed upon Demosthenes in the theatre at the Dionysia, with a proclamation to the effect that he consistently spoke and acted for the true good of the People of Athens, and a commemoration of his public services; and that Æschines had indicted this as illegal. The indictment had had the effect of suspending the operation of the decree, which became void at the end of the year in which it had been moved. Some difficulty has been caused by the fact that in the Speech against Ctesiphon

Æschines clearly assumed that unless Ctesiphon was condemned, Demosthenes would be crowned at the next Dionysia; and certain historians have been led by this to suppose that Ctesiphon's decree had again been brought forward at the time of the Spartan rising, and that this led Æschines to repeat his indictment. But there is no evidence of this; and it seems more natural to suppose that every one assumed, as a matter of course, that if the jury acquitted Ctesiphon his motion would be formally reintroduced and carried into effect. Others have suggested that Demosthenes' own party, in the confident expectation of an acquittal, forced Æschines to proceed with his indictment, by threatening to prosecute him and demand the infliction of a fine upon him for having failed to carry out his sworn intention earlier. But of this also there is no evidence; and it is inconceivable that if such threats had been used, neither orator should have made the barest allusion to them.

It is much more likely that Æschines thought that an opportunity offered itself, in the temporary humiliation of Demosthenes owing to his failure in regard to the Spartan rising, of inflicting a crushing defeat on his rival; and that the revived prosecution of Ctesiphon is to be connected with the prosecutions of anti-Macedonian leaders in other States, perhaps with the approval of Alexander or Antipater. Demosthenes himself saw such a connection.[1] "At the same time as the irre-

---

[1] *De Cor.*, § 197.

concilable enemies of Athens, Aristratus in Naxos and Aristoleos in Thasos, are bringing the friends of Athens to trial, Æschines in Athens itself is accusing Demosthenes." But Æschines had under-estimated the strength of Demosthenes' position. The sympathies of the People, of whom the jury that would try the case would be representative, were still with Demosthenes and antagonistic to the Macedonian rule. Even before the trial began Æschines must have been conscious of this; for he actually attempted to enlist the good-will of the jury by alleging, as among the offences of Demosthenes, that he had let slip a number of occasions upon which he might have opposed the Macedonians, and by continually insinuating that Demosthenes' opposition to Macedonia had been a sham. The result of the trial was to afford Demosthenes his last and most signal triumph.

Æschines assailed the proposal of Ctesiphon on three grounds. He alleged first, that it was illegal to crown a statesman who had not passed the public scrutiny to which all public officials were liable on laying down office, and that Demosthenes, who at the time of the decree had been a Commissioner of fortifications and of the festival-fund, had not passed this scrutiny; secondly, that it was illegal to proclaim the crown in the theatre in the manner proposed; and thirdly, that the reasons which were given by Ctesiphon for the award of the crown, and which it was proposed to proclaim, were false. It was a case in which the jury had not only to give the verdict, but also, if they condemned the accused, to fix the penalty. Never within the memory of man had any trial aroused such interest throughout the Greek world, and the court was thronged not only with Athenians, but with strangers from all parts of Greece.[1]

The prosecutor addressed the court first. After an introduction, in which he emphasised the importance of punishing illegal proposals, in order to safeguard the constitution at a time when all constitutional principles were falling into neglect,[2] he proceeded at once to explain the technical grounds upon which he relied. He first cited the law which forbade the crowning of an official still liable to scrutiny, and defended it on the ground that a proposal to confer a crown, even if the reservation were made (which Ctesiphon had omitted to make) that the ceremony should not take place until after the scrutiny had been held, was bound to prejudice the issue of the scrutiny in favour of the recipient of the crown.[3] He further replied to the argument which he expected Demosthenes to use, to the effect that the office which he held was not a public office in the technical sense, and that the public money of which he had charge was his own gift, for which he could not reasonably be called to account.[4] It may be suspected that some of these passages (like some which occur

[1] Æsch., *in Ctes.*, § 56.
[2] §§ 1–8.
[3] §§ 9–12.
[4] §§ 13–31.

28

later in the Speech) were inserted in it for publication after Demosthenes had spoken; but there can be no doubt that up to this point Æschines' case was a good one in point of law.

With regard to the second technical question, there is not much more doubt. There appears to have been a law which forbade the proclamation of a crown in the theatre, and ordered that a crown, if awarded by the Council, should be proclaimed in the Council-chamber, if by the People, in the Assembly. But there was apparently another law, regulating proceedings at the Dionysia, and forbidding proclamations in general at the festival, but permitting those crowns to be publicly conferred in the theatre which had been granted to Athenian citizens by other States, if the People gave permission. This law Æschines expected Demosthenes to wrest to his purpose, by arguing that coronation in the theatre was lawful if the People consented to it, and omitting to mention the restriction of this permission to the case of crowns conferred by other States. Accordingly he warned the jury against such sophistry, and protested against the notion that, with all the safeguards provided by the constitution against contradictory laws, such a contradiction as the anticipated argument implied would have been permitted to remain.[1]

It is highly probable that here also Æschines was on firm ground. But both he and Demos-

[1] §§ 32–48.

thenes were well aware that the case would not be decided upon purely technical grounds, and though he dealt with these grounds fully, and (so far as we can judge) straightforwardly, the greater part of his Speech was devoted to the attempt to prove that the reasons which Ctesiphon had given for conferring the crown on Demosthenes were false, and that Demosthenes had not deserved well of the State.[1]

After a brief reference to some of the early incidents of his rival's career, he divided his life into four periods—the first, the time of the Peace of Philocrates; the second, from the Peace of Philocrates to the renewal of the war with Philip; the third, the time of the alliance with Thebes; and the last from the battle of Chæroneia to the time of the trial. He attempted to show that in all four periods the policy of Demosthenes was corrupt and detrimental to Athens. We have considered these charges in reference to the events of the several periods in their place, and need not do so again. The most significant points in Æschines' attack are his insinuation that Demosthenes, in spite of his patriotic professions, had more than once acted in subservience to the Macedonian interest, and his attempt to prove, not only that Demosthenes had worked in harmony with Philocrates (in which there was some truth), but also that the alliance which he had negotiated with Callias and the Eubœans was dictated by sordid

[1] §§ 49–176.

self-interest; that he had claimed undue credit for the alliance with Thebes, and had granted the Thebans terms which were highly disadvantageous to Athens; that his policy at that time had led directly to the battle of Chæroneia and the destruction of Thebes; and that since these disasters he had pursued a cowardly, but not less mischievous, course. In a striking passage,[1] Æschines imagines the scene at Dionysia, if, when the orphans of those who had fallen in the service of their country were presented with a suit of armour by the State, Demosthenes, whose policy had made them orphans, was crowned with gold. At another point[2] he enumerates the qualities of a true "friend of the People," and finds that neither in his parentage nor in his character has Demosthenes any of these marks of the democratic spirit.

In the latter part of the Speech, Æschines first argued that whereas in old times rewards had been but rarely bestowed by the People, and had therefore been highly esteemed, the indiscriminate bestowal of honours was tending to diminish their value.[3] He then returned to the topic of the importance of trials for illegal proposals, and declared that in cases where the proof was necessarily so straightforward, and required only the comparison of the incriminated proposal with the letter of the law, the accused ought not to be allowed to employ an advocate to mislead the

[1] §§ 152–158. [2] §§ 168–176. [3] §§ 177–191.

jury—that Demosthenes, in short, ought not to be permitted to speak on behalf of Ctesiphon, or at least ought to be strictly confined to the legal questions at issue, and to the order of topics laid down by the prosecutor.[1] There follows in the Speech as we have it, a series of brief arguments in reply to those which Demosthenes was expected to use—most of them, in all probability, inserted after the trial, as a reply to arguments which Demosthenes actually had used—together with passages designed to arouse the animosity of the jury against Demosthenes himself or against Ctesiphon.[2] In conclusion, Æschines insisted upon the moral effect which the verdict of the jury must inevitably have, and besought them to put an end to the acquisition of excessive power by individuals and to the corruption of statesmen by Persian gold.[3] A passage of real power ends with a sadly frigid and artificial appeal:

And now, O Earth and Sun and Virtue and Intelligence and Culture, whereby we distinguish the honourable from the shameful, I have given you my aid and have spoken. If I have accused him well, and as the charge deserves, I have spoken as I desired; if inadequately, as well as I could. Do you consider the arguments which I have used, and those which I have passed over, and give the vote which justice and the interest of the city require.

Had the reply of Demosthenes been lost, it may be that Æschines' Speech would have been given

[1] §§ 191–214.   [2] §§ 215–242.   [3] §§ 243–259.

a higher place in the estimation of later ages than has usually been assigned to it. There are indeed in it passages of overwrought rhetoric and digressions of disproportionate length; yet his case is, on the whole, strongly presented, and its personalities do not transgress the limits which Athenian taste allowed. But Demosthenes' defence of Ctesiphon throws his rival's oration utterly in the shade. It is not only that, except upon the technical points, which no one present can have regarded as of serious importance, his case is overwhelmingly good; his Speech as a whole stands on a moral level which is incomparably higher. Certain reservations must doubtless be made, and those not unimportant. The replies to the several portions of Æschines' accusation are interspersed with passages of personal attack, which are almost savage in their vehemence, and are irrelevant to the main issue. Probably no such language was ever used by a politician about his opponents on any other occasion even in Athens, and the brilliant dramatic power which some of these passages show does not excuse their untruthfulness.[1] There are, moreover,—chiefly in those parts of the Speech which deal with the Peace of Philocrates,—misrepresentations of the truth, due to the orator's desire to disclaim all share in a transaction which was now discredited in popular estimation. On the points of law which Æschines' adduced, the

[1] Comp. esp., §§ 159, 198, 209, 257–264 (the famous account of Æschines's earlier days—probably almost entirely false), 308.

reasoning of Demosthenes can only be called sophistical and evasive. At best it could only be urged that the law had been broken before on many occasions, sometimes in Demosthenes' own favour. But when all that can be said in criticism of the Speech is fully allowed for, the greatest difference between it and that of Æschines remains. Æschines scarcely ever rises above the level of the party politician, the legal prosecutor, the personal enemy. His Speech reveals no breadth of outlook, no worthy ideal of national policy. Its whole effect is negative. It attacks one act of Demosthenes after another, cleverly indeed, but from the standpoint of no general principles, no far-sighted aims; and sometimes—more particularly in those passages in which it seeks to disparage the terms of the alliance with Thebes, or those in which Demosthenes is accused of favouring the Macedonian interest [1]—a meanness and an insincerity are revealed which are utterly unworthy of a statesman.

Demosthenes, on the other hand, speaks in the tone of a statesman who has attempted wholeheartedly to carry out his own highest ideals, and those of his countrymen, and who can appeal with confidence to the best side of their national character, convinced that he has not interpreted it wrongly. He claims to be judged, not by the

[1] Demosthenes did not reply to the charges so far as they referred to the most recent times—doubtless because of the danger he would have incurred had he tried to prove expressly his hostility to Alexander.

familiar jargon about the "friend of the People," but by the highest standards of statesmanship.

Every investigation that can be made as regards those duties for which an orator should be held responsible, I bid you make. I crave no mercy. And what are those duties? To discern events in their beginnings, to foresee what is coming, and to forewarn others. These things I have done. Again, it is his duty to reduce to the smallest possible compass, wherever he finds them, the slowness, the hesitation, the ignorance, the contentiousness, which are the errors inseparably connected with the constitution of all city-states; while, on the other hand, he must stimulate men to unity, friendship, and eagerness to perform their duty. All these things I have done, and no one can discover any dereliction of duty on my part at any time.[1] . . .

Do you ask me [he demands] for what merits I count myself worthy to receive honour? I tell you that at a time when every politician in Hellas had been corrupted—beginning with yourself,—no opportunity that offered, no generous language, no grand promises, no hopes, no fears, nor any other motive, tempted or induced me to betray one jot of what I believed to be the rights and interests of the city; nor of all the counsel that I have given to my fellow-countrymen, up to this day, has any ever been given (as it has by you) with the scales of the mind inclining to the side of gain, but all out of an upright, honest, uncorrupted soul. I have taken the lead in greater affairs than any man of my own time, and my ad-

[1] § 246.

ministration has been sound and honest throughout all.[1] . . .

All these measures, men of Athens, will be found by any one who will examine them without jealousy, to have been correctly planned, and executed with entire honesty; the opportunity for each step was not, you will find, neglected or left unrecognised or thrown away by me; and nothing was left undone, which it was within the power and the reasoning capacity of a single man to effect. But if the might of some Divine Power, or the inferiority of our generals, or the wickedness of those who were betraying your cities, or all these things together, continuously injured our whole cause, until they effected its overthrow, how is Demosthenes at fault?[2] . . .

Not when my surrender was demanded, not when I was called to account before the Amphictyons, not in face either of threats or of promises, not when these accursed men were hounded on against me like wild beasts, have I ever been false to my loyalty towards you. For from the very first I chose the straight and honest path in public life; I chose to foster the honour, the supremacy, the good name of my country, to seek to enhance them, and to stand or fall with them.[3]

At every stage in the argument, Demosthenes puts the question, "What was the part which Athens was bound to play, if she was to be true to herself and her traditions?" and claims to have urged her to play that part.

Should she, Æschines, have sacrificed her pride and her own dignity? Should she have joined the ranks

[1] §§ 297, 298.   [2] § 303.   [3] § 322.

of the Thessalians and Dolopes, and helped Philip
thereby to acquire the empire of Hellas, cancelling
thereby the noble and righteous deeds of our forefathers? Or, if she should not have done this (for it
would have been in very truth an atrocious thing),
should she have looked on, while all that she saw would
happen, if no one prevented it—all that she realised,
it seems, at a distance—was actually taking place?[1]
. . . What language should have been used, what
measures proposed, by the adviser of the People at
Athens (for that it was at Athens makes the utmost
difference), when I knew that from the very first, up
to the day when I myself ascended the platform, my
country had always contended for pre-eminence,
honour and glory, and in the cause of honour, and for
the interests of all, had sacrificed more money and
lives than any other Hellenic people had spent for
their private ends: when I saw that Philip himself,
with whom our conflict lay, for the sake of empire and
absolute power, had had his eye knocked out, his
hand and his leg maimed, and was ready to resign any
part of his body that Fortune chose to take from him,
provided that with what remained he might live in
honour and glory? And surely no one would dare to
say that it was fitting that in one bred at Pella, a
place then inglorious and insignificant, there should
have grown up so lofty a spirit that he aspired after
the empire of Hellas, and conceived such a project
in his mind; but that in you, who are Athenians, and
who day by day in all that you hear and see behold
the memorials of the gallantry of your fathers, such
baseness should be found that you would yield up

[1] § 63.

your liberty to Philip by your own deliberate offer and deed.[1]

So he argues above all in justification of the policy which led to the battle of Chæroneia:

Even if what was to come was plain to all before-hand; even if all foreknew it; even if you, Æschines, had been crying with a loud voice in warning and protestation—you who uttered not so much as a sound—even then, I say, it was not right for the city to abandon her course, if she had any regard for her fame, or for our forefathers, or for the ages to come. As it is, she is thought, no doubt, to have failed to secure her object—as happens to all alike, whenever God wills it: but then, by abandoning in favour of Philip her claim to take the lead of others, she must have incurred the blame of having betrayed them all. . . . But this was not, it appears, the tradition of the Athenians: it was not tolerable; it was not in their nature. From the beginning of time no one had ever yet succeeded in persuading the city to throw in her lot with those who were strong, but unrighteous in their dealings, and to enjoy the security of servitude. Throughout all time she has maintained her perilous struggle for pre-eminence, honour, and glory.[2] . . .

It cannot, it cannot be that you were wrong, men of Athens, when you took upon you the struggle for freedom and deliverance. No! by those who at Marathon bore the brunt of the peril—our fore-fathers! No! by those who at Platææ drew up their battle-line; by those who at Salamis, by those who off

Artemisium fought the fight at sea; by the many who lie in the sepulchres where the People laid them—brave men, all alike deemed worthy by their country, Æschines, of the same honour and the same obsequies —not the successful or the victorious alone![1]

It is such sentiments that give its unique elevation to the Speech on the Crown. We have considered in the preceding chapter the justification of Demosthenes' policy at different stages in his career, and there is no need to repeat what has been said, nor to give a formal analysis of a Speech which every student of Demosthenes must read many times. The Speech began with an appeal to the gods; and the solemnity of its conclusion also is in keeping with the momentous character of the issue:

Never, O all ye gods, may any of you consent to their desire! If it can be, may you implant even in these men a better mind and heart. But if they are verily beyond all cure, then bring them and them alone to utter and early destruction, by land and sea. And to us who remain, grant the speediest release from the fears that hang over us, and safety that nought can shake.[2]

When the votes of the jury were counted, it was found that Æschines had not received one fifth of the total number. He thereby became liable to the penalties ordained by the law of Athens for malicious prosecution—a fine of 1000 drachmæ,

[1] § 208. [2] § 324.

and certain civil disabilities.[1] He could doubtless have paid the fine and faced the loss of rights; but he could not face the spectacle of Demosthenes' triumph, and therefore withdrew from Athens. He first went to Ephesus, where he hoped to obtain a favourable reception from Alexander,[2] but the hope was frustrated by the news of Alexander's death in 323. Then, if not before, he went to Rhodes, where he passed most of the remainder of his life. He is said to have taught rhetoric there, reciting to his pupils the very speech with which Demosthenes had overthrown him; and to have met their admiration with the remark, "Ah! but you should have heard the beast himself!"[3]

The division of opinion in Athens, or rather, the conflict in the public mind between interested caution and patriotic sentiment, is illustrated by the few facts, apart from the doings of Alexander, that have come down to us from the period immediately following the acquittal of Ctesiphon. On the one hand, the party of non-resistance remained powerful. Phocion continued to be re-elected general.[4] Demades retained his power in the Assembly.[5] On the other hand, Lycurgus was

---

[1] Plut., *Dem.*, xxiv.; comp., Dem., *de Cor.*, §§ 82, 266.

[2] *Vit. X Orat.*, 846 c.

[3] *Ibid.*, 840 d.; Schol. on Æsch., *de F. L.*, i., etc.

[4] As he was general forty-five times, he must have been re-appointed almost every year.

[5] Decrees of the years 329 to 323 in his name are known to us from *C. I. A.*, ii., 178, 193, 809, 811; *cf.* Dein., *in Dem.*, § 101.

in control of public finance down to 326, and Demosthenes himself exercised important influence,
since he was described by Hypereides as "director
of State-affairs in general."[1] Deinarchus also
complains of his power, and both Demosthenes and
Demades figure as leading statesmen in the melan-
choly episode which comes before us, when next
we are able to study the internal history of Athens
in detail. It is probably to be inferred, not that
any formal agreement had been made between the
rival parties, but that statesmen of opposite views
were able to exercise influence side by side, and to
divide the administrative offices between them,
because caution demanded that those who were
of the Macedonian party should not be discarded,
while the stronger popular sentiment was on the
side of Demosthenes and Lycurgus. Probably
there was little open friction; and it seems most
likely that the political life of Athens was confined
for some years to purely local questions, and that
its most notable expression was the carrying out of
the extensive building operations which had been
planned by Lycurgus.[2] For the rest, the citizens
went about their business, and enjoyed the distributions of festival-money, and the other pleasures
of a time of peace.

In one respect only did serious trouble arise.

---

[1] ἐπιστάτης τῶν ὅλων πραγμάτων. Hyper., *in Dem.*, col. xii.;
comp. Dein., *in Dem.*, §§ 5, 7.

[2] See von Wilamowitz-Moellendorf, *Aristoteles und Athen*, pp.
352, 353; Ferguson, *Hellenistic Athens*, pp. 8, 9, etc.

The price of corn rose about this time to a formidable height. The rise had begun even before the trial of Ctesiphon[1]; and it became so serious that a special fund was formed for the purchase of corn; Demosthenes was made corn-commissioner, and contributed a talent from his own capital to the fund.[2] The position was made worse by the action of Cleomenes, Alexander's representative in Egypt, who made a "corner" in grain, and sold it at very high prices in Athens, transferring his cargoes elsewhere whenever the price fell.[3] It is possible that a number of decrees proposed by Demosthenes, conferring honour upon various persons, are to be connected with their services in connection with the corn-supply. By these decrees,[4] a certain Diphilus was given the privilege of maintenance in the Prytaneum, and the honour of a statue in the market-place; a resident alien, named Chærephilus, and his sons, were given the citizenship of Athens, and so were the bankers Epigenes and Conon; and statues of the princes of the Bosporus, whose friendship with Athens was of long standing, were also erected.[5] Demosthenes was accused of embezzlement during his tenure of office, but was acquitted.[6] We hear also

---

[1] Dem., *de Cor.*, § 89.   [2] *Vit. X Orat.*, 845 c.

[3] [Dem.], *in Dionysod.*, § 7, etc.; see Boeckh, *Staatsh.*, i., p. 119, etc.   [4] Dein., *in Dem.*, § 43.

[5] We do not, however, know the date of their erection, and it may have taken place earlier.

[6] *Vit. X Orat.*, 845 e. Schäfer rightly observes that this notice cannot refer to the year 338; Æschines would not have

of an expedition under Miltiades in May, 324, to Western waters, to protect the Athenian trade in the West against Tyrrhenian pirates. The decree ordering the expedition was proposed by Cephisophon and supported by Hypereides,[1] and instructions were given for the founding of a colony on the Adriatic; but we know nothing of the fortunes of the expedition.

In 326 Lycurgus ceased to hold office. Whether he retired of his own accord, or whether he was rejected in favour of other candidates we do not know. The former alternative is possible; he was not living after 324, and his health may already have been failing. The other alternative is suggested by the fact that he was succeeded by a personal enemy, Menesæchmus, whom he had successfully prosecuted for impiety in a matter which had to do with the sanctuary of Delos.[1] It has also been suggested that the election of Menesæchmus marks the beginning of a division in the ranks of the patriotic party, since we afterwards find Menesæchmus associated with Hypereides in attacking Demosthenes; but there is no evidence to prove or disprove this supposition. Shortly before his death, Lycurgus caused himself to be taken to the Metroon and the Council chamber, to render an account of his long steward-

---

failed to notice any charge against Demosthenes of dishonesty in that year. [1] *C. I. A.*, ii., 809 a.

[2] *Vit. X Orat.*, 843 d. A speech for the defence was included in antiquity among the speeches of Deinarchus.

ship. Menesæchmus, who alone ventured to bring any charge against him, entirely failed to justify his allegations, and the stern but capable and honest old statesman was carried home to die.[1]

[1] *Vit. X Orat.*, 842 e.

29

CHAPTER XIII

THE AFFAIR OF HARPALUS AND THE LAMIAN WAR

FOR about two years (327 to 325) Alexander was engaged in his great expedition to India, and it was not until 324 that he returned to Susa. In his absence his deputies had governed as though they had expected him never to come back; and among the most shameless of these unfaithful viceroys was Harpalus, who, after a chequered career, had been left in command at Babylon. There he indulged in a long orgy of luxury and immorality. He sent to Athens for the famous courtesan Pythionice, and treated her as his queen; and after her death he buried her sumptuously, and erected statues of her both in Babylon and in Athens, where Charicles, the son-in-law of Phocion, acted as his agent in the matter. The "Tomb of Pythionice" was still to be seen in Plutarch's day on the road from Athens to Eleusis. Another courtesan from Athens, named Glycera, was soon installed in the vacant place, and the extravagances of Harpalus continued as before. Suddenly it was announced that Alexander was on his way back from India. Harpalus fled from Babylon without delay (in the winter of 325–4), taking with him a force of six thousand mercenaries, and the sum of five thousand talents out of Alexander's treasure, which had been in his charge.[1]

He first sailed to the coast of Attica with thirty ships, and anchored off Sunium, expecting that the People of Athens would receive him and join forces with him in a revolt against the Macedonian power.[2] There was some ground for his expectations, since he had influential friends in Athens, and in return for presents of corn which he had sent, the Athenians had already granted him the citizenship. But Demosthenes, who doubtless saw that there would be great danger in such an alliance, and that the assistance of Harpalus was not likely to be the means by which Athens could secure freedom, persuaded the People to reject Harpalus' offer (tempting as it must have been at first sight) to place his ships and men at the disposal of the Athenians.[3] Demosthenes' policy on this occasion is very like that which he had pursued in regard to the Peace of 346—a policy of refusing to break the Peace when the chances of success were too small for a prudent statesman to act upon. The general Philocles, who had charge of Munychia and the Peiræus, was ordered to prevent Harpalus from landing, and undertook upon oath to do so.[4]

Thus baffled, Harpalus departed with his ships

[1] Diod., XVII, cviii.; Theopomp., fr. 244, 245 (Oxford text); Plut., *Phoc.,* xxii. [2] Curt., x., ii. [3] Plut., *Dem.,* xxv. [4] *Vit. X Orat.,* 846 a; Diod., *l.c.*; Deinarch., *in Philocl.,* § 1.

to Tænarum, and landed his men there. He then returned with a single ship to the Peiræus, bringing with him a very large sum of money. Philocles, probably induced by a bribe, failed to prevent his entrance, and he now supplicated the People for aid, at the same time distributing bribes where he thought they would be effective.[1] The less cautious members of the patriotic party, and among them Hypereides, wished to take this opportunity of declaring war, being evidently convinced (perhaps by the statements of Harpalus himself) that many of the oriental satraps were ready to rise against Alexander, and would already have done so, had Athens not repelled Harpalus.[2] But this policy was opposed by Demosthenes, who, as before, thought the occasion unfavourable for the renewal of the war, and by Phocion, who spoke so plainly in regard to Harpalus' methods as to force him to cut short his distributions of money.[3] At the same time the surrender of Harpalus was demanded by Antipater and Olympias, and also by Philoxenus, Alexander's commander in southern Asia Minor. Philoxenus came personally to Athens for the purpose, and his advent caused the Athenians great alarm, of which Demosthenes took advantage. "If," he asked the People, "you cannot look a candle in the face, how will you face the sun when he appears?" (There is in fact

[1] Plut., *Phoc.*, xxi.
[2] Pollux, X, § 159; Hyper., *in Dem.*, col. xix.
[3] Plut., *Dem.*, xxv.; *Phoc.*, xxi.

reason to think that Alexander was just now
contemplating a great expedition against Athens,
in consequence of a rumour th.at had reached him
that Harpalus had been well-received there.[1])
Finally it was resolved, on Demosthenes' proposal,
not to surrender Harpalus (for probably public
opinion would not have permitted this), but to
keep him in confinement, and to take charge of the
money which he had brought, until Alexander
should send a fully accredited representative to
take both over.[2] Demosthenes also had the
question put directly to Harpalus by Mnesitheus,
how much money he had brought with him.[3]
Harpalus named seven hundred talents as the
sum; but the amount actually deposited next day
in the Acropolis was found to be no more than 350
talents. Demosthenes, who was one of those
charged with the duty of conveying the money to
the Parthenon, failed to inform the People of the
exact sum deposited.[4] The probable reason for
this omission will presently appear; but it soon
became known that a very large sum was missing.

Demosthenes next appears to have carried two
proposals—first, that those who had received

---

[1] Curt., X, ii. The rumour is alluded to in the fragments of a
satyric play named *Agen*, performed before Alexander, probably
at Susa, early in March, 324; Athen., XIII, p. 596.

[2] *Vit X Orat.*, 846 b; Dein., *in Dem.*, § 89; Hyper., *in Dem.*, col.
viii., ix.

[3] Hyper., *l.c.*, adds the interesting note that Demosthenes was
sitting "in his usual place, under the cutting" or Katatome.

[4] *Vit. X Orat.*, 846 c.

money from Harpalus should be allowed to escape
all penalty if they restored it[1]; and secondly that
the Council of Areopagus should enquire into the
whole affair, and should report to the People the
names of those who had taken presents from
Harpalus, with a view to their prosecution.[2] Just
at this moment, Harpalus succeeded in escaping
from prison—with whose aid or connivance there
is no evidence to show[3]—and returned first to
Tænarum, and thence sailed to Crete, where he
was murdered by one of his own captains, Thibron
of Sparta.[4] The Council of Areopagus took their
time before setting seriously to work at the investigation entrusted to them, and in the meantime
the situation became further complicated.

Before Alexander had set out on his march to
India in 327, he had been greeted as a god through
the flattery of the sophist Anaxarchus—or it may
have been Cleon—and divine honours had been
paid him; though Callisthenes, the nephew of
Aristotle and himself a distinguished historian, had
strongly protested, and in consequence had shortly
afterwards been put to death on a charge of
complicity in a conspiracy of the royal pages.[5]
Early in 324 Alexander demanded that the Greek

[1] Hyper, *in Dem.*, col. xxxiv.

[2] Plut., *Dem.*, xxvi.; Dein., *in Dem.*, § 4.

[3] It was notoriously easy to escape from prison at Athens;
comp. Plato's *Crito*, in which Socrates' friends offer to arrange
his escape.   [4] Diod., XVII, cix.

[5] Arrian, IV, x., §§ 7–9, xv.; Curt., VIII, v., viii.; Plut., *Alex.*, lv.

States also should recognise his divinity.[1] Probably the smaller States complied without making any difficulties; at Megalopolis, for instance, a shrine was dedicated to Alexander, and was seen several centuries afterwards by Pausanias.[2] Even the Spartans gave a contemptuous assent, agreeing to "let Alexander be a god if he liked."[3] At Athens the spirit of resistance was stronger. Lycurgus, who was priest of Erechtheus, asked the indignant question, "What sort of a god is he, at whose temple a man must purify himself on coming out instead of on going in?"[4] The demand was opposed by Demosthenes, who declared that the city should worship only the traditional gods.[5] It was also opposed by Pytheas, an orator who was at present on the anti-Macedonian side[6]; and in spite of Demades' warning to the Assembly,[7] "to take care lest in guarding heaven they should lose earth," the People refused to submit to the demand.

But with it came another and a more serious command from Alexander, which Demosthenes was at first prepared to resist even at the risk of war.[8] This was an injunction issued to all the

---

[1] Note 1 at the end of the Chapter.   [2] Paus., VIII, xxxii., § 1.
[3] Æl., *Var. H.*, II, xix.; Plut., *Lac. Apophth.*, 219 e.
[4] *Vit. X Orat.*, 842 d.   The question may have been asked in 327; if not, it is the last recorded utterance of Lycurgus.
[5] Polyb., XII, 12 a.   [6] Plut., *Præc. Ger. Rep.*, 804 b.
[7] Val., *Max.*, VII, xiii.
[8] Hyper., *in Dem.*, col xxxi.; Dein., *in Dem.*, §§ 69, 94; Diod., XVIII, viii.   See Ed. Meyer, *Kleine Schriften*, pp. 311 ff.

Greek States that they should receive back those
who had been banished from their several cities,
with the exception of those who were under a
religious ban. The command was given by the
King partly (so Diodorus explains) "for the sake
of his reputation." It was not creditable to his
rule that many thousands of his subjects should
be homeless exiles; still less, that his dominions
should be overrun by lawless mercenaries or
brigands, such as many of the exiles became. But
the explanation was partly that "he desired to have
a large number of persons in each State attached
to himself, as a security against the revolutions
and risings of the Greeks." On the other hand,
the order was a direct breach of the convention of
Corinth, by which the King had undertaken not to
interfere with the internal affairs of the Greek
cities; though it might be argued that Alexander
the god could claim authority to supersede the
terms of any mere human convention; and from
this point of view, the combination of the two
demands was an ingenious stroke of policy.
Even apart from the divine claims, the injunction
was an announcement that Alexander intended to
stand above the internal party-divisions of the
several States. But the fulfilment of the injunction was bound to lead to serious internal disturbances in each city—the more so because exile was
generally due to political causes. The Athenians
had special reasons for apprehension, since they
had driven out a number of the inhabitants of

Samos[1] to make room for Athenian settlers, and the King's order would compel them to restore these. In any case the order was bound to evoke the strongest resentment in Athens. It was virtually a demand that she should renounce her internal autonomy; and it was in accordance with Demosthenes' strongest political sentiments that he should think it right to resist it to the death. There is thus no reason to have recourse, for an explanation, to the motive suggested by his enemies,[2] that he desired to get up a war in order to divert the attention of the People from the enquiry entrusted to the Council of Areopagus, from which he had reason to apprehend danger.

The popular feeling was on Demosthenes' side, and he was appointed chief of the official representatives sent by Athens to the Olympian festival in July or August, 324, to which Nicanor of Stageira had been sent by Alexander to proclaim the King's pleasure to the assembled Greeks.[3]

In anticipation of Nicanor's proclamation, more than twenty thousand of the exiles affected by it had gathered at the festival, and they received it with great demonstrations of joy, which were not shared by the Athenians or the Ætolians; for, just as the former had occupied Samos, so the latter had

---

[1] Perhaps as recently as 326. *C. I. A.*, ii., 808 a, records the despatch of a fleet to Samos in that year.

[2] *E. g.* Hyper., *l. c.*

[3] Diod., XVIII, viii.; Justin, XIII, v.; Curt., X, ii.; Hyper., *in Dem*, col. xviii.

occupied Œniadæ, and expelled the inhabitants of
the town; and they now found themselves required
to restore it to them.[1]   Nicanor was instructed
not only to proclaim the restoration of exiles
(except those from Thebes, whose return to their
native land was explicitly forbidden[2]), but also, it
would seem, to forbid the federal meetings of the
Achæans, Arcadians, and Bœotians; and Antipater
was ordered to enforce the King's decree by arms
upon those cities which proved disobedient.   Demosthenes does not appear to have expressed the
feelings of himself or his fellow-citizens in any
conspicuous manner during the festival; but it is
mere malice on the part of Deinarchus[3] to treat
him as a traitor to his country, on the ground that
he was seen speaking to Nicanor.   The representatives of the most hostile powers may have the best
of reasons for meeting one another, and it may
even be that Demosthenes postponed the outbreak
of a crisis by diplomatic conversations.

But whatever Demosthenes' conduct at Olympia,[4] his visit seems to have caused him to regard
the situation as more dangerous than he had at
first believed.   He remained firm indeed as regards
the restoration of exiles; but he withdrew the im-
peachment which he had preferred against the orator Callimedon for associating with the Athenian
exiles, who were now assembled at Megara and were

[1] Diod., *l. c.*; Plut., *Alex.*, xlix.
[2] Plut., *Lac. Apophth.*, p. 221 a.
[3] Dein., *in Dem.*, §,103.   [4] Note 2.

THE TEMPLE OF ZEUS AT OLYMPIA

PHOTO BY ALINARI

demanding readmission to Athens[1]; and he also withdrew his opposition to the recognition of Alexander's divinity. "Let him be son of Zeus," he said, "or, if he prefers it, son of Poseidon, for all I care." He doubtless believed that if the Athenians gave way upon this point, which was of comparatively little political importance, Alexander might be content to ignore their neglect of the more serious injunction.[2] In consequence of this, Demades now proposed that Alexander should be added as a thirteenth to the twelve Olympian gods, under the title of Dionysus, whose mythical home at Nysa Alexander fancied himself to have discovered; and that a temple should be erected to him[3]; and this decree appears to have been accepted, since Hypereides, a year or so later,[4] alluded scornfully to this payment of divine honours to men.

A number of embassies proceeded about this time to Babylon, where Alexander received their congratulations and homage (accompanied by golden crowns) early in 323; he also considered the political and other questions which they submitted to him, and among them, their requests in regard to the return of the exiles.[5] It is probable that

---

[1] Dein., *in Dem.*, §§ 58, 94. Another Athenian, named Polyeuctus, was also prosecuted, though not by Demosthenes; but was able to prove that he had gone to Megara to visit his mother.

[2] Dein., *in Dem.*, § 94; Hyper., *in Dem.* col. xxxi.

[3] Val., *Max.*, VII, ii., E. 10; Ælian., *Var. Hist.*, V, xii.; Athen., VI, p. 251 b; Diog., L., VI, lxiii.   [4] Hyper., *Epitaph.*, col. viii.

[5] Arrian, VII, xix., xxiii., seems to distinguish two series of embassies; Diod., XVII, cxiii., groups all together.

the Athenians sent envoys among the rest; for we are told that Alexander at this time restored to the Greeks the statues and other works of art which the Persians had carried off at the time of Xerxes' invasion of Greece, and among others restored to the Athenians the statues of Harmodius and Aristogeiton, who had liberated Athens from tyranny in 510. But he probably refused to give way as regards the restoration of exiles, since various inscriptions of the time allude to the return of the banished to their several cities—to Samos among others.[1] Whether he insisted upon the reception into Athens of those who had been expelled we do not know.

Before the embassies were received at Babylon, the Harpalus affair came to an issue. It is plain that public excitement over the matter had been growing; the apprehension of danger from Alexander had also increased; and there was much impatience at the long delay of the Council of Areopagus in coming to a conclusion. They had indeed instituted a search in the houses of suspected persons, but without result. Demosthenes was openly charged by his enemies with receiving money from Harpalus; and in self-defence proposed a decree ordering an enquiry by the Council of Areopagus into the charge against himself, declaring himself ready to submit to the penalty of death if he were found to have taken the money.

[1] *C. I. G.*, ii., 2166, 2671, 2672, etc., and *Ditt. Syll.*, (Ed. 2) 162.

Philocles did the same.[1] That Demosthenes himself gave evidence before the Council appears from the circumstance that Deinarchus accused him of committing perjury before that body. At some point in the course of the proceedings, two persons, a father and son, were condemned to death and executed, on the proposal of Demosthenes; it is conjectured that they may have been the watchmen who had been set to guard the treasure.[2] Such was the nervousness of all parties, that those who had actually taken money from Harpalus were the first to accuse others of having done so, in the hope of saving themselves.[3] Even Hypereides, who was above suspicion, was mentioned by the comic poet Timocles (probably at the Dionysia in March, 324) as having received money, along with Demosthenes, Mœrocles, Demon, and Callisthenes. At last, six months after the enquiry had been ordered,[4] the Council reported that Demosthenes had received twenty talents of the lost money, Demades six thousand gold staters (also equivalent to about twenty talents), and that various sums had been accepted by Philocles, Cephisophon, Hagnonides, Aristonicus, Aristogeiton, and Charicles.

In consequence of this report, the Assembly

---

[1] Dein., *in Dem.*, §§ 8, 47, 82, 83, 86, etc.; *in Philocl.*, §§ 1, 2. Demosthenes perhaps trusted that this Council would be favourably inclined to him, as on some former occasions.

[2] Dein., *in Dem.*, §§ 8, 62, 83.

[3] Plut., *Dem.*, xxv.; *Phoc.*, xxi.   [4] Dein., *in Dem.*, § 45.

appointed ten orators to prosecute the accused on
behalf of the State. Among the ten were Hypereides, Pytheas, Menesæchmus, Procles, Stratocles,
and Himeræus.[1] Of these Menesæchmus was the
former assailant of Lycurgus; Pytheas, though
he had opposed the recognition of Alexander's
divinity, was shortly afterwards in the pay of
Antipater[2]; Stratocles had been described by
Demosthenes[3] as the most plausible scoundrel in
the world. What was Hypereides doing in conjunction with such men, and in antagonism to
Demosthenes? Probably the two had been drift-
ing apart for some time. The patient moderation
of Demosthenes, who was waiting for a really
favourable moment before renewing the struggle
for freedom, and the fact that he had been content
to divide the administrative offices with Demades
and his friends, may gradually have alienated
Hypereides; the original refusal of Demosthenes to
accept the overtures of Harpalus may have seemed
to Hypereides to be a sacrifice of a unique opportunity,[4] and the charge of bribery and embezzlement may have seemed to be a convenient way of
getting rid of so cautious a leader. It was perhaps for similar reasons that Hypereides attacked
Hagnonides and Aristonicus, who had also been
opponents of the Macedonian power.

The charge against Demosthenes was tried

[1] Dein., *in Dem.*, § 1; *Vit. X Orat.*, 846 c.
[2] Comp. Dem., *Ep.*, iii., § 29.
[3] *In Pantænet.*, § 48 (*circ.* 346–5 B.C.).   [4] Note 3.

first. The speech of Stratocles, in which the
proofs of the charge are said[1] to have been given,
has not come down to us; and we are therefore
ignorant what the nature of these proofs was.
The Council of Areopagus had only reported its
conclusions, not the grounds of them.[2] The
speech of Deinarchus, composed for one of the
prosecutors—probably Himeræus,[3]—followed that
of Stratocles. The speaker does not offer a vestige
of proof of any kind, being apparently content
with the findings of the Council. On the other
hand, he tries by every means to rouse prejudice
against Demosthenes, by recalling the destruction
of Thebes and other disasters and attributing
them to him, and by accusing him of taking bribes
on a number of former occasions. But the
meanest arguments, in a speech brimming over
with malice, are those which accuse Demosthenes
of having all along been working in the service of
Macedonia, from the time of the Peace of Philocrates onwards, and of having thrown away every
opportunity of opposing Philip and Alexander.
(The arguments of course show that the prosecutors were aware that the feeling of the jury would
be strongly anti-Macedonian.) The speaker
further urged the jury to remember that the eyes

---

[1] Dein., *in Dem.*, § 1.　　　　[2] Dem., *Ep.*, ii., § 1.

[3] Blass, *Att. Ber.*, III, ii., p. 310. Haupt thinks that the
speaker was Menesæchmus. Whoever he was, he had himself
been denounced for corruption by Pistias, an Areopagite, but
had succeeded in clearing himself.

of the world were upon them, and that it was important to punish corruption in the case of eminent men above all. What, he proceeded to ask, would happen if Alexander demanded to be paid the money brought by Harpalus? Would Demosthenes expect the Athenians to go to war, in order that he and others might retain what they had stolen? The Speech is marked throughout by vehement and impetuous but overwrought rhetoric; by way of additional insult, passages not only of Æschines' but of Demosthenes' own earlier orations are used with very little alteration against Demosthenes himself; and, whatever were the merits of the case, there is no public oration by a Greek orator which stands on quite so low a level as this.

At a later stage in the trial Hypereides spoke, and some not inconsiderable fragments of his speech are known to us. Hypereides like Deinarchus regards the finding of the Areopagus as sufficient evidence in itself, particularly as Demosthenes himself had proposed that its verdict, if given against him, should be conclusive. He asks whether it is likely that it was for nothing that Demosthenes had taken no proceedings against the custodians who had let Harpalus go, when it was he himself who had moved that he should be kept in custody? or that Harpalus would have bribed lesser men, and passed over Demosthenes, the manager of the whole affair? He also brings up against Demosthenes the scandal about the Persian gold, and the failure to help Thebes against Alexander.

What is more interesting is that Hypereides gives us the only information we have as to the line of defence which Demosthenes was expected to adopt, and which had no doubt become known before the trial. Demosthenes had demanded a detailed account of the sums which he was alleged to have received, showing from whom he had received them, and where—a demand upon which Hypereides throws scorn, saying that it is treating the Council's report as though it were a banker's account; but which seems in itself not unreasonable. He had also declared that the report of the Council of Areopagus was false, and that the Areopagites desired to get rid of him, by way of doing a favour to Alexander. The latter assertion is very likely to have been so far true, that the danger which the Athenians apprehended from Alexander's indignation may have been strongly urged upon them, and may have forced them to make a report, when they had probably hoped to let the matter drop, as they had done in the case of the "Persian gold." But what is of most importance is the statement of Hypereides that Demosthenes had made all his subsequent denials of the receipt of the money ineffectual, by having at first admitted that he had taken the money and by having tried to justify himself for doing so, on the pretext that he had borrowed the money for the festival-fund.[1]

---

[1] The interpretation of προδεδανεισμένος (Hyper., *in Dem.*, col. x.) given by Holm and others, who take it to mean that Demosthenes had advanced twenty talents of his own to the

(His friend Cnosion also hinted that if pressure were exerted, the result would be the revelation of a state-secret, and would be detrimental to the public interest.[1]) This defence Hypereides described as bringing discredit upon the People, by letting it be thought that they would apply Harpalus' money to their own public purposes. The verdict of the court was against Demosthenes. It was open to them either to condemn him to death, or to fine him ten times the amount alleged to have been received by him.[2] Instead of doing either, they inflicted a fine of fifty talents, committing him to prison until it should be paid.

The question of the guilt or innocence of Demosthenes has been, and still is, keenly disputed. It is impossible to discuss all the considerations which have been urged on either side; many of them are plainly invalid; but it may be well to state briefly the conclusions to which the very slender evidence seems to point. It can scarcely be denied in the face of Demosthenes' own admission (unless Hypereides is telling a downright falsehood) that Demosthenes received the money. It appears probable that he did not take it as a bribe from Harpalus. If he had done so, he could hardly have proposed to take Harpalus into custody and

---

festival-fund, and had repaid himself out of Harpalus' money, cannot be extracted from the Greek, though it may represent Demosthenes' plea.

[1] *Ibid.*, col. xiii.   [2] *Ibid.*, col. xxiv.; Dein., *in Dem.*, § 60.

put his money into safe keeping to be restored to Alexander. Plutarch indeed[1] tells a story to the effect that though Demosthenes had refused Harpalus' offers at first, yet, when Harpalus was in custody and the money being counted, he was moved with admiration of a golden cup, finely worked, which was among the treasure; and that the same night Harpalus secretly sent him this cup, together with twenty talents. Next day, when he was called upon to speak in the Assembly, and expected to maintain his former attitude towards Harpalus, he pretended to be suffering from loss of voice, and appeared with his throat elaborately muffled up; but the story leaked out; he and his friends thought it well to get Harpalus away from Athens, to prevent any possible disclosures; and the Areopagus then instituted the domiciliary search which has been mentioned. But if this tale were true, it is almost inconceivable that it should not have been alluded to in the speeches for the prosecution. Deinarchus would never have failed to take full advantage of so picturesque a story. Nor does Hypereides mention it when he alludes to the escape of Harpalus. Moreover, we are told that Harpalus' steward was captured by Philoxenus at Rhodes, and told him the names of the statesmen to whom Harpalus had given money, and that Demosthenes' name was not among the number.[2]

Demosthenes then did not receive the money

[1] Plut., *Dem.*, xxv.　　　　　　[2] Paus., II, xxxiii., § 4.

from Harpalus, but must have appropriated it
after the treasure had been transferred to those
appointed by the Assembly to take charge of it,
of whom he was one.   Further it is quite possible
that his statement that he had taken it "for the
theoric fund" was true, though he cannot have
formally transferred it to the fund; for then it
could have been proved by the accounts of the
fund.   He was evidently apprehensive of war with
Alexander.   In case of war, the theoric fund would
almost certainly be called upon to provide money
for military purposes; and it is far from improbable that Demosthenes hoped to lay the foundations of a reserve out of the money taken from
Harpalus; just as he had taken Persian gold to help
Thebes.   If this was so, he was at least not guilty
of an act of theft for his own personal aggrandise-
ment, however indefensible his action may have
been.   Indefensible, of course, it was.   The money
was the property of Alexander; the People had
resolved that it should be kept in the Acropolis
until Alexander sent for it, and had entrusted to
Demosthenes, among others, the execution of this
decree: the money was clearly not available for
the public purposes of Athens.   But it cannot be
doubted that if war with Alexander had broken
out, the People would have sanctioned the use of
Harpalus' treasure for the defence of Athens;
Deinarchus assumed that this was so[1]; and it is
not to be supposed that the Athenians felt so

[1] Dein., *in Dem.*, §§ 64 ff.

strongly about Demosthenes' action in taking
the money prematurely for the use of Athens as
modern judges of the case would feel. The comparatively light penalty inflicted indicates this.
Demosthenes then was guilty of an action based
on the same principle, and directed towards the
same end, as his acceptance of Persian gold, but
less justifiable, because it involved a breach of
faith. When, however, that is admitted, his fault
still remains far less ignoble than his critics, ancient
and modern, would have us believe. There is at
least no sufficient reason for supposing that he was
influenced by corrupt motives, or that he aimed
at his own personal gain; and we are justified in
preferring an interpretation of his action, which,
while it does not acquit him of a certain unscrupulousness as to means, is consonant with the patriotic aims which he pursued throughout his career.

The penalty inflicted was, as we have said, light
in comparison with that which the laws allowed.
But in itself a fine of fifty talents was a heavy one.
No doubt the court took into account not merely
the appropriation of the money by Demosthenes,
but also his failure to report the exact sum deposited in the Acropolis[1]; though there may be some
ground for his complaint[2] that he was treated more
harshly than the rest because his case was the
first to be tried, and that others who made precisely the same defence as he, got off unpunished.[3]

[1] *Vit. X Orat.*, 846 c.   [2] Dem., *Ep.*, ii., § 15.
[3] It must, however, be remembered that he occupied a position

However that may be, he was unable to pay so large a sum, and was cast into prison. But before many days he felt the hardships of the prison to be greater than his age and health could endure, and contrived to make his escape. Plutarch tells the story[1] that when Demosthenes was a little way from the city, he saw some of those with whom he had had differences following him, and tried to hide; but they called to him that they had followed him to bring him money for his journey, and urged him to bear his misfortune cheerfully; whereupon he burst into lamentation at his exile from a city where even his enemies were kinder than any friends he would find elsewhere. As he left the city, so Plutarch also tells us, he had cried aloud to Athena Polias, "O Lady of the City, why dost thou delight in three of the most cruel beasts— the owl, the snake, and the People?" and when young men came to talk to him during his exile, he dissuaded them from entering upon a political career, declaring that if he had a fresh start and two roads lay open to him, the one to the platform and the Assembly, the other straight to death, then, knowing, as he did, all that a political career involved—fears, jealousies, slanders, struggles,— he would take the road that led straight to death. He passed his time for some months partly in Ægina, partly at Trœzen; but he found Trœzen

---

of special influence and responsibility, and that less important persons might well be more leniently treated.

[1] Plut., *Dem.* xxvi.

an unsafe refuge, and moved to the island of
Calaureia, from which (as from Ægina) he could
see Athens and the Attic coast.[1] Hence he wrote
the Second Letter ascribed to him, in which he
pleaded earnestly with the People for restoration
to Athens. He recalled his long career of public
service, and claimed the same leniency as was
shown to his fellow-defendants; he protested his
abiding loyalty to his country; and asked to be
delivered, for the sake of the reputation of the
People, as well as of his own, from the hardships
and shame of exile.

As for the other accused persons, Demades either
did not venture or did not condescend to face the
jury; he was condemned and fined, but did not
leave Athens. Probably he was able to pay the fine
inflicted, and thus remained free to take part in political life. Philocles, who was held responsible for
the original admission of Harpalus to Athens, as
well as for his acceptance of Harpalus' money, was
driven into exile. Aristogeiton and the remainder
of the defendants appear to have got off free.[2]

Such was the history of this unhappy affair.
The result of it was that the party opposed to
Demosthenes had temporarily a free hand. Not
only Alexander, but also his deceased companion
Hephæstion, received official worship.[3] Mene-

[1] Dem., *Ep.*, ii., §§ 17–20. See Note 4.
[2] Dein., *in Dem.*, § 104; *in Aristog.*, § 15; Dem., *Ep.*, ii., §§ 15, 16.
[3] Hyper., *Epitaph.*, Col. viii.; Arrian, VII, xiv., § 7, xxiii., § 6;
Plut., *Alex.*, lxxii.

sæchmus prosecuted the sons of Lycurgus, claiming that they should make good that alleged deficit in the public accounts for which he had vainly tried to prove their father responsible; and they were actually condemned and imprisoned.   But shortly afterwards their cause was taken up by Democles, a pupil of Theophrastus, and by Hypereides, and was strongly supported by Demosthenes in a letter addressed to the People—the third of those ascribed to him—in which he declared that the People of Athens were being ill-spoken of abroad owing to their treatment of the sons of one of their most loyal and public-spirited servants; and that when Pytheas was suffered to riot in wealth and immorality, and those who had taken the patriotic side were driven into exile, it was plain that patriotism was unprofitable.   He quoted instances of generous treatment accorded to far less deserving persons, and at the close of the letter pleaded once more for himself, as well as for the sons of Lycurgus.   Whether owing to this letter or to the activity of the advocates of the condemned in Athens, the People were moved to remorse for their ingratitude towards one of their greatest benefactors, and the sons of Lycurgus were released.[1]

The enemies of Demosthenes did not long enjoy their ascendancy; for early in June, 323, Alexander died at Babylon after a short illness.   When first the rumour of his death reached Athens, Demades refused to credit it.   "If Alexander were dead," he

[1] *Vit. X Orat.*, 842 d, and Hyper., fragm. 118 (Oxford text).

declared, "the whole world would be reeking of his corpse"[1]; and Phocion tried to quiet the public excitement by saying, in the manner characteristic of him, "If Alexander is dead to-day, he will be dead to-morrow and the next day also; so that we have plenty of time to make our plans." In fact the situation was not at all clear, for there was no obvious successor to Alexander; but as the result of the deliberations of his generals at Babylon, it was decided that his half-brother Arrhidæus, a man of feeble mind, should be temporarily acknowledged King, saving the rights of the yet unborn infant of Alexander and Roxana, should it prove to be a boy; that Perdiccas should be regent; that Lysimachus should have the command in Thrace and the Hellespont; and that in Macedonia the supreme power should be divided between Antipater, as commander-in-chief, and Craterus, who shortly afterwards advanced as far as Cilicia, but did not at present proceed to Macedonia. Egypt was assigned to Ptolemy, and various provinces in Asia Minor to Eumenes, Antigonus, Leonnatus, and others.[2]

Their short experience of Macedonian government led many Greek peoples at this crisis to attempt to throw off the yoke. Risings took place in Rhodes, Chios, and Ephesus.[3] In Greece

[1] Plut., *Phoc.*, xxii., etc.

[2] Arrian, Suppl., §§ 3, 7; Diod., XVIII, ii.–iv., vi.; Dexippus, fr. 1.

[3] Diod., XVIII, viii.; Suid., *s. v.*, Ephorus; Strabo, XIV, p. 645, etc.; Polyæn., VI, 49.

proper, the first active steps were taken by Leosthenes, an Athenian, who had succeeded in keeping together at Tænarum some eight thousand of the Greek soldiers who had returned from Asia; and this force was increased by the discontented soldiers who flocked thither from all parts, as to a cave of Adullam.[1] On hearing the news of Alexander's death, he went to Athens and opened negotiations with the Council, which gave him fifty talents and a supply of arms, and sent envoys in his interest to the Ætolians, and obtained a ready promise of support. These actions of the Council were not at first made known to the People, and it was not until the fact of Alexander's death was placed beyond all doubt that a proposal to fight for freedom was brought before the Assembly, and recommended to it by Hypereides as well as by messages from Demosthenes.[2] The richer members of the Assembly advised the maintenance of the Peace, but were overborne by a large majority, the eloquence of Hypereides proving more effective than the cautious advice of Phocion, though some of Phocion's observations were only too well founded.[3] "Leosthenes' talk," he said, "is like a cypress-tree—tall but unfruitful." "When," asked Hypereides, "will you ever advise the Athenians to fight?" "When I see the young," said Phocion, "ready to do their duty, and the

---

[1] Diod., XVII, cxi.; XVIII, ix.; Paus., I, xxv, § 5; VIII, lii., § 5.
[2] Hyper., *Epitaph.*, col. ii.; *Vit. X Orat.*, 849 f.
[3] Diod., XVIII, ix.; Dexippus, fr. 2.

rich to pay taxes, and the politicians to abstain
from stealing public money." The army of
Leosthenes inspired no confidence in Phocion.
"It is good enough," said he, "for the short race.
I am afraid of the long—of the campaign; for the
city has no other funds or ships or soldiers." But
the Assembly was in no mood for caution. It was
resolved to equip 240 ships, and to put all Athenians under forty years of age into the field—those
belonging to three of the tribes to guard Attica,
those belonging to the remaining seven to serve beyond the borders. They further sent embassies to
other Greek States, in the hope of inducing them to
join in a general rising and to claim their freedom.[1]

So unpopular had the Macedonians become, that
although it seemed to many persons in the other
States that Athens was taking a premature and a
dangerous step, the envoys found support almost
everywhere. Besides the Ætolians, many northern Greek tribes gave their adhesion—among them
some of those Thessalian and neighbouring tribes
which had been reckoned the most faithful allies
of Macedonia. Bœotia and Eubœa were in the
occupation of Macedonian troops or were subject
to strong Macedonian influence; yet even in Eubœa the people of Carystus joined in the league.
In the Peloponnese, Sparta was powerless, or at
least unable to help; but the peoples of Argos,
Sicyon, Epidaurus, Trœzen, Elis, and Messenia
all promised their aid.[2] As for funds, the treasure

[1] Diod., XVIII, x.   [2] *Ibid.*, xi.; Paus., I, xxv., § 4.

of Harpalus was freely used.[1] Demades was prosecuted for making illegal proposals and for impiety, and particularly for his proposal to recognise the divinity of Alexander. He was heavily fined—ten talents according to one authority, one hundred according to another—and lost his civic rights.[2] Pytheas also was prosecuted and was imprisoned; but he escaped, and he and Callimedon betook themselves to Antipater, and were despatched by him to the Peloponnese to counteract the effect of the embassies sent thither by the Athenians.[3] In Arcadia Pytheas encountered Demosthenes, who, though in exile, used all his powers to aid Hypereides, Polyeuctus, and the other spokesmen of Athens. Pytheas (according to Plutarch's story) remarked that, just as asses' milk made mischief in a house, so an Athenian embassy was bound to cause disorders in a state. "No," replied Demosthenes; "asses' milk is a good medicine, and so is a visit from the Athenians."

So great were the services rendered by Demosthenes, that the Athenian People determined to recall him. The formal decree for this purpose was proposed by his nephew Demon; and since it would have been unconstitutional to remit the fine of fifty talents which the orator had been

---

[1] Diod., XVIII, ix.

[2] Diod., XVIII, xviii.; Plut., *Phoc.*, xxvi.; Athen., VI, p. 251 b; Ælian., *Var. H.*, V, xii.

[3] Suid., *s. v.*, Pytheas; Plut., *Dem.*, xxvii.

condemned to pay, he was ordered to prepare and decorate the altar of Zeus the Saviour for a forthcoming festival, and to enable him to meet this very slight expenditure, the sum of fifty talents was voted to him.[1] We may suspect that the money came out of the treasure of Harpalus. A trireme was sent to convey him from Ægina, and at the Peiræus he was met by a great concourse of his fellow-citizens, headed by the nine archons and the priests; and we are told that he raised his hands towards heaven and thanked the gods that he had been granted an even more honourable return than Alcibiades, since his restoration was not forced upon his fellow-citizens, but was their voluntary act.

Before this happy event took place, the war had probably begun. Leosthenes commenced operations by sending a force of eight thousand men by sea from Tænarum to Ætolia; here he was joined by an army of seven thousand Ætolians; and with the combined forces he marched to Thermopylæ and occupied the Pass without encountering opposition. The Athenians had by this time despatched a force of five thousand citizen-infantry, five hundred cavalry, and two thousand mercenaries to join him; but they were unable to effect a passage through Bœotia, owing to the strong resistance offered by the allies of the Macedonians, until Leosthenes marched southward with part of

[1] Plut., *Dem.*, xxvii.; *Vit. X Orat.*, 846 d; Justin, XIII, v.

his forces, defeated the enemy, and so enabled the Athenian troops to reach Thermopylæ.[1] He then moved northward to confront Antipater, who came to meet him with thirteen thousand infantry and six hundred cavalry, not waiting for the reinforcements which he had urgently requested Craterus and Leonnatus to send. The first engagement took place near Heracleia. In the middle of the battle, Antipater's Thessalian cavalry rode over and joined Leosthenes, and Antipater was obliged to throw himself into the fortress of Lamia, to wait for the expected reinforcements from Asia. He was blockaded by Leosthenes, who had no siege-train with him, and failed to storm the fortress, but hoped to starve the defenders out. Antipater was one time so hard pressed that he asked Leosthenes for terms; but Leosthenes would accept nothing less than unconditional surrender, and this was naturally refused.[2]

Leosthenes' forces had grown considerably through accessions of troops from the peoples of north Greece, but he could not draw Antipater into the field. A peculiarly severe winter proved even more trying to his soldiers than the petty fighting to which they were continuously exposed; the Ætolians made excuses and returned home; and finally Leosthenes himself was struck on the head by a stone, and died two days afterwards.[3]

[1] Diod., XVIII, ix., xi.; Hyper., *Epitaph.*, col. v.
[2] Diod., XVIII, xii., xviii.; Polyæn., IV, iv., § 2.
[3] Diod., XVIII, xiii.

THE ACROPOLIS OF LAMIA

PHOTO BY FRADELLE & YOUNG

The Funeral Oration in honour of Leosthenes
and others who had fallen in the campaign was entrusted to Hypereides.[1] The greater part of his
speech has come down to us, and is a striking
specimen of the type, which was peculiar to
Athens. The matter, and even the style, of the
speech were largely determined by convention—
the introduction, in which the orator apologises
for his own inadequacy; the praise of Athens, her
indigenous People and the noble upbringing of her
sons; the praise of the fallen, and the recital of
their services to their country; the prophecy of an
immortality of fame for them; the anticipation of
their meeting in another world with the glorious
men of old; the mingled congratulation and consolation addressed to the bereaved; and (as regards style) the series of those artificial antitheses
of which Gorgias had set the example. Yet all
these conventional elements are treated by Hypereides with a peculiar grace and no small imagina-
tive power; and the speech is a worthy monument
of the last struggle of the Hellenes for freedom.

Leosthenes was succeeded in the command by
Antiphilus, who, though he was an able general,
had not the commanding personality which was
particularly needed, if the depression caused by
Leosthenes' death was to be surmounted.[2] Not

---

[1] It is very doubtful whether Diodorus is right in saying that
Demosthenes had not yet returned to Athens. The reason for
the selection of Hypereides was doubtless that he (after Leosthenes) was the chief promoter of the war. (So Schäfer, iii., p. 374.)

[2] Paus., I, xxv., § 5; Justin, XIII, v.

long afterwards Leonnatus, in response to Antipater's urgent call, crossed to Europe and marched into Thessaly with more than twenty thousand infantry and fifteen hundred cavalry. Antiphilus abandoned the siege of Lamia and moved northwards at the head of twenty-two thousand infantry and thirty-five hundred cavalry. In a severe cavalry engagement, Leonnatus was defeated and slain; and the Macedonian infantry, not daring to face the Thessalian horse, withdrew into the hills. But on the following day Antipater joined forces with the relieving army, and marched northwards, unmolested by Antiphilus; and on the banks of the Peneius he was joined by Craterus and a large army.

At sea the Macedonian fleet proved victorious, and though the Athenians equipped all the ships they could, the total number which put to sea under Euetion was only 170; and they were twice severely defeated—the first time, probably, near Abydos (Euetion having proceeded thither to guard the Hellespont); the second time by Cleitus with 240 ships, near Amorgos.[1] But a force of Macedonians and mercenaries which landed on the coast of Attica near Rhamnus and laid it waste was repulsed with considerable loss by Phocion at the head of a citizen-levy.[2] At the same time

[1] The evidence of unpublished inscriptions is cited for these battles by Ferguson, *Hellenistic Athens*, p. 17; Diodorus assigns both victories to Cleitus. The Athenians had a larger number of ships, but could not man them. See also Beloch, *Gr. Gesch.*, iii., p. 76 n. [2] Diod., XVIII, xv., xvi.; Plut., *Phoc.*, xxv.

Phocion resisted successfully the proposal that an Athenian force should invade Bœotia.[1] Antiphilus remained in Thessaly; but his forces had been for some time falling away, many contingents leaving either because they thought that Leosthenes' successes had settled the war, or because the soldiers had affairs to attend to at home; and signs of discontent showed themselves in the camp. When Antipater and Craterus marched southwards with an army of nearly fifty thousand men in all, Antiphilus had less than thirty thousand to oppose to them. The two armies met at Crannon, on the 7th of Metageitnion (early in August, 322), the anniversary of the battle of Chæroneia. The battle was in itself indecisive, though the Greek loss was heavier than the Macedonian; but the council of war called next day by Antiphilus and Menon (who commanded the cavalry) rejected the proposal to request the Greek States to despatch reinforcements, and decided to send a message to Antipater, asking him to discuss terms of peace. But Antipater refused to recognise the anti-Macedonian league as a whole, and replied that each State must treat with him separately; while at the same time he proceeded to take the Thessalian towns one after another by storm, and Pharsalus among them. The result was that the States of northern Greece soon came to terms with him, being further encouraged to do so by his envoys, who promised favourable terms to those

[1] Plut., *Phoc.*, xxiv.; *Polyæn.*, III, xii.

31

who submitted; and before long, out of all the
members of the league which had been formed, the
Ætolians and Athenians alone were left.[1]

The Athenians now found it necessary themselves to ask Antipater for conditions of peace.
At what precise moment they first sent to him is
uncertain. It may have been after the taking of
Pharsalus[2]; but it was probably not until Antipater
and Craterus had crossed the Pass of Thermopylæ
and encamped in Bœotia. Then the Athenians,
in alarm, once more called upon Demades to get
them out of their difficulty, restoring to him his
civic rights, and cancelling the fine which had led
to his loss of them. He went to Antipater's camp
with Phocion and Demetrius of Phalerum; but
Antipater would agree to no terms except absolute surrender—the only terms which, in an
evil hour, Leosthenes had been willing to accept
from him at Lamia. That Antipater did not
march into Attica, as Craterus desired to do,
before dictating terms, was only due to his respect
for Phocion.[3]

The Athenians had no choice but to submit.
They had not even, as in former days, any supremacy at sea, and would have had no power to
withstand a blockade; and although Demochares,
the nephew of Demosthenes, entered the Assembly
with his sword and called his fellow-countrymen to

[1] Diod., XVIII, xvii.

[2] *Vit. X Orat.*, 846 e, does not really prove this.

[3] Diod., XVIII, xviii.; Plut., *Phoc.*, xxvi.

arms,[1] it was resolved to send Phocion and the other ambassadors back to Thebes, to announce to Antipater the unconditional surrender of the city. The philosopher Xenocrates, the head of the Academy, was sent with them, in the hope that being a friend of Antipater he might use his influence to advantage; but Antipater refused to hear him.[2] Antipater then announced that the Athenians would be allowed to retain possession of Attica, but not of Oropus, which was given to the Bœotians. Lemnos and Imbros appear also to have remained in the hands of Athens.[3] The question of the possession of Samos was referred to the regent Perdiccas, who subsequently restored the island to its former inhabitants, and ordered the Athenian settlers to withdraw. The Athenians were required to deliver up to Antipater the orators who had promotèd the war; and to revise the constitution in such a way as to restrict the franchise to citizens who had a property of at least twenty minæ. On these conditions they would be permitted to be the friends and allies of Macedonia. A Macedonian garrison was to be placed in Munychia, and a heavy war-indemnity was required.[4] Xenocrates is said, on hearing the terms, to have declared them to be reasonable terms for slaves, but harsh for free men; and

---

[1] *Vit. X Orat.*, 847 c., d. [2] Plut., *Phoc.*, xxvii.
[3] Diod., XIX, lxviii.; XX, xlvi.; *C.I.A.*, ii., 268, 592, 737, etc.
[4] Diod., XVIII, xviii., lvi.; Plut., *Phoc.*, xxvii.; Diog. Lært., X, i.

Phocion did his best to induce Antipater to give
up his determination to garrison Munychia, but
in vain. "I will do you any favour, Phocion,"
Antipater replied, "which does not mean destruction for you and for us"; and Callimedon, one of
Phocion's colleagues, and a man of strongly anti-
democratic sentiments, is said himself to have
opposed Phocion's request. The surest way to
quell any desire to resist the conqueror was to
disfranchise the greater number of those poorer
citizens whose inclinations were generally towards
war. On the day of the procession which escorted
the statue of Iacchus from Athens to Eleusis, at
the opening of the Eleusinian Mysteries (the 20th
of Boëdromion, in the middle of September, 322),
—ordinarily a day of joy and religious emotion,
—a Macedonian force under Menyllus occupied
Munychia, and the visible proof of the humiliation
of Athens was complete. By the constitutional
change imposed upon the city 12,000 citizens lost
the franchise, and 9000 only retained it. A very
large proportion of those who were disfranchised
were deported at Antipater's bidding to new homes
in Thrace and elsewhere.

The chief power in Athens was once more in the
hands of Demades and Phocion, with whom were
associated Pytheas, Callimedon, and others of the
Macedonian party. On the proposal of Demades,
sentence of death for high treason was passed
against Demosthenes, Hypereides, Himeræus, and

[1] Diod., XVIII, xviii.; Plut., *Phoc.*, xxviii.

CALAUREIA, VIEW NEAR THE PRECINCT OF POSEIDON

PHOTO BY MR. A. B. COOK

other patriotic orators.[1] The condemned had probably already fled from Athens; but the emissaries of Antipater were in pursuit, and did their work only too well, taking no account even of the privilege of sanctuary.[2] Archias of Thurii, surnamed "the exile-hunter,"[4] seized Hypereides, Himeræus, and Aristonicus in the temple of Æacus in Ægina, and sent them to Antipater at Cleonæ, where they were executed on the 9th of Pyanepsion (early in October).[3] Demosthenes took refuge in the sanctuary of Poseidon in the island of Calaureia. There Archias landed with some Thracian soldiers, and first tried to induce him to leave the sanctuary by promising that he should suffer no injury. According to Plutarch's story, Demosthenes had had a dream on the previous night, in which he thought that he was acting a tragedy, as the rival of Archias (who had been an actor by profession), and that though he won the favour of the audience, he failed in the end for lack of proper equipment. No offer that Archias could now make induced him to surrender. "Your acting, Archias," he said, "never convinced me yet, nor will your promises now." Archias then changed his tone, and began to use threats. "Ah!" said Demosthenes, "now I hear the voice from the Macedonian tripod; you were acting until now. Wait a little," he added, "until I have written a message to my friends at home." He

---

[1] Suid., *s. v.* Ἀντίπατρος.   [2] Polyb. ix., xxix.   [3] φυγαδοθήρας.
[4] Plut., *Dem.*, xxviii., etc.; comp. *Vit. X Orat.*, 849 b, c.

then retired within the temple and took a tablet, and biting the end of his pen, as he used to do when he was composing, he kept it between his lips for a short time, and then covered up his head. The soldiers thought that this was a sign of cowardice, and Archias again offered to effect a reconciliation for him with Antipater. But when Demosthenes felt the poison, which he had concealed in the quill, beginning to work, he cried, "Now, Antipater, the time has come when you can play the part of Creon, and cast my body away unburied. Dear Poseidon, I leave thy sacred precincts before I die; for Antipater and the Macedonians have not even left thy sanctuary unpolluted." So saying, he tottered forward. As he passed the altar he fell, and died with a single groan. The day was the 16th of Pyanepsion, the day on which the women celebrating the Thesmophoria held their solemn fast.[1]

NOTES TO CHAPTER XIII

1. Mr. D. G. Hogarth in the *English Historical Review* for 1887, p. 317, and (with some slight modifications) in his *Philip and Alexander of Macedon*, p. 198, attempts to prove that the demand for divine honours for Alexander was made not by himself,

---

[1] Plut., *Dem.*, xxix., xxx. Plutarch mentions some variations of the story which became current; *e. g.* that he imbibed the poison from an amulet, or took it from a bag which he carried around his neck. He adds that the heading, but no more, of a letter to Antipater was found upon his person when he fell, according to one version. Demochares stated some years afterwards that his uncle had not died of poison, but had been mercifully taken out of this life by the gods at this critical moment.

but by his supporters in the several cities of Greece, and was "a spontaneous outburst of adulation from various cities, led by the philo-Macedonian party in each, intended to greet the conquerer on the earliest occasion whereon an embassy could approach his presence." He points out that the only authority which expressly mentions a letter from Alexander as the occasion of the votes and debates in the several cities is Ælian., *Var. Hist.*, II, xix., who records how ἄλλοι μὲν ἄλλα ἐψηφίσαντο, Λακεδαιμόνιοι δ᾽ ἐκεῖνα, Ἐπείδη Ἀλέξανδρος βούλεται θεὸς εἶναι, ἔστω θεός. Arrian, VII, xxiii., describes the embassies which subsequently went to Alexander as garbed ὥσπερ θεωροὶ δῆθεν εἰς τιμὴν θεοῦ ἀφιγμένοι, but does not say that it was in obedience to a command from Alexander that they did so. It is true that Ælian is not always trustworthy; but it is surely not justifiable to discredit his story on the ground that the Spartan reply is too characteristically "Laconic" to be true—at least to be true of Sparta in 324. Nor is the fact that his head was not struck on any coin (for this was a mark of divinity) in his lifetime in itself conclusive, especially as he died so soon after the date of the alleged claim to divine honours.

Mr. Hogarth also tries to show that the προσκύνησις or adoration of Alexander in Bactria in 327 was due to a politic determination on his part to assimilate the habit of the two peoples—the Persian and the Macedonian—in their King's presence, and did not imply a claim to divinity. But those who were present certainly interpreted it in the latter way, if there is any truth in Arrian's account; and Mr. Hogarth's attempt to discredit Arrian's authority at this point is not very convincing.

At best, it must be left an open question whether Alexander himself claimed divinity or not. So far as the position in Athens is concerned, it makes little difference whether the demand was initiated by Alexander or by Demades; though it does affect our estimate of Alexander's character, which Mr. Hogarth is concerned to defend. (See also Ed. Meyer, *Kleine Schriften*, pp. 285 ff.; esp. pp. 330, 332.)

2. In Plut., *Dem.*, ix., and *Vit. X Orat.*, 845 b, c, we find the story of a brilliant address delivered by Demosthenes at Olympia, in reply to a sophist named Lamachus, who had uttered a panegyric on Philip and Alexander, combined with denunciations of the Thebans and Chalcideans; whose services to Greece Demosthenes

extolled, while attacking those who flattered the Macedonians. No date is given, and Schäfer assigns the incident to the present occasion; but it seems at least as likely that it took place in 332, though we have no independent evidence of Demosthenes' presence at Olympia in that year.

3. Haupt (*Die Vorgeschichte des harpalischen Processes, Rhein. Mus.*, xxxiv., pp. 377–387) thinks that the split in the anti-Macedonian party may have been of still longer standing. He notes that Hypereides gets his material for the denunciation of Demosthenes from as far back as the date of the destruction of Thebes; and that he and Deinarchus use virtually the same language about Thebes and about the alleged overtures of Demosthenes to Alexander and Olympias; and he argues that this means that Hypereides cannot have been in agreement with Demosthenes at that time. But all that it necessarily implies is that he was getting up the best case he could against Demosthenes, and using any material that would serve his turn. He may, however, have been alienated by Demosthenes' withdrawal of active support from the Peloponnesian revolt in 330, or by his acquiescence in the recognition of Alexander's divinity. It is also possible (see above, p. 448) that the substitution of Menesæchmus for Lycurgus in 326 was due to differences in the party; but the evidence does not permit certainty.

4. The genuineness of the Second and Third Letters ascribed to Demosthenes is disputed by Schäfer, Westermann and others. Absolute proof is impossible; but Blass (*Att. Ber.*, III, i., pp. 440 ff., and III, ii., pp. 406–7) makes out a very strong case for their genuineness, and I have felt at liberty to use them as historical documents. If they are not by Demosthenes, they probably date from very shortly after his time; and nothing of first-rate importance depends upon them. The genuineness of the First Letter is far more doubtful (it is an exhortation to internal unity after the death of Alexander). The Fourth and Fifth are probably spurious.

CHAPTER XIV

CONCLUSION

THE question how far Demosthenes was justified in the policy which he pursued has been discussed in the preceding chapters in relation to each of the principal crises of the struggle in which he played so large a part. His vindication of himself in the Speech on the Crown is more convincing than any discussion at the present day can possibly be, and very little more need be said.

The claim of Demosthenes to be ranked among the heroic men of the past rests above all on the constancy and sincerity with which he defended the noblest cause known to the Greeks—that of Hellenic liberty; and only those who have failed to recognise that most of what was best in the Greek, and, above all, in the Athenian character sprang from and was bound up with political liberty, can seriously censure his choice. If any cause was, to a Greek, worth fighting for to the death, that for which Demosthenes fought and died was pre-eminently so. Polybius indeed,[1] writing two centuries later, declared that the

[1] Polybius, XVII, xiv.

"crop of traitors" in the Greek cities, whom
Demosthenes so vehemently denounced, deserved
no such name, and that they were pursuing the
true interest of their several countries in submitting
to Philip and Alexander, and finding in subjection
to a common master that freedom from strife with
one another which they had failed to find so long
as they were autonomous. Yet such a solution
of their political problems can hardly be called an
honourable one; nor did these States ever bring
forth fruits comparable to those achievements by
which the Athenians, when they were most fully
inspired by the spirit of freedom, won the admiration of humanity.

Moreover, it is plain that the test by which
Polybius tried the policy of the statesmen of the
fourth century was simply that of success. Demosthenes' policy, he said, led to the disaster of
Chæroneia, whereas the Arcadians and Messenians enjoyed the blessings of peace. If success is
the true and only test of statesmanship, Polybius
was doubtless right. But if political liberty had
proved itself so precious that without it the
whole of life would have seemed to be lived on a
lower plane, success was an altogether unworthy
criterion by which to judge the actions of those
who were dominated by such a sentiment. Demosthenes was convinced that such was the persuasion
of the Athenians, if not of all other Greek peoples,
and that by struggling to the end for the freedom
of Athens, and causing the Athenians to struggle

for the freedom of the Hellenes, he was fulfilling their noblest instincts.

If, however, success is seriously taken to be the proper criterion of merit, it must not be forgotten that the policy of Demosthenes very nearly did succeed. Philip was actually discomfited before Byzantium; and the defeat of Chæroneia was due to nothing which it was in Demosthenes' power to provide against, nor even to the inferiority of the forces which he had brought together, but simply to bad generalship. Whether, supposing that Philip had been defeated at Chæroneia, the struggle would have been at an end, no one can say; and it is idle to speculate upon such questions; but at least the defenders of Hellenic liberty came near enough to success to justify their attempt, even from the narrow standpoint assumed by Polybius and by some modern critics. Nor is it without significance that Aristotle (who had no special liking for Demosthenes), when he desires to illustrate a common form of fallacy,[1] finds a conspicuous illustration in the statement that the policy of Demosthenes was responsible for all the evils that befell his country.

The principal causes of the failure of Demosthenes' plans have long been plain to us—the unsteadiness of the Athenian people; the lack of generals comparable in ability to the statesmen of the time; the disunion of the Greek States. For the second of these causes, no blame attaches to

[1] The argument *post hoc, ergo propter hoc:* Ar., *Rhet.*, II, xxiv.

Demosthenes, and it is not certain that he could have been aware of the inferiority of the Athenian commanders until they were put to the test. The disunion of the States he strove hard to overcome, and to a very remarkable extent he succeeded. The alliance of Thebes and Athens was a thing of which the most sanguine prophet could never have dreamed a few years before.

But ought Demosthenes to have recognised that his fellow-countrymen were no longer equal to the strain to which he desired to subject them? Is he to be blamed for taking too generous a view of their character? Certainly he was not unaware of their defects. No one ever pointed out more candidly than he, how far they fell short of the traditional ideal of Athenian citizenship, or realised more clearly their unwillingness to sacrifice pleasure and ease, and to undertake great personal risks for the sake of the national honour. The fickle and spasmodic nature of their patriotism, their liability to be carried about by alternate gusts of courage and alarm, were constantly before him. Yet even so, incapable of sustained effort and prolonged sacrifices as the Athenians were, it was a nobler thing to attempt to revive in them the spirit which they had lost, than to acquiesce in their degeneracy and levity, and to "despair of the Republic." Nor must it be forgotten that in this attempt also Demosthenes came nearly enough within reach of success to justify his policy in the judgment of any large-minded critic.

Demosthenes' ideal and his determination to maintain it, as the ideal not of himself alone but of his nation, stand in no need of vindication; and he well deserves our admiration for the courage with which, in pursuit of this ideal, he contended against those desires and prejudices of his fellow-countrymen which were inconsistent with it. In three important points at least, his policy ran directly counter to popular sentiment—in his demand that the festival-money should be given up for purposes of war; in his far-sighted desire to bring about an alliance with Thebes; and in his attempt to obtain the co-operation of the Persian King against Philip. Yet all these aims he pursued without faltering in face of attack and misrepresentation; and there can be little doubt that he was wise, as well as courageous, in so doing.

The question whether liberty and pre-eminence are political ideals which possess a universal value and need no justification is too large to discuss here. There are many who believe (as Plato and Aristotle probably believed) that these are secondary in importance to the good life of the individual in a peaceful society, and to whom militarism and imperialism are consequently abominable. There is something to be said for this view. But it must not be forgotten that in the Athens of Demosthenes' day it was a view which had not made its way into the region of practical politics, but was peculiar to philosophic circles. There is no evidence that it was desire for the good life, or for the refined enjoyment of art, literature, and philosophy, that made the majority of the Athenians unwilling to fight; or that any higher motives than business, pleasure, and love of ease were the cause of their reluctance. Nor is it an absurd contention that the life of the individual is itself greatly ennobled by membership of an imperial nation.[1] It may at least be doubted whether more than a handful of Athenians thought otherwise; and if so, it is a mistake to judge Demosthenes by a standard which is out of relation to the political life of his times.

The faults which sullied the character of Demosthenes as a public man are not only conspicuous, but are such as tend in many ways to alienate the sympathies of the modern world from him. The worst, perhaps, was an indifference to truth, which, while it was not incompatible with the larger sincerity manifested in his constancy to the supreme objects of his life, led him to deal very unfairly with his opponents, to falsify history, and to repudiate his own share in transactions which were perfectly proper, but which had come in time to be viewed with disfavour by the majority of the Athenians. Doubtless some of the blame

[1] It cannot of course be contended that the noblest element in British imperialism—the government of dependent races for the good of the governed, and the bringing of light to those who sit in darkness—was present in the imperialism of Athens, but this does not invalidate the contention stated in the text.

for this should be assigned to the People itself;
and Demosthenes' attempts to deceive the People
in regard to the past are in some degree excusable
when we consider that if he had spoken or admitted the whole truth, his policy in regard to the
present and future would certainly have been im-
perilled. It may be that absolute truthfulness
is not possible for the leader of a democracy. But
it is difficult not to feel that the misrepresentations
of which Demosthenes was guilty sometimes went
beyond anything that such considerations can
justify; that one who could lament over the
calamities of the Phocians, which he had done
nothing to prevent, and could ascribe them to the
man who (if any one had done so) had helped to mitigate them deserves the severest reprobation; and
that his scandalous inventions in regard to his rival's
history and morals are utterly atrocious. There
was also a certain *intransigeance*—amounting at
times almost to ferocity—in his absolute refusal
to consider even the most reasonable offers which
Philip might make, and in the steps which he
took to exacerbate the relations between Athens
and the King of Macedon. No doubt he was
whole-heartedly convinced that even if a compact,
as favourable to Athens as possible, were made
with Philip, it would mean at best that Athens
would be sure only of the second place in the
Hellenic world; and that whatever compact were
made, it would only be observed by Philip until
such time as he desired to break it. Yet Demos-

thenes, however sincere and patriotic he may have been, is sometimes repellent in the hatred which he displays, and at times this hatred led him to make false charges and to commit acts of cruelty which admit of no justification.

In his money-dealings he did not always observe the standard of correctness which a modern statesman is expected, as a matter of course, to observe. There is not, however, an iota of evidence that will stand criticism to show that he profited personally by any of the transactions that were alleged against him; and the worst of these transactions, the appropriation of Harpalus' treasure, was probably dictated, just as his receipt of the gold from Persia had been, by public spirit so intense as to render him unscrupulous about means. Judged by the standard of his times, he is almost beyond reproach. It is not unworthy of notice that within a few months of condemning Demosthenes for taking some of Harpalus' money, the People themselves took all that was left of it to pay the cost of the Lamian War. No one now asserts that the policy of Demosthenes was in the smallest degree influenced by considerations of gain or of gratitude for presents received. It is doubtful whether this could be said of some of the orators who opposed him.

To the enumeration of his faults as a statesman, it must be added that he seems to have been a man of an unsociable and unfriendly temperament, and a bitter and relentless enemy; in all that we learn about him from the ancients or from his own writings, there is no hint of any intimate friendship or domestic affection. So wholly was he identified with political aims, that he almost seems to have had no private life. He was, moreover, deficient in humour and in gentlemanly feeling; and both these faults reveal an unattractive narrowness of imagination.

But against these faults, public and private, is to be set a devotion to a great ideal, absorbing the whole man; a capacity for work unrivalled in the history of great statesmen; a thoroughness in all that he did, which cared for every detail, and left nothing to chance; a gift of language, penetrated and transformed into eloquence of the very highest order by the passion for a great cause; and a courage which rose superior to all physical weakness, and was not daunted by failure or danger. The greatness of his character in these respects more than redeems its unloveliness.[1]

Many years after Demosthenes' death, in the year 280 B.C., when there was a temporary revival of the spirit of independence in Athens, his nephew Demochares carried a decree that his statue in bronze should be erected in the marketplace, and that the eldest son of his house should always receive maintenance at the public cost in

---

[1] I have attempted a brief appreciation of the character of Demosthenes as an orator in the introduction to my translation of the Public Speeches, and need not repeat what is there said. See also Index, *s. v.* Demosthenes.

the Prytaneum. The statue which was erected was the work of Polyeuctus, and its character is familiar to us through the two great copies of it in marble which have come down to us. Of these one is in Lord Sackville's collection at Knole, the other in the Vatican. In both these the hands which hold a roll are substitutes for those which originally belonged to the statue. In the original the hands were clasped tightly, and a story is told of a soldier who deposited all his money in the hollow formed by these clasped hands; the leaves of a plane-tree which stood near fell into the hollow and concealed the gold for a long time; and when the soldier came back and found his money, the wits of the time vied in making epigrams on the orator's incorruptibility.[1] In the year 1901 a pair of clasped hands in marble was found in the gardens of the Palazzo Barberini in Rome. These proved to be the hands of a copy of the original work of Polyeuctus; and a cast of the Vatican statue which was made, with these hands in place of the well-known ones, proves the superiority of the original design.[2] The earnestness and strong emotion which the clasped hands betoken are in keeping with the character of Demosthenes as a politician and an orator. It is possible that the hands which hold a roll were substituted at some

[1] Plut., *Dem.*, xxx., xxxi.; cp. *Vit. X Orat.*, 847 a, 850 f.
[2] See illustration. The discovery and restoration were the work of P. Hartwig (see *Jahrbuch des K. Deutschen Archäologischen Instituts*, vol. xviii., pp. 28, 29).

THE STATUE OF DEMOSTHENES RESTORED BY HARTWIG

FROM THE JAHRBUCH DES DEUTSCHEN ARCHAOLOGISCHEN INSTITUTS, VOL.
XVIII, PART I, PAGE 28, PUBLISHED BY GEORGE REIMER, BERLIN, 1903

period when (the original hands having been lost) Demosthenes was regarded from the standpoint of his literary eminence, rather than of his political importance and moral force.

INDEX

*A Selection from the
Catalogue of*

G. P. PUTNAM'S SONS

**Complete Catalogue sent
on application**

Heroes of the Nations

A SERIES of biographical studies of the lives and work of a number of representative historical characters about whom have gathered the great traditions of the Nations to which they belonged, and who have been accepted, in many instances, as types of the several National ideals. With the life of each typical character will be presented a picture of the National conditions surrounding him during his career.

The narratives are the work of writers who are recognized authorities on their several subjects, and, while thoroughly trustworthy as history, will present picturesque and dramatic "stories" of the Men and of the events connected with them.

To the Life of each "Hero" will be given one duodecimo volume, handsomely printed in large type, provided with maps and adequately illustrated according to the special requirements of the several subjects.

For full list of volumes see next page.

HEROES OF THE NATIONS

The Story of the Nations

IN the story form the current of each National life is distinctly indicated, and its picturesque and note-worthy periods and episodes are presented for the reader in their philosophical relation to each other as well as to universal history.

It is the plan of the writers of the different volumes to enter into the real life of the peoples, and to bring them before the reader as they actually lived, labored, and struggled—as they studied and wrote, and as they amused themselves. In carrying out this plan, the myths, with which the history of all lands begins, will not be overlooked, though these will be carefully distinguished from the actual history, so far as the labors of the accepted historical authorities have resulted in definite conclusions.

The subjects of the different volumes have been planned to cover connecting and, as far as possible, consecutive epochs or periods, so that the set when completed will present in a comprehensive narrative the chief events in the great STORY OF THE NATIONS; but it is, of course, not always practicable to issue the several volumes in their chronological order.

For list of volumes see next page.

THE STORY OF THE NATIONS

240
6

1200   20

241000 1